This Great New Treasurehouse of Unusual Knowledge Includes:

—The latest fascinating evidence about the Loch Ness Monster, the Abominable Snowman, and other legendary creatures.

—Eerie case histories of feral children.

—The powers of aspirin and what we do not know about it.

—Startling experiments with extrasensory perception.

—New secrets of longevity.

—Both sides of the major arguments about UFOs.

—Curiosities of the brain.

—The amazing facts about biofeedback.

—An extraordinary interview with an eminent contemporary psychic.

—The dazzling mysteries of pyramid power.

—The formation of the bizarre Cargo Cult of Melanesia.

—And so much, much more in this comprehensive exploration of the world of the mysterious, the bizarre, the undeniably extraordinary. . . .

THE WORLD ALMANAC BOOK OF THE STRANGE

More MENTOR and SIGNET Reference Books

THE WORLD ALMANAC® BOOK OF THE STRANGE

BY THE EDITORS OF

The World Almanac®

A SIGNET BOOK

NEW AMERICAN LIBRARY

TIMES MIRROR

SIGNET TRADEMARK REG. U.S. PAT. OFF. AND FOREIGN COUNTRIES
REGISTERED TRADEMARK—MARCA REGISTRADA
HECHO EN CHICAGO, U.S.A.

SIGNET, SIGNET CLASSICS, MENTOR, PLUME, MERIDIAN AND NAL
BOOKS are published by The New American Library, Inc.,
1633 Broadway, New York, New York 10019

First Signet Printing, December, 1977

8   9   10   11   12   13   14

PRINTED IN THE UNITED STATES OF AMERICA

Acknowledgments

Among the many people who gave freely of their knowledge and advice in the creation of this book, several names in particular stand out. Ted Bloecher brought invaluable data and years of experience to the UFO material. Sabina Sanderson and Marty Wolfe of SITU proved valuable guides through the thickets of the unexplained, and Holly Johnson gave similar assistance in astrology. The librarian of the Eileen J. Garrett Library of the Parapsychology Foundation, Mrs. Grazina Babusis, helped with many details, while Charles Honorton provided an excellent general view of the parapsychology field. Among the critics, special thanks are due James Randi, Martin Gardner, Milbourne Christopher, L. Sprague de Camp, and Philip Klass.

Most of the research for the book was done by Stephanie Bernardo, Peter Kussi, Russ Rueger, and Charles Nydorf. Photo researcher James G. Burke and artist Ed Kudlaty provided the illustrations. *World Almanac* editors Hana Umlauf and Barry Youngerman wrote most of the book. Articles marked S.R. in the section on Astronomy were written by Stephen Rosen, author of *Future Facts* (Simon & Schuster, 1976).

Picture Credits

The editors and publisher wish to thank the following people and organizations for pictures which they supplied.

American Geographical Society; American Museum of Natural History, New York City; American Philosophical Society; Arica Institute; Backster Foundation; Bettmann Archives; James G. Burke.

Carl Cravatz; Countrywide Publications; L. Sprague de Camp; Dell Publishing Company, Inc.; Doubleday & Company, Inc.; French Government Tourist Office; Funk & Wagnalls Publishing Company, Inc.

Professor H. E. Hinton; Houghton Mifflin Company; Professor John Hyslop; International Meditation Society; Kirlian Photography Association; Bettye Lane; Library of Congress.

Madelaine Gill; Maimonides Hospital, Parapsychology Laboratory; Miller Services, Ltd.; Janet Mitchell; Museo Civico, Piacenza; Museum of Modern Art, New York City; Museum of the American Indian, New York City.

National Investigations Committee on Aerial Phenomena; National Library of Medicine; New York Botanical Garden; New York Public Library; Fima H. Noveck; Philadelphia Museum; Harold Puthoff.

Radio Times Hulton Picture Library; Dorothy Sara; *Scientific American*; J. M. Simon; Society for the Investigation of the Unexplained; Toronto Public Library; Toronto Society for Psychical Research.

United Nations Organization; United Press International; U.S. Department of Agriculture; U.S. Games Systems, Ltd.; *Washington Post*; Wide World Photos, Inc.; *Yankee Magazine*.

Preface

For those who seek wonders, the everyday world is full of amazing things. The sting of the jellyfish, the playfulness of dolphins, seventeen-year locusts, and hundreds of other phenomena should satisfy the most ardent seeker after wonders. Key-bending psychics, UFOs, lost continents, and ancient astronauts are mere curiosities compared to the genuine miracles of nature.

In fact, the *perceptive* seeker can slake the thirst for wonders by contemplating merely one living individual of one species. Looking into his or her own body and mind, without making up a single mystery or imagining even one miracle, the true wonderer can find material enough to fill a lifetime with amazement.

In spite of the presence of the astonishing in their daily lives, many people seem to need ever greater wonders. At its best, this need is one basis of science and leads to new discoveries about people and the universe. But too often the human need for mystery and miracles can lead to gullibility and delusion. Indeed, the human capacity for credulity and self-delusion is itself one of the most mysterious things about *Homo sapiens*. Some people will believe the most incredible things if only they are presented in the holy robes of pseudoscience or some other form of pseudoscholarship.

In recent years, the recurrent phenomenon of people hungering after the occult and mysterious has reached a new peak. In every major city there is at least one bookstore reaping profits from the sale of "secrets"—secrets of pyramids; secrets of Easter Island; secrets of visitors from outer space, secrets of mind control, of ancient mystics, of healing, of diet and exercise, of the stars, the palm, tarot cards and Chinese manuscripts, of Stonehenge, monsters, lost gold mines and buried treasures; and above all, secrets of power, wealth, beauty, happiness, success, bliss, and eternal life, not to mention sexual satisfaction. And all these "secrets" sell for less than $3 a bunch.

Ninety-eight percent of this stuff is balderdash. If it could be clearly labeled "entertainment," there would be little cause for concern. Unfortunately, these wild ideas are too often presented as proved facts in competition with established science, reputable researchers, and genuine wonders. The exploiters and profiteers, those who depend on ignorance and confusion, command handsome incomes; those who are seriously studying unusual phenomena, who are trying to diminish confusion and ignorance, have scarcely enough money to carry out their investigations.

Specifically, the field of parapsychology needs better funding to permit a wider range of repetitions of experiments in order to confirm, deny, or refine previous experimental findings. Likewise, although a reasonable person might conclude that the UFO phenomenon is vitally significant whether it is physical or psychological in origin, there is no adequately funded UFO research. There are also a number of biochemical and electromagnetic studies related to psychic phenomena, hallucination, and meditation that might be profitably pursued if there were adequate research funds.

The readers should not assume from the foregoing that this book speaks from a stern, rigidly scientific, Establishment point of view. On the contrary, the perspective expressed here is much more open to the unexplained than to the cut-and-dried. That is not because the editorial staff is personally persuaded of the validity of psychic phenomena, UFOs, or astrology, but because the excessively rationalistic approach seems to be so limited and restrictive as to be self-defeating.

Questions and uncertainty, however painful to the scientist *or* to the believer, are both more interesting and more promising than premature answers and those rigidly held opinions which are usually expressed with rising excitement and a determination to be right.

Certitude of that sort contributes to the lack of adequate study of unexplained phenomena. Research in unusual areas does not receive the kind of public airing and debate, the constant refining and retesting, which are the lifeblood of scientific progress. This can be blamed, in part, on believers' ignorance of excellent debunking studies.

But prejudiced attitudes on the part of some scientists and others also play a role in this confusion. For example, the procedural objections of C. E. M. Hansel to psychic phenomena have long since been overcome, but scientific debunkers continue to cite Hansel's book as the ultimate exposé. This prejudiced attitude is not a conspiracy—as paranoid occultists are too likely to assume. The attitude stems, rather, from an understandable desire not to waste time and reputation in an area filled with crooks, cranks, and paranoid occultists. One scientist who made thorough tests of pyramid power and spoke of his negative findings to a group of believers was told, "You must have done something wrong or your pyramids would have worked." A scientist can have only one or two experiences like that before he decides that these are matters of faith, not science, and best left to believers.

On the basis of such incidents, scientists sometimes assume that the general public is not intelligent enough to understand scientific method or grasp the subtleties of theoretical statements and experimental procedures. Because of communication problems scientists tend to appear and, at worst, even become priestlike, jealously protecting the purity of their secret knowledge.

Because truth cannot be determined by majority vote, science can never be democratic; science is an elitist process. But because the search for truth does not take place in a social vacuum, scientists are required to deal with the public's concerns with the detachment and objectivity appropriate to science. To avoid these concerns or to deal with them with unscientific arrogance is to invite increasingly severe waves of antiscience reaction.

The media—TV, radio, the daily press—are caught in the middle between skeptics, believers, and the public. The working newsman is seldom more able to judge the truth or falsehood of certain claims than is his listener or reader. In any case, the newsman's role is merely to report claims and not to exercise a kind of censorship against the incredible. In practice, as UFO stories so clearly demonstrate, the press is at the mercy of competing "experts" who usually interpret the data according to preconceived opinions.

The Book of the Strange hopes to serve as a guide to this perplexing conflict. In areas where clear-cut answers can't be provided—psychic phenomena and UFOs are outstanding examples—this book will, we hope, at least provide some guidelines for thinking about certain kinds of information.

And because overemphasis on the falsely mysterious is too common, *The Book of the Strange* will also pay a lot of attention to the strange things we sometimes encounter but take for granted—aspirin, unusual animals, lightning, Gypsies, strange religions, coincidences, and hundreds of other odd items.

It is nearly impossible today to keep up with all the information on the subjects covered here. For that reason the staff of *The Book of the Strange* hopes the readers, experts and lay-people alike, will help us keep up to date on information which ought to be in the book in its next edition. We can't promise to respond to all letters or to include all topics suggested, but we will do our best to respond quickly and accurately to the issues that seem uppermost in people's minds. Send your suggestions, questions, and criticisms to *The Book of the Strange*, 230 Park Avenue, Suite 410, New York, New York 10017.

GEORGE E. DELURY
Editor, *The World Almanac*

Contents

Nothing endures, nothing is precise and certain
(except the mind of a pedant); perfection is the mere
repudiation of that ineluctable marginal inexactitude
which is the mysterious inmost quality of Being.
—H. G. WELLS, *A Modern Utopia*

Civilized man, after centures of materialistic teaching,
has almost lost sight of the fact which is so evident
to the child of Nature—that the appearances and
phenomena surrounding him are all miraculous,
magical, inscrutable, unaccountable, unprovable,
and, under proper conditions, are resolvable into
invisibility and apparent nothingness.
—M. OLDFIELD HOWEY, "The Serpent as Amulet
and Charm," *Treasury of Snake Lore*, B. Aymar, ed.

For the world is not to be narrowed till it will go into
the understanding (which has been done hitherto),
but the understanding is to be expanded and opened
till it can take in the image of the world.
—FRANCIS BACON

To let understanding stop at what cannot be
understood is a high attainment. Those who cannot do
it will be destroyed on the lathe of Heaven.
—CHUANG TSE

THE HUMAN BEING

Strange Conditions

Anorexia Nervosa

Anorexia nervosa is a self-induced aversion to food and a manifestation of psychiatric illness.

Anorexia nervosa was first described in 1868 by Sir William Gall and was named in 1874. The disorder afflicts about 5 of every 100,000 Americans. These sufferers, all but a few of whom are female, have no physical disorder that would explain their loss of appetite. Refusal to eat usually begins between the ages of ten and fifteen. Body weight may drop to half of normal. Associated symptoms include various digestive disturbances, self-induced or spontaneous vomiting, and amenorrhea (failure to menstruate). Often, in contrast with victims of famine, anorexia nervosa victims feel no hunger; furthermore, they are able to maintain daily activities at a near-normal level and are unconcerned with their condition. From 5 percent to 15 percent will eventually starve themselves to death.

Since most people who refuse to eat do so for a variety of reasons, it is generally agreed that anorexia nervosa is best understood as a symptom rather than as a disorder or disease. The greater number of patients attribute their loss of appetite to an extreme desire to avoid getting fat, whereas a smaller number claim they don't eat because they are afraid of food or of eating itself.

Recently, however, given the greater awareness of roles forced on women by social structure, the traditional psychiatric approach to anorexia nervosa and other supposed mental illnesses common to women has been called into question. Psychiatrists with a profeminist orientation posit that it might be more correct to view a young women's loss of appetite as a social protest than as an illness. They note that young women suffering from the disorder commonly stop or fail to menstruate and are typically unconcerned about this situation.

Treatment of the disorder has been successful in many

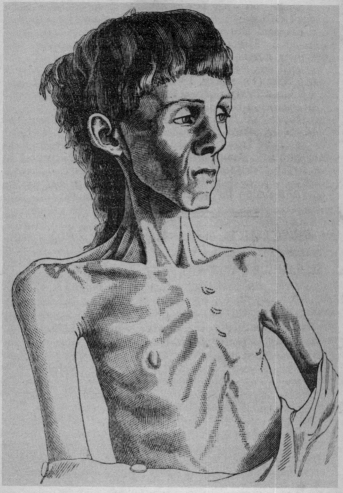

Fourteen-year-old victim of anorexia nervosa as shown in photo-engraving in The Lancet, *1888.*

cases. Some patients, however, develop intercurrent infection or chronic mental illness. Hospitalization in the early phases is generally imperative. The physician must have total authority to carry out effective treatment. Psychiatric consultation is advised in all cases and is absolutely necessary in some, especially in those where a dietary regimen fails.

For more information, see Lawrence C. Kolb, *Modern Clinical Psychiatry*, 8th edition (Saunders, 1973).

Feral Children

Feral children are children who have apparently been nurtured in the wild by animals.

In 1758 the great classifier Linnaeus listed *Homo ferus* (wild man) as a subdivision of *Homo sapiens*. According to Linnaeus, the characteristics of *Homo ferus* were movement on all fours, hairiness, and lack of speech. To be precise, these cases should be divided into two categories: feral man proper, brought up by animals, and isolated man, growing up without human contact.

Linnaeus knew of nine such cases. Since his day about thirty other cases have become widely known, though some of these cases may have simply involved people of a very low intelligence mistakenly thought to have been reared in the wild. Like Linnaeus' examples, these people moved on all fours and lacked speech; they were not particularly hairy, however, and they had one common feature not mentioned by Linnaeus— suppression of sexuality. (This would suggest that the development of sexuality is socially conditioned.)

Among the cases mentioned by Linnaeus were those of Wild Peter of Hanover and the Lithuanian bear-boy. Wild Peter was brought to England in 1724 by King George I and turned over to Dr. John Arbuthnot, a friend of Alexander Pope and Jonathan Swift. The Lithuanian bear-boy was found in 1661 living among bears. He was adopted by a Polish count, who attempted to "humanize" him.

Another well-known case was the wild boy of Aveyron, a child of about twelve, who was seized by three hunters in France in 1797 as he was climbing a tree. The child had been seen several years before—entirely naked, eating acorns and roots. The boy was dirty and inarticulate, and he trotted on all fours and grunted like a beast.

Brought to Paris and exhibited in a cage, he would rock back and forth and appear completely apathetic. The pioneer psychologist Philippe Pinel diagnosed the child as an incurable idiot and doubted the story of his wild origins.

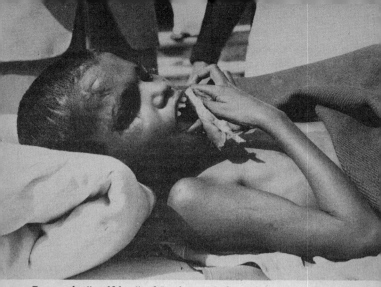

Ramu, the "wolf boy" of Lucknow, India, takes a bite of raw meat at Balrampur Hospital, where he underwent physiotherapy.

Despite Pinel's pessimistic prognosis, Jean-Marc-Gaspard Itard, a young physician and teacher of deaf-mute and retarded children, took charge of the boy's education. When he began, the child, given the name Victor, could not climb on a chair, his nose could be filled with snuff without making him sneeze, and he could pick up potatoes from boiling water without reacting to the heat. Itard was able to remove some of these disabilities, but not all. Victor learned to read and to obey simple commands, but he never learned to speak.

Itard was apparently never fully convinced that the child had been born with a normal intellectual capacity. In 1970 Victor's story was depicted in the acclaimed French film *The Wild Child*, directed by François Truffaut.

Another famous case, whose authenticity has been disputed, involved Kamala and Amala, two feral girls. Kamala, aged about eight, and Amala, one and a half, were found among wolf cubs in a giant abandoned anthill on the outskirts of a village in India in 1920. They looked and behaved almost like wolves, with calloused knees and palms and sharp-edged teeth, and their nostrils flared when sniffing food.

The children ate raw meat, and on one occasion they killed and devoured a chicken. They shunned other children, preferring the company of cats and dogs. Amala died within a year, but Kamala, who lived to be eighteen, learned to walk, wear clothing, and speak a few words. (See Bergen Evans, *The National History of Nonsense,* Knopf, 1946, for a criticism of the documentation of this case.)

Feral children present in dramatic form an old dilemma of psychology—the question of the relative roles of heredity and early environment in mental development. The limited studies that have been done with feral children suggest that social deprivation has its greatest effect on their personalities, with a more moderate effect on their intelligence and the least effect on their physical dexterity.

More specifically, the case of Victor tends to support the "critical period" school of language learning, which maintains that a first language must be learned somewhere between the age of two and puberty. Also, Victor's inability to direct his sexual energies toward another person, or even to understand the behavior of his sex organs, may indicate the major role of society, rather than instinct, in organizing sexual behavior.

For more information, see Harlan Lane, *The Wild Boy of Aveyron* (Harvard, 1976) and J. M. G. Itard, *The Wild Boy of Aveyron* (Appleton, 1962).

Hiccups

A hiccup is a spasmodic contraction of the diaphragm, leading to a massive intake of air, checked by the sudden close of the glottis, the closure of the windpipe.

When one breathes, the diaphragm contracts, enlarging the chest cavity and helping the lungs expand. The nerves that control the contractions of the diaphragm are the phrenic nerves, which pass from the upper part of the spinal cord in the region of the neck down to the diaphragm. If these nerves are irritated anywhere along their paths, a hiccup can result.

The word "hiccup" is of imitative origin. It has sometimes been spelled hiccough, influenced by the word "cough."

Hiccups may result from surgery following operations on the colon, the prostate gland, the gallbladder, or the stomach, usually involving men over forty-five years old.

In other cases, the condition is caused by infections of a portion of the brain or of the central nervous system, as in encephalitis. In such cases a neurological specialist must be

Robert Meier's eight-day siege of hiccups ended when a mysterious man suspended a water-soaked noodle over Meier's head (above), lighted two black candles, and made some curious motions with his hands.

consulted, and an early diagnosis may be lifesaving. Persistent hiccups may be a symptom of disorders of the intestines, kidney, heart, lungs, and nervous system. The cause of some attacks may never be determined.

The tempo of hiccups may be fast or slow. In dangerous, persistent types of affliction, the tempo is generally very fast, and the patient may become totally exhausted.

The home remedies for hiccups are legion, and for routine cases many of them are effective. Drinking water out of the wrong side of a glass concentrates attention and has psychological value, as does drinking gin or eating lumps of sugar. A sudden distraction to the hiccuping person often stops the spasm.

Holding one's breath, sipping cold water a few drops at a time, placing ice against the neck, swallowing dry bread or crushed ice, putting pressure on the eyeballs, placing a mustard plaster or ice bag to the abdomen, tickling the nose to induce sneezing, and breathing in a series of deep, regular breaths are among hundreds of often effective cures. Some of them have been in use at least since the time of Plato, judging from the *Symposium,* in which Aristophanes is cured of an attack by sneezing.

When an infant has the hiccups, it may be held on the shoulder and patted on the back, causing it to expel the air which may have been distending the stomach or esophagus.

One of the most effective and rational home remedies is breathing in and out of a paper bag, which builds up the carbon dioxide levels in the body to the point where the hiccup reflex is broken. In a variation used in some severe cases, a patient breathes an atmosphere high in carbon dioxide, produced by a special machine. A new remedy is a teaspoon of ordinary granulated sugar eaten without water. Many doctors recommend this cure for mild attacks.

For severe attacks, potent drugs, such as antispasmodics, muscle relaxants, and nervous system depressants, can be administered. Surgery to deaden the phrenic nerves has been used in some cases. This kind of operation deprives a person of one-quarter of his normal breathing capacity, but since one's natural capacity is generally more than adequate, this does not impose any significant handicap.

For more information, see B. Roneche, *The Orange Man* (Little, Brown, 1965) and A. Smith, *The Body* (Avon, 1968).

The Joseph Disease

The Joseph disease is a rare, hereditary form of degenerative nerve disease traced back to Antone Joseph, a Portuguese sailor.

The extremely unpleasant disease, called an autosomal dominant genetic disease in medical jargon, usually starts with a loss of coordination, a drunk-like staggering gait, and a gradual slurring of speech. The disease is generally fatal, with death occurring about twenty years after its onset, usually from a gradual paralysis of the muscles involved in breathing.

Only offspring of those actually afflicted can inherit the disease, and they have a fifty-fifty chance of contracting it. The disease is almost impossible to detect before it begins in the teens or, more probably, in the mid-twenties. By then many of those afflicted have already begun to have children, thus perpetuating the disease.

The history of the disease began with Antone Joseph, a Portuguese sailor who jumped ship in San Francisco in 1845. Preferring California to his home in the Azores, Joseph eventually brought his family there. By age forty-five Joseph was dead because he carried a defective dominant gene inherited from his father. Three of his six children inherited the gene and died as a result. Of Joseph's some 300 descendants, at least 48 have died as a result of his legacy.

In early October 1975 nearly 100 of Joseph's surviving relatives gathered at Children's Hospital Medical Center in Oakland, California, to discuss the disease. The unusual family reunion was the culmination of a massive search conducted by the National Genetics Foundation to trace all of Joseph's descendants. Of those present, 10 were found to have the disease, and 26 others, children of those who had the disease, may develop it.

According to Dr. William Nyhan, professor and chairman of the department of pediatrics at the University of California at San Diego, the disease will eventually appear in neurology textbooks as striato nigral disease. Doctors who have studied the Joseph family state that all that can be done is to attempt to relieve the symptoms of the disease with drugs and discourage its spread by urging victims to forgo having children of their own.

For more information, see *The New York Times* (September 30, 1975, p. 1).

Narcolepsy

Narcolepsy is a disease which brings on sudden, uncontrollable spells of sleep during the day, with disturbances of sleep during the night.

Narcolepsy, a disorder related to the malfunction of the sleep mechanism, is a chronic neurological syndrome that can last a lifetime. There is no known cure. Four symptoms, which may occur singly or in combination, are characteristic of the disease: attacks of sleep during normal waking hours; sudden loss of muscular tone and control, medically known as cataplexy; hallucinations during the hypnagogic, or transitional, state which precedes the onset of sleep; and sleep paralysis.

For example, one victim of a sleep attack fell asleep against a radiator and was awakened by a painful burn. During a "cataplectic" attack, which can be triggered by anger or fear, the individual may crumple and fall to the floor or the jaw or arm may sag for a few seconds. Some suffer such attacks hundreds of times in a single day, while others are affected only once or twice a month. The hallucinations take the form of very real and very frightening images. The victim of sleep paralysis is unable to move just as he is about to fall asleep. Narcoleptic symptoms may also occur in association with other disorders, such as brain tumors or psychological disorders.

Between 100,000 and 250,000 people in the United States suffer from narcolepsy. It occurs three or four times as often among men as among women, and it generally appears in the second or third decade of life.

When first described as a clinical entity a century ago, narcolepsy was regarded as a psychological disorder, but today physicians consider it a neurological problem with psychological components. A genetic factor may also be involved because the disorder tends to occur in several members of a family.

Although precise causes are still unknown, it is now clear that narcolepsy is intimately connected with the REM (rapid eye movement) phase of sleep—the phase in which dreaming normally occurs and which is characterized by paralysis of voluntary muscles. It has been shown that sleep attacks are actually episodes of REM sleep, and hypnagogic hallucinations appear to be nothing more than the vivid dreams that are normally part of REM sleep. At night, narcolepsy victims go directly into REM sleep, rather than passing through the non-REM phase, as is typical of normal people.

One theory about narcolepsy propounds that attacks result from "overinhibition" of certain impulses; for example, the sleepiness of a soldier under fire is typical of any situation in which there is conflict between the desire to escape and to fulfill a painful duty. One narcoleptic fireman fell asleep while holding onto a grab iron of a fire engine traveling at 70 mph. Thus, the theory surmises, the narcoleptic suffers from an undue susceptibility to inhibition of the cerebral cortex.

Psychotherapy can be used to treat narcolepsy caused by hostility and other emotional problems. Drugs that combat sleepiness, such as the amphetamines, may diminish the frequency of sleep attacks or paralytic attacks.

For more information see W. C. Dement, *Some Must Watch While Some Must Sleep* (Freeman, 1972) and *The New York Times* (November 19, 1975, p. 18).

Tourette's Syndrome

Tourette's syndrome is a nervous affliction characterized by motor incoordination and accompanied by involuntary repetition of words spoken by another (echolalia) and involuntary utterances of obscenities (coprolalia).

This rare disease was first mentioned in 1825 by the French physician J.-M.-G. Itard and subsequently recorded in greater detail in 1885 by Gilles de la Tourette, who described nine cases.

A typical victim emits an unnerving assortment of yips, barks, explosive burps, and other sounds. His face contorts, and various parts of his body are subject to tics. The victim may jump, squat, kick, lick his shoulder, punch himself, copy the words or actions of others, and obsessively touch things or people. Although the symptoms may wax and wane, they always recur. Approximately one-half of those afflicted have coprolalia. The syndrome is three times as prevalent among men as among women.

The first symptoms are observed in childhood, usually before the age of ten. In many cases, the onset of the affliction follows some precipitating factor—for example, an emotional shock or an operation, such as tonsillectomy. The echolalia is believed to serve the purpose of controlling emerging thoughts of an unacceptable nature, and often phrases such as "shut up," "don't say it," and "keep quiet" are uttered. In a number of cases the illness is progressive and leads to mental deterioration.

The Tourette Syndrome Association, founded in 1972, reports that there may be as many as 20,000 victims of the disease. The Tourette Syndrome Association is located at 42-40 Bell Boulevard, Bayside, New York 11361.

Tourette's description aroused interest around the world. Many local and probably related variants were reported: "jumpers of Maine"; *latah* on the Malay Peninsula, *myriachit* in Siberia, and *Schlaftrunkenheit* in Germany.

The cause of the disease has not yet been established. One school of thought, led by E. Ascher, holds that the disorder is primarily psychological. On the basis of an intensive study done in the 1940s, Ascher concluded that most of the symptoms could be understood in terms of the patient's relationship toward authority figures. Each of his patients had had difficulty with a domineering parent and had developed an obsessive character structure early in life. The coprolalia, Ascher believed, represents the release of hostile impulses toward authority figures.

Other authorities believe that psychological factors are insufficient to explain the disease and that some abnormality of the central nervous system must also be involved. In addition, the disease may be hereditary. Studies have shown it tends to be more common in certain families and among certain people, such as those of Eastern European Jewish backgrounds. Other theories point to enzyme deficiency, immunological abnormalities, and virus infection as possible causes.

Historically, treatment has reflected prevailing theories on the cause of the disease as well as predominant therapeutic methods popular in a given era. Generally psychoanalysis, hypnosis, and electroshock therapy have been disappointing; however, intensive psychotherapy, lobotomy, carbon dioxide inhalation, and sleep treatment have produced improvement.

Haloperidol (Haldol), a drug that restores enzyme balance by blocking the action of a potent neurotransmitter in the brain, has proved very promising. The drug, according to Dr. Arthur K. Shapiro, a psychiatrist at New York Hospital, is completely effective in relieving symptoms in 25 percent of patients and offers significant relief in another 50 percent. The drug's success strengthens the theory that the disease is due to enzymatic abnormality. Because of the bizarre symptoms of the disease, early diagnosis and treatment are stressed to prevent the development of psychological harm to the victim's personality.

In general, because of the shift in emphasis to research and treatment of physical causes, physicians today are much more optimistic about ameliorating the condition or, at least, preventing what was formerly a relentless downhill course.

Strange Remedies

Aspirin

Aspirin, effective against fever, pain, and inflammation, has become the most widely used drug in the world, even though scientists are still uncertain about how it works.

Hippocrates (ca. 460–377 B.C.), the "father of medicine," recommended extract of willow bark for rheumatic pains and fevers, and American Indians used willow-bark tea for the same ailments. In 1763 a paper on the success of treating malaria with willow bark was reported to the Royal Society of London. The active ingredient, salicylic acid, was later isolated, and by the 1860s practical methods of preparing salicylates synthetically in large quantities had been developed.

But the drug did not come into general use until after 1893, when Felix Hofmann, a chemist at the Bayer Company, found a simple way of making the acetyl compound of salicylic acid. Hofmann's father, a rheumatic, had complained about existing salicylate preparations. These compounds often caused serious irritation to the digestive tract and had an unpleasant taste.

Throughout the nineteenth century individual physicians reported remarkable results with varieties of the drug against certain pains such as neuralgia and headache, against fever in a wide range of infectious diseases, and against inflammation in some conditions, including gout. Aspirin (the trademark Aspirin was introduced by Bayer in 1899) even seemed to have some effect in preventing kidney stones. Its effectiveness in such a wide range of treatments made it the wonder drug of the era, and its popularity has never diminished. In 1964 the United States manufactured 27,000,000 pounds of aspirin, enough to fill four 100-car freight trains.

Some side effects do exist, however, as with all drugs. True, aspirin is nonaddicting, and it is difficult to commit suicide with it, since vomiting would be induced before any lethal effect could take place. But about 100 children die in the

United States each year of aspirin poisoning, and violent, even fatal, allergic reactions in adults are occasionally encountered.

More commonly, aspirin can cause gastrointestinal bleeding. Many patients lose about a teaspoonful of blood in the stool after taking aspirin. A 1969 study of 125 patients with acute gastrointestinal bleeding showed that 80 percent had taken ten aspirin tablets in the preceding forty-eight hours, but the connection has not been conclusively shown. Aspirin has been found to be capable of causing a deficiency of platelets, which play a part in the blood-clotting process.

This anticlotting action, though, may turn out to be invaluable in the prevention and treatment of heart and circulatory ailments. Studies are now in progress on the use of aspirin in preventing strokes and heart attacks caused by clotting. Of course, no one should pursue such an experiment without the careful supervision of a doctor, in view of the toxicity of the drug and the necessity of other types of treatment for these conditions.

Two groups of British researchers have recently shown that the antipyretic (antifever) and anti-inflammatory effectiveness of aspirin is due to its blocking action against prostaglandins. These are fatty acids which occur in many tissues and which—like hormones—seem to have a potent effect on various physiologic processes. Certain specific prostaglandins apparently induce fever. By blocking their synthesis, aspirin brings about a reduction of body temperature. Similarly, other prostaglandins that cause inflammation are prevented from being formed though the action of aspirin, and in this way aspirin exerts an anti-inflammatory action. The drug's analgesic effect (antipain) is still not fully understood.

For more information, see H. J. Weiss, "Aspirin—a Dangerous Drug?" *Journal of the American Medical Association* (August 26, 1974).

Placebo

A placebo is an inactive medication, generally given "to please" the patient or as a control in an experiment to test an active drug.

Derived from the Latin for "I shall please," a placebo, prior to the 1960s, was defined as a bland "sugar pill" or injection of plain salt water. Today the "placebo effect" can be applied to virtually any substance, therapy, or medical procedure—X rays, vitamins, antibiotics, surgery—that is used for its psychological or psychophysiological effect rather than for a specific medical function.

In use since antiquity, popular medical prescriptions considered placebos by modern standards included "theriac powder" and the legendary "bezoar stone." Until recent times most drugs prescribed by doctors owed their power to "placebo effect" rather than to a real pharmacological activity.

However, although more effective drugs are available today, use of placebos is increasing rather than decreasing. Recent estimates state that 35 percent to 45 percent of all prescriptions filled are for substances without any therapeutic effect on the condition for which they are used. This use has been ascribed to patient pressure to "get something." Extensive testing since the 1940s has shown the effectiveness of placebos in a wide range of diseases and postoperative situations.

H. R. Beecher, in the 1940s, gave harmless "sugar pills" to patients who believed they were receiving potent medicines. He found that in such diverse conditions as the common cold, postoperative pain, and angina pectoris, placebos produced "satisfactory relief" in about 35 percent of the patients.

In thirteen different studies of severe postoperative pain, about 30 percent of the patients got satisfactory pain relief from placebos, and placebos proved as effective as several standard drugs in relieving cardiac pain. In an eleven-year study conducted at the University of Mississippi Medical Center, in a group of patients with high blood pressure, placebo pills or injections were found to be as effective as several drugs commonly used to lower blood pressure. On the basis of these results the doctors concluded that there is a psychological factor in hypertension.

The ways and means of the placebo effect are still mysterious. Some persons seem predisposed to placebos, while others almost never respond. Typical placebo candidates are anxious, self-centered, and emotionally unstable. The placebo responder has a marked advantage when he has to take active drugs because he is generally more responsive to active drugs than the person immune to the placebo effect.

Studies have found, however, that the placebo effect is directly proportional to the effectiveness expected from the "real" drug by both the doctor and the patient. A study of analgesic effectiveness showed that the placebo was 56 percent as effective as morphine, 56 percent as effective as Darvon, and 54 percent as effective as aspirin. In other words, when the patients thought they were getting aspirin, the placebo gave them pain relief about half as strong as that which they would have got from aspirin.

Although some physicians assume that the placebo effect is due to suggestibility or gullibility, F. J. Evans ("Power of the Sugar Pill," *Psychology Today*, April 1974), asserts that "careful studies have failed to find any relationship between suggestibility, gullibility and sensitivity to placebo." He does concede that suggestion may play a part because it has been found that placebos that are brightly colored or have a "medicinal taste" are more effective than others.

The use of placebos in the trials of potent drugs have at times raised serious ethical questions because the procedure may mean that medication patients need is being withheld from them. For example, Dr. H. K. Beecher cited an instance in which the drug chloramphenicol was tested for its effectiveness in typhoid. The drug was given to one group of typhoid patients and withheld from another group. Of the latter group, 23 percent died, wheras only 8 percent of the group treated with chloramphenicol died.

Placebo therapy advocates, however, point out that there is a definite benefit to be derived from placebos. They are essential for controlled, unbiased evaluation of drugs; they can save patients money; they rarely cause side effects; and, above all, there is an impressive amount of evidence that they can relieve pain and provide other therapeutic benefits.

For more information, see S. Bok, "The Ethics of Giving Placebos," *Scientific American* (November 1974) and A. J. Snider, "Wonder Pill That Does Nothing," *Science Digest* (March 5, 1968).

Ionization

Unusual ionization in the air is supposed to produce an effect on humans and other creatures, according to some theorists.

In 1899 the German physicists Julius Elster and Hans Friedrich Geitel discovered ions in the air. An air ion is made up of from four to twelve uncharged particles. The ion is positive if its protons outnumber its electrons and is negative if its electrons predominate. Since it has become possible to measure the proportion of ions in the air, experimenters have been studying the effect on people and animals of an imbalance of either positive or negative ions.

In one type of experiment, single cells have been exposed to a higher than normal proportion of positive or negative ions. It was found that an imbalance tended to interfere with the growth of all kinds of single cells.

Some physicians report that patients with respiratory diseases improved with an increase in the proportion of negative ions in the air and grew worse with an increase in the proportion of positive ions. T. Winson and J. C. Beckett reported (see P. Krueger, W. W. Hicks, and J. C. Beckett, "Influence of Air Ions on Certain Physiological Functions," in *Medical Biometeorology*, S. W. Tromp, ed., [Elsevier, 1963] that positive ions produced "dryness, burning and itching of the eyes." They proposed that ions produce these effects by affecting the cells of the respiratory tract. Sections of tissue from the windpipes of mammals were kept alive outside the body and exposed to high proportions of positive and negative ions. The experimenters claimed that, as predicted, positive ions had a harmful effect on the tissue. The same tissue, the experimenters reported, flourished significantly in an atmosphere with a high proportion of negative ions, even in comparison to normal atmosphere. No explanation for the results has been found.

Other studies, publicized about 1960, purported to show the benevolent effect of negative ions on mood and visual acuity. At that time, the "Purotron," a widely advertised device, was promoted as a means of increasing the proportion of negative ions in the home.

Aging and Death

Extreme Longevity

Extreme longevity is a phenomenon of high concentrations of extremely long-lived persons in certain geographical areas.

Three areas of the world—Vilcabamba in Ecuador, Hunza in Kashmir, and the Caucasus Mountains region of the southern USSR—have high concentrations of extremely old people, many well over one hundred years old.

Javier Pereira, an Indian from Bogotá, Colombia, at the age of a hundred and sixty-seven years, clenches his fists in anger as photographers take his picture.

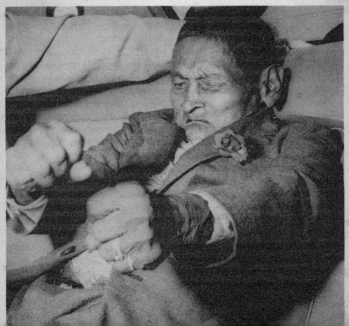

Vilcabamba, an isolated village in the Andes, according to its own 1972 census had a population of 819 persons, including 7 men and 2 women over one hundred. The people are of European descent. Vilcabamba's oldest citizen, Miguel Carpio, was still alive at one hundred twenty-nine in April 1976. Vilcabamba, situated in a valley 4,500 feet above sea level, lies 260 miles south of the equator and receives the sun's direct rays all year round.

The people of Vilcabamba practice subsistence farming and generally work into their nineties. People of all ages are physically very active. They live on low-calorie diets, particularly low in animal fats and proteins. Typical meals include beans, corn, potatoes, yucca (a starchy vegetable), banana soup, bread, fruit (such as papaya, oranges, and grapes), and very little meat. The people drink locally made rum and smoke tobacco. The old people have a high social status and are actively involved in the affairs of the community.

Hunza, administered by Pakistan since 1974, lies in the Karakorum Mountains of Kashmir and borders on Afghanistan and China. The Hunzakats, who number about 40,000, are ethnically different from other races in the region and are believed to be descendants of Alexander the Great's soldiers—their features are Caucasian, and they resemble southern Europeans. Their language, which is unlike any other, puzzles scholars.

Although no survey comparable to the Vilcabamba census exists, Dr. Alexander Leaf, chief of medical services at Massachusetts General Hospital and a Harvard Medical School professor, reported seeing "an unusual number of vigorous people who, though elderly in appearance, agilely climb up and down the steep slopes of the valley." Leaf found one man, Tulah Beg, who, in 1973, claimed to be one hundred ten years old. The next oldest, also a man, claimed to be one hundred five years old. Local legend claims that some people have lived to be one hundred forty years old.

The Hunzakats exercise strenuously, walking many miles a day. In the course of their work they are often forced to carry heavy loads up and down the steep slopes of their countryside.

The typical diet consists chiefly of foods made of grain, leafy vegetables, potatoes and other root vegetables, peas, beans, fresh milk and buttermilk, fruit (mainly apricots and mulberries), meat on rare occasions, and wine.

Like the aged people of Vilcabamba, the old people of Hunza are not isolated but maintain a high social status. The mir, the hereditary ruler, daily consults with a council of elders, a group of old wise men. The old people continue to perform useful duties, such as weeding the fields, feeding poultry, doing the laundry, and caring for the young children.

The Caucasus, unlike Hunza and Vilcabamba, covers an extensive region, including the Soviet republics of Georgia, Azerbaijan, and Armenia. The region best known for its high concentration of long-lived people is Abkhazia in southern Georgia. The Caucasus has the largest and best documented number of people over one hundred years old in the world. According to the 1970 census, between 4,500 and 5,000 centenarians live in the region. Of these, 1,844 persons live in Georgia, and 2,500 in Azerbaijan. Shirali Mislimev, acclaimed as the oldest person in recent times, died in Azerbaijan in 1973 at the claimed age of one hundred sixty-eight.

The climate of the Caucasus varies with altitude, from warm and humid along the Black Sea to drier and more continental inland and in the mountainous country. Although more old people are found in the mountains than in the lowlands, the warm sea-level parts of Georgia also have a large number of centenarians. The ethnic background of the centenarians is mixed; it includes Georgians, Russians, Jews, Armenians, and Turks.

Most of the aged people are found in agrarian settings, working as hunters, shepherds, and farmers. Like the long-lived people of Hunza and Vilcabamba, the centenarians of the Caucasus remain energetic and are honored and useful members of the society. Their diet, however, differs from that of the Hunzakats and the people of Vilcabamba. A study of the diets of 1,000 persons aged eighty years and more showed that 60 percent consisted of milk, vegetables, meats, and fruit. Some 70 percent of the calories were of vegetable origin, and the remainder from meat and dairy products. Milk, mainly sour milk and cheese, was the chief source of protein, and bread was the chief source of carbohydrates. The centenarians also continue to drink wine and vodka into old age and to smoke.

The first consideration in analysis of the phenomenon of longevity is documentation of the stated age spans. The extreme ages in Vilcabamba are believed accurate because they are verified by baptismal records in the local church. The number of centenarians in the Caucasus is generally

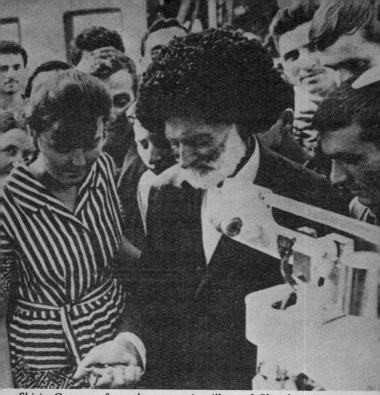

Shirin Gasanov, from the mountain village of Chereken, in Azer-baijan SSR, at the alleged age of a hundred and fifty years, visits a big city for the first time in his life.

considered well documented largely because of the work of Professor G. E. Pitzkhelauri, head of the gerontological center in Tbilisi, in the Georgian SSR. Pitzkhelauri divided sources of documentation into three areas. The first—documents giving dates of birth (mostly church baptismal and birth records, but also passports, letters, and carvings on doors and walls)—was given the highest credence. The second category included marriage dates, which are usually well remembered, time elapsed until birth of children, and the current ages of offspring. The third area of documentation encompassed the centenarians' memory of outstanding his-torical and local events. A correlation of ages determined first by the first category and then through the use of the second and third types of sources showed the latter sources accurate in 95 percent of 704 cases studied. The dating of the Hunzakats is more problematical. Since Hunza has no written language, no records exist. In some cases, the mir has verified ages based on his own knowledge of the state's history. Otherwise, reliance must be placed on the observations of qualified observers, such as Dr. Alexander Leaf.

One of the most striking factors common to all three concentrations of long-lived people is that they are generally rural, mountain people whose daily work entails a great deal of physical exertion. The constant physical exertion into old age combined with necessity of traversing the mountain terrain on foot seems to contribute to cardiovascular fitness, as well as to general muscular tone.

Dr. Leaf, who has studied the old people in all three areas, found that broken bones were a rarity. He determined that constant activity kept bones mineralized and consequently dense and strong. Since inactivity at any age causes bones to lose their calcium salts and leads to osteoporosis (porousness and fragility of bone tissue), common among the aged in the United States, Leaf concluded that constant physical exercise is "the most potent measure against this debility."

A Georgian cardiologist, Dr. David Kakiashvili, who has spent twelve years studying gerontology, feels strongly that continued exercise is a major factor in longevity. He tested the hearts and lungs of old people in the Caucasus and found evidence of all kinds of cardiovascular disease. Yet, because these people seem to withstand myocardial infarction much better than city dwellers, he concluded that their continued physical exertion improved cardiopulmonary function "so that the oxygen supply to the heart muscle is much superior to that in city dwellers." Although the old people of the Caucasus suffer heart attacks, the attacks are apparently silent and not felt by the victims.

Dr. Miguel Salvador of Quito, Ecuador, an internationally known cardiologist, led a medical team of cardiologists to Vilcabamba in 1969 and examined 159 old men and 180 old women. His examination found no incidence of aging in arteries or any heart disease in the family backgrounds. He noted that the village has no doctors or hospitals and that the people either fast or take herbs and other natural remedies to heal themselves. Dr. Salvador, however, associated the unique health of the old people to their predominantly natural-food diet, another widely studied factor in longevity.

The typical diet in Hunza and Vilcabamba is similar—low in protein and fat and high in carbohydrates—and violates the standards of nutritionists in the United States. The daily intake of calories is also lower than the daily intake suggested by the U.S. Academy of Sciences for people over age fifty-five. However, in both areas, there are no signs of obesity or malnutrition.

Dr. Guillermo Vela of Quito, Ecuador, studied the eating habits of the people of Vilcabamba and concluded that the low-fat diet offset atherosclerosis, the fatty deterioration of the heart and arteries. Current medical opinion concurs with this conclusion.

In the early 1900s, Dr. R. McCarrison, a British surgeon who was director of nutrition research in India in 1927, ran several nutritional tests in which he fed laboratory rats the typical Hunza diet (see R. Taylor, *Hunza Health Secrets*, Award, 1944). Over a period of two and a quarter years, none of the rats succumbed to illness or death from natural causes. When he put diseased rats on the Hunza diet, they all got well. When he put healthy rats on a typical British or Indian diet, they were afflicted with a variety of diseases. It must be noted, however, that it is notoriously difficult to compare human and animal nutrition requirements.

At first consideration, the typical diet of the Caucasus, which is less stringent and higher in animal protein and fat than in the other two locals, would seem to shake the dietary evidence found in Hunza and Vilcabamba. However, according to some of these centenarians, the diet of the Caucasus dwellers once consisted chiefly of beans and vegetables and has improved greatly in recent years. According to Leaf, well-documented experiments with animals have proved that a low-calorie diet during early life will extend total life span. Perhaps a low-calorie diet for humans in the early years is as important as is moderate consumption during the middle and late years.

The genetic factor has been considered by many scientists to be instrumental in longevity. Almost all the centenarians in Leaf's studies had at least one parent or sibling who had lived for more than one hundred years. Although there is no known gene responsible for longevity, it is believed possible that the simple absence of "bad" genes decreases the risk of fatal disease. Thus, hypothetically, in isolated, interrelated communities like Vilcabamba or Hunza, the individuals lacking "bad" genes may have become the progenitors of isolated pockets of centenarians. Although the Caucasus is not as isolated or ethnically pure as Vilcabamba or Hunza, it has been found that most of the centenarians there are also the progeny of long-lived parents.

Other common features of the enclaves of long-lived people are the high social status of the aged and the strong sense of family continuity. In general, the aged are esteemed for their wisdom, which is believed to be derived from long experience, and their word in the family group is usually taken as law. Nor is there any forced retirement age. In a study conducted in Georgia, it was found that the aged died quickly when they lost useful roles in the community.

Another interesting factor, documented by Professor Pitzkhelauri's study in the Caucasus, was the correlation of marriage and longevity. Of about 15,000 people aged eighty and over, only married people, with rare exceptions, reached extreme ages. He concluded that marriage and a regular, prolonged sex life were important to longevity. He also discovered that women who had more children lived longer.

For more information, see Alexander Leaf and John Launois, *Youth in Old Age* (McGraw-Hill, 1975) and A. Leaf, "Growing Old," *Scientific American* (September 1973) and "Every Day Is a Gift When You Are Over One Hundred," *National Geographic* (January 1973); also Paul Martir, "The Old Men and Women of the Mountains," *Parade* (April 1976) and Grace H. Halsell, *Los Viejos; Secrets of Longevity from the Sacred Valley* (Rodale Press, 1976).

The Rejuvenators

The rejuvenators are a group of twentieth-century physicians and scientists who have attempted to restore and maintain youthfulness and vigor in people through the administration of various preparations.

The first of the notable modern rejuvenators was Serge Voronoff, born in Russia in 1866. He became a surgeon and pathologist and, as a naturalized French citizen, performed notable surgery in military hospitals in World War I. Shortly before the war he had served as a physician to the khedive of Egypt and observed that eunuchs aged more quickly than other men. Voronoff concluded that absence of testicular hormones was responsible and that provision of this hormone through grafts of testicular tissue might retard the aging

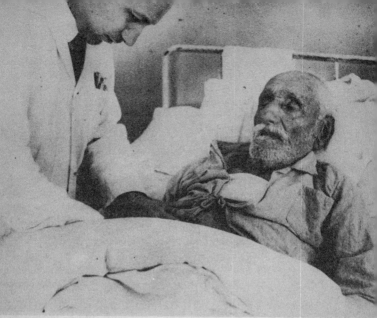

Turkey's Zaro Agha, at the age of one hundred and fifty-six years, receives treatment in Istanbul in preparation for age-fixing experiments arranged by Dr. Serge Voronoff, the Russian monkey-gland rejuvenation expert.

process. He experimented with animals and by the 1920s felt confident enough in his approach to treat humans. Since he could not obtain volunteer donors of testicular grafts, he used anthropoid tissue. According to O. Segerberg, author of *The Immortality Factor* (Dutton, 1974), a conference of 1,000 surgeons held in Austria in 1928 concluded that Voronoff's testicular implant procedure "afforded transient regeneration." Voronoff died an extremely wealthy man, at age eighty-five.

Another Russian rejuvenator was Elie Metchnikoff, born in 1845. Like Voronoff, Metchnikoff spent most of his life in France. He was a biologist who worked with Pasteur, and in 1904 he became deputy director of the Pasteur Institute. Metchnikoff was especially interested in the processes of immunity. His research on phagocytes, mobile cells that guard the body against outside attackers, won him the Nobel Prize in 1908.

Metchnikoff developed a theory that materials in the large intestine form poisons that debilitate and age the body; thus, to preserve youth and prolong life, a bowel detoxification program is necessary. Metchnikoff was largely responsible for the popularity of yogurt throughout Western Europe; his detoxification program made extensive use of yogurt, which he believed discouraged the appearance of toxin-producing bacteria in the intestine. Metchnikoff died in 1916.

Metchnikoff's work on rejuvenation was carried on by Alexander A. Bogomolets, who developed a serum which supposedly stimulated the body's natural immunity against agents of disease and aging. According to P. M. McGrady, Jr., author of a popular book on the rejuvenators, *The Youth Doctors* (Coward-McCann, 1968), the "antireticular cytotoxic serum" of Bogomolets won acclaim inside Russia but did not gain acceptance abroad. Also known as ACS, the serum was produced by first injecting human connective tissue into animals, then extracting the antibodies produced in the animal. These antibodies formed the basis of ACS.

Another famous rejuvenator, Swiss doctor Paul Niehans, developed a system of cellular therapy (CT) based on the injection of fresh or freeze-dried sheep cells. Notables treated by CT included Pope Pius XII, German Chancellor Konrad Adenauer, the eminent writers Thomas Mann and Somerset Maugham, and financier Bernard Baruch. In the late 1960s Niehans claimed to have performed more than 50,000 CT injections. CT therapy is practiced throughout the world but is not sanctioned in Great Britain or the United States.

No conclusive, objective studies on the results obtained with CT therapy are available. Opponents claim that the objectivity of CT researchers is suspect because their work is predominantly financed by Niehans and because the findings are not published in "reputable" journals. However, McGrady points out in *The Youth Doctors* that cellular therapy bibliography lists 753 monographs, 55 of them attributable to Niehans. According to McGrady, there is no evidence that conclusively disproves the major CT tenets, and some of the research by independent investigators is supportive of the Niehans approach. However, McGrady agrees that there are no conclusive data on humans.

CT may entail some risk to the patient, especially when performed by unskilled or unscrupulous practitioners. The injected cellular material represents foreign protein to which the body may respond with an anaphylactic reaction—a dangerous, often lethal form of shock. Infection is also a hazard in CT therapy. McGrady notes that during the wave of enthusiastic publicity for CT that followed the successful treatment of the Pope in 1953, thirty-five deaths attributable to CT were reported in Germany alone.

A rejuvenator enjoying some contemporary popularity, especially in Europe, is Dr. Ana Aslan, chief of the Geriatric Institute in Bucharest, Romania. Dr. Aslan is the inventor of gerovital, also known as H-3, a preparation based on the alleged ability of procaine to stimulate the body's regenerative processes. Gerovital contains procaine (widely used by American dentists as an anesthetic under the trade name Novocain), plus several other ingredients which presumably strengthen the effect. Once treatment with H-3 is given, it has to be repeated at intervals throughout the patient's life to prevent "backsliding." The results of the therapy are controversial. The American Medical Association, according to McGrady, has taken the position that H-3 is simply procaine by another name and that it is not especially effective as a rejuvenating drug.

According to British gerontologist Alex Comfort, the "rejuvenators" have not yet produced any unequivocally positive results, but they are pioneers who are trying to do something about retarding aging, rather than just talking about it. McGrady is optimistic that in the near future there will be a definite specialty of medicine entirely devoted to rejuvenation and to helping people "live longer better." What consciousness expansion was to the 1960s, McGrady believes, "life extension" will be to the 1970s and 1980s.

Submissive Death

Submissive death is the hypothesis that humans and animals tend to bring about their own death if put into situations which are intolerable and which they cannot change or control.

A growing body of evidence has been collected, on the basis of observations of a variety of experimental animals—rats, chickens, monkeys, and cockroaches—and human beings of varying ages in a variety of external conditions, to support the phenomenon of submissive death.

Major F. Harold Kushner, a physician who spent five and a half years in a Vietcong prison, has described prisoners who lost the will to live and consequently died of helplessness (see *Psychology Today*, May 1974). In one case a prisoner who was suffering from malnutrition and a terrible skin disease remained physically and mentally resilient because, Kushner deduced, he believed that he would be released in six months. However, when he realized his promised release was a hoax, he became depressed, refused food, lay in a fetal position sucking his thumb, and eventually died.

In 1954 Curt Richter, at Johns Hopkins Medical School, did some of the first experiments which linked the state of helplessness to sudden death. In tests with wild Norway rats forced to swim until they died from exhaustion, he discovered that rats which had gripped until they stopped struggling often, upon immersion, dived immediately to the bottom and drowned. Unrestrained rats swam for as long as sixty hours before dying.

L. S. Ewing made similar observations of submissive death among cockroaches. He discovered that in the dominance hierarchy of cockroaches, subordinate cockroaches which were repeatedly assaulted by dominant cockroaches died even though the assaults did not harm them.

In studies of human behavior, evidence of submissive death has been found in war prisoners, concentration camp inmates, and other people suddenly exposed to psychological states of helplessness.

Another example, cited by David Hendin in his book *Death as a Fact of Life* (Norton, 1973), is the higher death rate of widows and widowers than of their counterparts who have not lost a loved one. Dr. George Engel, a psychiatrist at the University of Rochester School of Medicine, who has studied the psychological causes of illness for two decades, terms this phenomenon the giving-up complex. He believes that a person who is in a "giving-up" state feels unable to cope with bereavement and succumbs to the stress. Occasionally the bereaved person may suffer from symptoms mimicking those that killed the spouse or relative.

R. Kastenbaum and R. Aisenberg, in *The Psychology of Death* (Springer, 1972), broaden the concept of submissive death to what they call the will to death. They consider the will to death to be a specific psychic factor that can be precisely identified and measured. In support, they cite studies of cancer patients in which this factor was measured and used to predict mortality rates.

Martin E. P. Seligman, associate professor of psychology at the University of Pennsylvania, believes that the evidence indicates that some species will deteriorate when they become helpless. Because the terminal causes in such incidents are extremely varied, he does not believe the cause can be traced to one physical event. However, he argues that this inability to pinpoint a physical cause should not stand in the way of attempting psychologically to prevent submissive death. Instrumental control, i.e., an individual's control over his environment, needs to be built into the lives of people thrown into situations of helplessness.

As a practical example of the latter, Seligman suggests that newly acquired wild animals, which frequently die en route to zoos, should be placed in situations which give them a sense of control. Al Markowitz of the Oregon Zoological Research Center in Portland has improved the health of apes by allowing them to control their own food supply instead of doling it out to them automatically. Similarly, aquatic animal trainers have found they can combat helplessness in newly captured sharks by leashing them and walking them back and forth across their pond. This teaches the sharks that they can act in what might seem a helpless situation.

Life After Death

The question of life after death has been the subject of speculation and belief for thousands of years. Recently Elisabeth Kübler-Ross, an internationally respected expert on the psychiatric dimensions of death and former University of Chicago professor, has stated that she is convinced "beyond a shadow of doubt" that there is life after death.

Kübler-Ross came to this conclusion following her work with terminally ill patients and interviews with subjects who were declared clinically dead and were subsequently resuscitated. These interviews included 193 cases of patients who had returned to life as much as twelve and a half hours after being declared clinically dead.

Kübler-Ross has said that she has always felt that something significant occurs within a few moments after death. She found that after clinical death some of her patients had "peaceful expressions" and that some, as they neared death, spoke to departed loved ones. She has come to believe that anyone dead whom you loved dearly in life will be at your deathbed to help you make the transition between life and afterlife.

All the patients whom Kübler-Ross studied seemed to have

three common experiences: a sense of floating out of the body or a shedding of their physical body; a feeling of peace and wholeness; and a meeting with someone who had died prior to their death. None of the patients who had "lived" through this type of experience was afraid to "die" again.

In one case, which initially spurred Kübler-Ross to further research, a patient who had been declared dead after last-minute resuscitation efforts came alive spontaneously three and a half hours later. The patient said that she had floated out of her physical body and watched the resuscitation process. She described in detail the efforts of the resuscitation team.

Dr. Raymond A. Moody, Jr., who is a doctor of both philosophy and medicine, believes that most near-death experiences cannot be explained as delusions induced by pain-killing drugs. However, unlike Kübler-Ross, he does not claim to have scientific evidence of an afterlife. In his book *Life After Life* (Mockingbird Books, 1976) he states that cases of this type are too clear and too similar to each other to be dismissed. He also states that cultural conditioning must be dismissed as an explanation because the experiences do not conform to contemporary American images of death. In fact, he states, the floating-out-of-the-body experience is remarkably analogous to images found in the *Tibetan Book of the Dead*.

Psychologist Karlis Osis of the American Society for Psychical Research in New York City has used a computer to tabulate interviews with 877 physicians whose patients have reported deathbed visions. In most cases the patients saw benign apparitions that had come for their souls. Osis is satisfied that patients whose brains were impaired by disease or high fever reported fewer visions than those patients who were fully alert. Osis is convinced that "so far it looks as if patterns are emerging consistent with survival after death" (see *Newsweek*, July 12, 1976).

There are, however, two related problems involved in the Kübler-Ross and Moody data. Death is medically defined as "irreversible." If a person has been declared dead and revives, the declaration was in error regardless of the clinical data that supported it.

If, then, the "dead" people were in some sense still living, the experiences they describe on reviving may be explainable as a major effort by the subconscious to deal with extreme emotional crisis.

Curiosities of the Brain

Brain Hemispheres

The brain is divided into two halves called the right and left hemispheres. Each hemisphere is, in superficial appearance, the mirror image of the other, just as the right and left lungs and kidneys are mirror images of each other. The brain is also divided into sections with half of each section in each hemisphere. Bundles of nerves, called commissures, run between the two hemispheres connecting the halves of particular sections of the brain in one hemisphere with the halves of the corresponding sections in the other hemisphere.

The cerebrum, the upper section of the brain, is particularly large in human beings. The skills and facilities necessary to function in society, particularly the use and understanding of language and tools, originate in the cerebrum. The two halves of the cerebrum are connected by several commissures, the largest of which is the corpus callosum, or great cerebral commissure.

The two halves of the cerebrum are known as the right and left cerebral hemispheres. Signals from the sense organs come to the cerebrum, which in turn sends signals out to the muscles. Generally, signals from the sense organs of the left side of the body go to the right cerebral hemisphere, and signals from the sense organs on the right side of the body go to the left cerebral hemisphere. The situation with the eyes is slightly more complex: the signals from the right half of the visual fields of each eye go to the left cerebral hemisphere, while signals from the left half of the visual field of each eye go to the right cerebral hemisphere. The left cerebral hemisphere sends signals to the muscles on the right side of the body, and the right cerebral hemisphere sends signals to the muscles on the left side of the body.

Various experiments have revealed that, in humans, the two cerebral hemispheres are not perfectly symmetrical. Each hemisphere is better than the other at performing certain tasks. Most people are right-handed—that is, their right is the "dominant hand." In right-handed people the left cerebral hemisphere is called the dominant hemisphere. The dominant hemisphere, usually the left, has greater ability to use language and to reason. It also regulates gestures made while speaking. The nondominant hemisphere, usually the right, has greater ability to perform motor tasks. It is also better at understanding and using nonverbal sounds, such as melodies. The nondominant hemisphere also has a better understanding of spatial relationships and is strongly related to creative work and the emotions.

Split Brain

A split brain is one in which there is no communication between the left and right hemispheres of the brain. Although in such an instance the right hand literally does not know what the left hand is doing, people with split brains generally seem normal. When there is no additional brain damage present, individuals with split brains show no obvious changes in intelligence, skills, or personality.

A split brain generally refers to a brain in which the corpus callosum and possibly other commissures have been severed. Some individuals are born without a corpus callosum, and in others it has been destroyed by illness or injury or severed by surgery.

The apparent normality of individuals with split brains spurred R. W. Sperry and others to begin experimentation in the field. Sperry's experiments with cats and monkeys in which the corpus callosum was deliberately cut drew attention to the phenomenon of the split brain. He eventually moved on to human subjects, leading to the discovery, in the 1930s, that surgical cutting of the corpus callosum could sometimes relieve epilepsy. Michael S. Gazzaniga, one of Sperry's co-workers, studied four patients who had been subjected to this drastic treatment. Gazzaniga's conclusions form the basis of most of the current discussion of split brains.

In his experiments Gazzaniga presented stimuli to the senses of the subjects in such a way that a given stimulus was transmitted to only one hemisphere in the brain. For example, the subject would touch something with his left hand that he could not see. Since the signals from the left hand go only to the right cerebral hemisphere and this hemisphere is cut off from the left cerebral hemisphere, the subject's response would depend solely on activity in the right hemisphere. Similarly, the subject was required to perform tasks using muscles controlled by only one of the hemispheres.

Once allowances had been made for the different abilities of the two hemispheres (i.e., since the left hemisphere controls language, it was not expected that a subject with a split brain would be able to name or describe a stimulus presented to his right cerebral hemisphere), the results of the experiments showed that each hemisphere functions as an independent brain with its own perceptions, thoughts, feelings, and memories. It was concluded that, just as in normal people, in most situations one hemisphere takes over at a particular task while the other hemisphere is inhibited. However, in some situations the two hemispheres try to do different things at the same time, with the result that the right-hand activities of the subject with the split brain interfere with the activities of his left hand. The positive aspect of this phenomenon is that under the right conditions such a subject can do two things at once, whereas a normal person must do them one at a time. Although the two hemispheres of a split brain are no longer in communication with each other, one hemisphere can often tell what is going on in the other hemisphere by watching the parts of the body controlled by the other hemisphere. This is similar to the way a person can often tell what is on another person's mind by watching his behavior.

These early studies with split brain subjects were valuable in determining the functions of the halves of the cerebral cortex. If a subject with a split brain was unable to perceive or do certain things, it meant that the half his cortex being tested was not able to do those things. From these experiments it was established that in most people the left hemisphere is necessary for understanding speech while the right hemisphere is unable to use language.

Since these early experiments were performed, it has been found that it is not necessary physically to split a subject's corpus callosum in order to make him perceive and perform tasks as though his brain were split. It is possible temporarily to turn any normal person into a subject with a split brain. This method of studying the functions of the hemispheres is called psychoanatomy—"psycho" because it involves purely mental activities, such as perceiving and acting, rather than surgery or drugs, and "anatomy" because it enables scientists to separate and study the parts of the brain as an anatomist would. Psychoanatomy has applications beyond causing the brain to function as if it were split. Using a technique called cyclopean perception, it can be employed to split off the parts of the brain that connect directly to the senses and muscles from those parts that are more central.

Marcel Kinsbourne, a psychologist, has done experiments using psychoanatomy. Although a single hemisphere has many different functions, Kinsbourne noticed that the whole hemisphere tends to become active at once. When one hemisphere becomes active, Kinsbourne noted, the other hemisphere tends to be less active. Thus, if an experimental subject is asked to perform a task for which one hemisphere is necessary, the entire hemisphere becomes active and the activity of the other hemisphere declines. Consequently the subject will have an easier time performing other tasks which involve functions for which the already activated hemisphere is needed. At the same time the subject will have difficulty performing tasks which require functions housed in the other hemisphere, the one whose activity is reduced.

In Kinsbourne's experiment the subject was required to keep six particular words in mind, i.e., activating the left hemisphere. At the same time the person was asked to notice certain things about visual patterns. The visual patterns were presented to the subject's eyes in such a way that certain parts of the patterns could be seen only with the right sides of eyes and certain other parts could be seen only with the left sides of the eyes. It must be noted that in the case of the eyes the left hemisphere is responsible for seeing out of the right half of each eye, and the right hemisphere for seeing out of the left half of each eye. Therefore, for the right eye, the left hemisphere is responsible for the half of the eye closest to the temple and, for the left eye, for the half closest to the nose. Since the left hemisphere is responsible both for activities connected with words and for seeing out of the right sides of eyes, Kinsbourne predicted that the subject who kept the six words in his mind would tend to see better out of the right sides of his eyes. The results bore out his prediction.

A similar technique has been employed to study the functions of the right hemisphere. It has been found that the right hemisphere is necessary for performing certain tasks that involve understanding spatial arrangements and is involved with emotional reactions to situations.

For more information, see R. W. Sperry, "The Great Cerebral Commissure," *Scientific American* (January, 1964);

Michael S. Gazzaniga, "The Split Brain in Man," *Scientific American* (August, 1967); Doreen Kimura, "The Assymetry of the Human Brain," *Scientific American* (March 1973); Marcel Kinsbourne, "The Cerebral Basis of Lateral Assymetrics in Attention," *Acta Psychologica* (Vol. 33, 1970); and Gary E. Schwartz et al., "Right Hemisphere Lateralization for Emotion in the Human Brain," *Science* (October 17, 1975).

Aphasia

Aphasia is the loss or impairment of the ability to use words as symbols. It results from damage to the brain.

One form, Broca's aphasia, occurs following injury to the left hemisphere of the brain. In one case, cited by Howard Gardner in *The Shattered Mind: The Person After Brain Damage* (Knopf, 1975), the subject lost most of his reading ability and the ability to speak clearly and coherently. The patient was able to read the words for specific things, such as "bee" and "oar," but could not read the concept words "be" and "or." When asked why he was in the hospital, he showed that his memory and reasoning faculties were unimpaired as he struggled to say "stroke."

Wernicke's aphasia occurs following injury to the left posterior temporal lobe. One patient could pronounce all the words he wanted, but what he said made little sense. He found it very difficult to name concrete things, although he often came close in calling a table a chair or a knee an elbow. Sometimes the word he wanted to say came out distorted—"clip" became "plick," "butter" was "tubber," and "comb" went through "close, saw it, kit it, cut, the comb, the came." He could carry out complex commands such as "stand up, turn around three times, and sit down." But he could not respond to the command "make a fist." When asked why he was in the hospital, the patient went into a rambling monologue that showed little understanding of the cause.

A patient suffering from another form of aphasia, anomia, could not remember the name of anything. When he was shown an object, he could not remember its name. When the name of an object was given first, he was not sure what the name might refer to. When he came into a room, he might say, "May I sit in this chair?" but when asked what he was sitting in, he couldn't say. The patient filled a huge notebook with word lists and descriptions including some of the following items: "chair: to sit on," accompanied by a simple sketch; "ceiling (top)"; "tile floor (bottom)"; "cane, caine: to help people walk"; "wrist-band: for watch."

Following damage to the right hemisphere of the brain, the patient suffers distortion of spatial understanding. Patients are unable to find their way from place to place and sometimes put their clothes on backwards or upside down. They tend to neglect the left visual field, sometimes shaving only the right half of the face or eating only the food on the right half of the plate. If severely crippled by a stroke on the left side, the patients are apparently not fully aware of the disability.

Biofeedback

Biofeedback training is a technique for achieving voluntary regulation over body processes which were formerly thought to be beyond the reach of conscious control.

It has long been assumed that body processes governed by the so-called autonomic nervous system (also known as the involuntary nervous system) were almost entirely automatic, outside a person's awareness or will. Typical of such functions are heartbeat, respiration, the work of the organs of digestion and elimination, regulation of body temperature, and maintenance of muscular tone. In recent years, however, it has been shown that through the use of biofeedback methods, people could learn to intervene in these supposedly automatic functions and make surprisingly delicate adjustments of the body's innermost mechanisms. The key to the technique is the use of electronic devices that monitor physiological processes and feed back this information in the form of simple, readily understood visual and auditory signals.

The term "biofeedback" is derived from the Greek word *bios*, meaning "life," and the modern engineering term "feedback," defined by cybernetics pioneer Norbert Weiner as "a method of controlling a system by reinserting into it the results of its past performance." The thermostat system controlling the temperature of a house is based on the feedback principle.

Pioneer work in biological feedback started as early as 1901, when J. H. Bair devised a successful feedback method for teaching subjects to twitch their earlobes, a skill that a majority of human beings have lost in the course of evolution. Another pioneer in feedback research was Dr. Neal Miller of Rockefeller University, who in the 1960s successfully taught experimental animals to control their own heart action. But it is only during the last decade that biofeedback has ceased to be a scientific curiosity and has rapidly come into its own as a practical method of therapy. Patients have learned to slow down racing hearts, to lower their blood pressure, to produce specific kinds of brain waves, to prevent headaches through muscular relaxation, and even to control the flow of stomach acid.

The more striking recent achievements of biofeedback research are described by biofeedback authority Dr. Barbara Brown in her book *New Mind, New Body* (Harper & Row, 1974). Asthmatic patients were shown pictures of flowers, pollens, and other common allergy-producing materials, while a device attached to their forehead was monitoring muscular tension and converting this information into audible clicks. At first the sight of the feared allergens produced great tension, shown by violent clicking of the monitor, but gradually the patients learned to relax in the presence of the pictures. As the muscular response to the allergens eased, the psychosomatic component of asthma was gradually brought under control.

A similar approach was used in tension headache. By learning to relax their foreheads, people suffering from tension headaches were able to reduce headache frequency and intensity by 50 percent after two weeks of training and by 75 percent after the fourth week.

To treat migraine by biofeedback, researchers set up instruments that measure the temperature of the hand as a function of blood flow and convert this information into a series of clicks. Guided by these auditory signals, migraine patients learned to channel the flow of their blood toward their hands and away from their congested, throbbing heads. Result: warm hands, pain-free heads.

At a New York hospital, thirty-six patients suffering from various neuromuscular diseases were treated with biofeedback methods, and all but two achieved significant improvement or full recovery.

Another extremely promising area of biofeedback is represented by the work of Canadian scientist J. V. Basmajian on muscular control. This researcher has perfected a technique of voluntary muscular control which is so sensitive that his subjects learn to activate a single motor unit while the rest of their body is relaxed. (A motor unit is the smallest neuromuscular unit, consisting of a single nerve cell plus the muscle fibers under its control. The gentlest, barely detectable movement of the thumb would involve the action of several motor units.)

Basmajian states that through biofeedback training his subjects not only learned to "fire" single motor units in various patterns and frequencies, but also retained that ability even after the feedback monitor was discontinued (see "Electromyography Comes of Age," *Science*, May 12, 1972).

Among the practical uses of this research, Basmajian cites the retraining of muscles in physical therapy and the design of prosthetic devices for the handicapped. Researchers at a Veterans Administration hospital in California reported successful control of four severely ill epileptic patients who had not responded to drug therapy. During a training period ranging from a few months to a year the patients learned to produce more normal brain wave patterns through biofeedback, with a resulting decrease in the number and severity of epileptic seizures. The device used was an electroencephalograph (EEG) especially modified so that patients could monitor their own brain waves.

In 1965 Dr. Barbara B. Brown set up an experiment on brain wave feedback using an EEG monitor hooked to a blue light in such a way that the light came on whenever the subject produced the type of brain wave known as alpha. The subjects, guided by the blue light, learned to produce more alpha waves. The brain was thus learning to control itself. Instead of the blue light, any other signal of alpha activity would serve as well. Dr. Brown hooked up a person's amplified brain wave output to a small electric train in such a way that the alpha waves made the train run and beta waves brought it to a stop.

Aside from such amusing diversions, the applications of voluntary brain wave control are numerous. The successful use of feedback in epilepsy has already been mentioned, and therapeutic applications in other diseases of the central nervous system are being studied.

The control of alpha activity is useful in meditation. There is strong similarity between the brain wave patterns of people in Yoga and Zen meditation and people demonstrating strong alpha activity. In both situations the mind and consciousness turn inward and the identity of the external universe is dissolved. Alpha activity through biofeedback increases susceptibility to suggestion and hypnosis and tends to foster mental imagery.

Although the field is barely a few decades old, there are now about 1,000 medical researchers working on biofeedback in the United States alone, and the literature on the subject is growing rapidly. To a large extent the method is still experi-

BRAIN WAVES	EXPERIENCES Physical and Emotional	GRAPH OF BRAIN WAVES
BETA 14 to 30 cycles per second	AWAKE STATE fully alert physical activity excitement fear tension anxiety	
ALPHA 8 to 13 cycles per second	PRE-DROWSINESS passive awareness composure pleasant mood deep relaxation of mind and body numbness of body	
THETA 4 to 7 cycles per second	DROWSINESS deep tranquillity euphoric mood very deep relaxation often unconscious	
DELTA .05 to 3.5 cycles per second	DEEP SLEEP STATE total unawareness unconsciousness sleep	

The four brain wave states.

mental, and results have not been generally confirmed. Nevertheless, impressive gains have already been scored, and in the words of one author, biofeedback training at last puts the patient back in the driver's seat. When such diverse work is going on into many areas, some surprising breakthroughs may well be anticipated. For example, one researcher suggests that when people learn selective control over their blood flow, they may be able to shut off circulation to a cancerous tissue and "starve" the malignancy away (*Biofeedback Syllabus*, B. Brown, ed., C. T. Brown, 1975). From a theoretical point of view, the breaking of the traditional barrier between "voluntary" and "involuntary" processes undoubtedly represents an important advance.

On the whole, biofeedback training seems safe, although in some areas, especially neurophysiology, special caution is required. Dr. Brown cautions that there are dangers to be faced when insufficiently trained people and improperly developed machines are used in alpha feedback. Certain diseases, such as epilepsy, produce brain wave patterns similar to alpha patterns, and there is some risk that in some people susceptible to epilepsy the production of alpha waves through feedback may have undesirable consequences. Biofeedback training should also be used with caution in people with behavioral problems and people taking certain types of medication.

There may also be a more fundamental problem involved in bypassing "the wisdom of the body" and subjecting more and more processes to conscious, direct control. One objection to Western civilization is that it is already too controlling and manipulative, and perhaps the headache which we attempt to cure through biofeedback had its origin in a too cerebral and controlled existence in the first place.

But from another point of view, biofeedback training has some parallels in Oriental culture and wisdom. There are some striking similarities between the results achieved with biofeedback and the ability of Oriental mystics such as adepts of Yoga and Zen to control such physiological processes as heartbeat and respiration. Recent studies, utilizing the same kinds of electronic monitors as are used in biofeedback, have shown that Indian yogis are in fact capable of achieving deep relaxation of the autonomic nervous system during meditation, without drowsiness or sleep, and that Zen meditation is accompanied by definite and specific changes in alpha brain wave activity (J. Kamijia, *Biofeedback and Self-Control*. Aldine-A Therton, 1971).

The Third Eye

The third eye, also called the pineal or parietal eye, is the eye or eyelike structure located on the top of the skull in some reptiles or amphibians.

Interest in a third eye can be traced back in history to the Cyclops in Homer's *Odyssey*, the Sister Three-Eyes in the Grimms' fairy tales, and to the Hindu "Third Eye of Enlightenment." Many nineteenth-century writers believed the human pineal gland was a kind of third eye that looked into the non-physical world. More recently, Tuesday Lobsang Rampa, who claimed to be a Tibetan lama but was actually Cyril Henry Hoskin, an Englishman, published *The Third Eye* (1956). In this purported "autobiography," Rampa described an operation that opened a third eye in his forehead. This eye heightened his clairvoyant powers, allowing him to see people as they really are, not as they pretend to be.

However, scientific interest in the third eye did not arise until 1872, when Franz Leydig discovered a lizard that actually possessed a third eye. Since then, it has been discovered that a surprisingly large number of vertebrates have one or two eyes on the tops of their heads in addition to the two lateral eyes— those located on the sides of the head. Many families of lizards have been found to possess third eyes, although some, notably the gecko, beaded lizard, and whiptail, lack it. The third eye has also been found in another reptile, the tuatara of New Zealand (a living fossil, the survivor of an order of reptiles widespread in the age of dinosaurs), in the sea lamprey, in some frogs, and in some fish. Judging from study of fossil remnants, the presence of a third eye in many extinct fish, amphibians, and reptiles is indicated by a hole—the parietal or pineal foramen—found on the tops of the skulls. Third eyes, however, are not found in mammals and birds.

The pineal or parietal eye in various reptiles and amphibians is a functional photoreceptor capable of detecting light and discriminating wavelengths. Studies have shown that this structure is an aid in regulating the amount of exposure to sunlight and that lizards with the parietal eye removed stay out in the sun longer than they ordinarily would (R. C. Stebbins and R. A. Eakin, "The Role of the 'Third Eye' in Reptilian Behavior," *Am. Mus. Novitates,* Vol. 1870, 1958). It has also been found that this eye may facilitate survival at high latitudes by playing a role in temperature tolerance and thermoregulation. Additionally, it has been found that the reproductive cycle is accelerated when the eye is blocked.

Richard M. Eakin, in *The Third Eye* (University of California Press, 1973), states that because it is known that the reptilian parietal eye plays a role in thermal regulation, it is likely in the case of mammals and birds that the evolution of mechanisms for thermal regulation rendered the third eye obsolete. Although the third eye itself disappeared through evolution, the epiphysis, or pineal body, survived in mammals and birds and, to this day, possesses ciliary photoreceptors similar to those found in the third eye. In birds these light receptors help synchronize the bird's internal biological clock with the passage of time as marked by the cycle of day and night and the annual cycle of the seasons.

The pineal gland found in higher vertebrates is a carry-over from the third eye. F. W. Turek ("Pineal Gland: Seat of Solar Readout," *Science News,* October 18, 1975) believes the pineal functions as a middle organ between the environment and the internal organs and that there is a link between circadian rhythms (twenty-four hour cycles) and the control of reproductive readiness.

The human pineal is a small, gray, cone-shaped endocrine gland lying deep in the brain. It is located at the top of the spinal column where the neck enters the skull. It weighs between 140 and 200 milligrams and is about the size of a mustard seed. It tends to decrease in size with age. The human pineal gland contains a number of amines, including serotonin and histamine. It is thought the human pineal may be involved in the regulation of the excretion of aldosterone, a steroid hormone very active in regulating the salt and water balance of the body. Little is known about the effect of light on the human pineal, but there are reports that women with irregular menstrual cycles have normal cycles if they sleep with a lighted 100-watt bulb in their bedrooms on the fourteenth to eighteenth night of their cycle. If the light is removed, their cycles become irregular again (see "The Pineal—Still Much to Learn," *Chemistry,* Vol. 46, No. 5, May 22, 1973).

Herophilus, the fourth-century B.C. Greek anatomist, believed the pineal was a sphincter that regulated the flow of thought. It has been noted that although LSD causes a schizophrenic-like condition in man, this reaction can be prevented by the administration of serotonin (see E. S. West, *Textbook of Biochemistry,* Macmillan, 1966). The LSD molecule produces its effects by depriving the brain of its serotonin content. Since serotonin does not enter the brain from the body, there must be a local site of manufacture in the brain. It is thought likely that this site is the pineal gland. Tests have shown that the average serotonin content of the human pineal gland is 3,140 micrograms per gram of tissue. When tests were performed on a schizophrenic patient and a patient suffering from delerium tremens, their serotonin levels were found to be significantly below this figure—.50 micrograms and 22.82 micrograms respectively.

Although much further research is necessary to establish

strong correlations between states of mind and the serotonin content of the brain, it is interesting to note that this is the same organ that Descartes believed to be the "valve" between body and soul. Although elsewhere in the body serotonin appears to promote blood clotting and muscular contraction, it appears that in the brain it may be crucial to rational thought.

Subliminal Perception

Subliminal perception, also called subception and unconscious perception, is the alleged result of stimulation of human vision below the level of visual perception.

The characteristics of subliminal perception include: (1) stimulation of the subject below some awareness threshold; (2) no reported awareness of the stimulus on the part of the subject; (3) responses evoked in the subject differing from those evoked when the subject is stimulated supraliminally (at the level of consciousness).

In 1956 the London *Sunday Times* reported that certain advertisers in the United States were experimenting with "subthreshold effects"—i.e., subliminal perception—to send messages to people below their conscious guards. As an example the *Times* cited the case of a movie theater that flashed ice-cream ads onto the screen during the film. The flashes of ads were supposedly too short to be recognized consciously but long enough to be absorbed unconsciously. According to the report in the *Times,* the result of the experiment was an increase in ice-cream sales. On the basis of this experiment the *Times* speculated that indoctrination might be possible without an audience being aware that any influences were at work. The *Sunday Times,* however, cited no sources for the experiment and, at a later date, reported that similar tests conducted by the British Broadcasting Company were only moderately successful.

Much controversy has surrounded such attempts to manipulate human beings by "getting at them below their level of consciousness." The initial, somewhat sensational reports stirred an epidemic of "Big Brother" and brainwashing phobias and prompted a sharp decline in the credibility of the hypothesis of subliminal perception. J. V. McConnell et al. (*American Psychologist,* Vol. 13, 1958) traced the controversy to the claims of a commercial firm that subliminal perception of messages—"Eat Popcorn" and "Drink Cola-

Cola"—fantastically stimulated the sale of these products. Consequently, despite the lack of any detailed reports on experiments of such a nature, the technique was seized upon as the newest of the "new look" aspects of the application of psychology to advertising.

Although some experimenters believe that there is a below-threshold stage in nonconscious perception which occurs prior to conscious awareness, some, I. Rock for one (*An Introduction to Perception*, Macmillan, 1975), contend that many of the better known experimental effects either have been shown to be results of uncontrolled factors or can be explained in other ways. Other experiments (see N. L. Nunn, *Psychology: The Fundamentals of Human Adjustment*, Houghton Mifflin, 1961) claim it is impossible to be certain if a presentation is a little above or a little below an individual subject's threshold because a threshold is usually determined statistically and individual variations are wide.

Although some people claim they have not seen a shred of valid published evidence supporting claims of increased sales of popcorn, ice cream, etc., D. Byrne conducted an experiment that showed hunger could be increased through subliminal messages (see "The Effects of Subliminal Food Stimulus on Verbal Responses," *Journal of Abnormal Social Psychology*, Vol. 59, No. 2, 1959). In the experiment, subjects were shown the word "beef" for one two-hundredths of a second every seven seconds during a supraliminal film. After the film the subjects were asked to rate themselves on hunger and to choose one sandwich from a variety being offered. The results showed a significant effect on subsequent hunger ratings, but no significant effect on choice—there was no significant move toward choosing beef sandwiches. Further experiments have supported the finding that subliminal stimuli do not change existing habits or preferences.

However, J. Zuckerman ("The Effects of Subliminal and Supraliminal Suggestion on Verbal Productivity," *Journal of Abnormal Social Psychology*, Vol. 60, No. 3, 1960) found that imperatives—command sentences—could exercise an effect on behavior as long as the suggestions were subliminal. At supraliminal intensity there was no consistent effect on performance. In Zuckerman's test, subjects were required to write stories that centered on TAT (thematic apperception test) cards on which were flashed either "write more" or "don't write." In this experiment, subliminal stimulus seems to parallel the way posthypnotic suggestion works, in that the individual experiences his behavior as self-generated and not caused by external pressure. It seems reasonable to conclude that in the absence of a strong existing habit, a subliminal stimulus can impart direction to overt behavior.

Testing in different contexts has shown that subliminal stimulation can affect dreams, memory, emotional responses, adaptation level, conscious perception, verbal behavior, drive-related behavior, and perceptual thresholds. The main snag, according to N. F. Dixon (*Subliminal Perception: The Nature of the Controversy,* McGraw-Hill, 1971), is that because of differences in individual thresholds, it would be almost impossible to determine an intensity or duration value for a "subliminal" message that guaranteed it would be subliminal for all subjects.

While the published data do seem to place the validity of the concept of subliminal perception beyond a reasonable doubt, the controversy continues. Dixon attributes the unwillingness to accept the validity of subception to a deep-rooted distaste for the idea of unperceived control, especially in a culture which values personal freedom above all. He finds it understandable that there have been so many attempts to cast doubts on this phenomenon in view of the threat it seems to pose to personal liberty.

Hypnosis

Hypnosis is a trancelike state which may render a person more susceptible to suggestion than is true in his normal state.

Hypnosis has been alternately known as mesmerism, animal magnetism, artificial somnambulism, and reverie. Although it continues to be used for the treatment of physical and psychological problems and for entertainment purposes, its nature and limitations remain controversial.

Techniques resembling hypnosis were used in the religious practices of such ancient peoples as the Greeks and Egyptians. Faith healers and magicians in many ages and cultures also probably used hypnosis.

The modern study of hypnosis, however, did not begin before the work of Franz Anton Mesmer (1734–1815), a physician who practiced in Austria and France. Mesmer believed he had discovered in himself a quality he called animal magnetism, which he described as a kind of fluid transferred to others through touch. Under his personal influence, patients would experience fits or trances; when they awoke, various symptoms would be eliminated or relieved.

An investigation by the French Academy in 1784 ruled that the cures had been brought about by the patients' imaginations. This insight, however, was not pursued, and Mesmer was considered discredited.

Nevertheless, French and British followers of Mesmer continued to explore the possibilities of influencing a mesmerized individual. By the 1840s they had discovered all the major hypnotic phenomena acknowledged today: automatic and suspended motion, amnesia, anesthesia, positive and negative hallucination, posthypnotic phenomena, and individual differences in susceptibility to hypnosis.

James Braid, a Scottish surgeon, coined the word "hypnosis" in the 1840s, from the Greek work *hypnos,* meaning "sleep." He concluded that hypnosis was a result of impressions made on the nervous system by the hypnotist and discarded the notion of mesmerizing fluids. Braid standardized the technique of hypnosis, using verbal suggestion systematically for therapeutic purposes. Despite the use of hypnosis continually since that time by therapists of many different schools, its effectiveness remains in dispute.

It is agreed that the best subject for hypnosis is one who is emotional, yet stable, who is trusting and likes to rely on guidance by professionals, and who has artistic interests and a flexible outlook. Only about half the adult population can be effectively hypnotized. The personality of the hypnotist is also important, as a rapport between hypnotist and subject is necessary for inducing a trance.

In a typical session the hypnotist encourages the subject to relax and ignore all thoughts or impressions but those he suggests. The subject is then asked to focus on a particular object. His visual receptors become fatigued, causing unusual halos, shadows, and other effects. This unusual experience enhances the prestige of the hypnotist, who then monotonously suggests that the subject is becoming drowsy. Sleep is a passive state, but the hypnotist suggests that unlike the situation in real sleep, the subject will be able to hear and obey commands.

After a while the hypnotist begins to test the suggestibility of the subject with simple motor commands. He may tell the subject to try to lift his arm at the count of five, suggesting that the harder he tries, the less he will accomplish. If this simple motor suggestion is successful, the subject begins to feel his body moving with a different quality from its ordinary nature. The arm seems to be exceptionally heavy or to move of its own will. By now the subject has, according to many students of hypnosis, achieved an altered state of consciousness, characterized by enhanced suggestibility. However, the precise transition point to this state is unknown.

From this point on the hypnotist gives the subject a series of tests, each involving a greater level of suggestibility, until he reaches the subject's limit; this varies greatly among different individuals. Along the way the subject may be told that he will not feel pain when he is pricked by a pin. He may be asked to imagine a blackboard and to write certain words on it. He may be told that he cannot recall the words, then that he can recall them. The subject may be told that after he awakens, he will not remember anything that occurred during hypnosis, or he may be given posthypnotic suggestions—instructions to perform certain acts after he is awakened. The hypnotist may tell the subject that he can see something which is not actually present (positive hallucination) and cannot see something that is present (negative hallucination). Only a small percentage of the population can reach the deepest levels of hypnotic trance.

There are two major current theoretical conceptions of hypnosis. One school believes that the hypnotic subject attains a sleeplike state distinct from waking consciousness. The state is said to persist even while the subject is not in the process of reacting to a particular suggestion, and it continues until the trance is broken by the hypnotist (or until the trance wears off in the absence of the hypnotist, within half an hour).

Others maintain that hypnotism is merely a special case of cooperative suggestion, similar to other institutionalized types of personal influence. These include the use by a physician of a placebo (any medicine with no real curative properties) to cure psychosomatic symptoms and the suggestions a stage director gives to encourage an actor to identify with a character in a play, in order to perform a role unself-consciously.

In support of this second theory, we may note that a subject of hypnosis cannot be induced to perform distasteful or dangerous actions he would not ordinarily engage in or to perform physical feats he is incapable of performing without hypnosis. Furthermore, no major physiological indicator of the hypnotic state has been found to date, and EEG (electroencephalogram or brain wave) patterns of hypnosis resemble those of the waking state, not those of sleep.

On the other hand, the effects of posthypnotic suggestion have been noted even when the hypnotist was no longer in contact with the subject. And hypnosis has been successful in the treatment of some emotional, psychosomatic, or physical problems that resisted other forms of treatment administered by the same therapist. For example, it has been used in psychoanalysis to stimulate free association, in dentistry to relieve the fear of pain, and in the treatment of cigarette addiction to reinforce a desire to quit smoking.

Perhaps more convincing of the distinct nature of hypnosis is the fact that the subjects of hypnosis later report that their subjective experience was of a state different from the ordinary waking state. Hallucinations were believed genuine, even when they would have been rejected as absurd by the same subject in a nonhypnotized state.

Whatever the reality of hypnosis, some of its uses have been challenged by recent researchers, especially Theodore X. Barber. Among these uses are those involving analgesia (antipain) effects, age regression, and criminal investigation.

Many cases have been reported of the use of hypnosis to conduct painless surgery without anesthetics. However, measurement of such physiological signs as heart rate and regularity of breathing indicate that hypnotized surgical patients do experience pain and anxiety. In any case, some patients have been able to undergo similar surgery without hypnosis or anesthetics, indicating that the pain of surgery may be popularly overstated.

In age regression experiments, the subject appears to be reliving moments from an earlier period in his life, enabling him to remember long-forgotten or repressed details. Recent studies indicate that such subjects usually show the reflexes and perceptual characteristics of their real age. Furthermore, their recollections, upon verification, prove no more complete or accurate than their waking memories.

These findings also call into question the use of hypnosis to obtain legal evidence. A noncooperative witness could easily resist hypnosis or, as has been demonstrated, lie willfully under hypnosis. Even cooperative witnesses may report memories in hypnosis that are actually false, though strongly and genuinely believed.

For further information, see Theodore X. Barber, *Hypnosis* (Van Nostrand-Reinhold, 1969); E. Fromm and R. E. Shor, *Hypnosis: Research and Developments and Perspectives* (Aldine-Atherton, 1972); M. M. Gill and M. Brennan, *Hypnosis and Related States* (Wiley, 1966); Ernest R. Hilgard, *Hypnotic Susceptibility* (Harcourt, 1965); M. T. Orne, "Hypnosis, Motivation, and the Ecological Validity of the Psychological

Experiment," *Nebraska Symposium on Motivation* (1970); and M. T. Orne and R. E. Shor, eds., *The Nature of Hypnosis* (Holt, 1965).

Hypnotic Regression

Hypnotic regression is the return of a person, under hypnosis, to an earlier age to recall or relive detailed episodes of the past.

The most famous case of hypnotic regression is that of Bridey Murphy. In the early 1950s Morey Bernstein, a Colorado businessman who was fascinated by hypnosis and the possibility of finding a subject who could "regress to a previous existence," found such a subject in Virginia Burns Tighe (alias Ruth Simmons in Bernstein's famous book *The Search for Bridey Murphy*, Doubleday, 1956). Under hypnosis, Tighe allegedly returned to a previous incarnation, Bridey Murphy, a woman living in Cork, Ireland, in 1806. As retold in Bernstein's book, Bridey Murphy recounted in vivid detail her life in Cork.

Bernstein was criticized on many grounds. Many attacked him because he was a successful businessman, noting that the whole affair was extremely lucrative—the book became a best-seller, went into nine printings, and sold 170,000 hardcover copies in 1956.

No psychiatrist or psychoanalyst ever had the opportunity to examine Tighe. Many experts on early nineteenth-century life in Ireland challenged the authenticity of Bernstein's experiment. The Chicago *American* found a Bridie Murphy Corkell who had once lived across the street from Tighe in Chicago. Tighe, however, claimed never to have spoken to her.

Many opponents have argued that all the information provided by Bridey Murphy could be traced to suppressed or repressed information acquired by Tighe in her childhood. The literature on the subject is extensive.

While many attempts have been made to discredit the possible paranormal elements in the Bridey Murphy case and attribute them to cryptomnesia (the appearance in consciousness of memory images which are not recognized as such but appear as original creations), Dr. Ian Stevenson believed these efforts have failed. Stevenson maintained that some of the information may have been obtained normally, but there is no proof that it was not obtained paranormally (see "A Scientific

Report on 'The Search for Bridey Murphy,'" *Journal of the American Society for Psychical Research,* January 1957).

E. Zolik (" 'Reincarnation' Phenomena in Hypnotic States," *International Journal of Parapsychology,* Vol. 4, 1962) conducted an experiment in which subjects were hypnotized, regressed, and instructed to remember a "previous life." Zolik then traced the origin of some of the information elicited from these fantasies and found that people had combined facts from people they had known and from books and plays.

Dr. Harold Rosen, in a similar experiment (*A Scientific Report on the Search for Bridey Murphy,* Julian Press, 1956), hypnotized a man who was able to utter words in a third-century B.C. Italian dialect, Oscan. However, when rehypnotized, the subject was able to recall once having glanced at an Oscan grammar book. Rosen concluded that the phrases had been registered in his unconscious and later found expression during the hypnotic state. Although Rosen and Zolik's experiments did not prove that all cases of hypnotic regression are either fantasies or attributable to forgotten memories from the past, they suggested a new interpretation of the phenomenon.

Elisabeth Kübler-Ross, the Swiss authority on the psychiatric aspects of terminal illness, has experienced age regression hypnosis and was impressed with the results. She listened to the tape from her experience, wherein she was regressed to the embryo stage, and found she had complained of the uncomfortableness of her quarters and her wish to get out. She was a triplet and the first to emerge. She felt the experiment was valid because she had not told the hypnotist that she was a triplet. However, it is possible that knowing the facts of her birth, she could have projected how it felt to be in the uterus.

The debate about hypnotic regression will continue to be a major element in UFO studies and in parapsychology. It does appear possible under hypnotic regression to recall material that has been practically forgotten, as in the case of the Oscan speaker. But it also appears likely that the hypnotized person will pick up minute clues from the environment—including the hypnotist's inadvertent suggestions—almost forgotten conversations, and even dream material to weave an acceptably realistic fantasy. There is no way of determining the authenticity of the regressed report unless it can be compared to physical evidence or verified by disinterested witnesses.

Parapsychology

A Short History

During the past forty-seven years, since Dr. Joseph Banks Rhine began his first experiments in parapsychology in 1930, a great interest has been generated in the scientific study of psychic phenomena, and experimental evidence has emerged for four psychic processes: telepathy, clairvoyance, precognition, and psychokinesis.

Parapsychology is an outgrowth of the modern spiritualism movement of the late nineteenth century. When the Society for Psychical Research was founded in London in 1882, followed by the American Society for Psychical Research in 1885, the research involved the study of mediums and mediumistic trances. Attempts were made to learn whether the information disclosed at séances was the result of contact with discarnate beings, or of telepathy or clairvoyance between the medium and the participants, or simply fraud.

The first laboratory experiments in parapsychology were conducted by J. B. Rhine at Duke University in Durham, North Carolina. With the publication of his book *Extra-Sensory Perception* in 1934, Rhine popularized the term "ESP" and created public and scientific interest in his experiments. In 1935 the Parapsychology Laboratory was separated from the Psychology Department of Duke, and the range of experiments expanded from simple tests for telepathy and clairvoyance to tests for precognition and psychokinesis.

Although Rhine's statistical methods were new, the subject matter concerned beliefs that had long been part of human folklore. Telepathy is a modern term for mind reading; precognition is similar to divination and premonition. Clairvoyance was once called second sight, and psychokinesis (PK) refers, in part, to the old idea of mind over matter.

Rhine and his wife, Louisa E. Rhine, standardized research methods in parapsychology by the introduction of Zener cards and the use of statistics to interpret test results. A set of Zener or ESP cards consists of twenty-five cards, each card bearing one of five symbols—a circle, a square, a star, a cross, or three

Dr. J. B. Rhine, founder of modern parapsychology studies, using statistical methods.

wavy lines. In each trial, the subject "guesses" which card will come up next or which card the agent is concentrating on, the target. If only guesswork is involved, the subject has one chance in five of making a correct call. A series of twenty-five trials is called a run. Five hits per run is the mean chance expectation, and the deviation is the number of hits above or below that expectation. Statistical methods are then used to determine the probability of that deviation's having occurred by chance alone. If the probability is small, the assumption is that ESP has been involved.

In *Extra-Sensory Perception,* Rhine reported that using these techniques, he tested eight subjects who were able to exceed the mean chance expectation on a regular basis. Out of 85,724 trials, they obtained 24,364 hits: 7,219 more than expected if chance alone determined the outcome. Impressive as these early results seemed, there were many criticisms of Rhine's work because the exact experimental conditions were not described in his book.

In face of this criticism, Rhine and other parapsychologists became increasingly sophisticated in their experimental design and attempted to eliminate any possibility of recording errors and unintentional sensory cues.

Classic Experiments

Certain experiments are considered classic proofs of the reality of ESP by Robert H. Thouless (*From Anecdote to Experiment in Psychical Research,* Routledge & Kegan Paul, 1972) and others. Among these cases are:

1. The Pearce-Pratt experiments conducted between August 1933 and March 1934 at Duke University.

2. The Pratt-Woodruff experiments at Duke conducted between October 1938 and February 1939.

3. The Soal-Goldney-Shackleton experiments conducted in London between January 1941 and April 1943.

The Pearce-Pratt experiments were basically tests of clairvoyance. Pratt began the experiment at an appointed time by placing one Zener card facedown in the center of the table, leaving it there for one minute and then placing it to one side facedown. This procedure was followed through one run.

Pearce, alone in another building on the Duke campus, began to write down his guesses at the appointed time, making one guess per minute. At the end of the run Pratt turned over his pile of Zener cards and recorded the order of the symbols. A total of 1,850 guesses was recorded. Chance would call for 370 correct responses, but Pratt obtained 588. The odds of this occurring by chance alone were calculated at 22 trillion to 1.

In the Pratt-Woodruff experiments, five different ESP cards were hung on pegs above the subject's side of a screen partition with a two-inch gap between it and the table. Before the experiment began, the subject would change the order of the five cards so the agent could not know in which order they appeared. The agent then shuffled a pack of ESP cards and indicated that the run was about to begin. He did not turn over the cards. The subject would point to a spot under the pegged symbol which he thought would match the top card. The agent's top card would then be placed at that spot facedown. At the end of the run the agent made a record of the cards in each of the five piles, while an observer made a record of the order of the subject's pegged cards. These two records were then inserted in a locked box. The screen was then removed, and the results were tabulated. The records in the locked box served as a safeguard against falsification or error in the records.

The Soal-Goldney experiments with the gifted subject Basil Shackleton were tests for telepathy. In this experiment subject and agent were seated in adjoining rooms, out of sight of each other. The experimenter and the agent sat across from each other at a table divided by a screen with a small hole in it at eye level. Before each run, five cards with different animal pictures on them were shuffled and placed facedown in front of the agent, out of sight of the experimenter. Using a random number table to designate a number, the experimenter would hold up before the hole in the screen a card bearing a number from 1 to 5. If the number was 2, for example, the agent would pick up the second card from his left, look at it, and place it facedown in its place. The experimenter would signal the subject to record his guess. A run in these tests consisted of fifty trials, so Shackleton had only 1 chance in 10 of guessing correctly.

When the guesses were checked against the targets, Shackleton was shown to have scored consistently above chance, but not the target card. His guesses were correct for the one or two cards which came up *after* the target card. In one series, he obtained 439 hits of this sort, compared with a chance expectation of 321. The odds against this occurring by chance are 100 billion to 1.

The Critics

Even with the elaborate precautions, there were strong criticisms of these parapsychology experiments. C. E. M. Hansel, in his book *ESP: A Scientific Evaluation* (Scribner, 1966), objected that Pearce was not supervised and could have sneaked back to the building in which Pratt was handling the cards, peeked through a glass transom, and adjusted his calls to the cards Pratt was recording. In reply to these objections, Ian Stevenson studied the position of the transom and states that spying would not have been possible since the desk at which Pratt sat could not be seen from that position (*Journal of the American Society for Psychical Research,* July 1967).

Hansel criticized the Soal-Goldney-Shackleton experiments because Shackleton was able to obtain extraordinary results with only three agents and, once the experiments were completed, was never able to score above chance again.

Hansel maintained that in the Pratt-Woodruff experiments, it might have been possible for the agent to note the original positions of the pegged symbols, keep a mental note of the order in which they were removed from the pegs, and figure out some of their positions after the subject had rearranged them. He could then give the subject extra hits by moving cards to the appropriate pile during the recording process. The agent would need to know the position of only one card to affect the results significantly.

Ten years before Hansel's attacks on the experiments one of the most famous attacks on psychic research was launched by G. R. Price in *Science,* the prestigious journal of the American Association for the Advancement of Science. In "Science and the Supernatural" (*Science,* August 26, 1955), Price accused the parapsychologists of collusion with their subjects and claimed they were dependent on clerical and statistical errors and the unintentional use of subtle clues. Skeptics widely quoted this article in the years that followed, but in 1972 Price made an apology in a letter to the editor of *Science*: "During the past year I have had some correspondence with J. B. Rhine which has convinced me that I was highly unfair to him in what I said. . . . The article discussed possible fraud in extraordinary perception experiments. I suspect I was similarly unfair in what I said about S. G. Soal in that paper" (*Science,* January 28, 1972).

Price's apology came too late, however, to stop the many critics from using Hansel's arguments to attack parapsychology. Hansel insisted that as long as there was any possibility that trickery might have been used, the experiments could not be regarded as conclusive proof of the existence of ESP. Hansel noted the following facts about parapsychology research:

1. During card guessing experiments, subjects have obtained scores that cannot be attributed to chance alone.
2. Some subjects taking part in ESP experiments have used trickery.
3. Subjects who obtain high scores are not always capable of doing so.
4. Subjects tend to lose their ability. Often they exhibit high scores only for the duration of the experiment.
5. Successful subjects are sometimes unable to score above chance when tested by skeptical investigators.

6. Some investigators obtain high scores with many subjects, while other investigators fail to get high scores with any.

7. Subjects may be able to get high scores under one set of conditions and be unable to do so when the conditions are changed.

8. No subject has ever demonstrated the ability to obtain high scores when the testing procedure is completely mechanized.

Hansel concluded that the hypothesis which best explains these eight facts together is one of trickery: "Thus the set of facts given above display lawful interrelationships when interpreted in terms of the hypothesis of trickery, but they are difficult to reconcile with an hypothesis based on the existence of ESP." Hansel also concluded that a few additional facts would also suggest that experimental error is common in parapsychology.

Hansel's reference to a mechanized test of ESP concerned VERITAC, the first fully automated test of ESP, conducted in 1962 at the Air Force Cambridge Research Laboratories. A digit between 0 and 9 was selected randomly as the target. A printout was made of the target number, the subject's guess, the time of each trial, the total number of trials, the number of hits, and the subject's response time. There was no deviation from chance in the calls of thirty-seven subjects who underwent five runs of 100 trials each.

Price had also complained in his article in *Science* that testing should be automated with targets generated randomly and the guesses recorded automatically before the target was displayed. It seemed that a successful experiment using automatic electronic equipment would be the ultimate in ESP experimentation and provide a fraud-proof experiment to satisfy the critics.

Machine Tests for ESP

Dr. Helmut Schmidt became the pioneer in automated ESP tests. He designed an apparatus that provided random target selection based on the decay of radioactive material, considered one of the most random processes in nature. Schmidt's equipment also provided for the automatic recording of guesses and hits, thus eliminating the possibilities of experimenter error in recording and experimenter cuing by his mere presence in the room where the test was taking place. The experimenter could leave the subject alone with the machine, free to work when he was in the mood, and with no sensory clues to what the target might be. Schmidt's machine also paved the way for the development of an ESP teaching machine based on the principle of biofeedback training.

There are many variations of the Schmidt machine. Basically it is a quantum mechanical random number generator. The decay of the radioactive source delivers electrons randomly to a Geiger counter. Simultaneously, a high-frequency pulse generator advances a switch rapidly across target-choice positions. Lamps representing target choices are each coupled with a switch position. An electron reaching the Geiger counter stops the switch in one position, illuminating the lamp corresponding to that position. Each lamp has an equal probability of being the next target.

The subject registers his prediction of which lamp will light up next by pushing a button on the console. This opens the channel between the radioactive source and the Geiger counter, thus enabling a lamp to light soon after a call is made and not before. A mechanical counter advances to record the trial, the hit or miss, and the number of each lamp lit and button pressed. The recording is done on paper tape. To forge a recording, the subject or experimenter would have to open a sealed unit containing the tape, advance the trial counters, and carefully punch properly coded holes in the tape.

In an experiment reported in the *Journal of Parapsychology* (June 1969), three subjects attempted to predict which of four differently colored lamps would be lit next. No distinction was made between precognition and psychokinesis (influencing the radioactive decay process), and presumably a subject could succeed by using either method. Chance would expect the subject to be correct one-fourth of the time. Three subjects made correct calls at a rate of more than 500 million to 1 above chance.

New Criticisms

The Schmidt machine seemed to be the answer to all the charges the ESP critics had voiced in the past. However, the critics have raised further objections to parapsychological research—objections which a further refinement of experimental methods cannot overcome.

The first two objections both assume fraud. The critics charge collusion in the unautomated experiments between the experimenters and the subjects to produce positive results. To overcome this charge, parapsychologists would have to submit to twenty-four-hour surveillance and who would watch the watchers?

The debunkers' primary criticism in fully automated experiments, is that there is no assurance that parapsychologists are not just throwing out the records of runs which do not support their theories. Only a few would have to be discarded to raise the odds against chance to significant levels. Again, the only remedy for this possibility would be day-and-night observation and the constant services of a notary public to produce an independent record of every run.

Finally, the critics raise the problem of the law of large numbers. It is conceivable, for example, that a run of fifty coin tosses could produce fifty "heads." The odds against it are astronomical, but it is not impossible. However, probability theory maintains that if the run is continued, sooner or later enough "tails" will show up to balance the odds at the expected chance level that is, one to one. Some critics maintain that with a sufficient number of runs, the results of experiments which tend to support the existence of ESP would be canceled out.

Thus, although the evidence for parapsychological phenomena is massive, statistical problems and the potential for fraud and self-delusion continue to be as large an obstacle to progress as the elusiveness of ESP itself. Parapsychologists today have stopped trying to prove the existence of ESP; they believe it has been proved far beyond any reasonable doubt. They are now devoting their time to careful evaluation of the nature of ESP and the conditions which help bring it about and to ever clearer descriptions of what actually occurs in psi, the general term which parapsychologists now use to name both ESP and psychokinesis, which they believe work together and follow similar principles.

Three Characteristics of Psi

Three characteristics of psi have been studied now in considerable detail: the decline effect and the importance of rapid feedback; the psi-conducive situation; and the sheep-goat difference.

The problem of the successful experimental subject's inability to maintain high scores after a series of runs or even within one run the—"decline effect"—was commented upon by Charles Tart ("Card Guessing Tests: Learning Paradigm or

Extinction Paradigm," *Journal of the American Society for Psychical Research*, January 1966). Tart pointed out that the average parapsychological experiment was similar to techniques used to snuff out learning in animals. Tart suggested that to overcome this "extinction" process, experimenters should provide virtually immediate feedback on every trial so the subject can learn what a hit feels like and to encourage him to make more hits. Experiments should also try to make the test situation intrinsically motivating either by encouragement or by using materials of real interest to the subject. Finally, Tart said, the mechanics of test target selection, recording, feedback should be as unobtrusive as possible. Tests conducted to confirm or disprove Tart's contentions have supported his view overwhelmingly.

At about the same time that Tart made his suggestions, the concept of altered states of consciousness began to receive widespread attention. With the advent of hallucinogenic drugs and the appearance in the United States of a variety of forms of meditation, psi researchers began to examine the relation of altered states of consciousness to psi functioning. Experiments in telepathy, clairvoyance, and precognition used hypnosis, dreams, sensory deprivation, and meditation to produce a psi-conducive situation. Generally, these methods do improve psi functioning, but attempts to relate psi to certain kinds of brain wave activity, particularly alpha waves, have been inconclusive.

These explorations of ESP suggest that psychic communication is facilitated by a more inward focus of awareness. The psi-conducive syndrome seems to involve muscular relaxation, decreased arousal, and reduced sensory distraction. Many of these characteristics correspond with current knowledge about the functioning of the brain's right and left hemisphere. There has been a growing experimental interest in investigating whether an increase in right hemisphere functioning would result in an increase of psi communication (see Adrian Parker, *States of Mind: ESP and Altered States of Consciousness*, Taplinger, 1975).

In the 1940s, long before these elements of psi were discovered, parapsychologists, particularly Dr. Gertrude Schmeidler, began a long series of experiments to find out what sort of people do best in psi tests. Schmeidler's foremost finding was the difference between believers in ESP—sheep—and the skeptics—goats. Sheep consistently scored higher in ESP than did goats. Schmeidler and others have discovered that the sheep-goat distinction extends to experimenters as well. They also discovered that psi was more likely to appear in well-balanced, uncritical, flexible, spontaneous, and extraverted people (see Schmeidler and R. M. McConnell, *ESP and Personality Patterns,* Yale University Press, 1958).

Parapsychology Comes of Age

The three characteristics of psi outlined above are only a small portion of the wide range of discoveries and hypotheses developed by the sophisticated, interdisciplinary research in progress today. Most of C. E. M. Hansel's points against parapsychology have either been refuted or explained in ways consistent with the general public's experience of psi. The acceptance of the Parapsychological Association into the American Association for the Advancement of Science (AAAS) in 1969 marked the coming of age of a discipline which fewer than fifteen years earlier had been savagely attacked in the AAAS journal.

What the future holds for parapsychology is best expressed by Dr. John Beloff, director of the psychology department of the University of Edinburgh in Scotland:

> There are, at the present time, two guiding philosophies within parapsychology. According to the one, the concept of the paranormal has no permanent validity but is simply an expression of our ignorance. In the fullness of time, parapsychology will be integrated into a unified conceptual framework embracing all the sciences. Such a framework may have to be extended in various unexpected ways, but there is no danger of its being stretched to bursting-point. According to the other school of thought, which has been the dominant one in parapsychological history, the significance of the paranormal is precisely that it signals the boundary of the scientific world-view. Beyond that boundary lies the domain of mind liberated from its dependence on the brain. On this view, parapsychology, using the methods of science, becomes a vindication of the essentially spiritual nature of man which must forever defy strict scientific analysis. Which of these two antithetical philosophies will prevail remains a question for the future. In the meanwhile, there is no reason whatever why both parties should not cooperate in furthering our knowledge in this, the most perplexing

field of inquiry ever to engage the curiosity of our species. [*Handbook of Parapsychology,* B. B. Wolman, ed., Van Nostrand-Reinhold, 1977].

Major Parapsychological Organizations

American Society for Psychical Research (established 1885; reorganized 1905), 5 West Seventy-third Street, New York, New York 10023; 2,500 members, open to the public. President: Montague Ullman, MD; executive secretary: Laura F. Knipe. Publishes quarterly *Journal of the American Society for Psychical Research.*

New Horizons Research Foundation and *Toronto Society for Psychical Research* (established 1970), 10 North Sherbourne Street, Toronto, Ontario M4W 2T2, Canada; 200 members, open to the public. President: Allen Spraggett; secretary: Iris Owen. Publishes occasionally *New Horizons.*

The Society for Psychical Research (established 1882), 1 Adam & Eve Mews, Kensington, London W8 6UG, England; 1,100 members, open to the public. President: Dr. John Beloff. Publishes quarterly *Journal of the Society for Psychical Research.*

Parapsychology Foundation, Inc. (established 1951), 29 West Fifty-seventh Street, New York, New York 10019; not a membership organization. President: Eileen Coly; administrative secretary: Robert R. Coly. Publishes bimonthly *Parapsychology Review.*

Parapsychological Association (established 1957), Box 7503, Alexandria, Virginia 22307; 250 members, limited to established professionals in the field. President (1977): Dr. Charles Tart. Publishes annual proceedings under the title *Research in Parapsychology* (Scarecrow Press, 52 Liberty Street, Metuchen, New Jersey 08840).

Altered States of Consciousness and Psi

Altered states of conciousness—dreaming, meditation, deep relaxation, and the hypnagogic state just preceding or following sleep—have been shown to facilitate psi performance. In a long series of experiments conducted at the Parapsychology Division of the Maimonides Medical Center in Brooklyn, New York, and elsewhere, researchers have demonstrated clearly that psi information transference occurs with greater regularity during periods when the perceiver has less conscious sensory input to deal with.

Charles Honorton, director of research at Maimonides, in his presidential address to the Parapsychological Association in 1975, pointed out that before psi communication can occur, the perceiver must be able to sense the presence of and pay attention to stimuli of a very weak and tenuous nature. It is hardly surprising that with the constant bombardment of our senses by much stronger visual and aural stimuli, psi stimuli are seldom noticed.

In dreams and some forms of deep relaxation, however, the conscious mind no longer manipulates incoming stimuli according to conscious anticipations and purposes. In these states the more subtle psi stimuli can gain a place among the random images that flit through the brain.

Honorton has performed a series of experiments using *ganzfeld* stimulation, a form of sensory deprivation that allows the brain freely to bring images to consciousness and thus creates a clearer channel for possible psi information flow. In these experiments the subject's eyes are covered with the halves of a Ping-Pong ball. He can keep his eyes open but can see nothing except a soft rosy glow caused by a red lamp directed at his face. Isolated in a soundproofed room, the subject lies back in a recliner chair and, through earphones, listens to "white noise," a low-level shhh similar to mild static but without any irregularities that might gain the attention of the listener. After a relatively brief time in the *ganzfeld* (whole field), the subject is unable to tell if his eyes are open or closed and a variety of images and thoughts begin to stream through his mind. Among these may be some that are deliberately sent by psi to the subject from another participant in the experiment. As the images go through his mind, the subject describes them aloud, and his descriptions are transmitted by an intercom system to another room, where they are recorded by a monitor.

The subject spends about one-half hour in the *ganzfeld,* and for five or ten minutes of that time a "sender" in another room concentrates on the pictures in a View-Master slide reel, attempting to transmit their subject matter to the person in the *ganzfeld.* All the pictures on a reel are related to a single topic. The reel is one of four in a packet, and all four reels are thematically distinct. The packet of four reels is chosen at random from a pool of thirty-one packets, and the sender is the only one who knows the contents of the target reel.

At the end of the *ganzfeld session,* the subject's descriptions are read back to him to provide him with a review of his impressions. After this he is given the packet of four View-Master slide reels and asked to rank the reels from "most like" to "least like" his *ganzfeld* images. The subject, of course, does not know which reel was the one used by the sender. After the ranking is completed, the sender enters the room and names the reel he was trying to send to the subject.

In four series of experiments conducted by Honorton, fifty-one subjects went through 124 ganzfeld sessions. Overall, there were fifty-seven correct first-rank choices. The odds against this happening by chance are 845,000 to 1.

Since Honorton began these experiments, other independent researchers have repeated the same sort of experiment ten times. Only three of these repetitions had significant results, but even if all ten sets of results are lumped together, the results go against chance by 295,000 to 1.

Details of Honorton's work can be read in *The Journal of the American Society for Psychical Research,* Vol. 68, No. 2 (April 1974) and Vol. 70, No. 2 (April 1976). Details of the independent experiments are in the same *Journal* in Wood and Braud, "Free Response GESP Performance . . .," Vol. 69, No. 2 (April 1975) and in articles by R. L. Morris and L. Raburn in *Research in Parapsychology 1976* (Scarecrow Press, 1977).

Psi-Mediated Instrumental Response

Psi-mediated instrumental response (PMIR) is a theory, proposed by Dr. Rex G. Stanford, director of the Center for Parapsychological Research in Austin, Texas, which asserts that spontaneous use of psi can occur without the intention or awareness of the user and that it tends to work to the benefit of the user. The theory holds that ESP-PK is a system by

Two hits in the ganzfeld experiments with the subjects' descriptions prior to seeing the slides.

Target: "Lancelot Link Secret Chimp." Response: ". . . a chimpanzee from 2001 jumping up and down . . ."; ". . . apes and prehuman life-styles . . ."; "The images of prehistoric gods, prehuman apemen, what a rough existence they must have had. An image of a family friend who is a policeman, blue uniform, and badge. . . ."

which the individual scans the environment for helpful information and then acts or influences the environment to produce beneficial results or to avoid unpleasant or dangerous situations.

The term "psi-mediated" means that a person uses psi, and "instrumental" means that he or she carries out his or her purpose in "response" to the environment. PMIR may sometimes explain "good luck."

If the theory is correct, PMIR can occur naturally in people and in animals at any time. It can occur without any conscious effort to use psi, without any conscious knowledge of even the existence of the circumstances to which one is responding psychically, and without any awareness that something extraordinary is happening.

Target: "Rare Coins." Response: ". . . now I see circles—an enormous amount of them. Their sizes are not the same . . . some are really large, and others are very tiny—no longer than a penny. They just keep flashing in front of me—all these different sized circles"; "Now I see colors—a complete array of colors. Two in particular—gold and silver seem to stand out more than all the others. I sense something important. I can't tell what, but I get a feeling of importance, respect, value."

PMIR can work in a variety of ways. Unconscious timing may cause a person to miss a plane which subsequently crashes. Forgetting to do some task may cause the postponement of a decision which would not be helpful. A mistake such as dialing a wrong number may bring needed help to the person who answers the call. Remembering a friend and calling spontaneously may bring unexpected helpful information.

When a person is aware of a need for help, PMIR is likely to be of assistance through PK. This is most likely to happen when the individual (1) is not focusing on exactly what needs to be done, (2) feels incapable of doing something himself, (3) believes that he has properly appealed to an outside force, usually supernatural, for help and (4) believes that it is now up to that outside force to act or not, and (5) feels that things are already working out helpfully.

Sometimes PMIR is not present. This may be due to psychological factors such as behavioral rigidity, inhibitions, stereotyped thinking and acting, compulsiveness, and strong preoccupations. Again PMIR may be used by an individual to harm himself if he is very neurotic, has a negative self-image, or harbors strong feelings of guilt and feels a need to be punished.

The PMIR theory appears to fit most of the experimental and anecdotal data about psi in everyday life and in normal— not psychically gifted—people. The theory is unusually useful because it suggests many different ways to prove or disprove the theory in experiments with normal people.

Indeed, one of the most interesting experiments has been designed by Dr. Stanford himself. In this study, male college students were assigned the extremely boring task of operating a pursuit tracker at its slowest speed for forty-five minutes. A pursuit tracker is similar to the driving test game in a penny arcade, but at a slow speed it is as unchallenging as stirring a bowl of soup.

While the student worked on the pursuit tracker, a random-event generator was operating in another room. This generator, similar to a computer, would randomly turn on one of six electric switches every second. The experimenter arbitrarily chose one of those switches as the "correct" one.

The student was not told there was a random-event generator operating in another room. Nor was he told that he could escape his boring task and be asked to study some sexy pictures if, in any block of ten consecutive random events, seven of them turned the "correct" switch on.

The odds of getting 7 hits out of 10 trials are more than 3,700 to 1. Since each person could have had 2,700 trials or 270 blocks of 10 in his forty-five-minute test period, the odds against any single person escaping the boring job were 13 to 1. Since forty students were tested, chance alone would give three of the students relief from the chore and the opportunity to look at sexy pictures. In fact, eight students were able to do so. The odds against that are 144 to 1.

Skeptics will claim that this result was a momentary statistical aberration that would disappear if many more subjects were put through the trials.

It is certainly true that years of experiments will be required to prove the PMIR theory. But the results of the Stanford

Subject using pursuit tracker.

experiment are already backed up by similar results for other experiments designed to demonstrate nonintentional PK or PK in animals.

These studies are: H. Schmidt, "Observation of Subconscious PK Effect With and Without Time Displacement," *Research in Parapsychology, 1974,* J. D. Morris (ed.), Scarecrow Press, Metuchen, New Jersey, 1975; H. Schmidt, "PK Experiments with Animals as Subjects" in *Journal of Parapsychology,* No. 34 (1970); and G. K. Watkins, "Possible

Dr. Rex Stanford at the random-event generator.

PK in the Lizard Anolis sagrei" in *Proceedings of the Parapsychological Association,* No. 8 (1971). The account of Stanford's experiment appeared in "Psychokinesis as Psi-Mediated Instrumental Response" in the *Journal of the American Society for Psychical Research,* Vol. 69, No. 2 (April 1975). The full account of Stanford's PMIR theory appeared in the same *Journal* in Vol. 68, No. 1 (January 1974) and No. 4 (October 1974).

A Clairvoyance Experience

In a remote-viewing experiment in 1976, physicists Harold Puthoff and Russell Targ at Stanford Research Institute (SRI) in Menlo Park, California conducted more than fifty tests with nine subjects. The tests demonstrated the possibility of accurate paranormal viewing of places and objects at distances greater than one mile. The tests showed that this ability does not decrease with distance and that electrically shielding the remote viewer in a Faraday cage does not block the phenomenon. Correct information tended to be descriptions of the shape, form, color, and material rather than of the names or the uses of the items being viewed.

In the first series of tests, three subjects were either gifted psychics, including Ingo Swann (see An Interview with Ingo Swann, Psychic) or persons experienced at remote viewing. Three other subjects were learners. On each occasion the subject was isolated with an experimenter while a "target team" was issued a target-location description, selected at random from a set of 100 that had been prepared by a person not otherwise associated with the experiment. The subject and his observer were unaware of the contents of the 100 descriptions and of the particular description selected for the occasion. The target team (two to four other experimenters) were usually ignorant of the appearance of the target location until they arrived there; they, too, did not know the contents of the 100 location descriptions. No target location was used more than once during the entire experiment.

All the locations were within a thirty-minute drive from SRI. Thirty minutes after the team left, the subject was asked to describe his impressions of the site where the target team was now located. The subject's impressions were recorded on tape, and he was asked to make drawings of his impressions whenever helpful. After fifteen minutes the test was ended. Later an informal comparison of the results was made, and the subject was taken to the site to provide feedback.

After a subject had completed eight or nine tests, packets of the unedited transcripts of the tapes with their associated drawings were given to a research analyst. The packets were in random order and unlabeled. The analyst, upon visiting each site in turn, was asked to rank each packet on a scale of

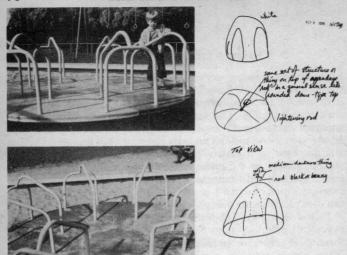

Merry-go-round target (left) and subject drawing (right) of target by remote viewing.

similarity or dissimilarity to each site. Thus, for subject No. 1 there were nine packets—one for each remote-viewing site. The analyst rated each packet on a scale from 1 to 9 at each site. The analyst on this occasion placed seven out of the nine packets in the first rank at the correct sites.

The researchers estimated the odds against chance for these placements very conservatively by considering them as a whole. For the series of rankings described above, the odds against chance were more than 33,000 to 1. After other tests with other subjects, five packets were ranked first and four were ranked second out of nine in one set of tests (more than 5,000,000 to 1); and three were ranked first and three were ranked second out of eight in another set (2,500 to 1). The results of a fourth set of tests did not differ significantly from chance.

In a second series of tests twelve experiments with five subjects were carried out, using only seven targets. Part of the aim of the experiment was to see if descriptions of one target by several subjects would improve an analyst's ability to identify the target. The targets in this case were pieces of equipment somewhere in the SRI complex. Similar judging procedures were used, except that all descriptions of the same machine were put in the same packet. There was one correct first and four correct second ranks out of seven. The odds against this were conservatively estimated at 26 to 1.

From a random arrangement of the original twelve separate results, a visiting scientist chose one at random and submitted it to an engineer for independent analysis, with a request for a guess on what was being described. The engineer, on the basis of the subject's taped remarks and drawing, said the item was "man-sized boring machine." The target was a drill press.

A third set of experiments involved precognitive remote viewing. The experimenters outlined their procedures as follows:

Experiment Protocol: Precognitive Remote-Viewing Time
Schedule Experimenter/Subject Activity

10:00   Outbound experimenter leaves with 10 envelopes (containing target locations) and random number generator; begins half-hour drive.

10:10   Experimenters remaining with subject in the laboratory elicit from subject a description of where outbound experimenter will be from 10:45–11:00.

10:25   Subject response completed, at which time laboratory part of experiment is over.

10:30   Outbound experimenter obtains random number from a random-number generator, counts down to associated envelope, and proceeds to target location indicated.

10:45   Outbound experimenter remains at target location for 15 minutes (10:45–11:00).

After four tests with one subject, three judges, working independently, were each able to match packets to targets without error. The odds against this were very conservatively estimated at 20 to 1.

With its wealth of pictures and other detail, the report on these experiments is strikingly persuasive about the reality of remote viewing. It is also persuasive in the authors' conclusion that "the principle difference between the experienced subjects and the inexperienced volunteers is not that the latter never exhibit the faculty, but rather that their results are simply less reliable. This observation suggests the hypothesis that remote-viewing may be a latent and widely distributed, though repressed perceptual ability."

The authors also point out that "the often held belief that observations of this type are incompatible with known laws *in principle* is erroneous, such a concept being based on the naive realism prevalent before the development of modern quantum theory and information theory." They conclude their report by stating that "the working assumption among researchers in the field is that the phenomenon . . . is consistent with modern scientific thought, and can therefore be expected to yield to the scientific method."

The appearance of this description of parapsychological experiments in the *Proceedings of The Institute of Electrical and Electronic Engineers* (Vol. 64, No. 3; March 1976) marked a major breakthrough in the publication of parapsychological data in reputable scientific journals. The article itself is unusual in the care used to describe procedures, the thoroughness of the theoretical background presented, and the detail of the bibliography.

"P" Values

A "p" value is a statistical indicator of the significance of the results of an experiment. Translated into ordinary English, a "p" value indicates the odds against those particular results appearing by chance. The layperson is unable to determine those odds unless he knows a little bit about statistics. It is maddening to read an interesting account of a parapsychology experiment and to begin wondering just how positive the results were, only to be told near the end of the article that the experiment found "a significant ($p < .02$) positive deviation" or that the results were "significant at $p = 3.8 \times 10^{-4}$." How significant is that? What do these "p" values mean in "odds against chance?"

The layperson can find out by doing two simple arithmetic processes. In the case of "$p < .02$, the "$<$" means "less than" and indicates that "p" really equals something like .0199999 etc.; ignore it. To determine odds against chance subtract the .02 from 1:

$$
\begin{array}{r}
1.00 \\
- .02 \\
\hline
.98
\end{array}
$$

Then divide the results, .98, by the subtrahend, .02:

$$\begin{array}{r} 49 \\ \hline .02 \overline{\smash{).98}} \end{array}$$

The odds against chance in this example were 49 to 1.

This same procedure is followed anytime the "p" value is a simple decimal: .02, .042, .007, .0009. The more zeros immediately after the decimal point, the greater are the odds against chance.

When the "p" value is a number (3.8) followed by figures like "$\times 10^{-4}$," the following procedure is used. The small negative number after the 10 indicates the number of zeros which should follow the 1 and precede the decimal in the first operation, the subtraction, thus:

$$\begin{array}{r} 10{,}000.0 \\ 3.8 \\ \hline 9{,}996.2 \end{array}$$

Then, as in the first example, the result is divided by the subtrahend, 3.8:

$$\begin{array}{r} 2{,}630.6 \\ \hline 3.8 \overline{\smash{)9.996.2}} \end{array}$$

The odds against chance in this case were about 2,630 to 1.

The procedure applies whether the other figure is 10^{-5}, 10^{-8}, or 10^{-15}. The higher the small negative number, the more significant are the results.

Occasionally, results are so significant they may simply be written like this: $p = 10^{-30}$. That means that the odds against chance are so great we don't even have a name for the number involved (in this case, a 1 followed by thirty zeros). If the small negative number is not too great, as in 10^{-6} for example, just write the specified number of zeros after 1 to find the odds against chance: 1,000,000 to 1, in the example.

Sometimes, the experimenter will say the "p" value is "one-tailed" or "two-tailed." Ignore that; it is only shoptalk that tells other statisticians what method was used to determine the "p" value.

The Levy Affair

Dr. Jay Levy, who received an MD from the Medical College of Georgia in 1973, had worked since 1969 on various projects for famed parapsychologist Dr. J. B. Rhine at the Institute for Parapsychology in Durham, North Carolina. Levy, only twenty-six, had gained wide recognition for his work on precognition in rats and, as director of the institute, was considered by many the heir apparent to Rhine. Among Levy's major achievements had been the automation and computerization of experimental designs to test ESP. It had been hoped that his "hardware" approach would help legitimize the struggling field of parapsychology by removing experimenter influences. Ironically, it was Levy's tampering with his own apparatus that led to his downfall.

The experiment in question involved rats that had been implanted with electrodes in the pleasure centers of the brain. At first, the rats were taught to self-stimulate the brain's pleasure center through bar pressing. This procedure was then replaced with a computer which stimulated the rats' pleasure zones at random intervals. The experiment was designed to test the hypothetical psychokinetic (PK) ability of rats to influence the apparatus to obtain stimulation. On a purely random basis the creatures would be expected to receive stimulation half the time. However, in early May Levy's instruments were recording stimulation 54 percent of the time.

Several assistants observed Levy tinkering with the test apparatus for no apparent reason. Consequently, the assistants erected duplicate recording devices and planted a hidden observer. Levy was caught manually interfering with the automatic equipment in order to obtain a higher frequency. The duplicate instruments only recorded a 50 percent chance score.

When Levy was summoned by Dr. Rhine, he immediately confessed his guilt and resigned. He explained that he had been obtaining significant results for some time, but suddenly they had gone wrong. He claimed that he falsified the data in order to keep interest in this line of research alive at other institutions. He maintained that this was the only instance of deception in all his work.

Subsequent revelations, however, made Rhine suspect that "Levy's deception was much more extensive than had first been discovered." One assistant discerned possible tampering with apparatus in a Levy experiment on precognition in gerbils. When the published reports of Levy's automated maze tests with human subjects were compared with the computer record, they also diverged, with the latter showing no statistical significance. "Apparently, a completely different set of results had been invented," Rhine admitted. Still another

Levy experiment—testing chicken embryos for PK effects—revealed long strings of "hits"—very similar to his admitted rat deception. With the strings removed the results were not significant, just as in the rat tests.

These discoveries brought into question the results of all the work Levy had done from 1969 to 1974. A list of Levy's publications was compiled by J. B. Rhine, "Second Report on a Case of Experimenter Fraud" (*Journal of Parapsychology,* Vol. 39, No. 4, December 1975, pp. 323–24).

Jim Kennedy, Levy's assistant in the rat experiments, was unable to obtain significant results in a continuation of this work. However, when it was learned that the electrode implantation process itself was faulty, all replication attempts by the Rhine Institute ceased. The APA [American Psychological Association] *Journal Monitor* reported that the electrodes had deteriorated over time, thereby lessening the pleasure stimulation after a few months. Levy, unaware of this, used his rats for six months at a time, which could have accounted for the fall in results which led him to resort to trickery.

Kennedy and other researchers attempted to replicate Levy's chick embryo PK results, but failed. Other experimenters conducted replication studies of Levy's main "claim to recognition in parapsychology," his precognition experiments with small rodents. Researchers Jerry Levin and James Terry worked with gerbils and obtained significant results in only a small percentage of cases. Although their work was suggestive, it certainly "does not constitute independently confirmatory evidence," according to Rhine.

In other tests, Hans J. Eysenck demonstrated that certain strains of rats evidenced precognitive ability to anticipate mild electrical stimulation. Other ESP experiments on rats—by James Davis and Joseph Sanford—have seemed less than conclusive, although Sanford claims that his "experiments have provided evidence that seriously supports the idea that animals have ESP and can learn to use it to their advantage in the environment."

Rhine indicates that certain other contributions by Levy, such as the human subject automated-maze technique and the random behavior analysis are "still on trial," and may possibly be confirmed in the future. In summarizing the situation, however, Rhine states flatly that "nothing definitely confirmatory has so far come out of all the attempts made here since his [Levy's] departure."

People familiar with psychic research believe that the

Levy incident made more waves in the press than in the community of parapsychologists. Two effects of the Levy affair can be inferred from the literature. Few parapsychologists have either the inclination or aptitude for Levy's sophisticated automated-computerized style. Thus, the prospect of reliable replication of tests and scientific legitimacy has been set back. On a more human level, the search for a worthy successor for the aging Rhine once again has become a problem.

As in most fields, research has its own impetus, and, besides making fraud a clearer concern in the laboratory, the Levy case, as Rhine indicates, "will probably not arouse that much interest. No one in or out of the field ever even asked the gloomy question: 'Is this going to ruin parapsychology?'," he said, adding that "the forthright exposé seemed rather to increase public confidence." As evidence, he indicated that a generous support grant was donated to the institute at the time of disclosure to boost morale.

Perhaps, most crucially, the Levy affair will add fuel to parapsychology's critics. By creating an air of disreputability, the Levy debacle could lessen the acceptance of parapsychology and hinder the interdisciplinary research essential to the growth of the field.

In a curious development (which, according to *Time,* August 26, 1974, revealed that "Rhine lacks one of his own favorite phenomena: precognition"), Rhine had published a lengthy discussion on "security and deception in parapsychology" immediately before the Levy disclosure (see "Security Versus Deception in Parapsychology," *Journal of Parapsychology,* Vol. 38, 1974). In that paper, he said that the last attack on a new discipline is the charge of fraud. In other words, when other critiques (e.g., of methodology) have failed, detractors cast doubts on the honesty of the experimenters. Rhine said that charges of fraud in parapsychology had begun in the mid-1950s.

In an appendix to his "security and deception" article, Rhine noted a discussion by Dr. Theodore Barber of the Medfield Foundation in Massachusetts that deals with "investigator and experimenter effects" in the field of psychology (see Theodore X. Barber, "Pitfalls in Research: Nine Investigator and Experimenter Effects," in *Second Handbook on Research and Teaching,* R. Travers, ed., Rand-McNally, 1973). Although the article addresses itself to possible pitfalls in research, Barber speaks of the dilemma of data "fudging." Scientific and academic pressures to derive "meaningful" results create an atmosphere in which deception, innocent or not, can occur. Rhine himself revealed that in the early stages of his research he caught several experimenters " 'redhanded' in having falsified their results." These obvious frauds, he says, are characteristic of a young discipline and adds that "fifty or more years ago, there were notorious cases of experimenter fraud in physics, biology, and medicine, among other fields."

An instance of deception in another scientific field, in the spring of 1974, involved Dr. William Summerlin, an immunologist working at the Sloan-Kettering Institute for Cancer Research in New York City. He performed skin grafts between genetically incompatible black and white strains of mice and claimed that he had overcome the continuing problem of antigens rejecting foreign tissues. It was discovered that Summerlin had used a pen to color the grafted areas in order to make it appear that the transplants had taken. His deception resulted in a terminal leave of absence.

Outright fraud, however, is only a small, though highly visible, aspect of data manipulation. With present developments in behavioral science data collection and analysis—including statistics and probability theory, factor analysis, multidimensional scaling, and analysis of variance—possibilities abound for data manipulation. Often, most of the controversy in modern research involves misuses of mathematical tools.

ANIMALS
AND PLANTS

Mammals

Talking Chimpanzees

A chimpanzee named Washoe in 1966 began to learn to communicate in American Sign Language, or Ameslan, the primary language used by deaf people in North America. Five years later, at age six, she had learned 160 words, which she was able to use singly or in combinations in a variety of conversational situations. Washoe's teachers during this period were Beatrice and R. Allen Gardner, behavioral psychologists at the University of Nevada at Reno.

Before the Gardners' success with Washoe, attempts to teach apes to talk verbally had not shown much success. In the early 1950s Keith Hayes (see Eugene Lindon, *Apes, Men, and Language*, Dutton, 1974) attempted a comparative study of the problem-solving abilities of a chimp, Vicki, and several human infants. Although Vicki proved capable of matching the human infant's performance in figuring out the locks of latchboxes and discriminating colors and form, she was able to learn to utter reliably only four words.

The Gardners, after viewing extensive films of Vicki's training, suspected that the problem was not that apes were not smart enough to learn language, but rather that physical differences between the vocal organs of man and apes made it difficult for apes to pronounce words. The Gardners speculated that a chimpanzee, however, might be able to learn a sign language. They chose to work with a chimpanzee because chimps are reputed to be most easily trained of the great apes. They chose Ameslan, in which gestures play the role of words, because it has proved to be practical, it is accepted as a bona fide language, and its acquisition by the deaf has been carefully studied.

The Gardners installed Washoe in a trailer in their backyard. The Gardners did not insist on a particular teaching method but experimented with several until they hit on a combination of methods that worked. At the outset they rewarded Washoe when she successfully approximated the sign being taught. However, after the first year, they discovered that guidance or molding—actually forming the gesture with the chimp's hands—was the most effective method. Washoe's first word was "more," a gesture made by repeated touching of the fingertips with the palms toward the signer. The Gardners spoke no English around Washoe but conversed consistently in Ameslan about the activities they were involved in—playing, eating, washing, etc. Once Washoe realized that she might get what she wanted, e.g., be tickled or fed—by asking for it in Ameslan, she began to take an active part in her education. She began to initiate conversations and to ask the signs of the things she was interested in. Washoe used her first combination, or multisign sequence, in April 1967, when she was just two years old, about the same age at which human infants utter their first two-word sentences. From then until June 1969 she was observed to use ninety-four different combinations.

In 1971, when Washoe reached adulthood and became too unruly to handle, she was sent to the Institute for Primate Studies in Norman, Oklahoma, where, under the supervision of Roger Fouts, the Gardners' former chief assistant, she was to continue her education. By this time Washoe could apply a sign correctly in a new context; for example, having learned the sign for dog, she could apply it correctly to a picture of a strange dog. She could make up new signs for things she had never encountered; when she saw a swan for the first time, she called it a "water-bird." She was able to use language to lie; when she was angry at her trainer, she concealed her anger and seductively signed for him to come to her and then attacked him. She could grasp the way word order conveys meaning—that is, she understood which sign had to come first if she wanted to be tickled instead of tickling her teacher, and she used this understanding to create new grammatically correct sentences. People familiar with Ameslan testified that in conversing with Washoe, they soon forgot that she was an animal and felt that they were simply talking with a child.

Since the Gardners' initial experiment, they and other scientists have continued to apply their methods to teach Ameslan to other apes. In a further experiment the Gardners started with two chimps, Major and Pili, who were only a day or two old, placed them in homes of either deaf people or with a couple whose parents were deaf and who had learned sign language in infancy. They discovered that the chimps were learning words at a rate comparable to that of human infants in deaf homes (Boyce Rensberger, "Chimps Learning Signs Faster with Deaf," *The New York Times*, February 2, 1975). They also discovered that the chimps were building their vocabularies faster than chimps that were not exposed to Ameslan until they were one year old or older. Although the chimps' vocabulary did not yet exceed that of other chimps trained in Ameslan, the Gardners felt their rate of progress promised spectacular achievements in language acquisition as they grew older.

Research conducted at the National Institute for Primate Studies, now loosely associated with the University of Oklahoma, has done much to support, as well as to further, the pioneering work of the Gardners. Roger Fouts' work with Lucy, the oldest of the institute's chimps currently being raised in isolation from other chimps, has centered on how she understands words. For instance, in one experiment Lucy was asked to classify twenty-four different fruit and vegetables. At that time the food-related words in Lucy's vocabulary were "food," "fruit," "drink," "candy," and "banana." Lucy knew "banana" referred specifically to banana and used "food," "fruit," and "drink" in a generic manner to refer to those three classes of items. When speaking of citrus fruit, Lucy tended to call them "smell fruit," referring to their distinctive odor. In distinguishing between fruits and vegetables, Lucy preferred "fruit" for fruit and "food" for vegetables. In the case of watermelon, Lucy particularly showed her descriptive abilities. She liked watermelon and called it "candy drink" three times, referring both to its sweetness and to an attribute of the fruit we recognize in our name for it. Another time, calling it a "drink-fruit," she came very close to the creative symbolization that produced the English word "watermelon."

In another experiment at the National Institute for Primate Studies a chimp named Ally learned to recognize ten words spoken in English. He was then taught, in response to the spoken words, the same ten words in Ameslan. Thus, when Ally was shown a spoon, he could identify it in Ameslan. He had learned cross-modal transfer, the ability to link a gesture, learned from hearing the word, with a visual stimulus. In other work at the institute, chimps isolated on an island began to talk to one another in Ameslan and, apparently finding it a useful means of communication, are using it increasingly to communicate with one another. In the future, when the first infant is born of a Ameslan-speaking chimp

"sweet/candy"

"drink"

Lucy, using Ameslan, invents her own word for "watermelon," using the sign for "sweet" or "candy" and the sign for "drink."

mother, possibly Washoe, the institute plans to study how Ameslan will affect the mother-infant relationship and determine whether the mother will actively teach the child the language.

Some investigators have used different techniques to teach language to chimpanzees. David Premack, a psychologist, working at about the same time as the Gardners, used strictly behavioralist methods to teach language to Sarah. He taught Sarah to communicate by using plastic tokens to write on a magnetic board. At the outset Premack manipulated Sarah's desire for treats. She had to write "give Sarah apple" in order to get an apple. He then taught her the token "name of" and taught her new words by placing "name of" between the new token and the object. He determined that Sarah understood the symbolic nature of tokens by asking her to describe an object represented by a token. She described an apple, which is represented by a blue triangle, with characteristics such as redness and roundness. Premack was also able to exploit Sarah's specific tastes, by teaching her the conditional—"if . . . then"—type of sentence. For instance, Sarah was given a choice between an apple and a banana. Only if she chose the apple would she be given a prized piece of chocolate. After some frustrating trials Sarah learned to read the sentences.

At the Yerkes Regional Primate Research Center in Atlanta, Georgia, Duane Rambough has invented an artificial language called Yerkish for Lana, another chimpanzee (Boyce Rensberger, "Talking Chimpanzee Asks for Names of Things Now," *The New York Times,* December 4, 1974). Lana communicates with a system of symbols that are displayed on a computer terminal. She makes sentences by hitting the appropriate keys in the correct order. Not only has she learned to ask for concrete objects by the names she has been taught, but she has also learned, like Washoe, to ask for the names that represent objects whose names she does not know.

At Stanford University Penny Patterson, who is working on a doctorate in psychology focusing on the comparative cognitive skills between apes and humans, has taught Ameslan to a gorilla, long considered less intelligent than chimpanzees (see Sandra Blakeslee, "Koko the Gorilla Gives Hints of Being Smarter Than the Chimpanzees," *The New York Times,* June 27, 1975). Patterson claimed Koko is learning signs at a rate faster than Washoe's. Also in a recent test, gorillas scored

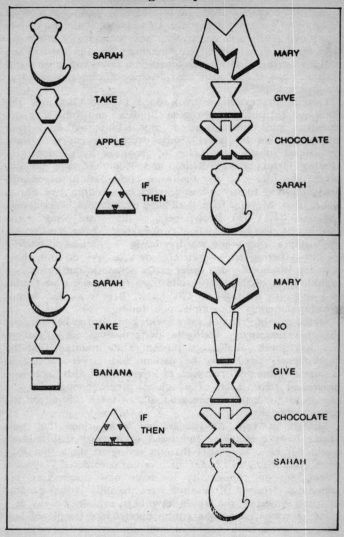

Sarah, presented with these two symbol sentences, an apple and a banana, understood that if she chose the banana, her favorite fruit, she would not also get the greatly desired piece of chocolate.

higher than chimpanzees in set learning tasks—a method designed to test ape intelligence. In addition, Patterson claims that Koko uses words creatively: "She occasionally makes up new words [signs] which are amazingly appropriate and she is able to string known words together in novel and meaningful constructions. Koko also has a sense of humor and plays word games."

Despite the extensive work done by the Gardners, the National Institute for Primate Studies, and others, many scientists and philosophers do not admit that apes have learned human languages. Some psycholinguists who have specialized in the acquisition of language by children, including Ursula Bellugi-Klima and Roger Brown, do not accept the idea that the multisign combinations of chimps are similar to multiword utterances by children (see Stuart Baur, "First Message from the Planet of the Apes," *New York*, February 24, 1975). Brown believes that word order is the crucial criterion in syntactical competence. Brown has argued, for instance, that while word order is "as natural to a child as nut-gathering to a squirrel," data as yet do not show whether Washoe's word order has a semantic nature or is a cranking out of the appropriate signs to achieve a particular end—e.g., to be tickled. The latter, Brown argues, is not creating sentences, but simple conditioning.

In the case of Premack's work with Lana, critics have argued that her seemingly intelligent performances could just as well have been taught to a pigeon. They maintain that the experimenter need only be patient and clever enough to break down the performances, as Premack did with Lana, into individual steps, each of which is simple enough for the pigeon to master, and then gradually to teach the pigeon the entire sequence.

Linden, in *Apes, Languages, and Men*, argues that most critics have been more interested in proving that animals could not have languages than in trying to show that they could. According to Linden, such critics considered Washoe a threat, not an opportunity to make new discoveries. He concludes, "Indeed, if Washoe were the only chimp capable of using Ameslan, she would have been explained away as a freak; however, once one chimp entered the temple of language others soon followed and it became increasingly difficult to get them out."

Rats

Rats are a genus of rodent whose great adaptability has enabled them to penetrate almost all human communities.

Of the 500 kinds of rats (not counting other varieties of rodents often mistaken for rats), the best known are the black rat (*Rattus rattus*) and the Norway rat (*Rattus norvegicus*).

The black rat has been associated with the earliest-known settlements in Asia. It reached Europe no later than the Crusades, helped spread the bubonic plague, and appeared in South America by 1540. The Norway rat (also called the wharf, sewer, or brown rat) probably originated along stream banks in northern China, eastern Mongolia, and eastern Siberia. A skillful swimmer, the animal spread south along man-made canals and irrigated rice fields and may have reached Europe in the Middle Ages, though the first definite European appearance was in 1553. Norway rats were found in North America by 1775 and had spread to all the states by 1923. The world rat population probably equals the human population in number.

On the whole, Norway rats have replaced black rats as the dominant species, for reasons that are not clear. Nevertheless, the two species coexist in several areas in the United States, including the Southeast and the Pacific coast. The black variety is found in trees, roofs, and upper stories, while the Norway rat inhabits cellars and underground burrows.

Rats are social animals and live in large packs. About 45 percent of Norway rat packs have more than 60 members, and some have more than 200. Strange rats that attempt to join an established pack are often threatened and attacked by members of the pack. The rejected rats usually die within a few days even if no physical injury is inflicted. Since these dead rats show enlargement of the adrenal glands, it has been theorized that death is caused by overreaction to severe stress.

Rats are a major pest in many countries, consuming a large portion of crops and stored grains, as well as poultry and game. They can also carry more than two dozen diseases. Control is made difficult by their rapid proliferation, with a single rat capable of bearing up to seven litters a year, each containing two to twenty-two offspring.

Half-grown rats face an unusual danger sitting close to

Rats, which in India's desert state of Rajasthan are thought to be the earthly representatives of a Hindu deity, the Holy Ganesha, the god of prosperity, swarm to the altar of the temple sanctuary of rats at feeding time in Deshnoukh.

each other in their nest. Their tails may become intertwined in a knot known in German as a *Ratten König*, or rat king. Their attempts to pull free only bind them tighter together. As many as twenty rats have been known to die as a result.

Laboratory studies which showed a remarkable learning ability in rats have been challenged. Some researchers argue that the experiments really demonstrated the ingenuity of the experimentors in breaking down tasks into steps easy enough for rats to learn. However, more recent studies of rats under natural conditions have tended to confirm, in general, the rats' problem-solving abilities.

Groups of rats exhibit ways of obtaining food which are learned and passed on to younger members of the pack, according to *Grzimek's Encyclopedia*. Some packs seem to have learned to fish by extending their forepaws into flowing water and making a sifting motion. Others have learned to hunt for birds, behaving in ways remarkably similar to the instinctive hunting behavior of carnivores.

One of the bases of this learning ability is the rat's curiosity and penchant for exploration. This penchant is so strong that according to Samuel Barnett, in *The Rat*, rats in the laboratory can be taught to perform tricks when the only reward they receive is the opportunity to explore new surroundings.

This learning ability aids rats in avoiding poison. If the first rat in a pack to explore some food rejects it, he marks it by depositing urine or feces, according to *Grzimek's Encyclopedia*. His pack-mates will then avoid the food, adding their own deposits. On the other hand, if the first rat eats the poisoned food, the others will often follow suit.

But even an individual rat has an ability to detect poison through taste and smell and perhaps through another sense. Rats whose sense of smell is destroyed by experimenters are sometimes able to avoid poisoned bait even without tasting it, according to Barnett.

For further information, see Samuel A. Barnett, *The Rat: A Study in Behavior* (Aldine, 1963); Ernest P. Walker, *Mammals of the World,* Vol. II, 3d ed. (Johns Hopkins University Press, 1975); E. O. Wilson, *Sociobiology* (Harvard University Press, 1975); and *Grzimek's Animal Encyclopedia*.

Dolphin Intelligence

In 1960 John C. Lilly predicted that within the next decade or two the human species would establish communication with another species, "nonhuman, alien, possibly extraterrestrial, more probably marine; but definitely highly intelligent, perhaps even intellectual." In 1975 Lilly said the prediction has not yet come true. He added, however, that he was returning to his work with interspecies communication to try a new approach and hoped to have an answer by 1980.

Although Lilly has not made the claim, his extensive writings on dolphins—*Man and the Dolphin* (Doubleday, 1961), *The Mind of the Dolphin* (Doubleday, 1967), and *Lilly on Dolphins* (Doubleday, 1975)—have been widely accepted as showing that dolphins are at least as intelligent as humans, have their own language, are capable of learning human language and are, therefore, the nonhuman creatures with whom people will establish communication.

Although he does not attempt to dampen the belief and enthusiasm of his followers, Lilly thus far has made clear that his assumptions about dolphins are conjecture. In *The Mind of the Dolphin,* Lilly does endorse the assumptions of his co-worker Margaret C. Howe. Howe, who has done extensive work with dolphins, believes that "dolphins are capable of communication with man on the level of high intelligence." However, much of Lilly's writing on the intelligence of dolphins and other cetaceans is anecdotal and speculative. In one instance, he tells of the quickly learned ability of killer whales in Antarctica to discriminate whaling boats from fishing boats even though they are nearly identical. He speculates that the first killer whales that learned the difference between the two may have described the difference to other killer whales and the warning eventually was spread to the entire population of killer whales.

Lilly's work with dolphins has encountered considerable criticism. Karen W. Pryor ("Behavior and Learning in Cetaceans," *Naturwissenschaften,* 1973) is a zoologist who has done extensive observation of and experimentation with dolphins. Along with her co-worker, the influential communications theorist Gregory Bateson, she was initially enthusiastic about Lilly's assertions and set out to confirm them. However, after years of research, she reported that there is no clear evidence that dolphins exhibit intelligent behavior of a kind superior to that observed in dogs or horses. Nor did she find evidence of a dolphin language.

Forrest G. Wood, another zoologist who has worked with dolphins for many years, has also criticized Lilly's work. Although it must be considered that Wood may be biased against Lilly because Lilly criticized work Wood did for the Navy, his arguments have merit. Wood (*Marine Mammals and Man*, Luce, 1973) pointed out that Lilly has not provided adequate documentation for the anecdotes he uses to support his assertions. Specifically, he questions Lilly's suggestion that there is a dolphin language. He questions, as do many scientists, the assumption that there is such a thing as general intelligence. If, in fact, there is not, Wood argues that it is not possible to compare the intelligence of different species of animals. His own intensive review of research on dolphin communication, he states, has failed to produce evidence of a dolphin language. Wood also questions Lilly's assumption that brain size can be correlated with intelligence. He pointed out that although an elephant's brain is larger than that of a horse, it is difficult, if not impossible, to devise tests of intelligence in which an elephant does better than a horse.

One of the strongest criticisms made of Lilly's work has been made by Edward O. Wilson in *Sociobiology* (Harvard University Press, 1974). He writes, "Lilly's books are misleading to the point of bordering on irresponsibility." Wilson criticized Lilly because he felt other zoologists have simply ignored his work, allowing him to have a great influence on the public and scientists in related fields. According to Wilson, "It is important to emphasize that there is no evidence whatever that delphinids are more advanced in intelligence and social behavior than other animals. . . . The communication and social organization of delphinids generally appear to be of a conventional mammalian type."

Insects

"Killer" Bees

"Killer" bees are a crossbred species found in Brazil that is reputed to be exceptionally aggressive. It is supposed to be expanding its range at a rate that will bring it to the United States by 1990.

Brazilian "killer" bee (Apis mellifera adansonii).

The "killer" bee is a cross between the mild European honeybee and the aggressive African strain which was imported into Brazil about 1955. The African bees are more productive than their European cousins, working longer hours in worse weather. They also have a greater tendency to abscond from beekeepers' hives and turn wild.

An African hive first absconded in São Paulo in 1957. These bees soon mated with the European strain and began to expand rapidly across Brazil. The bees' range now covers an area greater than that of the United States less Alaska.

News stories about the bees have recounted cases of mass

attacks by the bees on men and animals, and several fatalities have been reported. In spite of the alleged danger, Brazilian farmers have redomesticated many "killer" hives and, pleased with the bees' greater productivity, have resisted attempts to make them more tractable by crossing them with a mild-mannered Italian variety.

Estimates by some experts see the wild "killer" bees' range expanding by 200 miles a year. If the bees do reach the United States and interbreed with domestic bees, some reports have suggested they will constitute a menace to human and animal life in all agricultural areas and, from time to time, even in large cities.

Many experts hold that the aggressiveness of the bees has been overstated. Roger A. Morse, professor of agriculture at Cornell, says the bee is no more aggressive than at least one other species, the Cyprian bee, that is often raised by beekeepers. The hybrid bees are less ferocious than their purebred African ancestors.

The ferocity of the insect seems most apparent in its mass attacks on humans and animals, yet these attacks, according to bee experts, are the result of chemistry and statistical chance rather than of any innate viciousness on the part of the bees. When a disturbed bee stings and flies away, it leaves its stinger, with some of its viscera attached, in the victim. The viscera contain a chemical, isoamyl acetate, whose odor tends to attract other bees to the site. If the victim panics, he is likely to crush some of the bees, thus increasing the amount of the chemical odor in the air. Since the new Brazilian bees tend to move in larger clusters than do other bees, it is statistically more likely that more of them will respond to the odor and home in on the terrified victim.

Professor Morse also maintains that the "killer" bee cannot adapt to temperate climes. He points out that North American bees, adapted to tropical and subtropical conditions, do not have the "winter cluster" trait in their behavioral repertoire. Thus, the temperate zones of North and South America will block the expansion of these bees.

For further information, see *Scientific American* (January 1976); C. D. Michener, *The Social Behavior of Bees* (Harvard University Press, 1974); and E. O. Wilson, *The Social Insects* (Harvard University Press, 1971).

Seventeen-Year Locusts

Seventeen-year "locusts" (*Magicicada septendecim*) are insects that live underground for seventeen years and suddenly, as if on a common signal, emerge in late May.

The insect, not a locust at all, is a cicada and belongs to the order Homoptera. Also called a periodic locust, it is the strangest of some 2,000 cicadas known to science and has the longest life span of any insect. There is another periodic locust, the thirteen-year cicada, which is found only in the southeastern United States.

In the spring and early summer the female uses her sawlike ovipositor to make punctures in twigs and dry branches to deposit her eggs, usually 12 to 20 in each insertion, for a total of 400 to 600 eggs. The eggs hatch in six to seven weeks, producing wingless larvae, which drop to the ground and burrow their way into the soil. Although the drop may be 1,000 times the length of the larvae, they are light, and the air cushions their fall. Once in the soil, the larvae dig their way—approximately eighteen to twenty-four inches below the surface—toward a rootlet from which they subsequently nourish themselves by drinking the sap. The larvae stay underground for seventeen years, then make their way to the surface. In May of the seventeenth year the larvae come close to the surface and, on one warm night, as if on a common signal, they all come out of the ground and climb up nearby trees and bushes to prepare for their transformation. In a few hours they have turned into pale white winged creatures of the air. By morning the creatures which emerged during the night have turned dark. They have brilliant eyes and glistening parchment wings with yellow veins. Tremendous numbers up to 40,000 may emerge from beneath a single tree. Adults live about thirty to forty days, during which time they live by sucking sap from trees. During this period they mate and deposit their eggs to begin a new cycle.

In some localities the seventeen-year cicada appears every couple of years. This is the result of there being several broods, each brood following a precise seventeen-year cycle. In all, about thirty different broods are known. Brood X, the most carefully observed and studied, has a complete record dating from 1715. It is the largest brood and covers almost half the United States east of the Mississippi. Everywhere throughout this immense area the members of brood X appear at the same time on the same day.

E. W. Teale, in *Grassroot Jungles* (Dodd, Mead, 1937), stated that he believed civilization—the building of concrete highways over the larvae's underground "waiting room"—would in time render the insect and its quaint reproduction system extinct.

The Pilgrim Fathers, in 1634, named the seventeen-year cicadas "locusts." They heard the typical wail of the cicadas and thought what they saw emerging from the ground was a plague of locusts as had occurred in biblical times. The biblical locust—the eighth plague of Egypt—was, in fact, a true locust (*Schistocerca gregaria*), which is periodically responsible for enormous depradations, especially in Africa.

For more details, see A. H. Verill, *Strange Insects and Their Stories* (L. C. Page, 1937).

Sea Life

Electric Eels

The electric eel (*Electrophorus electricus*) is undoubtedly the most powerful and dangerous electric fish known; it is capable of producing an electric shock strong enough to stun a man.

The electric eel is not an eel at all, lacking the sinuous grace and streamlined contours of the American eel and its relatives. Practically nothing is known about the eel's life history. A young eel does not produce enough electricity to defend itself and procure food until it reaches a length of five or six inches. At a length of three feet, it reaches maximum voltage, and subsequent growth serves to increase amperage. The maximum length reached is about nine and a half feet, and the maximum weight is about ninety pounds. Strictly an air breather, the eel will drown if held underwater for any length of time. It uses its electric power for navigation, locating prey, obtaining prey, and self-defense.

Although the electric eel is sensitive to electricity, it is not harmed by its own discharges or by those of its fellows. On the contrary, when an individual eel discharges electricity, all other eels in the vicinity converge to the spot, apparently searching for food. Whenever an electric eel moves about, it produces a series of low-powered discharges, which are used as a kind of radar to locate objects in its environment. A number of electric fishes use a low-power electric field in the same manner.

The mature eel can produce a discharge of 550 volts at one ampere, with average discharges running at about 400 per second, and the fish can keep it up for days, although frequency drops as time passes. According to R. A. Caras, in *Dangerous to Man* (Chilton, 1964), the eel is probably the only electric fish capable of killing on contact a full-grown man in good health and of knocking down a horse at a distance of twenty feet.

Of the world's thirty-five to forty known varieties of electric fish, only the eel and the torpedo ray are capable of

Dr. Christopher W. Coates, at the Bronx Zoo, in New York City, trains electric eels to give off the kind of electrical discharge he needs for research on human nerve disorders, such as epilepsy.

injuring large mammals or man; the rest are harmless.

The eel's power comes from the fact that it has a greater number of special cells—contained in more than one-half of its body—for the production of electricity than other fishes.

All animals, from the primitive worm to the human, produce electricity, but in all but the electric eel and other electric fishes, this ability remains primarily an internal phenomenon. All of the fish's vital organs are in the front 20 percent of the body, with the remaining 80 percent devoted to electricity production. Each of the electric cells in the special tissues produces one-tenth of a volt. The eel has a total of about 500,000 electric "plates," each with a tiny nerve coming from a group of nerves in the belly region. The electroplates are situated one behind the other in close rows side by side and are "wired" in parallel. The power is additive and is released in the form of discharges under the control of the central nervous system.

In spite of its great power, the electric eel could not operate ordinary electric appliances or light fixtures. This is because each discharge lasts only two one-thousandths of a second, while an incandescent light, for example, takes as long as one-fiftieth of a second to heat up enough to become visible. The current generated by an eel is always direct current, and the front end of the fish is always the positive pole.

We feel, hear, smell, taste, see, and move electrically, but only fish—living in a medium which is a natural conductor of electricity—are capable of transmitting this current to the external world in appreciable strength.

Fossil fish have been found with what appears to have been tissue identical to the electricity-producing structures of contemporary eels. Thus, the ability to produce electricity is probably a very ancient refinement, even though it is a remarkable and bizarre adaptation of the nervous system.

For more information, see F. Drimmer, ed., *The Animal Kingdom* (Doubleday, 1954).

Hermaphroditic Fish

Hermaphroditic fish are found in various species in which the individual is capable of playing both the male and the female role in sexual reproduction, either with other individuals of the species or by itself.

Within the past fifteen years many accepted beliefs about fish have been overturned. Hermaphroditism (the ability of an individual to function, either in sequence or simultaneously, as a fertile male and a fertile female) has been found to be much more widespread among fish than had previously been suspected.

The Serranidae (sea perch), the Sparidae (sea bream), and the Maenidae families of fish have one two-part sex organ; one part produces eggs, and the other part sperm. The two parts may mature at different rates, but once they reach maturity, either half can be used at any one time.

Serranellus subligarius, a small sea perch that lives in the reefs off Florida, practices cross-fertilization. During the spawning season, one individual will take the male role, fertilizing the eggs of another individual taking the female role. The two fish then reverse roles.

Another type of sea perch, the grouper, appears to go through two gender changes in the course of a normal life cycle. Beginning sexual maturity as a male, the grouper goes through a period when it is both male and female, then spends the rest of its life functioning as a female. A reverse process occurs in the bluehead wrasse, among which females become males as they grow older.

The ultimate in self-sufficiency is the *Rivulus marmoratus*, a topminnow found in the brackish waters and tidal floodplains of Florida and the West Indies. Generally, it reproduces by releasing its eggs and then secreting sperm over them, but some individuals are able to fertilize their own eggs inside the body.

In one tropical Pacific species, the cleaner wrasse (*Labroides dimidiatus*), sex change seems to be inhibited by a peculiar process of dominance and submission. The male cleaner wrasse dominates all the females in his harem, but there is a rigid pecking order among the females themselves, with one dominant female to which the others defer. If the male dies, the dominant female becomes a male and takes over the harem and its territory. D. Ross Robertson, who studied these fish, believes that a female cleaner wrasse has a tendency to turn into a male, but the experience of being dominated inhibits the physiological processes that cause the sex organs to change. When the dominant female is left without a dominant partner, the change is allowed to occur.

Many hermaphroditic fish are deep-sea denizens, thus making it difficult to locate a mate for breeding purposes. Self-fertilization could solve that problem (although it also reduces the amount of variation, and a less varied population is also less able to survive changes in the environment). Dual-gendered fish have one major evolutionary advantage. When two individuals do meet, both can be fertilized. If they were single-gendered, one, at the most, could be fertilized (none at all if they were of the same gender).

An intriguing hypothesis about the bluehead wrasse (*Thalassoma bifasciatum*) was proposed in 1969 by Michael T. Ghiselin, of the University of California at Berkeley. The females of this species tend to become male as they grow in size. Large males of this species attract mates more readily than do small males, although small females are as likely to mate as large females. Individuals who have the genetic trait of living as a female when small and as a male when large thus have the maximum opportunity to mate and pass the trait to subsequent generations. They mate more than permanent males, which are at a disadvantage while young, and more than permanent females, which never achieve the optimal reproductive stage of large malehood.

For more information, see N. B. Marshall, *The Life of Fishes* (Universe, 1966) and R. Reinboth, ed., *Intersexuality in the Animal Kingdom* (Springer-Verlag, 1975).

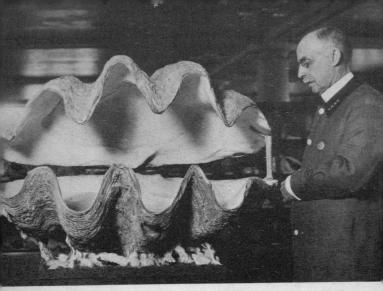

Giant clam (Tridacna gigas) *shell from Philippine Islands, at the American Museum of Natural History.*

The Giant Clam

The giant clam (*Tridacna gigas*), also known as the killer clam and man-eating clam, is the largest known bivalve. It may grow to over four feet long and reach a weight of 500 pounds.

A native of the seas off East India, the giant clam is greatly relished as food, and one clam can feed many people. Generally found on coral reefs or on sand in shallow lagoons, the clam feeds upon an immense population of single-celled algae, which live symbiotically in the tissues of the clam's brillantly colored mantle margin. The algae get some food from the clam and, in turn, provide it with extra energy.

The clam has been widely assumed to be a ferocious, dangerous animal. C. M. Yonge, in his report *A Year on the Great Barrier Reef* (Putnam, 1931), claimed that men have been killed by the *Tridacna* clam. Dr. Bruce W. Halstead, in *Dangerous Marine Animals* (Cornell Maritime), makes the same claim and offers instructions on how a person can release himself from the clam's hold by severing the great adductor muscles with which the animal closes its shells. The *U.S. Navy Diving Manual* also considers the clam dangerous, stating that the clam "traps legs and arms between shells."

The clamshells are very popular for use as washbasins and baptismal fonts, as well as for use in interior decorating. Occasionally, the clams produce a nonprecious pearl that may be as large as a golf ball.

Most experts dispute the giant clam's ferocious reputation. R. A. Caras, author of *Dangerous to Man* (Chilton, 1964), surveyed a large number of experts on marine zoology. The general consensus was that the clam was not at all aggressive. None of those surveyed could cite an authenticated death which could be attributed to the clam. They all agreed that a person's leg or arm could get caught in the animal's shell but felt that this, too, was unlikely for two reasons: (1) The clam's brightly colored mantle is difficult to miss, and (2) the clam does not snap its shells shut quickly, like a bear trap, but closes them rather slowly.

Those who disagree with the foregoing consensus point out that, although the mantle is colorful, it is often well camouflaged, and the clams live in a region where there are numerous other brightly colored organisms, making it easy for an unwary diver to overlook the giant clam.

Nematocysts

Nematocysts are the stinging cells of jellyfish, fire coral, and sea anemones, so small that as many as 80,000 can be found on one centimeter of jellyfish tentacle.

The nematocyst (or nettle cell) is grown by many varieties of coelenterates, the lowest and simplest form of multicelled animal. The nematocyst is a sealed unit with a minute, mechanical trigger, which opens a "lid," allowing a threadlike tube to snap out, like a jack-in-the-box, with enough force to penetrate laboratory gloves. The tube penetrates the skin and injects a venom which can cause a variety of ills ranging from irritation, pain, and swelling to cramps, chills, fever, and psychological disturbances. In the case of jellyfish called sea wasps, or box jellies (*Chironex fleckeri* and three species of *Chirosalmus*), commonly found in the South Pacific, contact can kill an adult human within minutes. These jellyfish, particularly the *Chironex fleckeri*, may be the most venomous animals in the world. The poison of the *Chironex* can kill mice even when diluted 10,000 to 1. Because the cells are self-contained and operate mechanically, they remain potent wherever the producing animal leaves them—on fishnets or anchor lines, even on the flesh of the dead jellyfish. Certain sea slugs, which are otherwise without defenses, can absorb these cells and utilize them to kill unwary predators.

The precise chemical composition of nematocyst poison is not known; it varies among the twenty-odd varieties of these "booby traps of the sea."

The sea slugs' use of the cells is not intelligent tool use, but a complex evolutionary adaptation. Some of the slugs which use the cells have developed bright coloration to warn predators that they are armed.

The well-known Portuguese man-of-war produces nematocysts but is seldom, if ever, venomous enough to be lethal. Deaths usually attributed to the man-of-war have either been caused by the less-colorful sea wasp or by complications resulting from the sting. In a recent case in Florida the agony of a man-of-war sting caused a heart attack in an elderly man (see Roger Caras, *Venomous Animals of the World*, Prentice-Hall, 1974).

Coelacanth

The coelacanth is a type of fish once thought to be extinct and is related to a suborder that may have been the ancestor of all four-limbed land animals.

Prehistoric coelacanths were a group of large, bony fish having a pair of lobe-shaped fins used for crawling around the ocean bottom in search of prey. These fins had an unusual bony and muscular development.

The first living specimen was discovered in 1938 near East London, South Africa, in the catch of a fishing boat. About eighty-five other examples, all of the same species, have since been found in Indian Ocean waters. These examples, larger than the fossil variety, are up to six feet long and weigh up to 150 pounds. They are steel blue to purple-brown in color, with irregular pink spots. The species is called *Latimeria chalumnae*, after Miss M. Courtenay-Latimer, who discovered it, and after the Chalumna River, near which it was caught.

Special anatomical features include a hollow spine ("coelacanth" is based on the Greek term for hollow spine) in the forward dorsal fin; large, rough, bony scales covered with mucus; and a fatty lung used to aid in floating. Coelacanths have many sharp teeth and a special joint in the skull that moves in coordination with the lower jaw, making the fish a

Cast of a coelacanth.

powerful carnivorous predator, difficult to land when hooked.

Coelacanth females are ovoviviparous—that is, they bear their young already hatched. This fact was recently discovered by ichthyologists at the American Museum of Natural History in New York, after they dissected a specimen that turned out to be pregnant.

Fossil remains show that the coelacanths first appeared about 350,000,000 years ago and spread over much of the world. Originally freshwater fish, the coelacanths gradually became sea dwellers. The most recent fossil coelacanths are about 70,000,000 years old.

The coelacanths are relatives of the suborder Rhipidistia, now extinct, which is thought to be the ancestor of amphibians and thus of all land vertebrates. Recent biochemical research has found that the connection with Rhipidistia is not as close as had previously been believed.

For additional information, see C. Larett Smith et al., "Latimera, the Living Coelacanth, Is Ovoviviparous," *Science* (December 12, 1975).

Miscellaneous

Slime Molds

Slime molds are single-celled organisms which sometimes aggregate to form colonies that resemble individual, multi-cellular organisms.

Slime molds constitute a group of organisms that belong to neither the animal nor the plant kingdom. One order, the cellular slime molds, has excited a great deal of interest because the individual cells sometimes group together to resemble multicellular organisms.

TIME (HOURS)

The life cycle of the slime mold society. The actual time of development may cover several days.

Dictyostelium discoideum, the most thoroughly studied cellular slime, was discovered in 1935. The individual organism of this order resembles a member of the genus *Amoeba*. The aggregation of the individual cells into colonies proceeds in two stages: The first looks like a crawling slug; the second resembles a fruit supported by an upright stalk.

At the beginning of the process, spores land on moist topsoil, rotting wood, or fallen leaves. Each surviving spore develops into an amoeba—about half the size of a human white blood cell—which lives by feeding on bacteria. The amoeba reproduces by dividing at intervals of three to four hours. As the amoebas in one area begin to multiply, they begin to use up the supply of bacteria that serves as their food.

At this point something new occurs. Some of the amoebas become attractive to others, which begin to migrate toward them. The migrating amoebas begin to form a single body, the pseudoplasmodium, which is sausage-shaped and averages between one-half to two millimeters in length. At this stage it resembles a multicellular organism, although it is, in fact, a colony of individual single-celled organisms.

The pseudoplasmodium has a distinct front and rear end. It is able to crawl and move accurately in the direction of sources of light and heat. After moving about in this stage for up to two weeks, the pseudoplasmodium turns into a fruiting body, which consists of a thin upright stalk, up to two millimeters in height. A tiny ball at the top of the stalk contains thousands of spores, each of which is a dormant cell from the colony. The ball breaks up, releasing the spores into the air. The spores drift until they come to a favorable spot, and the cycle starts anew.

This two-stage life-style permits the species to make maximum use of the food supply in a particular area and then to disperse to find food in new areas. The single-cell amoeba is a fast eater because its surface, through which it eats, is large in proportion to the volume (as compared to the volume/surface ratio of the pseudoplasmodium to a multicellular organism) and reproduces quickly, creating more amoebas to eat a given supply of food. The pseudoplasmodium can travel to a good spot to release the spores, which can then disperse to utilize food supplies in new areas.

Research is currently progressing toward an explanation of how the single-celled *Dictyostelium discoideum* amoebas are attracted to each other to form a colony when their food supply diminishes. Basically, the amoebas give off a chemical —adenosine-3', 5'-cyclic monophosphate, cyclic AMP for short—when they have been deprived of food for a period of time. When deprived of food, the amoebas also become attracted to cyclic AMP, resulting in their tendency to move in directions in which the chemical is more concentrated. Thus, an amoeba attracts other amoebas when food is short because it gives off an increased amount of cyclic AMP, and it is drawn to other amoebas because of the cyclic AMP they emit.

This explanation is incomplete, however, because it is not sufficient to explain how the amoebas move together. As an amoeba emits cyclic AMP, the chemical spreads and becomes less highly concentrated farther away. Thus, if an amoeba moves away from the spot where it has been emitting cyclic AMP, it is moving away from the area of highest concentration of cyclic AMP. One would logically expect the amoeba to stay in its own place rather than to be attracted to other amoebas. Actually, *Dictyostelium discodeum* has an elegant way of solving this problem. The amoebas do not emit cyclic AMP steadily, but in pulses which come at 300-second intervals. After each pulse the amoebas send out an enzyme that breaks down the cyclic AMP surrounding the amoeba in order that the next pulse will emit a sharper increase of AMP in relation to the remaining AMP. When an amoeba detects a pulse from another amoeba, it sends back an answering pulse after an interval of about 15 seconds. Then, for about 100 seconds, it moves toward the first amoeba. While it is moving, it does not respond to later pulses. Thus, the amoeba responds not only to the simple concentration of cyclic AMP, but also to periodic jumps in its concentration.

For more information on cellular slime molds, see John Tyler Bonner's *The Cellular Slime Molds* (Princeton, New Jersey, 1967).

Magnetism and Animal Navigation

Several species of animals, according to various studies, are able to detect the magnetic field of the earth and use that information to orient themselves. In other words, they use the same method a person uses when he consults a magnetic compass.

It is a well-known fact that homing pigeons are able to tell direction from the position of the sun in the sky. Recent research by William T. Keeton and his associates at Cornell University has determined that even at night or in heavy overcast, when the position of the sun is obscured, pigeons are still able to orient themselves. The researchers hypothesized that under such conditions pigeons rely on the earth's magnetic field for cues to direction.

The Cornell investigators attached bar magnets to pigeons to alter the magnetic field around them. They found that on sunny days the magnet-carrying pigeons were able to orient themselves normally, but that they tended to become disoriented on totally overcast days. A control group of pigeons —pigeons carrying nonmagnetic bars of the same size and shape as the magnets—were still able to orient normally on overcast days (William T. Keeton, "The Mystery of Pigeon Homing," *Scientific American*, December 1974).

Subsequently, Charles Walcott and Robert Green of the State University of New York at Stony Brook performed more refined experiments with pigeons. They designed an apparatus that enabled them to distort the magnetic field surrounding a pigeon's head in a controlled way. Thus, on overcast days they were able to make the pigeons orient themselves in a way that would be correct if the magnetic poles of the earth were reversed.

In further experiments Keeton has attempted to measure the sensitivity of the pigeon's magnetic sense organ and has found it to be extraordinarily sensitive.

Similar studies have been conducted by Friedrich Merkel and Wolfgang Wiltschko of the University of Frankfurt. They found that European robins—which are not closely related to the American robin—also can use cues from the earth's magnetic field to orient themselves. William Southern at Northern Illinois University has found that magnetic activity affects the orientation of ring-billed gulls. However, no one yet knows what the magnetic sense organ of birds is like or where it is located in the body. Since the magnetic field can penetrate the body, it may be an internal organ.

Experiments conducted by Martin Lindauer and Herman Martin at the University of Frankfurt have shown that the honeybee also uses the earth's magnetic field for orientation. Honeybees have been found to change their orientation in response to fluctuations in the magnetic field at least as small as those detected by pigeons. Again, the nature and location of the magnetic sense organ are not yet known.

Animal Mimicry

Animal mimicry is a biological phenomenon in which one animal resembles another animal, usually biologically un-related, and derives an advantage merely from having the similar appearance. There are many varieties of animal mimicry.

In one form of mimics, called bogeys, the mimic gains advantage by structurally resembling the model. One such bogey is the *Fulgora lucifera,* one of several bugs of the genus *Fulgora,* which has an appendage on the front of the head that resembles the head of an alligator—more precisely, a caiman, the South American relative of the alligator. These bugs are in danger of being eaten by birds or monkeys. Birds

The bogey, Fulgora lucifera.

The caiman, a South American relative of the alligator.

and monkeys, in turn, are endangered by caimans. The *Fulgora*'s false caiman head is, of course, much tinier than the real head of the caiman, but it appears to be frightening to birds, which apparently avoid that particular shape regardless of size.

Another bogey is the pupa, or chrysalis (the inactive stage a caterpillar passes through before turning into a butterfly), of the *Spalgis epius*, a butterfly found in India. The pupa, which is only 4.5 to 6.5 millimeters long, attaches itself to twigs, branches, or leaves. The pupa resembles the head of a local monkey, the rhesus macaque, and thereby frightens birds, its natural predators. The African butterfly *Spalgis lemolea* is a close relative of the Indian butterfly. Its pupa also resembles the head of a monkey—in this case, a local African monkey.

Batesian mimicry, another variety of mimicry, was described by H. W. Bates, an English naturalist and explorer in the mid-nineteenth century. Batesian mimicry is found in species which are not poisonous or nauseating but which resemble species that are. A predator is likely to mistake the mimic for the poisonous or nauseating species and avoid it. One example of a Batesian mimic is the tropical American membracid beetle. Its body is covered by a structure that looks like the cocoon of a moth which is nauseating to insect-eating birds. A group of Philippine cockroaches (genus *Prosoplecta*) mimics ladybird beetles (Coccinellidae) and leaf beetles (Chrysomelidae) which are inedible and marked by prominent colors, usually with contrasting spots.

Another very common form of mimicry is Mullerian mimicry, named after its discoverer, Fritz Müller, a nineteenth-century German-Brazilian naturalist and explorer. A Mullerian mimic is a poisonous or nauseating species that resembles another poisonous species that is closely related. In this form of mimicry, both species, the model and the mimic, benefit in that a predator that has had a bad experience with one will tend to avoid the other as well. For instance, in South America, inedible butterflies of many subfamilies (Daninae, Ithomiinae, Acraeinae, and Heliconiinae) all share the same warning coloration.

Natural selection explains the evolution of animal mimicry, and animal mimicry is important to the theory of evolution in that it offers an ideal test case which shows the operation of natural selection in the evolutionary change of living organisms.

It has been reconstructed that originally one animal in the mimic species happened to resemble another animal (i.e., the model) and was thereby more likely to be left alone by its predators. That mimic would have been more likely to survive long enough to have more offspring than the other members of its species. Some of the offspring will inherit their parent's mimic traits—a frightening, warning, or repulsive appearance—and in turn will have a greater possibility for survival and for propagation of the species. Consequently, from generation to generation, the proportion of animals that are mimics will increase until, eventually, all animals of that species will be mimics.

For more information, see E. H. Gombrich and R. L. Gregory, eds., *Illusion in Nature and Art* (Oxford University Press, 1974) and Julian Huxley, *New Bottles for New Wine* (Harper and Brothers, 1957).

The Gaia Hypothesis

The Gaia hypothesis holds that living matter, the air, and the oceans are a part of a huge system able to control conditions on earth and thus create an optimum situation for the survival of the biosphere.

The Gaia hypothesis, named after the Greek goddess of the earth, was proposed in the early 1970s by British scientists Dr. James Lovelock and Dr. Sidney Epton, in collaboration with the American biologist Dr. Lynn Margulis (see *New Scientist,* February 6, 1975). Although it has been recognized that conditions on earth must remain within narrow limits in order that life can continue, no one, before the Gaia hypothesis, had attempted to explain how the necessary conditions had been maintained.

The hypothesis states that organisms living on earth control such conditions as the amount of water on earth, the chemical composition of the atmosphere, the earth's surface temperature, the amount of ultraviolet radiation that penetrates the atmosphere, and the salinity and acidity of the soil. Furthermore, all living organisms, according to the hypothesis, *cooperate* to regulate these conditions and keep them within limits, making it possible for life to continue on earth. The system, according to Lovelock, seems to exhibit the behavior of a single organism.

Since the influence of organisms (for example, the fact that green plants release oxygen into the atmosphere) has long been known, it is the latter aspect—that organisms have actually acted together to maintain certain conditions—that is novel.

In specific terms, for example, the hypothesis states that organisms have kept the earth's temperature suitable for life by regulating the amount of heat-retaining gases, such as ammonia and carbon dioxide, in the atmosphere. By so doing, the organisms have maintained the earth's temperature within a narrow range despite the fact that the sun has become significantly hotter since life began on earth.

The Gaia hypothesis is still in its infancy and faces various difficulties. Some critics have stated that the theory is so general that it can explain any condition on earth and that it must be more specific so that its assumptions can be proved true or false. As it stands, according to critics, the theory does not add to our knowledge. Lovelock himself doubts that the hypothesis will ever be accepted because it is difficult to see how it could be disproved. He counters that the Gaia idea "has proved an extremely fruitful source of experimental suggestions."

Another difficulty with the hypothesis is that it is difficult, given our present knowledge, to explain how organisms could come to cooperate in regulating conditions on earth. The theory of evolution, which is used to explain how conditions came to be as they are, assumes that the environment—the conditions in which organisms live—is not affected by the organisms and that organisms adapt to conditions as they exist. It has always been recognized that organisms do change the world in which they live, but these changes have been generally explained as the accidental products of organisms adapting to conditions.

ASTRONOMY

Big Bang Theory

The big bang theory is a theory in cosmology based on the premise that all the matter in the universe came from a tiny superdense object (sometimes called a primeval atom), which hurled its fragments in all directions at enormous speeds following a cataclysmic explosion 10 to 20 billion years ago.

As the universe expands, it thins out. Thinning out means that the number of stars and galaxies in a given volume of space is diminishing. Since the postulated original explosion, the fastest-moving galaxies would have gone the farthest, and the slower-moving ones not as far. Thus, from any one place in the exploding matter, all other moving objects would seem to recede at speeds proportional to their distances. The more distant, and therefore faster, objects would indicate their speed and distance by the red shift (a reduction in the frequency—an increase in the wavelength—of the light emitted).

Energetic radio sources, identified with visible stars, are called quasi-stellar sources, or quasars. Quasars are identified by the vast amounts of radio energy they radiate, their small size, and the enormous changes in their energy output over intervals of months or less. Examining their red shifts indicates that quasars tend to be at great distances at the outer reaches of the primeval explosion. It is as if quasars were produced *only* at the time of the explosion, tending to confirm the existence of a big bang.

If there were a big bang that started the universe's expansion, we ought to be able to observe some of the original radiation from it. That radiation would have been very dense, hot and opaque, a primeval fireball, shortly after the big bang occurred. Subsequent expansion would thin out this radiation and the red shift would reduce its energy. The equivalent temperature of the fireball now would be about −270 degrees celsius, and it should appear to be equally intense in all directions (isotropic). Radiation apparently matching these requirements was recorded on sensitive instruments in 1965 and 1968 and consequently could indeed be the glowing embers of the big bang.

Because every galaxy is fleeing from the center of the presumed big bang and because the radiation is uniform in all directions, then there is no direction given to a center of the universe. That center is all around us. (S.R.)

Neutron Star

A neutron star is a possible end product of stellar evolution, composed entirely of neutrons compressed to extremely high density.

Neutron stars are interstellar objects emitting considerable amounts of nonvisible energy. A neutron star of one solar mass, a mass equal to the mass of our sun (2×10^{33} gm, or 2.2×10^{27} English tons), would have a radius equal to 1 kilometer (⅝ of a mile). The superdensity resulting from this would be tantamount to a billion billion tons of neutrons occupying a space the size of a teaspoon.

A neutron survives only a few minutes in its free or unbound state before it decays into a proton and an electron. But under extremely high pressures, a neutron is stable. If all the electrons in a star could be forced into their atomic nuclei where the protons reside, all the matter in the star would become neutrons. These neutrons, crowded into a small space at high pressure and density, are called a degenerate neutron gas, which does not behave like a normal gas. The neutrons are not free to move randomly, for example, because they would encroach on regions already occupied by other neutrons.

The pressures responsible for creating a neutron star may arise from a mechanism within the star such as a supernova explosion. This violent event could eject the outer layers of a normal star at the same time that the inner regions were compressed to neutron star densities. Another possible route to a neutron star status is via gravitational contraction as the star's nuclear sources of energy become exhausted. If the star's mass is less than two solar masses, strong repulsive forces between neutrons are set up, causing a rapid rise in pressure, halting the gravitational contraction, and stabilizing the neutron star.

It is not impossible that a star more massive than two solar masses might continue to contract indefinitely. Eventually, the star would become so small and superdense that the velocity needed to escape from its surface would equal that of light, and so light or photons could escape no longer. The object would "disappear" from the universe; it would be a black hole.

The size of a tennis ball, a black hole would weigh as much as the earth. Not only would it be invisible, but any object

that came within its range of gravitational attraction would
fall into it, be absorbed, and vanish. (S.R.)

Black Hole

A black hole is a theoretical object of such great mass and
small proportion that its gravity is stronger than any other
force on the astrophysical level. An area around the object is
also included in the concept of a black hole.

A black hole would be formed in the collapse of a red giant
star when it had expended the last of its nuclear energy. A
red giant is little more than a vast sphere of hot gas. Its size
is due to the expansion of gas as a result of the radiation of
nuclear reactions. Gravity keeps it from flying apart. When
the nuclear fuel is consumed, the star cools and gravity begins
to pull the gas inward.

If the red giant is massive enough, probably more than
three times the mass of the sun, and if it is unable to throw
off some of that mass in its last nuclear gasps, the force of
gravity will be so great that the material of the star will be
compacted indefinitely. Theoretically, the end of the process,
the center of the black hole, should have infinite density and
zero volume. This appears to violate known physical law, but
Einstein's theory of gravity demands just that result.

The existence of a black hole has not yet been confirmed,
but there is a strong candidate for the role. It is known as
Cygnus X-1 to radio astronomers and as HDE 226868 to
optical astronomers. To the radio astronomers, Cygnus X-1
is a powerful, flickering X ray source. X rays are emitted by
stellar objects when gases are compressed to great densities.
The flickering suggested to astronomers that the source was
very small, and the only small sources that can emit X rays
are neutron stars and black holes. Perhaps Cygnus X-1 is a
neutron star.

Optical astronomers found the source of the Cygnus X rays
to coincide with a visible double star system. The star they
can see is a supergiant, a hot blue star, probably thirty times
more massive than the sun. This monster moves so eccentrically
that astronomers have been forced to conclude that it has a
small, unseen companion. To push that blue giant around, the
unseen object would have to be at least five times as massive
as the sun. Since neutron stars can only be three times more
massive than the sun, the blue giant's companion must be a

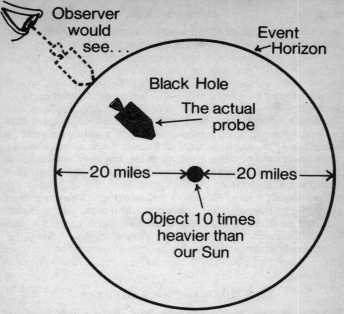

As a space probe entered a black hole, an observer would see an image of the probe stopped at the event horizon, while the actual probe continued toward oblivion in the hole itself.

black hole—if all the theoretical assumptions are correct. Astronomers believe the small black hole is pulling gases away from the supergiant, compressing them, and so emitting X rays.

A black hole can never be seen. It does not shine, and it will not reflect light. Light cast on the surface of the object would not be able to escape its gravity and, thus, could not return to our eyes. That is why the object is called black; it is called a hole because anything entering it will disappear.

If the center of a black hole were about ten times the mass of the sun, it would be surrounded by a screen, about 40 miles in diameter, called an event horizon. That horizon marks the point at which the power of gravity of the hole exactly equals the escape velocity of light. Within that horizon, light particles, or photons, would be inexorably trapped, unable to travel to a distant observer. If we were to launch a space probe toward the hole, it would appear to move more and more slowly as it neared the event horizon, because the hole's gravity would slow down the photons returning to us, the observers. At the edge of the event horizon the probe would appear virtually to stop as the photons escaped the intense gravity with almost infinite slowness. The probe itself would hurtle into the hole to be infinitely compressed in millionths of a second.

Various speculations have been advanced to suggest that the black hole may be a passageway into another universe, a space warp, or a spot where all known physical laws are in abeyance. None of these are impossible, but they appear to be irrelevant, since no one who enters a black hole can ever return to tell about it.

For details, see William J. Kaufmann, *Relativity and Cosmology* (Harper, 1973); Harry L. Shipman, *Black Holes, Quasars and the Universe* (Houghton Mifflin, 1976); and K. S. Thorne, "The Search for Black Holes," *Scientific American* (December 1974).

The Edge of the Universe

Is there an edge to the universe, and if so, where is it? In 1973 observations of some of the most distant objects yet discovered seemed to indicate that there was an edge and that it had been found. But that is a matter of interpretation.

The term "edge" implies a brink—some discontinuity in the "here"—and a beyond. That would lead to the idea that the universe is limited in size, that it is finite and bounded. But if a boundary is found, what can there be beyond it? Such an imponderable query is the direct result of human experience with boundaries and beyonds.

So great is the quandary about a beyond that some people have rejected "finite and bounded" in favor of "infinite and unbounded." This is another mind boggler because it would permit no limit anywhere. Everything would become infinite: volume, mass, time, and energy.

A third possibility avoids these two dilemmas. Perhaps the universe is finite but unbounded. The surface of the earth is finite in area, but it has no boundary. The surface is strictly a two-dimensional area; the curvature is merely a feature of the surface and does not affect its basic two-dimensional quality.

In the universe all three dimensions are curved. This is difficult to imagine, but the effects of this curvature will show up in the laws dealing with the geometry of space and affect the way the universe is surveyed, just as the earth's curvature affects the rules used to survey its surface.

Astronomers have long known that some astronomical objects are moving away from earth. Today it is known that those objects are entire galaxies like our Milky Way and that the farther away they are, the faster they are moving. The speed of these galaxies can be measured by the red shift of their light. The red shift refers to a change in the wavelengths of light very similar to the change in the pitch of a train whistle as it passes and moves away from the listener. The more distant galaxies show a greater red shift, indicating that they are moving away at a greater speed. In fact, the relationship between their speed and distance is exactly linear—twice the distance, twice the speed.

This process is usually called the expanding universe, but the "dispersing universe" might be a better term. The galaxies seem to be dispersing into the universe, and the universe—the domain in which physical laws can operate—seems to be waiting out there for the galaxies to arrive.

This matter of dispersion raises another question. If all the galaxies are moving away from one another, they all must once have been together at one central point in the universe. By measuring their recessional velocity and working backward, astronomers have deduced that the galaxies were together about 12 billion years ago. The implication is that at that time a gigantic explosion hurled the mass of the universe out of a central core (see Big Bang Theory).

In the early 1960s radio astronomers discovered small but bright sources of intense radio waves. Optical astronomers were at first puzzled by the properties of quasi-steller radio sources, or quasars. The puzzle was solved when their strange light was interpreted as the result of a very great red shift. But if the red shift was as great as it appeared, it meant that two or three of the quasars were moving away from us at a velocity equal to 92 percent of the speed of light. If the expansion law is still linear at that speed—and no one really knows—those quasars are about 11 billion light-years away from us. They are very faint, but fainter ones could be seen if they were there, and fainter ones would be even farther away from us and moving faster. If nothing is found farther away from us than the two or three quasars that astronomers have already seen, those quasars may be at the edge of the universe.

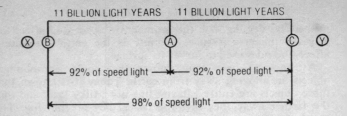

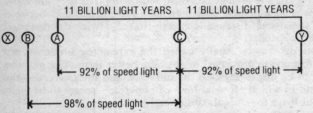

Seen from galaxy A, galaxy Y appears to be relatively near galaxy C; but from galaxy C, galaxy Y is seen to be as far away as galaxy A.

But this interpretation must be refined even more. Consider the viewpoint of an observer at one of those distant quasars. Looking back at our galaxy, he would see us receding from *him* at 92 percent of the speed of light. But if he looked beyond our galaxy to the other edge that we can see from here, he would not see a galaxy moving away from him at twice the speed of light. Instead, the red shift he perceived would indicate that the extremely distant galaxy was moving at 98 percent of the speed of light. This must be his interpretation in spite of our belief that we are halfway between his position and the distant galaxy at the other edge and that we are 11 billion light-years from both. Thus, galaxies at great distances would seem to be bunched up, and the appearance of an edge may be only the result of this curious visual compaction.

Perhaps, too, we are not looking at a distant edge of space, but at a distant edge of time, the beginning. For when we look out into the universe, we look backward in time. The light we see from that most distant quasar began its journey to us 11 billion years ago. Since we can see nothing beyond these quasars, we may be looking back into the murk of the first billion years, into the time before anything else could have taken form out of the primordial nuclear material of the big bang.

Immanuel Velikovsky

Immanuel Velikovsky has launched theories about the universe which challenge some basic tenets of contemporary science.

Immanuel Velikovsky was born in Russia in 1895. A trained psychoanalyst, he studied and practiced in Palestine and a number of European countries. In 1939 he came to the United States to do research for a planned book on "Freudian heroes" (Moses, Oedipus, Ikhnaton). This work took him in an unexpected direction, for in the course of his research he conceived the daring idea that the catastrophes described in the Bible—and paralleled in similar accounts by such widely scattered peoples as the Egyptians and Central American Indians—might be not fanciful myths but reports of actual cosmological events.

Velikovsky expounded this catastrophe theory of cosmology in a series of books which achieved worldwide popular success but which the scientific community greeted with skepticism and even hostility. Velikovsky's central thesis can be summed up as follows:

1. The earth has undergone repeated catastrophes, which have periodically wiped out animal and human life, changed the rotation of the planet and reversed its poles. 2. Several of these catastrophes occurred in recorded history; one of the most devastating took place in the second millennium B.C. 3. Venus was formed by breaking away from Jupiter and settled into its present orbit as late as the first millennium B.C. 4. The catastrophes which the earth experienced between 1500 and 800 B.C. brought about violent upheavals; parts of the earth melted, the seas boiled and evaporated, continents were raised causing great floods, and hurricanes swept over the surface. According to Velikovsky, this is supported by a wealth of quotations from the Old Testament, the Vedas, Greek and Roman mythology, as well as folk traditions and myths of a variety of peoples.

The core of Velikovsky's theory was presented in *Worlds in Collision*. This book, published in 1950, promptly became a

Immanuel Velikovsky.

worldwide best-seller. According to Velikovsky, "the archaeological, geological, and paleontological evidence" for the
theory was collected and presented separately in *Earth in
Upheaval,* published in 1955. Here Velikovsky catalogued
various findings from all over the world which supported his
view that evolution was a misnomer and that the so-called
evolutionary process was in reality a series of cosmic upheavals.

Some key pieces of evidence: islands in the Arctic sea containing bones of animals associated with moderate climate
(for example, the horse); coral and coal deposits near the poles;
the relative youth of the world's great mountain chains; signs
of polar shifts, reversed magnetic polarities, sudden changes in
sea level. All these findings indicate, according to Velikovsky,
that our planet had a revolutionary—rather than evolutionary—
history, marked by repeated global cataclysms.

A persuasive argument for the validity of Velikovsky's work is the confirmation of predictions stemming from his theories:

Prediction	Confirmation
Venus is hot and has an atmosphere of gaseous hydrocarbons.	In 1963 Mariner II measured Venus temperature at 800 degrees, and detected a sizable hydrocarbon layer.
Venus emits radio noise (1953).	Noise from Venus recorded (1955).
The last glacial period was three times more recent than believed heretofore.	Need for revising dating of glacial period confirmed by radiocarbon studies (1952).
The moon's surface contains molten material only a few millennia old, as well as hydrocarbons and radioactive substances.	Presence of these materials confirmed by Apollo moon missions.

These are only a few of the many predictions made by Velikovsky which conflicted with established views of science but which have subsequently been proved correct. In addition, support for Velikovsky has come from a small group of scientists, such as Soviet astronomer and director of the Kiev Observatory Sergei Vsekhsvatii, who believes it possible for a comet to have been ejected from Jupiter and to have passed close enough to the earth to have caused major catastrophes.

In general, however, the response of scientists to Velikovsky has been adverse. His facts have been questioned, his theories derided, his predictions dismissed as lucky coincidences. Advances of conventional science have taken some of the steam out of his theories by providing simpler explanations; for example, the finding of remains of animals or plants in regions not normally associated with those species can now be explained on the basis of continental drift. Velikovsky has been taken to task for going "to the public" instead of publishing in scholarly journals. The eminent American astronomer Harlow Shapley has characterized Velikovsky's theory that a comet had made the earth stand still as "rubbish and nonsense," pointing out that there are written observations of Venus dating back to about 2000 B.C.

Gerald Hawkins, the British astronomer, states in *Beyond*

Stonehenge (Harper & Row, 1973) that computer projections of present orbits indicate that Venus and Mars came nowhere near the earth in 700 B.C. or in 1500 B.C., contrary to Velikovsky's belief. American astronomer Donald H. Menzel, former director of Harvard College Observatory, described Velikovsky's reordering of history as "wild speculation." With regard to Velikovsky's apparent anticipation of the discovery of the Van Allen belt, Menzel declared: "Velikovsky forecast nothing resembling the Van Allen radiation belt. He implied that the earth's magnetic field would be more intense outside the ionosphere; actually, it is weaker." Cecilia Payne-Gaposchkin, a Harvard University astronomer and one of Velikovsky's severest critics, called attention to numerous errors in his work and concluded: "Even errors of information could be excused if the thesis of the book [*Worlds in Collision*] were reasonable. But the conclusions that Mr. Velikovsky draws are utterly impossible."

Carl Sagan, author of *The Cosmic Connection,* was quoted in *Newsweek* (February 25, 1974) to the effect that many of the things that are right in Velikovsky are not original, others are so broad as to lend themselves to a variety of interpretations, and others simply contradict known physical laws. Sagan has also pointed out that while much attention has been paid to Velikovsky's correct predictions, little has been said of the many more predictions that have been proved wrong.

It will probably take years before a definitive verdict is passed on Velikovsky's theories. Velikovsky himself seemed optimistic of ultimate vindication when he said in a *Newsweek* interview (February 25, 1974), "My old critics no longer ignore my ideas, and today's young scientists are open-minded enough to listen to me."

In addition to the sources mentioned in the text, the following material may be of interest:

Velikovsky's Works
    Worlds in Collision, Doubleday, 1950.
    Earth in Upheaval, Doubleday, 1955.
    Ages in Chaos (Vol. 1), Doubleday, 1952.
    Oedipus and Akhnaton, Doubleday, 1960.

Review Material Generally Favorable to Velikovsky
   A. de Grazia, ed. *The Velikovsky Affair*, University Books
   1966.
   The Editors of Pensée. *Velikovsky Reconsidered*, Double-
   day, 1976.
   Harpers, October 1963 and December 1963.

Review Material Generally Unfavorable to Velokovsky
   C. Sagan. *The Cosmic Connection*, Amber Press, 1973.

Miscellaneous
   Science Forum, April 7, 1974.
   Chemistry, October 1971.
   The American Behavioral Scientist, September 1963.
   Saturday Review, April 22, 1950.
   Popular Astronomy, June 1950.

STRANGE
PEOPLES

Phoenicians

The Phoenicians were the greatest traders of the ancient world whose accomplishments reached a high degree of sophistication.

Knowledge about the Phoenicians is mainly derived from other peoples because they left practically no records about themselves. A very damp climate that destroyed papyrus and clay tablets and the frequent sacking and destruction of the Phoenicians' strategically located cities are the chief reasons for the lack of records.

There never was an empire known as Phoenicia, but rather a collection of cities—Tyre, Byblos, and Sidon—which spread across a region corresponding to modern Lebanon and adjoining parts of modern Syria and Israel. It seems that no large-scale federation of the cities ever took place. From all indications, the government was a kingship whose power was limited by wealthy merchant families. The Phoenicians, who were Canaanites, came into the area around 3000 B.C. Under the influence of first Egypt and then Syria, the Phoenicians became independent and prospered from roughly 1200 to 900 B.C., a period of overseas colonizations. The Phoenician colonies, of which Carthage—founded on the North African coast at about 820 B.C.—was the most important, spread around the entire Mediterranean Sea. Phoenicia came under the rule of the Persians in 538 B.C., then under Alexander the Great; in 64 B.C. it was incorporated into the Roman province of Syria.

The Phoenicians were known for the manufacture of Tyrian, or royal purple, a colorfast dye that did not fade. It was greatly admired and in some countries was worn only by kings. The dye was made from the liquid removed from the glands of snails, which were abundant in the coastal waters in the region of Tyre and Sidon. It took the glands of 60,000 snails to produce one pound of dye. It has been calculated that one pound of silk, dyed according to the highest Tyrian standards, would cost close to $30,000 in modern currency. The dye industry eventually died out because of prohibitive costs. The Phoenicians also manufactured quality glass and had great skill in metalwork, woodwork, and stone.

The Phoenicians were skilled dentists. As evidence of their skill, the jaw of a woman, which was found in a sarcophagus, contained a pair of teeth taken from another individual and fastened to her teeth with a gold wire. In a sarcophagus excavated at Sidon, a man was found with six teeth held in place with a strand of gold wire expertly woven around the other teeth that acted as an anchor.

Perhaps the Phoenicians' greatest contribution to civilization was the development of a twenty-two-letter script alphabet, which was adopted first by the Greeks, later by the Romans, and is the ancestor of the modern Western alphabet. Gerhard Herm, in his recently published book *The Phoenicians: The Purple Empire of the Ancient World* (William Morrow, 1975), says that without the easily learned Phoenician alphabet, "we would perhaps still have to learn from two to four hundred different characters, as Japanese or Chinese schoolchildren do, in order to be able to read our daily paper." Herm, an amateur historian, believes that the alphabet had a great deal of practical significance for the Phoenicians, who, because they were primarily merchants, needed a practical system of notation.

Herm believes that the Phoenicians actually sailed as far west as America. He cites as evidence the yet-unconfirmed theory of Brandeis University Professor Cyrus H. Gordon that the ancestors of the Melungeons—a light-skinned Indian tribe

Model of Phoenician sailing vessel.

of East Tennessee—came, as they themselves believe, from Phoenicia two and half millennia before Columbus.

Herm also cites the Greek historian Herodotus to the effect that as a result of the order in 609 B.C. of the Egyptian Pharaoh Necho, Phoenician sailors circumnavigated Africa, stopping periodically on land to grow and harvest crops. This would have been about 2,000 years before Vasco da Gama opened up a sea route around the Cape of Good Hope from Portugal to India. Herodotus recorded that the Phoenicians claimed—he didn't believe it, but many others did—that on their voyage around Africa they had the sun to their north. Herm believes this last statement is "clear proof that this journey must have actually taken place" because otherwise, the Phoenicians could not have known that in the Southern Hemisphere the sun would pass to the north of the celestial pole. Herm further states that Pharaoh Necho was so impressed by the Phoenicians' circumnavigation of Africa that he embarked on another ambitious project—the building of a canal from the Mediterranean to the Red Sea. "He must have certainly used Phoenician specialists," Herm writes, "and it seems reasonable to assume the original idea came from them, too." Construction of the canal was halted after Necho received an unfavorable prophecy.

R. Herker, in a review of Herm's book in the *Christian Science Monitor* (September 5, 1975), characterizes it as "a skillful collation of circumstantial evidence and intelligent speculation based on wide study." He agrees that the Phoenicians sailed around Africa 2,000 years before Vasco da Gama and "may well have been the chief artificers of the Suez Canal." Samuel W. Matthews, assistant editor of *National Geographic,* supports Herm's view that the Phoenicians sailed around Africa (see *National Geographic,* August 1974). The *Times Literary Supplement* (September 1975), however, sharply attacked the book as a "jejune and unsystematic presentation of a certain amount of Phoenician material in which fact is often obscured by fantasy and by journalistic rhetoric."

For additional information, see M. A. Edey, *The Sea Traders* (Time-Life, 1974).

Ainu

The Ainu were the Caucasoid population that inhabited much of Japan within historic memory and whose few remaining descendants live mostly on Hokkaido, the northernmost of the four major Japanese islands.

The Ainu had pale skin and brown hair and were short in stature. Their extremely profuse body hair may account for the fact that the Japanese are the hairiest of all the Mongoloids. Today only about 12,000 Ainu survive, almost all of whom live on Hokkaido (with a few on the Kurile Islands and Sakhalin). Almost none of them is pure Ainu, and most are physically indistinguishable from other Japanese.

The Ainu language and traditional culture are today practiced by residents of a few "cultural villages." The language is unrelated to any other known tongue, though elements of the culture are shared by other peoples of eastern Siberia and the Soviet Far East.

Among cultural elements that have survived (mainly as tourist attractions) are woodcutting, bark-cloth clothing, and the bear dance—a remnant of the most important religious ritual. In earlier times a bear would be caught while still a cub and would be tended by women and even suckled by them.

Ainu elders at a traditional ceremony.

After it reached adulthood, it would be sacrificed in the course of an elaborate ceremony.

Other aspects of the Ainu religion, sometimes similar to primitive Japanese religion, include the worship of rain and fire (called *fuji*), and of local mountains and rivers. The Ainu were subject to a form of religious ecstasy known as Arctic hysteria, characterized by compulsive mimicry by either a group or an individual.

One unique Ainu custom concerns the kut, a belt worn by every Ainu woman under her clothes. A specific type of kut, with its own special material, design, and length, is inherited by each woman from her mother. Various types are associated with various deities. A kut is never shown to a man and is treated with caution even among the women. It is assumed to have magical powers; for example, it could calm storms, hold back tidal waves, or repel smallpox. No woman may marry a man whose mother had the same type of kut as she has.

In the past women often had "mustaches" tattooed around the mouth.

Ainu power and geographic distribution have steadily declined for well over 1,000 years, in the face of many wars with the Japanese. By the late nineteenth century Japanese control was complete, and the traditional Ainu occupations of hunting, fishing, and trapping were replaced by sedentary agriculture. Large-scale Japanese migration to Hokkaido, leading to intermarriage despite some discrimination, assured the nearly complete assimilation of the Ainu.

There are several hypotheses explaining the origin of the Ainu. One theory, developed by Dr. Kindaichi of Tokyo University, maintains that the Ainu are a parent stock of the American Indians. Deriving originally from northern Europe, according to this theory, the Ainu migrated across Greenland and Iceland into North America, where some of them amalgamated with Mongoloid tribes. Others continued on through the Aleutians and Kuriles into Japan, untouched by Mongoloid influence.

Another theory holds that the forerunners of the Ainu penetrated eastward across Asia. Still another holds that the Ainu were the original race of East Asia.

Scholars had long speculated that the Neolithic cultures of Japan were related to the Ainu. But investigation of bone remains has shown that other groups, racial ancestors of the Japanese, were the dominant aboriginal people of Japan.

For additional information, see C. Etter, *Ainu Folklore*

Gypsy pilgrimage to the annual festival at Saintes-Maries-de-la-Mer, France.

(Wilcox & Follett, 1949) and N. G. Munro, *Ainu Creed and Culture* (Columbia, University Press, 1963).

Gypsies

Gypsies are a nomadic people, probably of Indian origin, who have spread throughout much of the world while retaining their unique language and culture.

There are about 3,000,000 Gypsies throughout the world, the large majority of whom live in Europe. All Gypsies speak some variation of Romany, a language akin to Sanskrit, and all belong to fairly close-knit tribal groups. The English word "Gypsy" derives from the misconception that the group came from Egypt. The Gypsies call themselves Rom, their word for man.

About 1,000,000 Gypsies now live in the Soviet Union. Bulgaria, Romania, and Hungary each have between 200,000 and 250,000, and Yugoslavia has about 115,000. Turkey and Greece together have about 200,000 Gypsies; Czechoslovakia has 150,000, and Poland has 15,000.

Gypsies may be descendants of outcast groups in India. They first appeared in Persia in the ninth century and in Bulgaria by the eleventh. They did not appear beyond the Balkans until the fifteenth century, when they spread across Europe. By that time they had also traveled through North Africa. Like other Europeans, many Gypsies have emigrated to the Americas and Australia.

Though many Gypsies live a nomadic existence, others have settled down for long periods in one place. In parts of Spain and Britain sedentary Gypsy populations have undergone some assimilation. The various Romany dialects, as well as Gypsy folklore and other cultural elements, have been strongly influenced by the countries through which the Gypsies have passed or in which they live.

The three major Gypsy tribes are based on geographic distribution—the Kalderash from the Balkans and central Europe; the Gitanos from southern France, Spain, Portugal, and northern Africa; and the Manush, or Sinti, from France and Germany. Marriage is usually within the tribe or subtribe. Further divisions are ultimately based on bands ranging from a few to a few hundred families, headed by a chief chosen for life.

During the second World War the Nazis murdered 400,000 to 500,000 Gypsies. This climaxed a 500-year history in which Gypsies were often objects of fear and persecution in various parts of Europe. Just as often, however, they were accepted as a peculiar but useful group, filling various low-status jobs such as entertaining, undertaking, and fortune-telling, despite their reputation for petty thievery.

Gypsies have acquired a veneer of Christianity or Islam but retain elements of a religion of their own, with a benevolent Great Spirit, a less-powerful unclean spirit, and a multitude of female spirits and fairies. Forms of ancestor worship help strengthen the Gypsies' very strong family ties, which are further enforced by a body of customary law.

Dogs and cats are considered ritually unclean, as are women, especially following childbirth, although many Gypsies no longer observe these taboos. Among the customs and superstitions that have been recorded are several concerning hair. For instance, witches are said to be able to do great harm using a lock of hair; therefore, hair found on one's coat should be burned to prevent harm to oneself, according to Gypsies. Also, a person will become insane if he steps on hair that came from an insane person, and if a wife wants to ensure her husband's continued love, she must bind some of her own hair to some of his by moonlight, repeating the ritual three times.

According to the author Jan Yoors, who grew up among Gypsies, the customs of fortune-telling and begging were adopted as defenses against outsiders and are never practiced among Gypsies themselves. Similarly, their disheveled appearance is a protective device.

In the past it was believed that Gypsies had introduced playing cards and palmistry into Europe. In fact, both customs were probably borrowed by the Gypsies from Europeans.

For additional information, see J. Yoors, *The Gypsies* (Simon & Schuster, 1967) and C. G. Leland, *Gypsy Sorcery and Fortune Telling* (University Books, 1972).

The Williamsons

The Williamsons are an inbred clan of "gyp artists," numbering about 2,000, that fleeces people all over the United States.

The clan is descended from Robert Logan Williamson, a Scotsman who came to the United States around the turn of the century. Although not members of the traditional European Gypsies, the clan leads a nomadic Gypsylike existence. The families rarely own their own homes, and the children rarely attend schools. The clan is known to the police as the Terrible Williamsons. Although Williamson is the name most frequently used, eight to ten other names, including McDonald and Stewart, are also used by the clan. Marriages of cousins are common, and marriages outside the clan are practically unknown. Police throughout the United States have adopted Williamson as a generic term for "itinerant hustlers."

The clan holds a convention annually in May in Cincinnati, Ohio. Cincinnati was chosen in the twenties because it is strategically situated in the middle of the country and is easily accessible. According to the *Saturday Evening Post* (October 27, 1956), the clan does not engage in swindles during this convention period, but other accounts dispute this point. There is general agreement, however, that the Williamsons spend a great deal of money in local stores and purchase new cars during the annual May convocation.

No matter where a Williamson dies, the body is sent to Cincinnati for burial. Generally, the final resting place is Spring Grove Cemetery, but the clan owns blocks of cemetery plots at various locations in Cincinnati. According to *The New*

Above left: Christina Williamson, twenty-nine, arrested for vagrancy in Miami Beach in 1952; released.

Above right: Margaret Williamson, Thirty-four, arrested in 1952 in Miami Beach for vagrancy; released.

York Times (May 16, 1971), the Williamsons used to keep bodies of deceased clan members in storage until they could hold a common funeral service in Cincinnati during the annual May meeting. Now fast cars and rapid transportation have made it possible to hold funerals the year round. Security at funerals is strict, and all visitors must give the clan password. Families rival one another in the lavishness of their funerals.

The usual activity of the clan consists of confidence tricks and "gyps" rather than violent crime. For example, in a classic maneuver, a few men will drive up to a house in a tank truck. They will say they have just resurfaced a roadway and, in order not to waste their leftover blacktop material, offer to resurface the driveway at a bargain. The homeowner accepts. Later, when the rain washes the gunk off the driveway, the homeowner realizes that the "blacktop" was crankcase oil. The Williamsons also install "lightning rods," which are actually wood or rope painted to look like metal. A standard routine for Williamson clan women is to elicit sympathy by holding a crying baby in their arms while trying to sell worthless merchandise. Since the Williamsons are generally excellent actors, they can portray a variety of characters as part of their sales pitch.

In *The Golden Fleecers* (Doubleday, 1966), W. Wagner describes a gang operating in California, which seems similar, if not identical, to the Williamsons. Wagner describes the gang, a clan of Gypsies, as the most colorful operating in Southern California suburbs. He says they are approximately 2,000 strong and are known by police departments from coast to coast. From 100 to 150 of them hit Southern California each year between Thanksgiving and Christmas, posing as roofing repair and blacktop driveway contractors. The women, according to Wagner, work assorted rackets, usually selling imitation Irish lace.

Newspaper reports from Cincinnati and other cities indicate that the clan's operation continues to the present time. The most recent report, from the Cincinnati *Enquirer* (May 6, 1976), states that they have a new gimmick—a Bicentennial Special—which involves the coating of concrete patios and similar areas.

The police and the Better Business Bureau claim that it is difficult to take effective action against the Williamsons because they are always on the move and routinely jump bail as part of their "operating" expenses. *New York Times* writer George Vescey states that many of the "gyps" fall into the "gray" area between sharp business practice and outright fraud. Because their offenses are generally not serious in legal terms, punishment is usually no more than a fine or a light sentence. In many cases, the victims are too ashamed of their gullibility to prosecute. The clan itself is proud of its ancestry and seems to have no particular sense of wrongdoing in fleecing the gullible.

The Better Business Bureau claims that the average annual take of the clan exceeds $1,000,000. It is reported that many of the clan members are well off. This evaluation stems from reports of clan members using $100 bills, wearing mink coats, and driving new Cadillacs.

Most accounts of the Williamsons are invariably mocking and hostile and make a loose identification between them and Gypsies. Similarities do exist—both groups like to travel, drive fancy cars, and hold opulent funerals. The Williamsons, however, despise Gypsies and make a practice of staying away from Gypsy encampments (see *Parade*, September 11, 1955).

STRANGE
GROUPS

Secular Groups

The Para Committee

The Para Committee, officially called the Committee to Investigate Claims of Paranormal and Other Phenomena, was recently formed by a group of scholars, scientists, and investigators to challenge and evaluate psychic phenomena, the occult, and pseudoscience. The formation of the committee was officially announced on April 30, 1976, at the meeting of the American Humanist Association in Buffalo, New York. Initially, the committee will be sponsored by *The Humanist*.

Committee co-chairman Paul Kurtz, professor of philisophy at the State University of New York at Buffalo and editor of *The Humanist*, states that as the public interest in paranormal phenomena has grown enormously—ranging from psychic healing, psychokinesis, immortality, reincarnation, Kirlian photography, orgone energy, psychic surgery, faith healing, astrology, "chariots of the gods," UFOs, dianetics, astral projection, exorcism, poltergeists, to the "talents" of Uri Geller, Edgar Cayce, and Jeane Dixon—the case for these phenomena has been presented on radio and television and in newspapers, books, and magazines. "Often," Kurtz states, "the least shred of evidence for these claims is blown out of proportion and presented as 'scientific proof' " (see *The Humanist*, May/June, 1976). Because of this alarming growth and its potential consequences, the individuals forming the committee believe it is necessary to develop a strategy of refutation.

The committee has outlined five major goals: to establish a network of people interested in investigating such claims; to prepare bibliographies of published works that carefully examine such claims; to encourage and commission objective and impartial inquirers to research in areas where investigation is needed; to publish articles, monographs, and books that examine such claims; and to hold conferences and meetings. However, according to Kurtz, it is not the purpose of the committee "to reject on *a priori* grounds, antecedent to inquiry, any or all such claims, but rather to examine them openly, completely, objectively, and carefully."

Many of those involved in the committee have done extensive research and writing on pseudoscience and cults, and many are active critics and debunkers. They believe there is a shortage of critical thinking today. And unfortunately, many scholars have not been willing to take the time and effort necessary to point out the errors in both fact and logic that are present in many pseudoscientific theories. Many scientists consider such efforts beneath their dignity, and others find them useless. This has created a gap which the committee hopes to fill.

The committee, besides co-chairmen Kurtz and Marcello Truzzi, professor of sociology at Eastern Michigan State University, includes:

George Abell, professor of astronomy at UCLA

Isaac Asimov, author

Richard Berendzen, dean of the College of Arts and Sciences at American University

Brand Blandshard, professor of philosophy at Yale University

Bart Bok, emeritus professor of astronomy at the University of Arizona

Daniel Cohen, author and former editor of *Science Digest*

L. Sprague de Camp, author

Charles Fair, author

Antony Flew, professor of philosophy at The University, Reading, England

Martin Gardner, author and member of the editorial staff of *Scientific American*

Sidney Hook, at the Hoover Institution at Stanford University and professor emeritus of philosophy at New York University

Richard Hull, associate professor of philosophy at State University at Buffalo

Lawrence Jerome, science writer

Philip Klass, author

Marvin Kohl, professor of philosophy at State University College at Fredonia, New York

Ernest Nagel, professor emeritus of philosophy at Columbia University

Lee Nisbet, special projects editor of *The Humanist*

James Prescott, neuropsychologist at HEW

W. V. Quine, professor of philosophy at Harvard University

James Randi, author, magician, and escape artist

B. F. Skinner, professor of psychology at Harvard University
Marvin Zelen, professor of statistical science at the State
University of New York at Buffalo.

A partial bibliography of notable "debunking" and critical
books and other works dealing with paranormal and other
phenomena follows:

Astrology

B. Bok and M. Mayall, "Scientists Look at Astrology," *Scientific Monthly* (Vol. 52, March 1941).

L. Jerome, "Astrology and Modern Science: A Critical Analysis," *Leonardo* (Vol. 7, 1974).

J. Barth and J. Bennet, "Astrology and Modern Science Revisited," *Leonardo* (Vol. 7, 1974).

G. Abell, "Astrology: Its Principles and Relation and Nonrelation to Science," *Science Teacher* (December 1974).

H. King, *The Background of Astronomy* (George Braziller, 1958).

J. Lindsay, *Origins of Astrology* (Barnes and Noble, 1972).

R. Gladeau, *The Origin of the Zodiac* (Castle, 1968).

Objections to Astrology (reprint of *The Humanist,* September/October 1975; Prometheus Books, 1976).

UFOs

C. Sagan and R. Page eds., *UFO's: A Scientific Debate* (Norton, 1972).

E. Condon et al., *Scientific Study of UFO's* (Bantam, 1969).

J. Hynek, *The UFO Experience: A Scientific Inquiry* (Regnery, 1972).

P. Klass, *UFO's Explained* (Random House, 1975).

K. Jacobs, *The UFO Controversy in America* (Indiana University Press, 1975).

Velikovsky's Worlds in Collision

O. Gingerich, *Science Year* (*World Book Encyclopedia Supplement 1975,* p. 249).

S. Gould, "Velikovsky in Collision," *Natural Science* (March 1975).

R. Bracewell, "Velikovskian Vermin," *The Galactic Club,* Chapter 2 (Freeman, 1974).

Von Däniken and "Ancient Astronauts"

R. Bracewell, "The Chariots of von Däniken," *The Galactic Club,* Chapter 11 (Freeman, 1974).

Erich von Däniken, one of the Para Committee's prime targets.

E. Krupp, "The von Däniken Phenomenon," *Griffith Observer* (April 1974).

R. Lingeman, "Erich von Däniken's Genesis," *The New York Times Book Review* (March 31, 1974).

L. McIntyre, "Mystery of the Ancient Nazca Lines," *National Geographic* (May 1975).

Ronald Story, *The Space-Gods Revealed* (Harper & Row, 1976).

B. Thiering and E. Castel, eds., *Some Trust in Chariots: Views on Erich von Däniken's Chariots of the Gods?* (Popular Library, 1975).

Astro-archeology

L. Sprague de Camp and Catherine C. de Camp, *The Ancient Engineers* (Ballantine, 1974).

G. Hawkins, *Stonehenge Decoded* (Delta, 1965).

G. Hutchinson, "Long Meg Reconsidered," *American Scientist* (January/February and March/April 1972).

J. Eddy, "Astronomical Alignment of the Big Horn Medicine Wheel," *Science* (June 7, 1974).

F. Hoyle, *Stonehenge and Modern Cosmology* (Freeman, 1972).

General

Milbourne Christopher, *Mediums, Mystics and the Occult* (T. Y. Crowell, 1975).

Christopher Evans, *Cults of Unreason* (Farrar, Straus & Giroux 1973).

Martin Gardner, *Fads and Fallacies in the Name of Science* (Dover, 1957).

Joseph Jastrow, *Error and Eccentricity in Human Belief* (Dover, 1962).

Robert Silverberg, *Scientists and Scoundrels: A Book of Hoaxes* (T. Y. Crowell, 1965).

Forteans

Forteans are the intellectual descendants of Charles Hoy Fort (1874–1932), a newspaper reporter who, supported by a small inheritance, turned to the full-time collection of accounts of strange events which, if true, could not be explained by accepted scientific theory.

Fort carried skepticism to its outer limits. He doubted the validity of most scientific theories; he probably doubted the veracity of many of the reports he collected; he certainly doubted the wild theories that he delighted in presenting as potential alternatives to established scientific ideas. It was Fort's contention that nothing was ever wholly true or false. To him the human view of reality was a sandbox for him to play in, and every grain of sand—whether it was the idea of a spheroid earth or of a flying horse—was of equal value in his eyes. There were a few exceptions: He knew for a fact, for example, that Santa Claus did not exist.

Fort published four books based on his trove of notes: *Book of the Damned* (1919), a collection of mysterious occurrences which were ignored, "damned" by science; *New Lands* (1923), a general attack on orthodox astronomy and related disciplines; *Lo!* (1931), a continuation of the attack on astronomy as well as on archaeology and geology; and the posthumous *Wild Talents* (1932), which looked at accounts of people and animals who were reported to do impossible things. (These books are available from Dover Press.)

The *Book of the Damned* is almost a list of report after report of such strange things as red, blue, black, and lavender rains; falls from the skies of a combustible yellow substance and of fleshlike material; falls of rocks, or water, or fish or anything else out of nowhere in a very small area under clear skies; a fall of pyramidal stones; crosses found in Georgia with the inscription "IYNKICIDU" and Roman coins found in American Indian burial mounds; a blue child born in England; twenty-inch footprints found in sandstone near Carson, Nevada; shadows on the moon; strange wheels of light in the sky; and a report of seventeen tiny coffins, three to four inches long, found buried near Edinburgh. "Science is a turtle that says that its own shell encloses all things"—but not these things, says Fort.

In 1931 his leading admirer, novelist and advertiser Tiffany Thayer, founded a Fortean Society. The society included some of the most significant literary talents of the period: Theodore Dreiser, Booth Tarkington, Alexander Woollcott, and others. In 1937, the society, with Thayer's money, began to publish a magazine which later became *Doubt*. Thayer defined the editorial policy of the magazine as "the only 'doctrine' Forteanism has, that of suspended judgment, temporary acceptance and eternal questioning." *Doubt* ceased to publish at about the time Thayer died in 1959. The magazine's files, which included all of Fort's notes, went to the New York Public Library. Robert C. Warth and Carl Pabst have recently finished transcribing all 42,000 of Fort's notes and about 3,000 miscellaneous items in his files such as clippings, correspondence, etc. Warth says the notes are typical of the kinds of data which are found in Fort's published works.

Warth is the president of the most notable Fortean organization in existence today, the Society for the Investigation of the

Unexplained (SITU), founded by zoologist Ivan T. Sanderson in 1965. SITU publishes a quarterly, *Pursuit,* and maintains a collection of clippings about artifacts of unexplained phenomena.

A few examples of the kinds of data which SITU collects include: mysterious explosions in space, unusual precipitations of animals, rainmaking, sunken cities, strange crystals, bottomless ponds, earthquake oddities, unusual tornadoes, men with tails, winged cats, abominable snowmen, sea monsters, spontaneous human combustion, outbreaks of animal mutilations, bleeding statues, and, of course, UFOs. The library is open to the society's 1,250 members.

The society and its magazine show an admirable detachment from any dogma and a readiness to recognize debunkers of all stripes. A recent article in *Pursuit* condemned as irrational the "blind acceptance of one or more 'unexplained' phenomena as established fact, illogical espousement of 'unpopular' beliefs, [and] flat rejection of opposing arguments or evidence" (C. L. Weidmann, "Bias in Perception of Fortean Events," *Pursuit,* April 1976). Correspondence should be addressed to SITU, Columbia, New Jersey 07832.

An individual Fortean, William R. Corliss, has pored through volumes of scientific journals and magazines and books of all types and found hundreds of "those facts that do not fit the mold, those anomalies that should not exist. . . ." He has published several volumes of summaries of strange data in the fields of geology, archaeology and folklore, biology, astronomy, and electromagnetism. Corliss, unlike many Forteans, has a professional scientific background and thus has a better sense of what is truly unexplained. His books may be purchased from the Sourcebook Project, Glen Arm, Maryland 21057.

Also of interest to Forteans (as well as to many scientists) is the Foundation for the Study of Cycles (founded 1940) at 124 South Highland Avenue, Pittsburgh, Pennsylvania 15206. The foundation publishes a journal on cyclic phenomena and has about 1,800 members.

Another Fortean-like group is the Ancient Mediterranean Research Association, 1047 Gayley Avenue, Suite 201, Los Angeles, California 90049. AMRA does research in ancient history (worldwide, not just Mediterranean), prehistoric civilizations, and general archaeology. It provides expeditions, seminars, books, and research reports to its membership of about 500.

British zoologist Ivan T. Sanderson, founder of the Society for the Investigation of the Unexplained.

Forteans are so varied in style, intellect, and interests that no single description will fit all. It is possible, however, to say that while most modern Forteans are considerably less zany and entertaining than Charles Fort, they retain his inexhaustible capacity for gathering reports of unusual phenomena and are worth hours of fascinating conversation. Forteans also continue the tradition of "suspended judgment." For some "Forteans," unfortunately, "suspended judgment" has come to mean a preference for false mystery and the rejection of well-documented explanations.

Mystical Groups

Hare Krishna

Hare Krishna is a modern American revival of an Indian Krishna sect. Its saffron-clothed devotees are a familiar sight on streets of American cities, dancing in daily processionals and chanting their devotion to the Lord Krishna.

The Hare Krishna movement, officially known as the International Society for Krishna Consciousness (ISKCON), was founded in New York City in 1966 by Swami Prabhupada. The original Krishna sect on which this revival is based first appeared in Bengal about A.D. 1500.

Today the society claims about 3,000 members or devotees in the United States, mostly in the large cities. The society has about sixty-five centers or ashrams throughout the world: about thirty to forty in the United States; seventeen in Britain, France, the Netherlands, and Germany, eight in Commonwealth countries, and four in India.

The temple in New York City houses 120 devotees, including twenty women, ten of whom are married to men in the temple. The bulk are Americans, and about a third are from middle-class Jewish families. The average age is twenty-three.

Upon entering the movement, devotees consider their previous lives a closed chapter; they take on new names and forswear meat, fish, eggs, intoxicants, tobacco, extramarital sex, and thought and speech not authorized by Scripture.

The sect believes Krishna is the "Supreme Personality of Godhead," which resides in every spirit. By concentrating on him, by constantly chanting the Hare Krishna mantra (repeated about 2,000 times a day), and by denying material and sensual gratifications, one can be liberated from the endless cycle of disease, aging, death, and rebirth. To send this message around the world is the main task of the movement.

The Gurukula, the sect's school in Dallas, Texas, founded three years ago, is thriving. Children of devotees from all over the country come to live there and learn about the movement. The young children learn Sanskrit, rudimentary English,

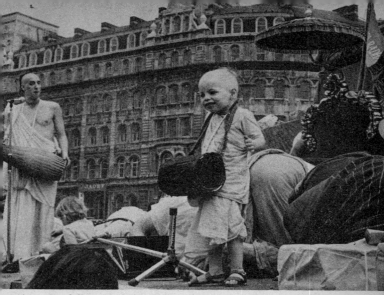

A young follower of the Society of Krishna Consciousness beats his drum at the Third International Hare Krishna Rathayatra Festival in London, England.

arithmetic, and some geography and history, but all in a Krishna context.

The movement's founder, Swami Prabhupada, born in Calcutta in 1896, gave up an active chemical business, his family and his contact in society, to devote himself entirely to the propagation of Krishna consciousness. He became a Hindu monk and in 1965, at the age of seventy, came to the United States. In New York City he began to work with derelicts and hippies on the Bowery, and he lectured on the Gita in the East Village, slowly gathering a following among hippie-oriented youth. In 1968 he opened a printing press. Today some half million copies of the movement's magazine are published monthly. Swami Prabhupada is highly respected by his followers, who believe he is part of an unbroken line of divine reincarnations that go back 5,000 years to the first appearance of Krishna himself as a supernatural cowherd boy with 16,000 wives. Devotees believe he is higher than Christ, Brahma, and Siva, surpassed only by Vishnu, who along with Brahma and Siva forms the trinity of supreme Hindu deities.

There are many signs that the Hare Krishna movement is

prospering and that its membership is growing. The movement's income stems from various sources: the sale of incense (the factory is estimated to earn about $1,000,000 a year), street collections (the New York ashram collects about $30,000 in one winter month), and donations from wealthy individuals.

For more information, see F. Levine, *The Strange World of the Hare Krishnas* (Fawcett, 1974).

Soka Gakkai

Soka Gakkai is an association of laymen who practice Nichiren-sho-shu Buddhism. The English translation of Soka Gakkai is Value Creation Society.

Soka Gakkai was founded in Japan in 1937 by Makiguchi Tsunesaburo, an educator. However, the practice of Nichiren-sho-shu Buddhism was not a new phenomenon in Japan. It is one of the sects that follows the teachings of the Japanese Buddhist saint Nichiren (1222–1282), a fervent nationalist who attacked the established contemporary religious and political institutions of Japan. Soka Gakkai revived Nichiren's strong nationalism and his dedication to improving political and social life.

After studying Buddhist Scripture, Nichiren concluded that only one Scripture gave the truth—the Scripture of the Lotus of the Good Law, also known as the Lotus Sutra. He developed three forms of devotion to the Lotus Sutra: the *honzon* or *gohonzon*, the *daimoku*, and the *kaidan*. All three still play a major role in the lives of the members of Soka Gakkai.

The *gohonzon* is a ritual drawing (mandala) on which names of the divinities mentioned in the sutra are arranged around the name of the Lotus Sutra. This mandala is placed on an altar in Nichiren temples, as well as in the homes of Nichiren Buddhists.

Daimoku is the practice of chanting *nam Myoho renge-kyo*—"salutation to the Lotus Sutra." The chant is the main religious act in Soka Gakkai.

The *kaidan* is the temple where the worshipers assemble to hear the teachings of Nichiren Buddhism and practice *daimoku*.

Nichiren's teachings gave rise to several sects, including Nichiren-sho-shu, which remained relatively insignificant until its revival by Soka Gakkai in this century. Nichiren-sho-shu differs from other sects in that it regards Nichiren as more

Soka Gakkai priests in ancient embroidered robes present a contrast to the severe modern lines of the temple of Daiseki-ji, located at the foot of Mount Fuji.

important than Sakyamuni, the historical Buddha. It is head-quartered at the temple Daiseki-ji, established at the end of the thirteenth century at the foot of Mount Fuji.

Makiguchi Tsunesaburo, the founder, believed that the goals of life are the values of beauty, gain, and goodness. He taught that religion was a practical means of attaining these goals.

During World War II Soka Gakkai suffered greatly from religious persecution by the Japanese government. Makiguchi died in prison in 1944, but his disciple, Toda Josei, revived the association in 1946 and gave it its present name. Since 1960 Ikeda Daisaku has led the organization.

Soka Gakkai, established a Japanese political party in 1964 known as Komeito (Clean Government). A nationalistic party, it won seats in both houses of the Diet, the Japanese national parliament. The party opposes extreme wealth and the rearma-

ment of Japan. In 1970 Komeito came under serious attack
for allegedly seeking to establish a fascist government with
Soka Gakkai as the state religion. Following this criticism, the
party was separated from Soka Gakkai in December 1970.

The membership of Soka Gakkai between 1951 and 1957
grew from 3,000 families to 765,000 families. Its membership
in 1974 was estimated at 10,000,000.

The phenomenal growth of Soka Gakkai in the 1950s
attracted worldwide attention. The increase in membership
was at least partly due to the association's strong emphasis on
conversion. Members are taught that conversion of new members, called *shakufuku,* is a practical way to attain desired
goals in their own lives. *Shakufuku,* which means "break and
subdue" in Japanese, involves unrelenting verbal persuasion,
according to James Dator (*Soka Gakkai,* University of Washington Press, 1969).

Soka Gakkai established the Nichiren-sho-shu Academy,
an independently incorporated Western Hemisphere affiliate,
in the United States in 1960. The organization actively seeks
non-Japanese converts. In 1976 the academy, headquartered
in Santa Monica, California, claimed a membership of 250,000
people, including many prominent sports and entertainment
personalities. On July 3, 1976, more than 15,000 members
from all over the United States staged a huge illuminated
night parade, featuring thirteen floats, in New York City as a
major part of that city's bicentennial celebration. The organization also staged a fireworks spectacular over Central Park.

The United States group has come under criticism from
Zen Buddhists for encouraging preoccupation with the desire
for worldly goals rather than with enlightenment, which
involves freedom from desire. They have also criticized the
association for valuing group support—the mutual encouragement and exhortation to practice their religion—instead of a
deep personal experience of enlightenment.

Arica

Arica is a latter-day mystical school intended to guide
individuals toward the highest possible self-awareness and
to develop methods for achieving universal understanding
and brotherhood. The Arica system is taught in a number of
centers in the United States and other countries.

The Arica system of thought and instruction was founded
by Oscar Ichazo, born in Bolivia in 1931. Early in life, Ichazo

Arica's founder, Oscar Ichazo.

was instructed in Zen, Sufism, the Kabbalah, and other mystical teachings by various Latin American experts. Later he traveled to Asia to study Oriental philosophies and occult practices. In 1971 Ichazo moved to the town of Arica in Chile, having made a decision to share the results of his knowledge and experience and to teach others in the system he had devised. In 1970 a group of about fifty Americans came to Arica to study with Ichazo, and they became the nucleus of the Arica Institute, which was organized in New York the next year. The Arica program expanded rapidly; by the end of 1975 close to 10,000 people participated in the program through about twenty-five centers established throughout the world.

An Arica student may enroll in one of four programs:

1. A forty-day training session.
2. A three-week intensive training (twelve hours per day).
3. A three-month training period described in Arica literature as "opening of the rainbow eye" and designed to

clarify the "entire spectrum of the elements of which human consciousness is composed."

4. An advanced program entitled "cutting of the adamantine pyramid" leading to a state in which "the liberated mind becomes the perfect container of total awareness."

The Arica system is based on Buddhism, Confucianism, Sufism, Christianity, and other elements, but it has qualities which are intrinsically its own. According to Ichazo, the aim is not to detach the people from this world but to train them to change it—to "slow down and love the earth before it is too late." The long and arduous training is intended to make a person realize a simple ultimate truth: He or she is already perfect, but does not realize it and does not accept the "radiant inner being." Accepting one's own reality means "understanding that the origin of our suffering is nothing but dependence upon the exterior."

As outlined in Ichazo's book *The Human Process for Enlightenment and Freedom* (Simon & Schuster, 1977), the method is extremely complex and couched in esoteric language. For example, this is a description of the first level of the Arica method:

> . . . we study the nine hypergnostic systems manifested in the three instincts, the four functions, and the two psychic poles which close the circle of the hypergnostic spectrum. At this point the method of karma cleaning machines is used, in which group processing has a considerable part. This accelerates the dynamic of losing our stratified mechanisms of defense around our point of fixation. Meditation is developed throughout the intensive and ritualized work.

The Arica method makes use of a variety of techniques and devices to facilitate meditation and to speed progress in mystical understanding; these include Yoga, music, chants, incantations, and psychic diagrams known as yantras.

Oscar Ichazo has pointed out that although Arica makes use of various traditional methods and principles, it represents an entirely new approach, particularly in its attempt to deal with mysticism and the human psyche in a rational, standardized way. Ichazo believes that psychology has not yet reached the level of an exact science and thus is unable to offer precise descriptions of such phenomena as consciousness and enlightenment. Ichazo claims the Arica method achieves the precision and reproducibility lacking in traditional mystical approaches and in modern psychology. It is difficult to judge whether Arica indeed transcends the sum of its parts, and until objective studies of the results achieved are available, the validity of Arica's far-reaching claims cannot be determined.

Dervishes

A dervish is a member of any of the Islamic religious fraternities which seek mystical experiences through special exercises such as meditation, prolonged dancing, or chanting.

The dervish orders appeared in the twelfth century as formalized versions of already-existing, informal Sufi fraternities. (Sufi is a generalized term for the mystical tradition within Islam.) There are said to be thirty-two dervish orders; but some of these have disappeared, and others have been subdivided into numerous suborders. The orders tend to be much less formally organized than Christian religious orders, though some of the larger orders have chapters in many countries. The central chapter of an order is often built around the tomb of its founder.

Dervishes can be residents in a community, travelers from place to place, or simply lay members. Varying degrees of asceticism are often practiced, but celibacy is not typical.

The most distinctive aspect of dervish practice is the dhikr (or kikr), the "remembering" of God. Details vary among the different orders, but a common feature is the attainment of a state of ecstasy through some hypnotically repetitive activity, often to the accompaniment of music, and sometimes through the use of hashish. Through the dhikr, which can be practiced individually or in a group, the dervish can attain spiritual perfection and, according to some, a spiritual union with God.

The famous "whirling" dervishes belong to the Mawlawi order founded in Turkey by the thirteenth-century Persian poet Jalal ad-Din ar-Rumi. The dancers wear tall conical hats and wide robes that flare as they dance. They begin by sitting in a circle, reciting poems, in the center of the tekke, an octagonal hall. They then slowly rise and move across the floor, spinning rhythmically. As they rise, the dervishes shed their black robes, a sign of death, to reveal pure white dancing robes beneath, a sign of resurrection.

Head back, arms extended, they whirl at increasing speed, until they attain a trancelike state. After an interval of rest the

The famous "whirling" dervishes.

ceremony may be repeated, followed by a prayer and a procession. The dance is said to symbolize the circling of the heavenly spheres and the circling of the soul as it vibrates with the love of God.

Other orders use controlled breathing exercises in the dhikr, possibly influenced by similar Indian (Yoga) practices. In one example, reported by an observer of Algerian members of the Rahmaniya order, the dervishes sat in a circle and recited the name Al-lah (the Muslim name of God), exhaling on the first syllable and inhaling on the second. This was done in unison, with sixty paired strokes a minute for about eight minutes and then repeated at a slightly slower pace.

The two routines were repeated three times, with the aid of a leader and religious professionals who helped maintain the rhythm. Members performed a fourth repetition on their knees, rocking back and forth, after which they touched the floor with their foreheads and remained in a mystical state for several minutes.

The word "dervish" comes from the Persian word for beggar, and some orders are composed of wandering beggars. Some of these dervish mendicants, especially those from lower social classes, were famed in the past for extraordinary physical feats. According to *Caravan,* by Carlton Coon (Holt, Rinehart & Winston, 1958) and other sources, the Rifay "howling" dervishes, found in Morocco and in American circuses in the past, would bite off the heads of venomous puff adders, lick hot irons, slash their limbs with long knives, and swallow hot coals, all in the frenzy of dancing. These practices have become less common in recent times.

The dervishes, like Sufis in general, are theologically diverse, and some avoid theological speculation altogether. In the context of Islam, they have usually acted as an emotional counterpoise to orthodoxy. This may help explain why the mystics flourished mainly among the non-Arab peoples of Islam, such as Turks, Persians, Berbers, and Indians.

The major religious and social roles that the dervish orders played in the Middle Ages were paralleled in modern times by their influence in rallying opposition to foreign rule, as in Sudan in the nineteenth century and in Libya in the twentieth. By now, however, the orders have lost much of their independence to centralized, bureaucratic governments.

Early Western travelers who noted the popular esteem accorded to dervishes attributed their reputation to their ability to heal the sick and interpret dreams. But the Muslims themselves believed the dervishes had a more important, mystical function. Without the presence on earth of a number of men who had transcended ordinary humanity, the cosmos might fall from its orderly cycle and be destroyed. The whirling of the Mawlawis is a physical expression of this role or even a form of sympathetic magic.

Kabbalah

Kabbalah, or cábalo, is a tradition of Jewish mystical thought and practice that flourished in the late Middle Ages and early modern era.

The term "Kabbalah," literally "received tradition," did not come into prominence until the twelfth century, but there were mystical currents within Judaism before that time which can also be called Kabbalistic, since they contained the basic principles of what later came to be identified as Kabbalah proper.

Judaism makes a distinction between "black" and "white" magic. The black variety is expressly and repeatedly forbidden by the Bible. The white, though not always encouraged, has often been condoned.

Jewish mysticism is concerned with trying to attain immediate communion with God and with explaining such matters as the connection between God and His creation and the existence of evil. Originally the discipline was esoteric and aristocratic, but the rise of Kabbalah in the Middle Ages created broad public interest. In the sixteenth century, after the expulsion of the Jews from Spain in 1492, Kabbalah became a popular movement, often involving the use of magic formulas and of amulets inscribed with the sacred names of God.

The earliest Kabbalistic works appeared in Palestine between the first and the sixth century A.D. Mystical teachings were transmitted via Italy to Provence, where the Kabbalah proper was developed. From there it spread to Spain, where it reached its highest achievement in a treatise called the *Zohar*. Compiled around the year 1300, it has been the basis of all Kabbalah down to the present time.

According to the *Zohar*, God makes his existence known to mankind through ten *sephirot*, or emanations of the *ein sof*, or Infinite. These emanations, such as wisdom, intelligence, beauty, etc., were charted and depicted in various ways, such as a tree with branches, or as the physical parts of Adam Kadmon, primordial man.

The *Zohar* is an optimistic book. Man is seen as the acme of creation, an earthbound incarnation of Adam Kadmon, and a microcosm of the universe. In a later development, another world was posited corresponding to Adam Belial, the opposite of Adam Kadmon. This world also had ten emanations, but it was demonic and inhabited by evil spirits.

Kabbalah teaches that each soul exists in a state of complete knowledge before it reluctantly accepts a body. Kabbalah also believes in metempsychosis, the transmigration of souls.

Kabbalists prefer symbolic to literal interpretations of the Bible. Various methods for extracting arcane meanings include computations based on the numerical value of Hebrew letters (each letter represents a numeral), acrostics using initial letters of words, and permutations, whereby one letter is substituted for another by using charts of letter correspondences.

By the sixteenth century Safed, in Galilee in Palestine, had become the chief center of Kabbalism, under the leadership of the scholar Isaac ben Solomon Luria. Luria explained the exile of the Jews as a withdrawal of the Infinite into Himself. He said this could be overcome by praying with an intense mystical feeling.

Kabbalah provided a point of contact between Judaism and other philosophical traditions. The main theories were heavily influenced by Neoplatonism and perhaps by Babylonian and even Indian speculative systems. Kabbalah, in turn, had an important influence on Christian mystics and philosophers, especially on the adherents of the "Christian Kabbalah" of the fifteenth and later centuries.

Within Judaism, Kabbalah served as a refuge from the rationalist and scholastic traditions and helped enliven the emotions and imagination of the faithful. In this context it contributed to the rise of Hasidism, a pietist movement, which started in Eastern Europe in the eighteenth century and continues to exert an influence on modern Judaism.

On the other hand, Kabbalah has over the centuries been condemned for introducing superstitious practices and false messianic movements among Jews.

For more information, see C. Ponce *Kabbalah* (Straight Arrow, 1973) and B. Pick, *The Cabala* (Open Court, 1974).

Occult Religions

Theosophy

Theosophy is a complex of philosophical and religious ideas centering on an attempt to gain access to the universal spiritual reality beyond material existence, popularized by the century-old Theosophical Society.

The modern theosophical movement began in 1875, when the Theosophical Society was founded in New York City by Helena Petrovna Blavatsky, a Russian noblewoman and occultist, along with Henry Steel Olcott, a journalist and student of spiritualism, and a variety of other mystics, Kabbalists, and occultists. The headquarters of the society was subsequently moved to Adyar, near Madras, India, where it remains.

Blavatsky became the guiding spirit of modern theosophy, through her writings, wide travels, forceful personality, and claimed psychic abilities. After her death in 1891 there emerged other leaders, in particular the British social reformer Annie Besant. Despite factional disputes, splits, and changes of emphasis, the society remains active with a worldwide membership of about 35,000.

Blavatsky and other modern theosophists claimed to be reviving an ancient mystical tradition that had often surfaced in Western philosophy and religion and, they claimed, had been the dominant strain of Indian intellectual history. Spiritual ancestors included Pythagoras, Plato and the Neoplatonists, the Gnostics, various medieval and Renaissance mystics, and the early-seventeenth-century philosopher Jakob Boehme. In India and Ceylon, Blavatsky and Olcott studied Buddhism and Hinduism in collaboration with Hindu revivalists and Buddhist sages. The two also claimed to communicate with certain spirits called masters.

The masters were said to be people who had reached the higher stages of perfection but remained on earth (mostly in Tibet) to help guide the world's spiritual revolution (see Dalai Lama). This aspect of theosophy, which generated

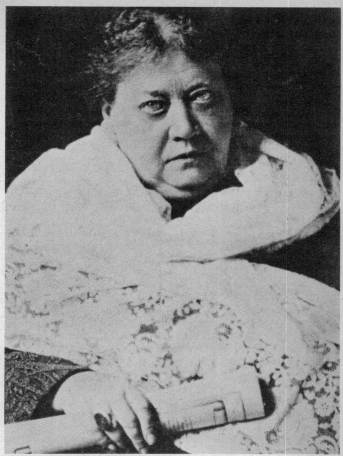

Helena Petrovna Blavatsky.

controversy and charges of fraud, became less important over the years, as did other paranormal phenomena, but the basic philosophy, including such ethical principles as universal love and the brotherhood of mankind, was retained.

Theosophy postulates one immutable, all-pervading principle which is at the root of all phenomena in the universe. This one principle includes the dual aspects of spirit and matter, life and form, positive and negative. Man, being a part of the whole, is evolving toward the perfect manifestation of the divine characteristics latent within him. Each higher stage brings more knowledge of the universe, visible and invisible, and higher moral and psychic powers. The unfolding of man's powers is slow and requires repeated reincarnations. The choices made in one's life determine the soul's condition in the next incarnation, according to the principle of karma, the law of cause and effect. Those souls reaching final liberation from the cycle of rebirth may return to earth, where some of them become the founders of great religions, all of which are said to share the same fundamental teachings.

Writing in the period of great debate over Darwin's evolutionary theories, Blavatsky posited that the entire universe evolves through seven worlds, or planes, and that people must experience a similar evolution through seven "root races," of which the current generation was the sixth.

For eighteen years early in the twentieth century, Annie Besant, who then headed the society, believed she had found the person through whom a World Teacher would come to lead people into their seventh and last stage. This person, an Indian youth named Jidda Krishnamurti, was to be inhabited by the master who had supposedly inhabited Jesus and would also be a reincarnation of the Buddha. The Order of the Star, founded to spread the word, attracted thousands of followers in India and in the West, but Krishnamurti himself dissolved the order in 1929, renouncing all divine claims.

The Theosophical Society was probably the most important agent in introducing Eastern thought to large Western audiences, and it helped break down Western attitudes of condescension toward non-Western cultures. It also played a significant role in stimulating Hindu and Buddhist revivals in Asia.

In its early years, the society was also the most important source for the spread of occult beliefs, perhaps because of its size and its respectability. But the combination of antidogmatic religion and nonmechanistic science has proved to be the most enduring element of theosophy.

For more information, see C. J. Ryan, *What Is Theosophy?* (Theosophical Press, 1941) and C. Jinarajadasa, *First Principles of Theosophy* (Theosophical Press, 1960).

Wicca

Wicca (alleged to mean "wisdom" but probably meaning "bent") is the term preferred by modern witches for their

Alexandrian queen witch "calling down the moon."

pagan beliefs, rituals and crafts. The term "warlock," sometimes defined as a male witch, is seldom used by wiccans, whose male adherents are also called witches.

Wiccans are polytheists and believe in the superiority of the mother goddess, who personifies the fertility of nature and the processes of birth and growth. A horned god, representing nature, death, and the afterlife, is also usually recognized, along with many lesser deities. Wicca emphasizes harmony with nature and usually does not assert any ethical doctrine beyond a simple appeal to that harmony.

Contrary to popular belief, modern witches are not Satanists or devil worshipers; they regard devils and Satan as fictions created by Christianity. Most of the avowed witches, particularly those who actively and publicly seek disciples or make public claims of their psychic powers are commercial hucksters and not associated with wicca covens.

Initiation into a coven, as each small group of worshipers is called, involves taking an oath of secrecy, adopting a special witch name, and receiving the tools of the craft from the high priestess. The initiate thus becomes a witch, the first degree of three. After further study and practice, the wiccan advances to the level of queen of witches or magus (for men), and beyond that lies the degree of high priest or priestess. A newly created high priestess is expected to leave her original coven and begin one of her own. The covens are matriarchical with the high priestess at the top of the hierarchy.

Ritual turns on invocations of the goddess and the gods and on joyous celebrations of life. Sexual imagery is very common in the ritual, but actual sexual activity in the rites is rare except in those few covens which emphasize it. A holy communion-like ceremony, using cakes and wine blessed by the high priestess, is very common. Some covens perform their rites "sky clad"—i.e., in the nude—while other covens are robed. There is no reliable information on which form is more common.

Esbat rituals are held at least once a month, especially at the time of the full moon; these are the regular services of wicca. Sabbats are rituals and festivities associated with the seasons. The greater Sabbats are Halloween, Candlemas or February Eve, Beltane or May Eve (the Walpurgis Night of medieval times, also called Roodmas) and Lammas or August Eve. The lesser Sabbats are celebrated at the equinoxes and solstices.

Many covens, but not all, practice mild forms of white magic, believing in the efficacy of love potions, healing rituals, and incantations against perils. Most covens also practice various forms of divination.

Belief in an afterlife seems to be rather vague in the tradition, though there is some suggestion of a mystical union with the deity. Many covens have adopted Oriental ideas of karma and reincarnation.

Wicca is of recent origin, although some wiccans claim descent by birth or teaching from medieval witches, who were allegedly practicing their ancient pagan faith in defiance of the Roman Catholic Church.

Such claims were not made, however, until after the

appearance of Margaret Murray's *The Witch Cult in Western Europe* in 1921 (available from Oxford University Press in New York in a 1962 paperback edition). Murray argued that medieval witchcraft was a survival of northern European pre-Christian paganism. Modern wicca strongly reflects her description of the beliefs and practices of the old religion. Murray's theory was given wide currency in her article "Witchcraft" in the 14th edition of the *Encyclopaedia Britannica* (1929). In her *God of the Witches* in 1931 (Anchor, 1960), she elaborated on the theory and traced the religion back to Paleolithic times. While the theory was soon discredited as historically and anthropologically unsound, it did lend a degree of respectability to subsequent efforts to revive fertility cult paganism.

A major credit for this revival must go to Gerald Gardner, a retired British customs official and a disciple of Aleister Crowley. Shortly before Crowley died, Gardner approached him for assistance in devising a pagan witchcraft ritual. Crowley responded with the *Book of Shadows*, a high-sounding blend of material from his own religion, Thelema, and materials from C. G. Leland's *Arcadia, or the Gospel of the Witches* (1899), supposedly derived from Italian witchcraft folklore, and *Gypsy Sorcery and Fortune-Telling* (1891). The *Book of Shadows* and its derivatives are still the most common ritual handbooks in wicca.

In 1954 Gardner published *Witchcraft Today* (London, Rider), in which he claimed that there still existed witchcraft covens which had direct links to the ancient religion of the Murray theory. Almost overnight, covens sprang up in England and looked to Gardner for advice and leadership. Gardner's second book, *The Meaning of Witchcraft* (London, Aquarian Press, 1959), cemented his influence on the movement.

With Gardner's death in 1964, the movement broke into many fragments. His chief heir, Mrs. Monique Wilson (the Lady Olwen, as her adherents call her), is the titular head of those who still follow Gardner's views closely. One major splinter group, the Alexandrians, borrowed heavily from other occult traditions and is particularly strong in the United States. Many covens dropped some of the more bizarre aspects of Gardnerism, such as the use of the scourge. A few covens, especially in England, claim hereditary descent from the medieval witches and scoff at both the Gardnerians and the Alexandrians.

Most American covens have adopted a mixture of anything that seems interesting in the fads of the moment. Compared to what the imagination might conceive and contrary to the suggestion of ecstatic experience in the *Book of Shadows,* most covens' rites are almost sedate and, at times, even spiritless—as if the witches did not quite believe their games are real. Dan Greenburg in *Something's There* (Doubleday, 1976) has two hilarious accounts of coven meetings he attended.

Cultural Religions and Sects

Druids

Druids were the priests and learned class of the Celtic people of Gaul and the British Isles.

Most of what is known about the Druids is derived from Greek and Roman sources, many of them secondhand, and from early medieval Irish sagas.

At the time of the Roman conquests of Gaul and Britain, the Druids were flourishing as the only unifying institution of the Celts. Because of their unity and because they appear to have resisted Romanization, the Druids were largely suppressed, except in Ireland, which the Romans never conquered. The Druid practice of human sacrifice may have also encouraged the Romans to suppress the cult.

The word "druid" is probably related to the Celtic word for oak tree—*daur*. The oak was, in fact, sacred to the Druids, as was the mistletoe, and, in early times, Druid rites were performed in oak forests. Although there were both male and female Druids, very little is known about the latter. A lower-ranking priesthood, the vates, were prophets and bards.

The Druids, who were recruited from the warrior class, were exempt from taxes, manual labor, and military service and occupied the highest rank in society. Thus, they had no trouble attracting new recruits.

The Druids were responsible for the education of young warrior nobles, as well as for the perpetuation of their own oral tradition. According to Julius Caesar, they spent as many as twenty years in learning verses, refusing to commit any of them to writing, though the Greek alphabet was familiar to them by Caesar's time.

The Druids possessed some knowledge of astronomy and medicine and had a mythology and a natural science of their own. They also taught the doctrines of immortality and the transmigration of souls.

The notorious Druid sacrificial rites were conducted with human victims, who were burned in huge wicker structures as offerings to aid the sick or those going into battle. When

Welsh Druids collect the sacred mistletoe.

criminals and prisoners (normally used as sacrifice) were unavailable, innocent victims were apparently used. Animals were also used at public and private sacrifices.

The Druids also served as chief judges, according to Julius Caesar, and all public and private quarrels, as well as criminal cases, were brought before them, often at their annual assemblies at Carnutes (which they believed to be the center of Gaul). Those who disobeyed their decrees were excluded from the sacrifices, which was considered a severe punishment. The Druids of Gaul had a single chief, chosen for life.

Though druidic tradition was in part preserved in Irish epic for some centuries after the Christianization of Ireland and faint echoes remain in Welsh folklore, the practices and doctrines of the Druids disappeared from Europe early in the Middle Ages. During the Renaissance interest in the Druids revived. But the cult was romanticized, especially in Elizabethan England, and the Druids began to be seen as the possessors of a great, lost wisdom.

In the seventeenth century it was believed that the Druids had built Stonehenge (this has since been attributed to a much earlier culture). In the following century there became popular a theory in which the Druids were considered followers of the religion of the Hebrew patriarchs, in its purest form.

Within the past two centuries modern druidic cults have arisen in England. They bear no genuine relation to the cult of the ancient Druids, but nevertheless, parts of this new ritual have been incorporated into the eisteddfod, the traditional Welsh festival of poetry and music, while midsummer druidic ceremonies at Stonehenge have become a tourist attraction.

Some historians have drawn parallels between the Druids and the Brahmans of Hindu tradition, whom they believe to be collateral descendants of a hypothetical Indo-European priesthood. However, the Druids probably incorporated some practices or beliefs of earlier European cultures as well.

For more information, see S. Piggott, *The Druids* (Praeger, 1968); A. L. Owen, *The Famous Druids* (Clarendon, 1962); and W. W. Reade, *The Veil of Isis—Mysteries of the Druids* (Ecklon, 1924).

Thugs

Thugs were a secret religious society of professional thieves, said to have plagued India for centuries until their suppression by the British in the 1830s.

The British East India Company, which at that time was virtually the sovereign power of India, directed a military and police campaign from 1828 to 1837 against the thugs, a purported secret criminal society that had robbed and mur-

dered Europeans as well as Indians. Sir William Henry
Sleeman, who led the campaign in cooperation with police
authorities in several of the princely states, later wrote
extensively of his experience.

According to Sleeman and other British authorities, the
thugs were a tightly organized, secret cult, largely hereditary
in membership, consisting of both Muslims and Hindus, but
dedicated to the worship of Kali, the Hindu goddess of
destruction.

Each band consisted of a handful to several hundred members. Thugs would infiltrate a group of travelers, gain their
confidence, and, at the first chance, strangle their victims,
usually with a length of cotton which they called the hem of
Kali's skirt. After removing a victim's possessions, they would
bury him and move on.

Thugs spoke a special argot and could recognize fellow
members from all parts of India. Deriving mostly from lower
castes, they would sometimes exempt low-caste travelers
from their attacks. Women sometimes belonged to thug bands,
and in general, women were not molested. However, no one
who witnessed a thug attack could be sure of escaping with
his or her life. Children would be sold into slavery.

The thug movement was said to have dated from at least

*The goddess Kali or Durga—worshiped as the destructive power
of nature—dances upon the body of Siva, her husband.*

the thirteenth century, but it flourished especially during the power vacuum that followed European colonial advances in the seventeeth and eighteenth centuries, preceding the final British takeover. The society evaded suppression not only because of its excellent organization and secrecy, but also because it paid protection money to local authorities.

During the campaign against the thug society, hundreds of adherents were killed in the field, 412 were hanged, and nearly 3,000 others were imprisoned. Individuals suspected of being thugs, as well as their families and relatives, were required to register under a Criminal Tribes Act and remained under police surveillance.

No subsequent incidents were attributed to the thugs, and after India gained independence in 1947, the new government repealed the registration law.

Many aspects of the generally accepted account of the thugs have been challenged. The Indian historian H. Gupta has maintained that the only reality behind the story was that the economic dislocations in the early nineteenth century led to the formation of scattered bands of brigands, responsible for random, small-scale crime. According to Gupta, the thugs did not constitute a religious fraternity, nor did they have a central or even regional organization.

The word "thug" in Hindi means "cheat" or "swindler." Random references to groups of thugs in Indian records prior to the nineteenth century need not refer to any specific cult. Sleeman, it has been pointed out, thought he had uncovered several other secret criminal conspiracies in India but did not have sufficient proof for these charges and even grossly misrepresented the character of the Sikhs, a legitimate religious movement.

The methods used by Sleeman to track down the thugs, violating both British and Indian canons of justice, were not conducive to discovering the whole truth. A suspected thug was given the choice of being hanged or at least severely punished, on the one hand, or of supplying the name of another thug, often in another part of the country, on the other hand. The resulting chain of accusations was apparently never subjected to independent trial or investigation. No attempt was made to recover the body or stolen property of a thug victim, nor were a victim's relatives questioned.

Until more definite evidence of a thug conspiracy is uncovered, most aspects of the traditional account will remain in doubt. Fictionalized accounts, such as the 1939 U.S. film

Gunga Din, are to be mistrusted even more, because they belong to the fading romance of the White Man's Burden.

For further information, see W. H. Sleeman, *Ramaseeana* (G. H. Huttman, 1835) and *Rambles and Recollections of an Indian Official* (Oxford University Press, 1974) and H. Gupta, *Journal of Indian History,* Vol. XXXLII, p. 167.

Voodoo

Voodoo is the folk religion of Haiti, originating in Africa but including some Roman Catholic, Carib Indian, and local Haitian elements.

Voodoo can rightly be called a religion, because it deals with questions of creation, the gods, death, and immortality and prescribes rituals for all the major events of life, such as marriage, birth, sickness, and the consecration of houngans, the voodoo priests.

Almost all Haitians have at least a sentimental attachment to certain aspects of voodoo lore, but the full practice of the cult separates the Creole-speaking masses from the French-speaking, educated elite.

African slaves brought Voodoo to Haiti, probably from the region of present-day Benin (formerly Dahomey). Most of the primary divinities, or loa, are African, though some are indigenous to Haiti, the result of the deification of powerful ancestors. There are hundreds of loa, both good and evil, each with its own dwelling place either under the water or within snakes, trees, or fire. Their powers were given them by the Great Master, the single god who judges people and distributes his powers according to his supreme will. The loa are his intermediaries.

Voodoo rites often involve possession by a loa. At a typical Saturday evening ceremony in a houmfor, or Voodoo temple, the houngan begins with a mixture of Voodoo and Catholic prayers. The possession culminates the ceremony, after sacrifices of food or animals have been made. All this occurs to the accompaniment of dancing, singing, chanting, and drums. According to some accounts, sexual promiscuity is sometimes practiced during these ceremonies.

The loa can possess a houngan, a mambo (priestess), or even one of the worshipers, in which case the spirit is said to "mount his horse." During the trance, which may begin with shouting, trembling, or convulsions, the possessed individual has special knowledge of the present and the future. He or she may assume the voice, gestures, and even the general physical characteristics of the god. The loa can induce the possessed to lie, steal, strike or caress a person without the possessed taking responsibility for the action.

Voodoo also maintains a tradition of private magic, accomplished through potions and spells, that can cure insanity, recall the dead as zombies, ruin or enhance a person's luck, arouse passionate love, repel werewolves, or secure the death of an enemy.

Of all the mysteries connected with Voodoo, the one that arouses the most discussion is the death spell. Some physicians, including Dr. Theodore X. Barber of the Boston University School of Medicine, have claimed that there is no evidence based on actual observation that death has ever been directly caused by sorcery. Some instances of supposed Voodoo death, Barber has said, were actually caused by poison or organic illness, while in other cases it appeared that the victim, believing that death was imminent, refused food and water and died of starvation and dehydration.

But anthropological evidence collected from many societies suggests that victims who strongly believe in the efficacy of

During a Brazilian voodoo ceremony, Oxossi, the Voodoo saint of the hunt, is one of the three saints represented in the ritual dance Saida dos Santos. Oxum (right) is the Voodoo saint of war.

the spell are deprived of the confidence and social support of their neighbors and may actually die of terror. The persistent excessive activity of the sympathetic nervous system, leading to very rapid pulse and respiration, combined with the lack of food and water, may kill the victim.

As for sticking pins into dolls resembling the prospective victim, the practice is not as central to Voodoo as is commonly believed in the United States, judging from the scarcity of references to this practice in the literature on Voodoo. The custom may have been developed by slaves simply to relieve their frustration at their impotence against cruel masters.

For more information, see A. Metroax, *Life in Haiti* (Schocken Books, 1972) and F. Husley, *The Invisibles: Voodoo Gods in Haiti* (McGraw-Hill, 1966):

Cargo Cults

Cargo cult is part of a religious and social movement among the blacks of Melanesia, a group of islands in the South Pacific northeast of Australia.

The cargo cults are a curious manifestation of increasing tension between the poor and rich areas of the world. Members of the cargo cults believe: (1) white people stole from God the secret of producing material goods; (2) ships, planes, and even rockets will deliver such goods to believers at no cost; (3) a messiah will come to make this possible; (4) when this occurs, they will never have to work again; (5) their dead ancestors will accompany the goods delivered to them; and (6) white rule will be succeeded by native rule.

The first cargo cults, led by prophets who claimed to have seen visions, appeared late in the nineteenth century. With the outbreak of World War I in 1914, the natives looked to the Germans as their saviors; they believed the millennium would occur when German cargo ships arrived. In 1919, on Papua, New Guinea, there occurred an outburst of cultism known as the Papuan Vailal Madness.

Between the First and Second World Wars, the natives began to regard Americans and Japanese as the people who would deliver them from domination by the British and French. In the late thirties, as international tensions increased, there appeared a new form of the cargo cult led by a native

The leader of a cargo cult, Mathias Yaliwan, poses with some of his followers and a Christian Bible, which they believe is a sacred book.

messiah, John Frum. He predicted that the islands would soon be visited by American cargo ships.

His prediction came true in 1942, when ships of the American Navy arrived to carry on the war against Japan. This caused a sensation among the islanders. The Americans obviously were further advanced technologically than the British or French; they paid native workers more than the Europeans did; the Navy included American blacks, which the natives regarded as proof that blacks could learn from whites how to produce great wealth.

After World War II, cult members staged nonviolent demonstrations, which disturbed their European overlords. When the British and French jailed their leaders, the natives were convinced that their own beliefs were shared by the whites who, otherwise, would not consider their ideas dangerous.

To prepare for "instant" paradise, they refused to work, ceased tending their gardens, killed their pigs, and destroyed their food stocks. They built wharves, warehouses, and landing strips for the endless supply of cargo goods they expected to receive from supernatural sources.

In a well-publicized cargo cult incident in 1964, 1,000 natives on the island of New Hanover, a small British protectorate, voted for Lyndon Baines Johnson as their representative on the local government council. When LBJ failed to appear, the natives raised $1,600 to buy him. They built an imitation airfield to attract his plane. Since 1964, however, the cult has taken a more practical approach. It has organized itself into an association devoted to agricultural development and invested in an Anglo-Australian copper plant on the island of Bougainville in the Solomon Islands.

Christianity has had a considerable influence on the cargo cults; it, too, teaches about a messiah and the coming of a millennium. Even the most objectionable features of the cults—the refusal to work and the sudden expenditure of resources—were advised by Christ, who believed the millennium was imminent. For example, Christ said, "Consider the lilies of the field, how they grow; they toil not, neither do they spin."

The situation in Melanesia makes some elements of the cult easier to understand. The cult maintains that the version of the Bible they have been given is incomplete. The natives claim that biblical descriptions of God's revelation of the magic which produced material wealth are being kept secret by the white man. In fact, the missionaries do use incomplete Bibles because the task of translating the entire Bible into the native languages is immense. The natives are told that white men obtain wealth through hard work alone. Yet the white men on the islands work less than the natives. Currently, the white officials in the New Hebrides are involved in their own kind of cargo cult. Despite the inadequate facilities on the island, they have embarked on a tourism campaign which lures tourists by magic (advertising) rather than by work.

· For additional information, see Peter Worsley, *The Trumpet Shall Sound* (Schocken, 1968; Peter Lawrence, *Road Belong Cargo* (Humanities, 1965); and Edward Rice, *John Frum He Come* (Doubleday, 1974).

Miscellaneous

The Unification Church

The Unification Church, founded in Korea in 1954 by the Reverend Sun Myung Moon, teaches that Moon is a modern-day John the Baptist who is preparing for the Second Coming of Christ, which will occur in Korea in 1980.

The basic message of the movement, which employs an austere regimentation, is based on three principles: Obey a puritanical moral code, fight communism, and believe in the Bible. The church teaches that Jesus accomplished man's spiritual salvation but could not complete man's physical salvation. According to Moon, whose teachings are summed up in a 536-page bible of the movement, *Divine Principles,* there are three stages in the historical process of revelation: the age of Judaism, which is still looking for the Messiah; the age of Christianity, which is awaiting the return of Christ; and the age of the Moon church. *Time* (September 30, 1974) characterized Moon's theology as a mixture of Christianity plus "occultism, electrical engineering, Taoist dualism, pop sociology and opaque metaphysical jargon."

Within the movement, some followers believe that Moon himself is the new Christ. Communication with the dead is sometimes practiced, and Moon has held séances with a medium to invoke departed spirits. Great emphasis is placed on the sanctity of marriage, although divorce is permitted. Moon must approve each marriage and performs weddings in mass ceremonies. There is a deemphasis of the sexual side of life—married couples are asked to remain chaste for forty days.

The Unification Church is involved in a variety of projects. It has sponsored and financed several scientific meetings dealing with science and human values. It has held free mass rallies in the United States, including one in Madison Square Garden in 1974 which drew an overcapacity crowd and one at Yankee Stadium in 1976 which drew a disappointing 25,000 spectators. The Yankee Stadium meeting was pre-

The Reverend Sun Myung Moon speaks at Madison Square Garden on September 18, 1974.

ceded by an extensive street-cleaning campaign by movement members in New York City.

The Unification Church now claims about 2,000,000 members and followers throughout the world, most of them in Japan and South Korea, and 30,000 members in the United States. Most of the members are young people in their twenties and thirties, and many live in church centers, of which about 120 are scattered in cities throughout the United States. Children are sometimes placed in church-operated nurseries. Members devote most of their time to fund raising.

They tend to be enthusiastic and hardworking. The members live frugally and share their goods in a communal way.

The Unification Church seems to be thriving. It owns real estate throughout the United States and has an interest in a number of diverse organizations. Moon is said to be worth $15,000,000, but his defenders maintain this is not personal wealth but the assets of the movement. According to the Washington *Post,* the church receives contributions amounting to $6,000,000 per year. In the last few years the church has purchased two mansions, in Tarrytown and Barryville, New York, estimated to be worth about $3,000,000.

Moon was born in 1920 in what is now North Korea. The son of Christian parents, Moon originally belonged to the Presbyterian Church. On Easter Sunday, in 1936, when he was sixteen years old, Christ came to Moon, according to his own testimony, and commissioned him as a prophet. Moon studied engineering in Japan for a time. Through prayer, he discovered "the process and meaning of history, the inner meanings of the parables and the symbols in the Bible, and the purpose of all religions." He began preaching when he was twenty-six years old. His messianic message brought him into conflict with the government of North Korea, which imprisoned him for three years. He was once arrested by the South Korean police as a draft dodger and later charged with promiscuity. None of these charges have been proved, and his followers blame them on persecution.

In addition to evangelizing, Moon has built a multibillion-dollar network of industries. By 1974 he was board chairman of firms in South Korea, Japan, and the United States dealing in pharmaceuticals, air rifles, titanium, and tea.

According to Moon, God told him to take his religious message to America, and when he arrived in New York City in 1972, he found it so godless that he wept. He has now obtained a permanent resident visa and resides in a large mansion in New York State. He periodically goes on lecture tours, having spoken in all fifty states and throughout the world.

Both Moon and his movement have a great admiration for the United States and its leaders. Moon once asserted that the United States, under the divinely ordained leadership of Richard M. Nixon, could bring other nations to God, provided that America repented its moral transgressions. In January 1974, about 1,000 Moon disciples marched on Capitol Hill with placards reading PRAY FOR NIXON and

FORGIVE. On February 1, Moon had an audience with Nixon and reportedly told him, "Don't knuckle under to pressure. Stand up for your convictions." *Progressive* (April 7, 1974) pointed out that part of the political ideology of the Moon movement is a "throwback to the Americanized version of Christian imperialism," typical of the nineteenth century. Moon has said, "This nation is God's nation, and the office of the President is therefore sacred."

Moon and the Unification Church have come under increasing attack from a variety of sources. The church has figured in stories about attempts to "deprogram" young members, allegedly subjected to psychological conditioning. In a court case in Washington, D.C., the parents of an eighteen-year-old girl claimed that the church had exercised so much influence over their daughter that she no longer functioned under her own free will. Witnesses at the trial also testified that disciples of the Church regarded Moon as the messiah. During the Moon rally at Madison Square Garden in New York City, a seventeen-church coalition was formed to oppose the movement's distribution of literature, stating that he is not really a Christian and encourages worship of himself as Christ.

In February 1976 more than 300 parents from groups throughout the country went to Washington, D.C., in an attempt to bring about government investigation of the Unification Church and similar groups. The parents contended that these movements were deceptive and dangerous and had "brainwashed" their children. A psychiatric social worker who has seen more than 150 young people who have left the movement asserted, at the Washington hearings, that half of them are either schizophrenic or have a borderline psychosis. One young woman testified that as a Moon follower she had sold candy and dried flowers for a nonexistent drug program and a nonexistent program for underprivileged children.

Scientology

Scientology is a religious movement founded by La Fayette Ronald Hubbard in the early 1950s. It claims to be based on scientific knowledge.

Scientology evolved from dianetics, a method of introspection and discussion invented by Hubbard and originally presented as a means to attain mental and physical health.

Hubbard first published the theory in the pages of *Astounding Science Fiction* magazine in 1950.

Dianetics divides the mind into two parts—the analytic and the reactive. In moments of unconsciousness or distraction caused by stress, the reactive mind makes emotional records of what happens. These records, called engrams, influence people's attitudes and actions in inappropriate ways. A person does not understand why he reacts as he does because his conscious, analytic mind does not have access to the engrams. The aim of dianetic processing is to make the person aware of the contents of his engrams so that they no longer influence his life. After processing, the person should be a well and happy individual who is no longer irrationally concerned with potential threats to his well-being. Hubbard claimed that as an indirect result of dianetic processing, IQs could be raised, bad eyesight corrected, and the common cold cured.

Faced with financial problems, a decline in public interest, and organizational disputes, Hubbard withdrew from the original, medically oriented Dianetics Organization and in the mid-1950s established the Church of Scientology.

The transition to a religious point of view came about because of new concepts introduced by Hubbard. Chief among these was the idea of the Thetan, the immortal self which is endlessly reincarnated. The Thetan accumulates engrams from each of its previous lives, and a person must become conscious of his previous lives if he is to be free of these engrams.

Upon joining the Church of Scientology, a person may undertake dianetic processing to free himself from his engrams and to increase his awareness of his spiritual being. During processing, the subject, called a pre-Clear, holds two tin cans wired to an E-meter, a device which registers changes in the electrical resistance of the skin. A change supposedly indicates when the pre-Clear is reexperiencing stressful moments in his past. The auditor who guides the pre-Clear through this process asks a series of questions about any item of discussion which causes the pre-Clear stress. The E-meter ostensibly acts as a biofeedback mechanism; when the pre-Clear attains full awareness of a disabling engram, the E-meter no longer shows signs of stress. Although brochures offer twelve and one-half hours of "Life Repair" along with E-meter sessions for $625, it may cost some pre-Clears as much as $5,000 to reach the Clear stage and even more to ascend to Operating Thetan. The church will refund unused portions of fees paid if a request is made within ninety days of withdrawal from processing.

The United States Church of Scientology is incorporated in California. Headquarters of the U.S. and all other Scientology churches is the Saint Hill Organization in England, called the Mother Church. U.S. branch headquarters of the Saint Hill Organization are in Los Angeles. A subsidiary organization called Flag, presently located in Clearwater, Florida, is responsible for general management. Flag certifies the orgs (local churches) and authorizes the sale of courses, literature, and E-meters. The church claims 3,000,000 members in the United States and another 1,000,000 abroad. A related organization, the Sea Org, is a voluntary association of Scientologists similar to a monastic order in its relation to the church organization.

All Scientology churches contribute 10 percent of their income to the Saint Hill Organization. Most of that contribution goes to the U.S. Church of Scientology Trust, which uses it to develop new churches and to defend Scientology against attack by the media or government agencies.

Hubbard was born in Tilden, Nebraska, in 1911. He studied engineering at George Washington University for two years. Best known as a science-fiction writer until 1950, he ostensibly discovered dianetics in 1938. He then began the research which led to the publication of *Dianetics: The Modern Science of Mental Health,* still one of the basic texts used by Scientology. Hubbard withdrew from the church directorate in 1966 and today lives in retirement in Ireland.

Scientology has been widely attacked and subjected to official government inquiries in Great Britain, Australia, and South Africa. Following the inquiries in Great Britain and Australia, all restrictions on the church were lifted. The South African inquiry is still in process. In 1963 the U.S. Food and Drug Administration raided a church in Washington, D.C., and seized all its E-meters on the grounds that Scientology falsely promised to cure neuroses, psychoses, and psychosomatic ills. Scientology avoided a charge of illegal medical practice by demonstrating that its practices were religious and had nothing to do with medical treatment. In the United States today Scientology is recognized as a religion by the federal government.

The church has been highly critical of such psychiatric practices as electroshock and lobotomy. The church, through task forces in various regions in the United States and elsewhere, has engaged in a variety of reform activities in the handling of the mentally retarded, the mentally ill, convicts, and narcotics addicts. Narcanon, which claims an 85 percent success rate in drug addicts' rehabilitation, was originally founded by the church.

Many of the practices of Scientology have been attacked as authoritarian. One practice, called Fair Game, was interpreted by some members and outsiders to mean that a person who left the church could be sued, cheated, beaten, or destroyed without regard for Scientology ethics. Hubbard later withdrew his Fair Game directive, stating that it had been intended to deprive the apostate of any recourse to the Chaplain's Court, a procedure within the church to settle disputes between members.

Another practice of the church, which angers journalists, is that of issuing extensive "false report corrections" of proposed articles or books written about the church. The "corrections" accompany Scientology's reputation for bringing suit against false reports. Many of the suggested "corrections" are petty quibbles over wording or opinions, some are factually misleading, and some are well grounded. In the early 1970s Scientology won a case in Britain against *The Scandal of Scientology* by Paulette Cooper and succeeded in having the distribution of the book stopped and the remaining books destroyed. The church also received a cash settlement.

Some critics have also attacked Hubbard's personal motives, suggesting that money was one of his major interests from the beginning. Hubbard is apparently a wealthy man today. When he gave up his direct control of the church in 1966, he asserted that he had not personally profited from the income of Scientology and had in fact forgiven debts of $13,000,000 owed him by the church. He continues to collect royalties on his books, including *Dianetics*, which are sold in all Scientology churches. In a 1949 speech to a convention of writers Hubbard is reported to have said, perhaps in jest, "If a man really wanted to make a million dollars, the best way would be to start his own religion" (*Time*, April 5, 1976).

For additional information, see Omar V. Garrison, *The Hidden Story of Scientology* (Citadel, 1974) and Christopher Evans, *Cults of Unreason* (Farrar, Straus & Giroux, 1974).

STRANGE
PLACES

Lourdes

Lourdes, one of the most popular of all Roman Catholic shrines, is reputed to be a place of miraculous healing.

Located in the region of the Hautes-Pyrénées in southwestern France, Lourdes today has a population of about 17,000. Annually, about 3,000,000 pilgrims, including about 50,000 sick and disabled people, visit the shrine of Our Lady of Lourdes and the spring, the waters of which are believed to have miraculous healing powers.

Between February 11 and July 16, 1858, fourteen-year-old Bernadette Soubirous (1843–1879) experienced eighteen visions at the grotto of Massabielle, in Lourdes. In the visions she spoke with a radiant woman who identified herself as the "Immaculate Conception." The apparition disclosed to Bernadette a muddy spring, the waters of which she was to drink and use to wash. The apparition conveyed a message stressing the necessity of prayer and penance for the conversion of man. Although the message gave no indication that the waters had healing properties, by the end of March the bishop of Tarbes, in whose jurisdication Lourdes lay, reported three cures. In 1862, following rigorous examination, the church declared the visions authentic and a chapel was erected on the site of the grotto and spring. The reputation of Lourdes as a place of healing grew rapidly despite the church's strenuous caution and demand for considerable evidence before recognizing "cures." In 1870 the Church of Notre Dame was raised to the rank of a minor basilica. Bernadette was canonized in 1933. Her feast is celebrated on April 6, and February 11 is dedicated to the Feast of Our Lady of Lourdes.

To aid in the accommodation of pilgrims, the underground church of St. Pius X was consecrated on March 25, 1958. The immense prestressed-concrete church, with a seating capacity of 20,000, is one of the largest churches in the world.

Since 1858 only sixty-three cures (eight in 1858) have been certified by the church as miracles. Analysis of the spring water, which the pilgrims drink and in which they bathe, has uncovered no unusual chemical properties.

Assessment of the authenticity of Bernadette's vision and the subsequent cures presents difficulties.

Although Bernadette's vision was declared authentic, count-less other devout Catholics' visions at the site have been dis-

*The grotto of Massabielle, at Lourdes, where Bernadette Soubirous
said the Virgin appeared to her.*

counted. It has been suggested that the bishop of Tarbes, who
had a reputation for using all means possible to advance the
influence of his see, had political motivations for promoting
the acceptance of such a wondrous happening.

As for the authenticity of the cures, it is reasonable to be skeptical of the early ones. The awe and excitement of the unexplained visions could have made the early enthusiasts poor witnesses.

Since the early cures, requirements for a miracle have been very strict, requiring specific evidence. First, proof, including X rays, physical examinations, and chemical tests, must show the patient was suffering from a specific illness which produced an observable abnormality in the body. Secondly, the signs and symptoms must disappear within a few hours of the alleged divine intervention. The improvement or "cure" must be sustained for several years. It must also be determined that there was no likelihood the cure had been caused by any treatment the patient was undergoing at the time of the divine intervention. If these conditions are met, two medical tribunals then judge the results. If the majority of the first tribunal—composed of a staff representative of the Lourdes medical bureau and of other doctors on hand—accepts the cure, a second tribunal—an eleven-member international medical tribunal selected by the bishops of Tarbes and Lourdes—reviews the facts after several years. If the tribunal accepts the cure by a majority vote, the dossier of the case is sent to the bishop of the diocese in which the patient who was cured lives. If the canonical commission concludes that the cure was an act of divine intervention, the bishop may then declare a miracle.

Despite the judgment of the two tribunals, several possible explanations for cures, beyond divine intervention, can be offered. For example, neurotics, who often suffer from a variety of debilitating symptoms, are suggestible, and have often been cured by hypnosis. Purely psychological factors, have been known to cause hysterical paralysis, blindness, and deafness. Some ailments are self-limiting and vanish when the illness has run its course. Careful study of cases of cancer (only two cures since 1858 reported) and other incurable diseases have shown that "impossible" cures sometimes occur.

Despite the lack of proof and the scarcity of accepted "miracles," pilgrims flock to Lourdes and patiently bear the overcrowded conditions in the village. When questioned, the majority of them say they come to seek solace and strength to bear their pain, rather than with the expectation of being miraculously healed.

For additional information, see Alan Neame, *The Happening at Lourdes: The Sociology of the Grotto* (Hodder & Stoughton,

1967) and Helen Flanders Dunbar, *Mind and Body* (Random House, 1955).

Fatima

Fatima is a Roman Catholic shrine in the central Portuguese village of the same name where, in 1917, three peasant children had visions and, on October 13, 1917, 70,000 persons witnessed a "miraculous solar phenomenon."

On May 13, 1917, three illiterate children, Lucia dos Santos and her cousins Francisco and Jacinta Marta, were tending their sheep when they were surprised by a bright flash. They went to the nearby Cova da Iria, a large pasture, to investigate. There, in the midst of a bright, glowing light, they saw a little woman. She said she was from heaven and told them to return every month until October when a public miracle would take place "so that everyone may believe."

On June 13 fifty spectators came to witness the phenomenon. Lucia, the oldest child, carried on a dialogue with an unseen entity whose responses were not heard. After the dialogue ended, the witnesses heard an explosion and saw a cloud rise from a tree in which all the succeeding manifestations would appear.

On July 13, before a crowd of 4,500 witnesses, the three children saw a terrifying vision of hell and heard two prophecies, one that was revealed and one that was not. The first stated that the war would end, but another would come, in the year Pope Pius XI would die (he died in 1939; World War II began the same year). The prophecy continued that when an unknown light was seen in the sky, it would be a sign from God that He would punish the world for its crimes through war, famine, and the persecution of the church and the Holy Father. The children told the secret prophecy to church authorities, who sent it to the Vatican under seal.

In the succeeding months the visions continued and the crowds grew in number. On October 13, 70,000 people gathered in pouring rain to witness the public miracle. On that day the children reported they saw the lady alight from the sky in a cloud and then rise again. According to Jacques Vallee in *The Invisible College* (Dutton, 1975), the spectators reported seeing a spinning flat disk that eventually stopped spinning and plunged downward in a zigzag fashion to the earth and then reversed direction and disappeared into the

The Fatima Basilica and 1951 Holy Year pilgrims.

sun. The crowd, who had been drenched in the rain, realized
that they, as well as the ground, were dry.

In 1930, after initial opposition, the bishop of Leiria
accepted the children's vision as the appearance of the Virgin
Mary. Construction of a basilica had begun in 1929, and it
was consecrated in 1953. About 1,000 pilgrims visit the
shrine each year, and on May 13, 1967, the fiftieth anniversary

of the first vision, a crowd, estimated at 1,000,000, gathered to hear Pope Paul VI say mass and pray for peace. Numerous cures have been reported at Fatima, but they are not generally publicized.

The 1976 *Catholic Almanac* states that the secret prophecy has not been revealed, but "Church officials have decried a morbid concern about it." However, Vallee states that Pope John XXIII opened it in 1960, was deeply shaken, and did not reveal the contents.

Vallee, a computer specialist who has done extensive research into UFO phenomena, compares the witnesses' descriptions of the physical phenomena connected with the children's visions with UFO data. He concludes that the various reported elements—the luminous flying disk or globe and its motion (falling-leaf zigzag trajectory), light effects, thunderclaps, buzzing sounds, strange fragrance, and "angel hair"—all are constant parameters of UFO sightings everywhere. He compares the mixture of seriousness and absurdity in the prophecy with the tone of experiences in several cases involving contact with UFO occupants.

He also indicated that unknown to most people, the events of 1917 were preceded in 1915 and 1916 by series of sightings of an angel by Lucia and some other children. The children were overwhelmed. According to Joseph Pelletier in *The Sun Danced at Fatima* (Assumption College, 1952), "This power is so intense that it absorbs and almost completely annihilates them. It practically deprives them of the use of their bodily sense . . . their bodies are subject to a mysterious, depressing force that prostrates them." This effect, Vallee argues, could be applied to the entire spectrum of close encounters with UFOs.

Santuário de Chimayó

Santuário de Chimayó is a 160-year-old Roman Catholic shrine in New Mexico, sometimes called the American Lourdes.

Located in the foothills of New Mexico's Sangre de Cristo Mountains, the twin-towered wood-and-adobe shrine lies twenty-eight miles north of Santa Fe. Annually about 35,000 pilgrims from all over the world come to the shrine, seeking help ranging from good crops to cancer cures.

The pilgrims enter through a sacristy whose walls are lined

with crutches, braces, and letters—all testimonials from previous pilgrims. The pilgrims say a prayer and enter a tiny white-washed antechamber. Here is located the "hole of the holy earth." The pilgrims take handfuls of soil from the eighteen-inch hole and either spread the soil on the ailing parts of their bodies or carry it home in various receptacles. Many claim that the cure has worked on everything from arthritis to broken bones and has even produced hair growth.

Although local tradition credits two religious statues—Our Lord of Esquipulas, a bloody figure of Christ, and the Holy Child of Atocha—with curative powers, the hole is the center of attraction for the pilgrims.

Belief in the powers of the shrine originated with local Indians who worshiped a hot spring for its curative powers. When the waters of the spring dried up, Bernardo Abeyta, a local settler, built the shrine in 1816. In 1929 the shrine was given to the Roman Catholic Church. The "hole of the holy earth" is situated on the approximate location of the hot spring.

The local priests make no claims that the adobe earth from the "hole of the holy earth" has curative powers and openly refill the hole when it is empty. The pilgrims, nevertheless, continue to flock to the shrine and insist the hole is miraculously replenished.

Oak Island

Oak Island, off the southeastern coast of Nova Scotia, is the site of a series of mysterious shafts and tunnels that may conceal a buried pirate treasure.

The search for buried treasure on Oak Island in Mahone Bay, Nova Scotia, has continued intermittently since 1795. In that year three local youths discovered a deep, filled-in, vertical shaft on the uninhabited 130-acre island. They abandoned an initial dig, after going 30 feet down, for lack of adequate equipment, but they returned in 1804.

Every 10 feet the diggers encountered a platform of oak logs, some tightly sealed with putty or with coconut fiber, which must have come from a tropical climate. At about 90 feet, a flat stone slab with a cipher message that has never been decoded, was discovered. At 100 feet the shaft became flooded with seawater up to the 35-foot mark. It later became clear that two water tunnels led to the shaft from an elaborate artificial drainage system underneath a beach about 500 feet away.

On the assumption that the system had been built to conceal buried treasure, numerous digs were organized in subsequent years. Six lives have been lost and $3,000,000 expended, but neither the treasure nor the mouths of the water tunnels have been found. The syndicate that now owns most of the island and the individual who owns the remainder have plans for further explorations, both in the original "money pit," as the shaft is commonly called, and elsewhere on the island.

Among the artifacts that have been uncovered are several tiny gold chain links, pieces of iron and cut wood, and two small pieces of parchment. Other signs of human habitation, including ring bolts for mooring ships, have turned up on the island.

The purpose of the Oak Island shafts and the identity of its builders are as much a mystery today as they were when the first discoveries were made, although it is widely believed that the network was built to conceal treasure.

The most popular theory is that the island was used as a "bank" for pirates, perhaps including the notorious Captain Kidd, who was known to frequent local waters long before the neighboring mainland was settled. A similar network, dating from the early eighteenth century, was uncovered on Haiti in

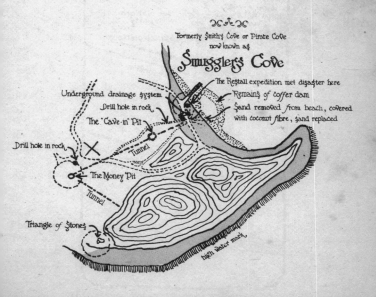

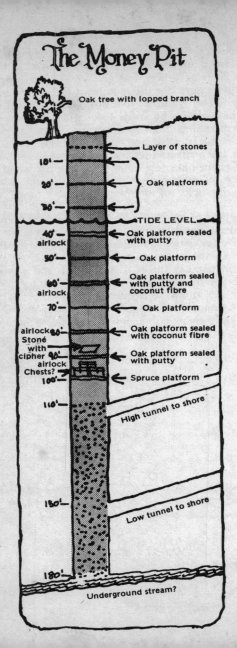

The Money Pit

Oak tree with lopped branch

Layer of stones

18' — }
20' — } Oak platforms
30' — }

TIDE LEVEL

40' — airlock — Oak platform sealed with putty

50' — Oak platform

60' — airlock — Oak platform sealed with putty and coconut fibre

70' — Oak platform

airlock 80' — Oak platform sealed with coconut fibre
Stone with cipher 90' — Oak platform sealed with putty
airlock
Chests? 100' — Spruce platform

110' — High tunnel to shore

130' — Low tunnel to shore

180' —

Underground stream?

1949. This network included a vertical shaft and water tunnels, as on Oak Island. Different bands of pirates dug horizontal tunnels out from the shaft at varying depths and deposited their loot at the end of the corridors. More than $50,000 in Spanish coins was reported to have been discovered at the Haiti site.

Other theories attribute the complex to: Sir Henry Clinton, British commander in chief during the Revolutionary War, who may have used Oak Island to protect his war chest during a threat against New York in 1778; French authorities of Canada, who may have transferred their gold reserve (known to have been removed from the fortress on Louisburg 240 miles north, in 1758) to the island; the Norsemen; and the Spanish conquistador Pizarro. More fanciful theorists say the islands are the repository of the crown jewels of France, the treasure of the Abbey of St. Andrew's Cathedral of Scotland (suppressed in 1560), the Holy Grail, or the supposed plays of Francis Bacon.

For additional information, see John Goodwin, *This Baffling World No. 1* (Bantam Books, 1968) and Steve Schwartz, "Update on the Money Pit," *Yankee* (March 1976).

Easter Island

Easter Island is a 150-square-mile island in the Western Pacific noted for immense faces carved from volcanic rock. It is a Chilean dependency.

Easter Island was discovered by Jakob Roggeveen, a Dutchman, in 1722. Contact between the islanders and Europeans was sporadic until the late nineteenth century. In 1862 a large portion of the population was killed or transported by Peruvian slavers. By the time Europeans came to study the island peoples their social order had been destroyed; their knowledge of a strange writing, probably priestly, lost; and the meaning of the great faces forgotten.

Island tradition holds that two different peoples lived there—Long Ears, who came from the east, and Short Ears, who came from the west. The Short Ears were enslaved by the Long Ears until a rebellion occurred (in 1680 according to carbon dating; between 1722 and 1774 according to some interpretations of European visitors' reports). The Long Ears were massacred, and many of the great faces were overthrown.

The faces and other sculptures can be divided into three periods. In the earliest period, perhaps beginning about A.D.

300, there are a variety of small to medium-sized stone statues and a solar observatory oriented to annual movements of the sun. This architecture is similar to that at Tiahuanaco in Bolivia. In the middle period, beginning about A.D. 1100, the stylized stone faces with long ears appeared, erected on top of platforms called ahus. The earlier solar temples were destroyed to provide material for the platforms. Throughout this middle period the statues became progressively larger. The biggest standing statue is about thirty-two feet tall and weighs about eighty-two tons. An unfinished statue, still attached to the volcanic mountain from which it was being quarried, stands sixty-eight feet tall. Once a statue was raised on an ahu, deep oval eye sockets were carved in the face and a cylindrical topknot of red stone was balanced on the head. The eighty-two-ton statue mentioned above had an eleven-ton topknot.

Experiments by the Thor Heyerdahl expeditions in 1955 and 1956 showed that twelve islanders could move and raise a twenty-five-ton statue in eighteen days with no tools except two logs used as levers and stones to hold the statue in place. Tradition and archaeology suggest that the statues represented dignitaries that were deified and revered after death.

The third and most recent period of Eastern Island sculpture was associated with a bird cult, portrayed in a variety of small statuary and wood carvings.

Another mystery of Easter Island is the writing, called rongo-rongo. The meaning of these signs, which were carved into wooden tablets, has been lost. There is considerable doubt that the writing is a language; the signs may be merely memory aids used in the performance of religious rites.

An imaginative attempt to translate the writing was presented by Jean-Michel Schwartz in *Mysteries of Easter Island* (Avon, 1975). Schwartz's rongo-rongo text is an exact copy of one brought back by Thor Heyerdahl, except that Schwartz's version is missing several lines contained in Heyerdahl's. Schwartz does not seem to be aware of Heyerdahl's work and seems uninformed generally about the history of Easter Island.

Signs similar to the rongo-rongo have been found on seals of the Indus Valley civilization (2000 B.C.) around Mohenjo-Daro and Harappa in modern Pakistan. The similarity of the symbols may be merely coincidental, but the imagination is stirred by the fact that Mohenjo-Daro and Easter Island are very close to being on precisely opposite sides of the world. Mohenjo-Daro is at 27°23′ North and about 69° East; Easter Island is at 27°08′ South and 109°23′ West.

Indus Valley	Easter Island	Indus Valley	Easter Island	Indus Valley	Easter Island	Indus Valley	Easter Island
I	II	III	IV	V	VI	VII	VIII

A comparison of a few of the many Easter Island written symbols with similar Indus Valley signs.

Despite claims to the contrary, the rongo-rongo writing has not been deciphered, the full meaning of the stone faces is unknown, and the origin of the Easter Island inhabitants is unclear, although there are strong indications that they were not homogeneous and came from a variety of areas around the Pacific. No mystery surrounds the carving or erection of the statues, this process being fully within the potential of people without sophisticated tools and using brute strength. The great gap in time and space makes it very unlikely that there was any connection between the Indus Valley civilization and Easter Island.

For further information, see Thor Heyerdahl, *Aku-Aku* (Rand-McNally, Chicago, 1958) and Heyerdahl's official report on the Easter Island expedition, *Archeology of Easter Island* (monographs of the School of American Research and the Museum of New Mexico, No. 24, Part 1, 1961).

Nasca Lines

The Nasca lines are a series of markings, whose origin and significance are obscure, north and south of the town of Nasca, Peru, about 200 miles south of Lima.

Sometimes referred to as Inca Roads, the markings are unlike the actual system of Inca roads because they do not lead to any particular place. Remarkably, the lines are barely discernible from the ground but are clearly visible from the air. Although it is estimated that the age of the markings ranges from 1,000 to 3,000 years, with most made about 1,500 years ago, the lines were first discovered in modern times, when airplanes began to fly over the area. Francisco Pizarro and his Spanish soldiers, as well as the conquistador Francisco Hernández, did not notice the markings while they were in the area. It is also common for modern travelers to drive through the area without noticing anything unusual.

Some of the markings form various kinds of geometric shapes, such as rectangles and triangles; others form designs of humans, animals, and unknown objects. One immense figure depicts a whale, with a harpoon through one of its eyes; other shapes include a stylized monkey, spider, and bird. In size, the markings range from several hundred feet to several miles in length. They cover a total area more than sixty miles long.

Depending upon the terrain, the markings consist of furrows, scrapings on rocks, series of small hillocks, and areas cleared of stones and pebbles. The geometric designs were made by clearing away blackened stones that litter the ground, with the result that the lines appear whitish against the darker background. The lines are clearly visible when one stands astride them and views them in an exact lengthwise direction. But if one stands just a few feet to either side, the lines disappear. The straight lines show a remarkable accuracy, according to G. S. Hawkins (*Beyond Stonehenge*, Harper & Row, 1973), with an average deviation of less than four yards per mile.

In general, the landscape of the area is similar to that of the moon—the ground is flat and barren. In addition, there is practically no rainfall and little climatic change.

Another figure, the so-called candelabra of the Andes, an 800-foot carving resembling candelabra or a trident, can be seen on a cliff near Paracas, Peru, seemingly pointing in the direction of Nasca. When the Spaniards first encountered it, they found a rope attached to the central fork, as well as indications that other ropes had been present and that the whole thing was some sort of apparatus.

England also has two prominent figures cut into the countryside. The Cerne giant, an 180-foot-long figure of a man holding a huge club, was cut into the chalk of Dorset in Roman-British times. The White Horse Hill, a 374-foot-long

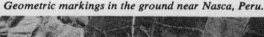

Geometric markings in the ground near Nasca, Peru.

figure of a horse, cut in the turf, is believed to date to about 100 B.C.

Charles Berlitz, in *Mysteries from Forgotten Worlds* (Doubleday, 1972), describes pictographs on the Colorado River in California, consisting of rows and ridges of scraped small stones which he states are similar to the Nasca lines. Although once called the Mohave maze, the Mohave Indians have disclaimed knowledge of them.

The significance and origin of the Nasca markings is a point of great, often fantastic speculation. V. W. Von Hagen, in *Highway of the Sun* (Duell, Sloan and Pearce, 1955), states that the people who created the markings could not possibly have seen them in their entirety from any position on the ground. The markings, Von Hagen writes, can be seen only from an altitude of about 1,000 feet. Louis Pauwels and Jacques Bergier (*The Morning of the Magicians,* Avon, 1968) and Erich von Däniken (*Chariots of the Gods?,* Bantam, 1971) say they look unmistakably like an airfield. Von Däniken suggests the markings could have been laid out on a giant scale by working from a model and using a system of coordinates or they could have been constructed according to instructions from an aircraft. He suggests further that perhaps the builders were sending a message to the gods: "Land here." (See Cargo Cults.)

Paul Kosok, a Long Island University researcher, and Maria Reiche, a German mathematician and geographer (see *Natural History,* May 1947), have concluded that a number of the lines point to positions of the winter and summer sun. The largest desert feature, a rectangle, points to the region of the sky occupied by the Pleiades A.D. 500–700. Thus, they conclude, the lines represent the "world's largest astronomy book" and were connected with the magical ceremonies associated with an ancient calendar. In support of this theory, it is known that sometime between A.D. 500 and A.D. 900 a people of the Tiahuanacan Empire invaded the coastal area and influenced the Nascan inhabitants with their interest in astronomy.

Charles Berlitz postulates that the lines may have been created as reminders to the gods to keep the world running on its proper course.

A group of researchers, including Gerald S. Hawkins (*Beyond Stonehenge,* Harper & Row, 1973), tested the astronomical theory, feeding measurements of the markings, taken from aerial photographs, into a computer to see if the lines would correspond with known astronomical data. The results did not support a linkage of the lines to positions of the sun, moon, or stars or to any use as a calendar.

Hawkins also dismisses the theory that the lines were constructed according to instructions from an aircraft and the idea that the lines identify certain topographic features because it does not fit with the observed data. He does suggest that the lines may have been intended as ceremonial pathways or walkways.

As for the "candelabra of the Andes," R. Charroux, in *One Hundred Thousand Years of Man's Unknown History* (University of California Press, 1963), suggests it may have been a tidal calculator or, perhaps, a seismograph, an apparatus for measuring and recording vibrations within the earth. Based on a hypothesis set out by García Beltran, Charroux states: "With counterweights, graduated scales and ropes that ran through pulleys, the system constituted a gigantic seismograph capable of precisely measuring earthquake vibrations not only in Peru, but from all over the globe." Charroux believes that the hypothesis is likely, given the frequency of earthquakes in Peru.

Guy Underwood, in *The Pattern of the Past* (Abelard-Schuman, 1973), presents an unorthodox theory explaining the British and other similar figures. He believes ancient peoples were sensitive to "geodetic lines"—electromagnetic lines of force that span the globe and depend on various subterranean and surface features. He posits that Stonehenge, as well as figures like the Cerne giant and White Horse Hill, originally represented tracings of the "geodetic lines."

Tiahuanaco

Tiahuanaco is a pre-Columbian ruin, located in Bolivia, whose origins are unknown.

Tiahuanaco lies 12,500 feet above sea level on a Bolivian plateau about 12 miles south of Lake Titicaca.

The surviving remains are divided into three sections: the Akapana, a large, terraced 50-foot-high pyramid of earth once faced with stone; the Kalasasaya, or so-called Temple of the Sun, a rectangular enclosure built with alternating tall stone columns and smaller rectangular blocks; and the Tunca-Puncu, also called the Palacio or Place of Ten Doors, a collection of remarkable stonework consisting of geometrically true squares,

Freestanding stone monolith at Tiahuanaco.

rectangles, and crosses. The most remarkable feature of the Kalasasaya is the Gateway of the Sun, a monolithic gateway cut from one piece of andesite, a very hard rock. It stands 11 feet high and almost 15 feet wide. The upper portion of one side is covered with a frieze carved in bas-relief. At the center of the frieze is a sun-god, presumably the principal Tiahuanacan deity, with sun rays radiating from his face in the form of puma heads. He holds two staffs adorned with puma and condor heads, and he is weeping tears shaped like condors and pumas. The sun-god is flanked on each side by twenty-four figures, all facing him and seemingly running toward him. The opposite side of the portal is covered with a severe geometrical pattern. According to A. Hyatt Verrill (*Travel*, September 1929), the various parts of the design are so mathematically exact that even by using a steel square and a millimeter scale, he could not find a deviation of more than one-fiftieth of an inch in the angles or surfaces. Large freestanding stone figures are also scattered throughout the site. Artifacts found among the ruins include metalwork and decorated ceramic pottery. Many pieces of the latter are modeled in lifelike images of men, birds, reptiles, beasts, gods, and inanimate objects.

The site lies midway between two ranges of hills, some six miles distant, which presumably could have been the only

Gateway of the Sun at Tiahuanaco, in Bolivia.

source of stone for the construction of Tiahuanaco. Ostensibly too high for intensive agriculture, Tiahuanaco is located far from any fertile area and has no easily accessible water source.

It is generally accepted that the construction of Tiahuanaco took place during several periods. The earliest construction, dating from 200 B.C. to A.D. 200, shows a stylistic similarity to the Pucara culture centered in southern Peru dating from the same period. Many of the major buildings are believed to date to the period of A.D. 200 to A.D. 600. Construction continued from A.D. 600 to A.D. 1000 during which time the spread of Tiahuanacan culture was seen at Juari and other areas in the central and southern Andes. E. P. Lanning (*Peru Before the Incas*, Prentice-Hall, 1967), a specialist in Peruvian archaeology, dates the Tiahuanacan Empire to A.D. 600–700 and states that it covered all the Titicaca basin, all of Peru south of the Majes Valley, and the coast and highlands of northern Chile.

According to another scholar, V. W. Von Hagen, sometime between A.D. 500 and A.D. 900 the Tiahuanacans and their allies invaded the coastal areas inhabited by the Nasca. The Tiahuanacans administered the entire Peruvian coast for more than 300 years before the empire collapsed for unknown reasons. Under the empire, Von Hagen states, what was originally Nascan disappeared and the pottery, wood carving, and weaving became Tiahuanacan. The motif of the weeping god dominated.

Whatever the date of or reasons behind the collapse of Tiahuanaco, its downfall came before the arrival of the Incas, who, according to the Spanish chronicles, found the area deserted. When Pizarro arrived in 1532, the Quechua and Aymara Indians who were then settled in the area knew nothing about the deserted city; their folklore said it had been built by gods.

According to E. P. Lanning, Tiahuanaco was one of several similar cities built during the Early Intermediate Period (200 B.C.–A.D. 600), each characterized by monumental buildings, plazas, and residential sections spread over an area of three to four square miles. The city's population was about 10,000. Although Tiahuanaco is the only city yet known in the broad region of the Tiahuanacan Empire, Lanning believes other large cities and ceremonial sites may yet be discovered. He states that the dramatic and sudden disintegration of the Tiahuanacan Empire may lie in events which affected all the

Andes—possibly peasant revolts in the provinces, barbarians at the periphery, or competition between empires.

V. W. Von Hagen (*Highway of the Sun,* Duell, Sloan and Pearce, 1955, and *The Desert Kingdoms of Peru,* Weidenfeld and Nicholson, 1964) believes that Tiahuanaco was not a metropolis but a religious center, extant between A.D. 400 and A.D. 1000, which was visited by pilgrims throughout the Andes. The Gateway of the Sun, Von Hagen states, "had more influence on art and religion than any other single element in the Americas." As the motif of the gate's weeping god spread through Peru, the tears changed from condors and pumas to snakes and human heads.

Beyond the obscurity of its origins and collapse, perhaps the greatest enigma of Tiahuanaco is that it was built at all and how. Charles Berlitz (*Mysteries from Forgotten Worlds,* Doubleday, 1972), states that Tiahuanaco was simply too high to grow the corn to support a population large enough to transport the building materials, build the massive structures, and carve the enormous stones. He fails to mention that the pre-Inca Indians were the people who first cultivated the potato and that the entire region is rich in animal life, particularly small rodents and llamas.

Verrill asserts that modern stonecutters equipped with steel tools and machinery would find it difficult to produce the accurately cut squares and rectangles and the carvings on the Gateway to the Sun. They probably would, especially if they tried to do the job in a few months with no more motivation than money. But with enough time, enough material, and enough energy, even the softest mineral can wear away hard ones. One need merely look at the Grand Canyon, where water has worn away thousands of cubic miles of stone. Bronze will slowly cut into andesite, and there are strong indications that the pre-Inca Indians had discovered bronze. In addition, the Andes abound in varieties of stones harder than andesite, and chips from these could be used to carve the most resistant of rocks. Finally, the precision of the design is not beyond the simplest geometry and the ritual care that would be devoted to the god's gateway over a period of decades.

One explanation offered for the transportation of the stones is that when Tiahuanaco was built and occupied, it stood on the borders of Lake Titicaca and that, subsequently, the waters receded. Remains which could have been docks or quays are cited as evidence. Verrill, however, states that there is no geological evidence to support this argument and, to the contrary, engineers believe that the water level of Lake Titicaca is rising. Artifacts found at the site also give no indication of a lake-faring race. Verrill also rejects as improbable the theory that the stones were transported across the lake via rafts.

He suggests, instead, that there is evidence—immense stone disks found at Tunca-Puncu—that the Tiahuanacans had discovered the wheel. With such wheels, attached to a fixed axle, the transportation would have been a fairly easy matter. This hypothesis, of course, contradicts the assumption that no ancient American peoples ever discovered the wheel.

The simplest explanation for the transportation of the stones is that large numbers of men used their own brute strength to pull, push, slide, or roll the massive stones from the quarry to the present site. Again devotion to the god and to his king, combined with the organization and sense of purpose which great leaders bring to their people, is sufficient to explain the motivation. Thus, the modern Chinese utilize masses of human laborers to accomplish major earth-moving and building projects. And for the last twenty years every adult American has contributed a little labor through taxes to the nonreligious task of putting men on the moon and a machine on Mars.

Berlitz, Jacques Bergier (*Morning of the Magicians,* Avon, 1968), and Erich von Däniken (*Chariots of the Gods?,* Putnam, 1970, and Bantam, 1971) all hypothesize visitors from outer space to explain the "mysteries" of Tiahuanaco. There is, however, no need to postulate "gods from the sky" to account for Tiahuanaco. And if such interference is not considered, the images of spacesuits and rocket ships which some people see in some of the carvings of Tiahuanaco appear once again to be merely incomprehensible religious symbols, of no more real significance than the crack in a wall which may suddenly look like a human face.

Finally, G. S. Hawkins (*Beyond Stonehenge,* Harper & Row, 1973) scoffs at the suggestion that the forty-eight symbols on the Gateway of the Sun are proof of a forty-eight-month year during an epoch when the moon circled the earth every seven and one-half days. This is impossible. Although the moon was once indeed closer to the earth and circled it much faster, the period when the revolution was as small as seven and one-half days was more than a billion years before the first person picked up his first tool.

Bimini Blocks

The Bimini Blocks are large underwater structures off the Bimini Islands in the Bahamas which, according to some sources were built by an ancient civilization that existed 10,000 to 15,000 years ago.

In 1969 two young American writers, Robert Ferro and Michael Grumley, set out to explore the area around the Bimini Islands for signs of Atlantis. Through exposure to Edgar Cayce's predictions—that signs of Atlantis would appear in the Bahamas in 1969—and "astrology, card reading, and psychic phenomena," Ferro and Grumley had become interested in the legends about Atlantis.

On February 26, Ferro, Grumley, and several others anchored at a spot about three-quarters of a mile off the west coast of North Bimini. Their Bahamian guide had indicated that there were some interesting rocks in the area which, until recently, had been covered by tidal sands. Viewed from the surface, the rocks seemed to form a geometrical pattern. After diving underwater, Ferro and Grumley reported that nearly all the rocks were gigantic and rectangular—the largest one about 18 to 20 feet long and 10 feet wide. The rocks appeared to be about 2 to 2.5 feet thick. The entire formation was approximately 700 feet long. It seemed that some of the stones had been moved or disturbed. The Bahamian guide said that many had been dredged up during the 1920s and used for construction in Miami, Florida.

Dr. Valentine, a member of the expedition described as an entomologist with a particular interest in beetles and an amateur archaeologist, dated the structure as 10,000 to 12,000 years old, on the basis of undisclosed evidence.

On the basis of their expedition, described in *Atlantis: The Autobiography of a Search* (Doubleday, 1970), the explorers proposed that the blocks are a wall which, though not part of Atlantis, was built by a fairly advanced civilization that existed about 10,000 to 15,000 years ago. Photographs, taken by Count Pino Turolla of Miami, "an archaeologist-explorer," are included in the book. Turolla also suggested 10,000 B.C. as the age of the ruins.

On July 12, 1969, Turolla and a group of divers discovered a group of pillars, some upright and others lying on the ocean bed, off the west side of Bimini. Analysis of a sample by "experts" indicated that it was not native Bahamian material but carved from a natural stone, possibly of South American origin. This led Turolla, as well as Ferro and Grumley, to speculate about a possible link between South American civilizations and an ancient civilization in Bimini. Turolla also discovered other underwater wall sections which curve around the tip of Bimini, suggesting that, possibly, at one time a wall encircled the Bimini Islands.

Charles Berlitz, in *Mysteries from Forgotten Worlds* (Doubleday, 1972), also gives a lengthy account of underwater structures in the Bahamas, but does not mention Ferro or Grumley. He ascribes the discovery, in 1968, of a "cyclopean stone construction about 35 feet underwater and about 1,000 yards from the shore of North Bimini" to the "initial efforts of Dr. Manson Valentine, anthropologist and archaeologist; Dimitri Rebikoff, inventor and underwater archaeologist; and Jacques Mayol, holder of the world's depth record for free diving." This group believes that these stones, which sound like the ones Ferro and Grumley discovered, are a wall which once formed part of a building.

Berlitz writes that underwater structures of unknown origin are prevalent throughout the Bahamas. He states that the initial discoveries came about because "two pilots" made a series of flights over the Bahama Banks in search of Atlantis. He gives no further detail except to say that the first underwater find took place in 1968 off the island of Andros near Pine Key. The first find was a "rectangular construction, outlined by beach grass and sponges fairly near the surface, divided into several sections by stone partitions." Berlitz cites numerous reports of sightings of underwater structures in the region, including a report by Robert Marks, "a diver, underwater explorer and archaeologist," of an underwater wall near Bimini with a large archway through the middle. If confirmed, Berlitz says, it would be an important discovery because true arches were presumably unknown to pre-Colombian peoples.

Some skeptics have claimed that these underwater stones are natural features. Berlitz claims that anyone who has seen them will have little doubt that they are man-made, adding that they bear a "striking resemblance to the pre-Inca masonry of Peru."

However, at this stage, the entire story of underground structures in the Bahamas must be treated with extreme caution. To date, there are no well-authenticated reports, either in a reputable scientific journal or by an accredited archaeologist.

The existing reports tend to be vague, uncorroborated, amateurish, and contradictory. Unquestionably, underwater structures do exist in the Bahamas, but their significance is still unclear.

Findhorn

Findhorn is a small community of mystics on Findhorn Bay, in northern Scotland, who claim that contact with spirits has led to remarkable agricultural success.

The Findhorn community was founded in 1962 by Peter Caddy, a former hotel manager, his wife, Eileen, and Dorothy Maclean, a former secretary and service worker. All three had been interested in mysticism for some time, and Maclean is said to have been in contact with voices that guided her spiritual life. Since 1962 the community has increased to about 100 people.

Though none of the founders had had previous agricultural experience and the soil at Findhorn was sandy and supported only sparse vegetation, the land eventually proved suitable to sixty-five vegetables, forty-two herbs, and twenty-one fruits, as well as to many kinds of flowers. The plants were said to reach enormous sizes—for example, forty-pound cabbages, sixty-pound broccoli plants, and eight-foot-high delphiniums.

When the founders first arrived, Maclean was contacted by the Landscape Angel, which was said to be associated with the general geographic area. This angel, or life force, would confirm or reject Peter Caddy's own intuition regarding such processes as the application of liquid manure, the making of compost, and the amount and frequency of watering.

Maclean then began to be contacted by spirits, or devas, associated with specific types of plants—a tomato deva, a dwarf bean deva, a spinach deva, and the like—one for each type of plant in the garden. The messages combined spiritual advice with such practical instructions as the time at which and the depth to which seeds should be sown and the spacing of the plants.

The devas' spiritual instruction stressed that harmony with the natural forces of the universe was as important in human life in general as it was in gardening.

Though the achievements at Findhorn are an impressive testimony to the possibilities of intensive organic gardening, some experts claim that similar results have been attained without mystical knowledge. Huge plants may not be unusual at a high latitude such as that of Findhorn, because of the long hours of daylight during the growing season.

For more information, see Paul Hawken, *The Magic of Findhorn* (Harper & Row, 1975).

STRANGE
CUSTOMS

The Sacred Cow

The cow, in the Hindu religion, is the most sacred of all animals and the personification of all the gods.

Tó Hindus of all sects and all four castes, everything about the cow, including its dung and urine, is sacred. The Hindus believe that the cow and the Brahmin were created on the same day and, therefore, are equally sacred. In Hinduism, killing a cow is a heinous sin, and the eating of beef is worse than cannibalism. The cow's mouth, however, is considered unclean because it was caught telling a lie by the god Brahma.

Hindus consider the feeding of a cow to be an act of great merit. Eating a mixture of milk, curds, butter, and cow dung and urine is believed to be purifying for a person's soul and body. In the streets of Hindu cities, according to R. Thomas in *Hindu Religion, Customs, and Manners* (Taraporevala Son, 1956), pious men and women of the lower classes follow cows, catching their urine in cupped hands and sipping it. No pious Hindu will pass a cow without touching it and then touching his own head in an act of homage.

Stray cows enjoy great liberties in Indian towns—they wander through the streets, break into private gardens, defecate on the sidewalks, and snarl traffic. The government maintains old-age homes for cows, and in Madras the police nurse sick cattle until they get well.

The Hindus venerate the cow as the mother of life, the symbol of everything that is living. Because they believe that every part of the body of the cow is inhabited by a deity, they consider every part of the cow, including the excreta, hallowed. The curious reverence for the cow is extremely ancient, dating to proto-Dravidian civilization (circa 1500 B.C.). Apparently, the Dravidians, the largest group of inhabitants in India before the advent of the Aryans, treated horned cattle with reverence.

The Hindu veneration of cows has not diminished through the centuries. Gandhi himself said, "Cow protection is the central fact of Hinduism. To me it is one of the most wonderful phenomena of all evolution; it takes the human beyond his species. The cow to me means the entire sub-human world. Man through the cow is enjoined to realize his identity with all that lives" (see N. Macnicol, *The Living Religions of the Indian People,* Student Christian Movement Press, 1934). In his autobiography, Gandhi described cow protection as includ-

A Hindu devotee caressing a cow at a cattle protection center.

ing cattle breeding, improvement of stock, humane treatment of bullocks, and the formation of modern dairies.

The origin of the repugnance to eating cattle may be economic. In India no other animal was available for tilling the soil or transporting agricultural products, and additionally, milk was a valuable food. Also, according to J. A. Dubois in *Hindu Manners, Customs, and Ceremonies* (Oxford, 1897), beef is nearly indigestible in a climate as hot as that of India. The eighteenth-century French writer Montesquieu wrote the following on the origin of the custom: "Cattle multiply but slowly [in India] and are subject to many diseases. Hence it is that a religious law which protects them is very necessary in that country. Hindu lawgivers felt it necessary to deify the animals in order to protect them."

Some experts, however, believe that cow worship is the chief cause of India's hunger and poverty because it keeps useless parasites alive. In 1959 the Ford Foundation concluded that about half of India's cows give no milk, and the milk production of the remainder is very low.

On the other hand, valid arguments can be made for the continued enforcement of the cow protection creed. Although India has a surplus of cows, there is a serious shortage of oxen, which are important as draft animals. Cows, therefore, are important as breeders of oxen. Cow dung is also an important economic asset. About half the cow dung produced is used as agricultural manure and the remainder as fuel. A paste made of cow dung is used as flooring material; it hardens into a smooth surface that can readily be swept clean. Cows that die of natural causes are eaten by low-caste Indians. Cows do not compete with humans for vegetable food because to a large extent they subsist on fodder, such as stubble and rice straw, that is useless for humans.

For more information, see M. Harris, *Cows, Pigs, Wars, and Witches: The Riddles of Culture* (Random House, 1974) and A. C. Bouquet, *Hinduism* (Hutchinson, 1949).

Fire Walking

Fire walking is a religious ceremony practiced in many parts of the world, including India, Malaya, Japan, Fiji, Tahiti, New Zealand, the Balkans, and Spain. It was also observed in classical Greece.

Fire walking takes various forms. The most common is that of walking swiftly over a layer of coals at the bottom of a shallow trench. Walking through a log fire and walking on red-hot stones are other forms.

The ability to increase the heat of the body by magic and achieve mastery over fire in order to prevent burning coals from harming the body is a marvel universally attributed to medicine men, shamans, and fakirs. Shamans and sorcerers worldwide are supposed to be "masters of fire," and they prove it by swallowing burning coals, touching red-hot irons, or walking over flames. Siberian shamans, for instance, swallow embers and run themselves through with swords. These feats are most completely manifested among the shamans of eastern Siberia and Manchuria, notably among the Tungus, but also among the Yakut, Samoyed, Koryak, Ostyak, and Chukchee. Insensibility to temperature, which renders both cold and heat tolerable, is considered a virtue, one that indicates the shaman has transcended the human condition.

The motives for fire walking are numerous: to ensure a good harvest; to attain purification through fire; to undergo an ordeal to prove innocence; to fulfill vows. Fire walkers believe that only those who lack faith will be injured. Injuries do happen, of course, but not as many as circumstances would seem to dictate.

Muslims believe that fire cannot harm something that is

Moslem fire walkers in Pakistan commemorating the martyrdom of Hussain, Mohammed's grandson.

holy or pure. In Sind, the southeastern province of Pakistan, stories are common about houses destroyed by fire in which nothing escaped save a copy of the Koran or about shrines in which all was destroyed but the tomb. Many sayids (Muslim aristocrats) believe fire cannot harm them; they step over a fire or dip their hands into boiling water.

No generally satisfactory explanation has yet been offered for the numerous cases of fire walking in which the participants have exposed themselves to extreme heat without suffering any pain or injury. Although some have alleged that fire walkers have unusually thick or calloused soles, in a number of instances, upon examination, fire walkers' feet have been found to be soft and flexible. At any rate, it is a fact that the fires and hot stones are sufficiently hot to char a pair of boots.

Other explanations include mass hallucination, psychical causes, the application of chemicals to the skin, the ingestion of narcotics or other drugs, and hydration (a special preparation of the skin).

One recent instance of fire walking, in India, in 1972 (described in *Natural History*, January 1974), was a failure and resulted in injuries. Although previous ceremonies had occurred without mishap, ten of the fifteen participants were severely burned. The failure caused great distress: "The villagers of Sunderpur believed that their magician was attempting to gain control over their local deities. . . . Other villagers were shaken because the deities in whom they believed and on whom they were dependent were about to be taken from them." Their confusion and distress seemed to demonstrate the intimate relationship between fire walking and the social, religious, and political life of the Indian village.

For more information, see A. Lang, *Magic and Religion* (Greenwood, 1969); J. Abbott, *The Keys of Power* (University Books, 1974); and V. Dioszegi, *Tracing the Shamans in Siberia* (Anthropological Press, 1968).

Hara-kiri

Hara-kiri is a traditional Japanese method of ritual suicide, either as a voluntary act or as a form of capital punishment.

The subject of voluntary hara-kiri (or seppuku, as the practice is usually called in Japan) kneels, stabs himself in the left side of the abdomen, draws the sword across his body, and turns the blade upward, releasing the intestines. A second stab below the chest, drawn down perpendicularly across the first cut, is also called for. Finally, the subject stabs his own throat. In obligatory seppuku (and often in the voluntary form as well), an assistant stands behind the subject and beheads him at the first sign of pain or change in the traditional seppuku posture.

The origins of the practice date from the wars of the eleventh century, along with the earliest development of the samurai code of conduct, later called bushido. This code, influenced by Zen Buddhist and Confucian attitudes, required of the samurai—the military class—strict martial honor and skill, discipline and self-composure.

The samurai was also expected to guard the peace as a just political administrator. He was required to follow rigidly standardized rules of behavior, covering every act—salutation, conversation, fencing, relations between husband and wife, and, *in extremis,* suicide. The most important rule was the complete absence of self-assertion before a superior.

A samurai would perform seppuku to avoid capture in war or to follow a feudal lord in death. He would carry two swords—a long one for the adversary and a short one for himself.

Seppuku could also be used to obtain release from shame or from conflicting duties. It could be an act of protest against a policy of a lord or of the government.

The use of seppuku as an honorable form of capital punishment arose in the sixteenth century, in order to spare samurai

An actor depicts the hara-kiri, or seppuku, posture.

the shame of being beheaded by a common executioner. It was applied when a samurai had committed a capital crime while revenging an injustice or insult or while protecting his lord. No one but a samurai could choose this method of execution. The practice was abolished in 1873.

The most famous recent case of seppuku involved the celebrated writer Yukio Mishima, who killed himself in 1970, after the failure of his attempted military coup d'état. A group of 1,000 soldiers had spurned his appeal to act against "corrupt politicians" and "American military hegemony." Before their eyes Mishima stabbed himself and managed to draw the blade seven inches across his abdomen before he was beheaded by his lieutenant.

The word "hara-kiri," used mostly by Westerners, literally means stomach cutting. The word "seppuku," preferred by the Japanese, emphasized not the cutting, but the stomach, which represents the inner self.

In Western culture, suicide is often considered cowardly, and slicing open one's belly may seem grotesque. In the Japanese context, however, it is an act of honor, courage, and self-sacrifice.

Seppuku developed as part of a general cultural pattern, which eventually influenced all levels of Japanese society. It supported an attitude that death must be faced squarely, with courage and tranquillity. Death was regarded not merely as an end of life, but as one of the most important features of life, capable of playing a positive role. If an individual were always prepared to die for duty or honor, his life would be considered meaningful.

For more information, see M. Anesaki, *History of Japanese Religion* (Tuttle, 1963) and C. A. Moore, *The Japanese Mind* (University of Hawaii Press, 1967).

Cannibalism

Cannibalism is the eating of human flesh by human beings. The word "cannibalism" is derived from a Spanish form for Carib, a West Indies tribe which practiced cannibalism. The practice of cannibalism is ancient and was widespread among primitive people on all continents. Peking man apparently ate other humans with no more compunction than he had in eating animal flesh.

Early cannibalism was largely motivated by the belief that the qualities of the people being consumed would be incorporated by the eating of their flesh and blood. In Mexico, for example, men representing the gods were periodically sacrificed and eaten, to identify the participant with the deity.

Reverence for ancestors was another motive for cannibalism. In Asia, as late as the fifth century B.C., certain tribes ate parts of a dead ancestor. Some ancient Scythians, some tribes of India, and, until recently, some tribes of the Amazon basin consumed bodies of relatives in a pious desire for the soul of the deceased to be reborn in the body of the consumer.

Population control has also motivated cannibalism; this is especially true in times of famine or among warrior tribes on the move, when a certain part of the population, often female children, is sacrificed or consumed.

Enemy eating was a common variety of cannibalism among the Aborigines of Australia, the Maoris of New Zealand, the Huron and Iroquois of North America, the Ashanti of Africa, and the Uscochi of the Balkans. Enemy eating is based on the desire either to incorporate the enemy's qualities or, as revenge, to destroy him utterly.

Throughout history, famine or the immediate lack of food has spurred otherwise noncannibalistic people to eat human flesh. Descriptions of several such cases follow:

PLACE: Russia.
DATE: 1812.
WHO: French soldiers.
NUMBERS: Unspecified, but presumably dozens or even hundreds.
CIRCUMSTANCES: Napoleon's retreat from Moscow.
DOCUMENTATION: Several eyewitnesses, including the Russian General Kreitz.
SOURCE: E. Tarle, *Napoleon's Invasion of Russia, 1812* (G. Allen & Unwin, 1942).

PLACE: At sea.
DATE: 1816.
WHO: Soldiers and civilians from the frigate *Medusse.*
NUMBERS: Unspecified, but presumably a dozen or more.
CIRCUMSTANCES: The *Medusse,* on its way to Senegal, sank in a storm, and the survivors drifted on a raft for many days.
DOCUMENTATION: Mainly from ship's surviving surgeon, Savigny.
SOURCE: The London *Times,* September 17, 1816.

PLACE: Western United States.
DATE: 1847.
WHO: The Donner party.
NUMBERS: Unspecified.
CIRCUMSTANCES: Party of settlers stranded in the Sierras in winter.
DOCUMENTATION: Several of the survivors agreed that cannibalism took place, although there was disagreement about details and precise circumstances.
SOURCE: R. Tannahil, *Flesh and Blood: A History of the Cannibal Complex* (Stein and Day, 1975).

PLACE: China.
DATE: 1901.
WHO: Chinese officer.
CIRCUMSTANCES: The inhabitants of a region of Kwangsi boiled and ate an officer sent to "pacify" them.
SOURCE: E. H. Parker, *China Review* (February 1901).

PLACE: Sumatra.

DATE: Nineteenth century.

WHO: Adulterers, traitors, spies, and deserters, etc.

NUMBERS: Unspecified.

CIRCUMSTANCES: Cannibalism was part of the judicial process of punishing malefactors.

SOURCE: E. M. Loeb, *Memoirs of the American Anthropological Association*, 1923.

PLACE: Haiti.

DATE: Nineteenth century.

WHO: Twelve-year-old girl.

CIRCUMSTANCES: The child was killed and eaten as part of a Voodoo ceremony.

SOURCE: S. St. John, *Haiti; or The Black Republic* (Smith, Elder, 1884).

PLACE: Germany.

DATE: 1924.

WHO: Twenty-seven boys.

CIRCUMSTANCES: Fritz Haarman, "The Hanover Vampire," was convicted of killing at least twenty-seven boys, making some of their flesh into sausages, and eating them.

SOURCE: *London News of the World* (December 21, 1924).

PLACE: The Andes.

DATE: 1972.

GROUP: Uruguayan airplane passengers.

NUMBERS: Unspecified.

CIRCUMSTANCES: A number of passengers who survived a plane crash ate the flesh of dead fellow passengers.

SOURCE: P. P. Read, *Alive: The Story of the Andean Survivors* (Lippincott, 1974).

Only in cases of famine does cannibalism spring from a single motive. Generally, two or more causes are required for survival of the practice. Whether the custom arose in a particular area through famine or other dietetic necessity, accident, or any other motives cited above, some reinforcement is needed to overcome the initial, instinctive repugnance and to confirm it into a regular mode of behavior.

Today cannibalism has died out in the world as a regular feature of religious or cultural life and breaks out only under special circumstances.

STRANGE
ACTIVITIES

Dowsing

Also known as divining or water witching, dowsing is a method of locating liquids, minerals, or living organisms by using a forked stick or other implement which supposedly moves in the presence of the object sought.

The practice of dowsing is said to date from antiquity. Moses, who brought forth water by striking a rock with a wand, is known as the first water dowser. The first authenticated evidence of dowsing with a forked stick comes from medieval Germany, where in 1556, in a posthumously published book, Georgius Agricola describes dowsing by miners to locate minerals and ores. Despite the opposition of Martin Luther and other churchmen, dowsing spread from Saxony to all parts of Europe. It was introduced into England during the reign of Elizabeth I by Saxon miners working in Cornwall, where dowsing is prevalent to this day.

The oldest and most commonly used device for dowsing, or divining, is a forked or loop-shaped rod made of wood, usually peach, willow, hazel, or witch hazel. A positive "signal" is obtained when the dowsing rod, which is held firmly in the palms of the dowser's hands, suddenly swings upward or downward. If a pendulum is used, the dowser may experience a deviation of the pendulum from the perpendicular plane or a rotation of the pendulum. However, most trained dowsers agree that the size, shape, weight, or composition of the rod or pendulum is of secondary importance. Wire coat hangers and metal tubing are commonly used today, and some dowsers operate without any mechanical device at all.

Evelyn Penrose, who has a worldwide reputation as a water and oil diviner, favors using a pendulum and a map. She believes her ability, effective over long distances from her home in Australia, is due to ESP and is a genuine gift.

Dowsers claim that the instrument they are using moves of its own accord in locating an object. Careful observation, however, shows that animation of the instrument is due to minute muscular movement by the dowser, generally on a subconscious level.

Despite extensive investigation of claims made by dowsers, including controlled studies, the results have been inconclusive and controversial.

E. Z. Vogt and L. K. Barrett, associated with Harvard

Onetime British Prime Minister David Lloyd George with a diviner, Mrs. David Wyllie, who dowsed for water with a hazel branch on his property; a 250-foot irrigation well was successfully located.

University, contend that field and laboratory tests have failed to establish the validity of dowsing. Judged by scientific standards, they concluded, the practice has little basis in fact. However, to offset their negative assessment, Vogt and Barrett noted that believers in dowsing attribute negative results of such studies to inadequacies in the scientific approach and also argue that dowsing cannot be expected to work in the artificial environment of the laboratory.

Others, including G. Underwood in *The Patterns of the Past* (Abelard-Schuman, 1973), argue that "scientific" tests are inconclusive because of the hostile attitude of scientists conducting the investigation or the reluctance of dowsers to expose their secrets. He notes that the success of dowsers in locating underground water has helped make large parts of the California desert productive. Underwood theorizes that the earth is covered by a powerful cosmic force and that underground deposits of water and minerals create "rifts" in this "earth force," to which dowsers respond. Animals, also sensitive to this earth force, use it to find their way and to locate suitable places for building their nests or dens.

Two authors, W. Barrett and T. Besterman, in *The Divining Rod* (University, 1968), posit that a dowser is a person endowed with a subconscious, supernormal, cognitive faculty of an unknown nature, which may be called cryptesthesia. By means of this faculty, knowledge of the object searched for enters the dowser's subconscious mind and is revealed by an unconscious muscular reaction.

In an article in *The Encyclopedia of Geochemistry and Environmental Sciences,* S. W. Tromp, who used orthodox geophysical methods over a span of twenty-five years to test dowsers, concludes that the ability is a true physiological phenomenon and is not caused by autosuggestion, but may be the result of the dowser's sensitivity to thermal radiations coming from the earth. Various tests showed that dowsers responded to changes in electromagnetic fields in a definite and specific way.

For further information, see Raymond C. Willey, *Modern Dowsing* (Esoteric Publications, 1976) and E. Z. Vogt and R. Hyman, *Water Witching U.S.A.* (University of Chicago Press, 1959).

Kirlian Photography

Kirlian photography, also known as high-voltage photography, is a method of supposedly photographing the coronal discharge or luminous "aura" of an object by using a high-frequency electric field.

High-voltage photography has a history that goes back almost 100 years. However, only since the 1930s has this technique achieved a degree of public recognition and acclaim. Major credit for pioneering high-voltage photography goes to Semyon and Valentina Kirlian, a Russian couple who have been working to perfect and popularize the method over the last forty years.

To obtain a Kirlian photograph, the object is placed between two condenserlike plates, a high-energy alternating current is applied, and the resulting "picture" is caught on photographic film. With certain suitable objects, such as the human finger, only one plate is used and the object itself is grounded to form one pole of the system. The photographs may be taken in black and white or color, and recently a technique for taking Kirlian motion pictures has also been developed.

Characteristically, Kirlian photos show a luminescent aura around the object, which varies in size, shape, and color. These variations are presumably related to the nature and inner state of the object. In the case of living organisms, the aura is believed to be determined by a variety of psychic and physiological factors. These are some of the noteworthy recent findings reported by researchers using high-voltage photography:

Kirlian photographs of the right feet of twin boys, taken on the same day. The boy whose foot appears at right was coming down with a forty-eight-hour viral infection.

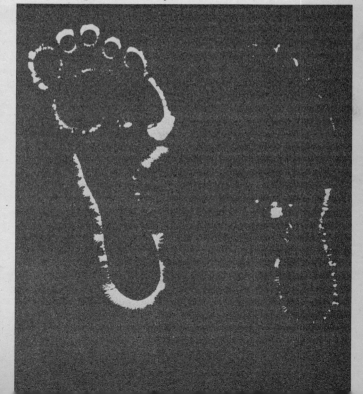

Psychological States

American researchers T. Moss and K. L. Johnson photographed the fingertips of about 500 subjects and found that each person had a characteristic aura which varied at different times, depending on emotional state. These workers also made high-voltage photographs of about 65 persons before and after the subjects used marijuana and reported that in a significant number of cases the emanations showed increased brilliance and width.

Mental Powers

Kirlian photographs taken of psychic healer Ethel E. Deloach by researcher E. D. Dean reportedly showed a distinct increase in the corona when the subject made an effort to concentrate her healing powers. H. S. Dakin conducted experiments with Uri Geller. The most noteworthy results of the experiments were Geller's apparent ability to create a variety of luminescent effects, including geometric figures, on the Kirlian photographs and to transfer "mental energy" from his finger to his wristwatch.

Medical Diagnosis

A current status report prepared by the International Kirlian Research Association (IKRA) cites evidence showing that specific changes in the Kirlian corona occur as a result of cancer and other diseases before these conditions can be detected by conventional diagnostic methods. Researcher J. B. Worlsey states that recent studies indicate the pathways depicted in Kirlian photographs of living tissues are related to the Chinese lines of acupuncture "meridians" and that flares seen in Kirlian photographs often issue from "acupoints" (key landmarks in the transmission of nervous energy according to the Chinese acupuncture system).

The "Phantom" Effect

Soviet researchers reported a phenomenon, known as the phantom leaf effect, whereby Kirlian photographs of a leaf taken after a part of it had been cut away still show the outline of the original leaf, with the removed part fainter than the rest but still clearly visible. This phenomenon was taken as supportive evidence for the existence of an "ethereal double" postulated by some Russian authors, an invisible network that supposedly regulates biological phenomena in living organisms. A few researchers outside the Soviet Union have reported having observed this "phantom" effect, but the majority of investigators have been unable to confirm the phenomenon.

Agricultural and Industrial Research

Success with Kirlian photography has been reported in a number of industrial and agricultural applications. For example, American researcher Thelma Moss claims 100 percent success using Kirlian photography to predict the ability of soybean seeds to germinate (see IKRA *Newsletter*, July 1976). High-voltage photography is being used to detect stress points in metals and to test a variety of industrial materials.

Doubts about the usefulness of Kirlian photography are mainly concerned with two questions: (1) What is the significance of the process and (2) how reproducible are the results?

With regard to significance, the basic objection raised about the validity of high-voltage photography is that the pictures may represent irrelevant results owing to the electric charges involved and may not be directly related to the object being photographed. Thus, some physicists claim the photographs merely represent displacement currents affecting the photographic emulsion, while others ascribe the corona and other Kirlian effects to the creation of water vapor by high-frequency currents (see *Science*, October 15, 1976, page 263). However, even if such side effects are present, this does not necessarily rule out the possibility that the biological properties of the object also contribute to the result.

From a practical point of view, the cause of the results is not as important as reproducibility. In the past, such reproducibility has been notoriously difficult to achieve, and some of the early results are open to serious question. For example, Dakin notes that the claim that Kirlian photography can detect pathological conditions earlier than standard methods is based on work done with inadequate controls and unstable equipment not capable of reliable, consistent data. According to Dakin, more recent studies have failed to show any significant correlation between Kirlian photographs and physiological states. Dakin believes that autosuggestion (the ability of a person to affect physiological processes through conscious effort) may explain the variability of the results.

Proponents of Kirlian photography agree that lack of standardized equipment has been a problem in the past, but they are confident that there is no intrinsic shortcoming in the Kirlian method itself that rules out reproducibility of results. With mounting interest in the subject and the growing sophistication of equipment, whether Kirlian photography can indeed make the transition from a fascinating toy to a reliable tool may soon be evident.

For details, see H. S. Dakin, *High-Voltage Photography,* (3101 Washington Street, San Francisco, 1974); S. Krippner and D. Rubin: *The Kirlian Aura* (Doubleday, 1974); and "Kirlian Photography: A Data Package" (prepared by Mankind Research Unlimited, Washington, D.C.). Information is also available from International Kirlian Research Association, 144 East Ninetieth Street, New York, N. Y. 10028.

Biorhythms

The biorhythm theory states that a person's vitality, emotional well-being, and intellectual alertness fluctuate in regular cycles.

According to proponents of the theory, a person can determine his emotional well-being, physical vitality, and intellectual ability on a given day by calculating where that day falls in the biorhythm cycles. Consequently a person can know on which days he will be most vulnerable to physical, emotional, or intellectual mishaps.

The biorhythm theory states that each cycle begins at birth. The emotional or sensitivity cycle lasts twenty-eight days. The first fourteen days are "plus" days as the cycle swings up from the average and drops back to it. The second fourteen days are "minus" days as the cycle swings down into a trough and then climbs back up to the average. The physical cycle is twenty-three days long, with eleven and one-half days on each side of the "plus" and "minus" line. The intellectual cycle is thirty-three days long. The day a cycle passes from "plus" to "minus" or vice versa is a "critical" day.

The plus days of the physical cycle are good for activities that require stamina; minus days are best kept for activities which require less exertion. The plus days of the emotional cycle are characterized by cheerfulness and the ability to

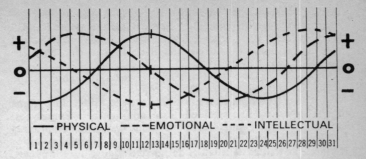

A biorhythm month with an especially critical day on the thirteenth.

cooperate with others and to think positively. On the minus days, a person is likely to be moody and have a negative attitude. Similarly, the plus days of the intellectual cycle are more conducive to creativity and intellectual pursuits than are the minus days.

The critical day of the physical cycle is ostensibly a day on which one is particularly accident-prone. On the critical day of the emotional cycle a person is both more accident-prone and more likely to be emotionally upset. On the intellectual cycle the critical day is not especially dangerous. A double critical day—that is, a day that is critical on two cycles—is particularly dangerous. Double critical days occur about six times a year and triple critical days about once a year. A day on which one cycle hits a peak or trough and which is also critical on the other two cycles is dangerous as well.

You can calculate your cycles by computing the number of days that have elapsed since your birth, being sure to add an extra day for each leap year. Divide that figure by the number of days in one of the cycles. The remainder will be the number of days that have elapsed since the most recent beginning of that cycle. The beginning of each cycle is the day it crosses the "plus" and "minus" line on the upswing. Follow the same procedure to find the other two cycles. If you were born in the late evening, use the following day as your birthdate.

Advocates of biorhythms regard Dr. Hermann Swoboda, who was a professor at the University of Vienna, and Wilhelm Fliess, a Berlin physician, as the founders of the theory. Both Swoboda, who published his work in 1904, and Fliess, who published his research in 1906, were responsible for the discovery of the twenty-three-day physical cycle and the twenty-eight-day emotional cycle. The thirty-three-day intellectual cycle is attributed to Alfred Teltscher, an Austrian engineer who did his work in the 1920s.

Although serious scientists have virtually ignored the biorhythm theory, it periodically enjoys great vogue. In late 1975 about 2,000 Japanese businesses were using biorhythms to cut down on the accident rate among their employees. United Airlines has put a computer at the disposal of employees interested in calculating their biorhythms. Books on biorhythms, as well as calculators designed to figure out the cycles, are selling well. Some shopping centers in the United States maintain computers that give personal biorhythm charts at a cost of fifty cents.

The enthusiasm of advocates continues to grow despite the negative findings of several studies that have attempted to relate biorhythms to accident rates. The Workmen's Compensation Board of British Columbia reviewed more than 13,000 accidents and discovered that biorhythms were apparently useless in predicting the day on which a person would have an accident. The negative finding was confirmed by the U.S. Tactical Air Command study of 8,625 air accidents (see "New Facts on Biorhythms," *Science Digest,* May 1976). A detailed discussion of the cycles can be found in George S. Thommen, *Is This Your Day?* (Avon, 1973).

POSSESSION

Possession

Possession, in some societies and religious beliefs, is a condition in which an individual's mind, body, or soul is taken over by a supernatural being.

Belief in possession is probably universal among human societies, primitive and civilized. Even in the highly developed countries of North America and Europe, some religious groups continue to believe in possession by the Christian Holy Spirit, and some practice exorcism of evil spirits from the demonically possessed. Communist societies may be the only societies in the world where such beliefs and practices are no longer acknowledged.

In primitive religion, possession is understood to be the result of special ritual invocations. The tribal religious leader, the shaman or witch doctor, in the course of a religious rite will enter a trance state and take on the attributes of a god. Sometimes this role falls to a worshiper or to an initiate into the rite. In at least one instance, an observer of a Voodoo rite involuntarily fell into a trance and was possessed by a god (see M. Deren, *Divine Horsemen: The Living Gods of Haiti*, Vanguard, New York, 1953).

One of the earliest accounts of possession is recorded in the ancient Greek tragedy *The Bacchae*, by Euripides, in which devotees of the god Dionysus become possessed and pursue the god or his stand-in through the woods. When they catch him, they tear him apart and eat him alive. Two words often associated with possession are derived from the Greek: "ecstasy" from *ex*, out of, and *histasthai*, to stand, thus, to stand outside oneself; and "enthusiasm" from *en*, in, and *theos*, god, or *enthoussiazen*, inspired or possessed by god.

The possessed person usually speaks in a different voice, sometimes in a different and unintelligible language, and displays a variety of spasmodic or graceful motions and other actions that would be nearly impossible for him to perform in the normal state (see Fire Walking; Dervishes). Frequently, the possessed may engage in aggressive or sexual acts that would not be permitted in the normal state. The worshipers usually believe that, through the possession, the god has come to join the group in its religious celebration, and the possessed person often dons a mask or other paraphernalia associated with the possessing deity.

In another variety of possession the possessed is taken ill. The illness may be explained as harassment by a purely malevolent evil spirit or as a spiritual punishment for violating some sacred law. In the former case a simple exorcism may cure the illness. In the case of a violation of taboo, a ritual cleansing of the sinner by a witch doctor will usually also involve a confession by the possessed, or his proxy, and probably some sort of penance or the payment of a penalty.

A common form of possession in the West during the last 150 years has been mediumistic possession. The medium enters a trance state fairly easily and is taken over by his or her control, a hypothetical discarnate spirit which uses the medium to communicate from the spirit world. The control mediates between the spirits of the dead and their concerned relatives gathered in the medium's parlor. Sometimes, however, the spirits are allowed to speak for themselves directly through the medium. Usually, the medium's voice and manner change radically, as the voice, accents, posture, and gestures of the controlling spirit are reproduced in the medium.

The most common form of possession in Christendom is possession by the Holy Spirit, a manifestation of the real presence of the divinity. Common to several Pentacostal sects of Protestantism and to some experimental groups in the major Protestant denominations and in Roman Catholicism, possession by the Holy Spirit usually takes the forms of physical seizures and glossolalia (speaking in tongues) and the interpretation of such speech.

Another form of possession in which Christians figure is demonic possession, a form most recently dramatized in *The Exorcist,* a book and film with much morbid interest in the unusual phenomena associated with possession. Demonic possession need not be sought out like divine possession or result from some moral transgression. It can be the consequence of simple malevolent seduction by an evil spirit (see Demonic Possession).

The usual experience of possession seems to follow after a prolonged or intense period of extreme mental or physical stress. This stress can be induced by drumming, chanting, dancing, special breathing, exercises, drugs, physical exhaustion, or physical debilitation through fasting or exposure. Intense stress of this sort can result in the dissociation of the mind from the body and of sections of the mind from each other.

In the case of shamans and mediums the ability often and

easily to enter a trance state and become possessed is the first requirement for the job, and there may be a preexisting dissociation in the personality of the medium or shaman. The trance can, in that case, be an easily adopted and eventually habitual alteration of consciousness.

Believers in possession maintain that the condition of dissociation that results from stress makes way for the god or spirit to take control of the mind and body. Those who adhere to a strictly psychological explanation and reject the supernatural regard possession as a form of hypnosis or autosuggestion.

Dr. William Sargant, a British physician who began to study dissociation during World War II, when he worked with battle-fatigued soldiers, finds the phenomenon of possession to be similar to such psychophysical crises as conversion, deep mystical experience, brainwashing, the excitement of mobs, orgasm, and the reliving of emotional trauma under psychiatric treatment.

In Sargant's view, extreme stress, beyond an individual's capacity to adapt to or bear it, causes the brain to enter a state of protective inhibition. This condition, or trance state, can be compared to a fuse's blowing out and closing down part of an electrical system when it is overloaded. A portion of the brain is isolated or the data contained there are wiped out, and the person is then open to suggestion from outside or to impulses arising from the unconscious areas of the mind. Frequently, even in cases of known autosuggestion, the "possessed" has displayed talents and abilities far exceeding his normal performance.

For further information, see T. K. Oesterreich, *Possession* (Kegan Paul, 1930) and William Sargant, *The Mind Possessed* (J. B. Lippincott, 1974).

Demonic Possession

Demonic possession, in religious belief, is a condition in which an individual's mind, body, and soul are taken over by an evil spirit that desires total control and, in Christian belief, the eternal damnation of the possessed.

The hallmark of demonic possession is a hatred and fear of the symbols of goodness and sanctity. Other signs include speaking in another voice and often in an unknown or unearthly language. According to Dr. Malachi Martin, a former

Jesuit priest who has participated in eleven major exorcisms, anyone can be a victim of possession regardless of psychological health, belief or unbelief, or strength of will.

Martin, in his book *Hostage to the Devil* (Reader's Digest, 1976), says possession begins when the evil spirit takes advantage of a character flaw or special psychological need of the victim. The victim feels an offer of special, nonhuman assistance and accepts it. The victim may soon feel he is on the verge of a breakthrough into new knowledge, a new reality, or a new and more expansive role to play in life.

At this point, according to Martin, the victim will clearly feel an alien pressure to accept outside control. If the victim yields (and physical consequences follow resistance), the promise of self-realization is withdrawn and "virtually all personal freedom ceases from that point on." Victims may gain some advantages in their profession, or increased personal safety, or popularity, but at the cost of an increasing loss of self-control and a decline in awareness of and concern for the self and others.

According to Martin, if the victim finally allows full control without conflict, perfect possession may occur. In this state the possessing demon no longer harasses the victim. The takeover is so complete that the possessed may appear perfectly normal, and the fear and hatred of religious objects may not be apparent.

Usually, however, a spark of resistance continues in the possessed, and the demonic harassment becomes so obvious that friends or relatives will seek help for the victim. Ultimately, if it can be established that the symptoms are not those of schizophrenia and no other diagnosis of mental illness seems appropriate, an exorcism may be performed.

In the course of a major exorcism the evil spirit at first maintains a pretense that it is not present and that the victim is normal. When the spirit is forced to drop that pretense and begins to speak for itself, witnesses sometimes hear "the voice," an unearthly babble of screams, groans, raucous laughter, whispers, cries, and other sounds. Ultimately, the exorcist forces the demon to declare its real name and commands the demon by name to depart in the name of God or Jesus. The clash of wills that ensues can go on for hours or days. It is during this period that a wide variety of paranormal phenomena is alleged to occur, as the demon contorts the victim's body and tosses furniture about. In one case recounted by Martin, the demon physically attacked the exorcist and put the priest in the hospital for a month. If the exorcism is successful, a sudden sense of the absence of evil marks the expulsion of the demon.

In early Judaism, Jehovah was understood to be the source of both good and evil spirits (I Samuel 18:10), and possession was not necessarily demonic. By the time of Jesus, possession was almost always thought to be of the demonic variety. Ecstatic possession by a good spirit or by the Holy Spirit was relatively rare in Christianity until the seventeenth century, when several Protestant sects revived the possibility.

In the meantime, from the fourteenth through the seventeenth century, Europe and New England were plagued by murderous outbreaks of demon hunting, exorcisms, and witch burnings. By the beginning of the eighteenth century allegations of demonic possession were seldom heard in public, though some churchmen maintain that the incidence of possession has remained relatively stable for years. Martin says that 125 major exorcisms were performed in the United States alone in 1975.

Evidence for genuine possession by an evil supernatural force is unavailable. Those who have supposedly been possessed insist on anonymity, and those who have participated at exorcisms refuse to reveal any details which might breach that anonymity and permit verification of some of the reported phenomena. Participants in exorcisms are usually also firm believers in demons and the efficacy of exorcism. Their testimony is undoubtedly colored by their beliefs; certainly their interpretation of events during exorcisms is based on their faith.

Martin, in a personal interview, claimed there was electroencephalographic evidence of anomalous brain waves in the possessed. He was unable to document this claim, and the interviewer's search for substantiation was fruitless. Martin was also asked if it would be possible for the interviewer to hear a tape of "the voice." Martin warned that hearing "the voice," even on tape, could be extremely dangerous—"You will never be the same afterward!" He stated that a tape of "the voice" was in existence, but he did not volunteer to arrange a playback for the interviewer, even though he often expressed his eagerness to prove the reality of demonic possession. In general, his exposition of the subject in his book is melodramatic and, at times, lurid. His discussion of the topic during the interview, while gracious and erudite, was marked by obvious dramatic techniques and forms of mystery mongering more likely to titillate the faithful than persuade the skeptic.

There may be circumstances when the victim's belief in possession would make exorcism the best method of ending a psychological disturbance. However, the lack of any evidence for the existence of demons makes it unlikely that possession is the result of an invasion by a real, alien force. It is more likely that psychological illness, a severely morbid imagination, and the collusion of believers create the circumstances in which the phenomena of possession and exorcism appear (see The Philip Phenomenon).

Another former Jesuit, Dr. Henry Asgard Kelly, writes: " . . . whether or not [demons] exist, it does not appear to be necessary to believe in them in order to cope with the problems of human life. Given the evils that belief in demonology has caused in the past . . . it would seem best to act as though evil spirits did not exist until such time as their existence is forced upon us" (*The Devil, Demonology, and Witchcraft: The Development of Christian Beliefs in Evil Spirits*, Doubleday, 1968).

On June 26, 1975, a special study by the Vatican's Sacred Congregation for the Propagation of the Faith asserted the reality of Satan, the chief evil spirit, but warned against a "morbid fascination" with devils. "It is easy to fall victim to the imagination, to get carried off course by inaccurate tales," said the study.

In general, demonic possession and exorcism seem far less dramatic and horrendous to Protestants than they do to Dr. Martin. Protestant exorcisms are more like counseling, therapy, and prayer sessions than the lengthy and elaborate Roman Catholic rites described by Martin. An evangelical Protestant view of demonic possession is presented by ministers, psychiatrists, and anthropologists in *Demon Possession*, J. W. Montgomery, ed. (Bethany Fellowship Inc., Minneapolis, 1976).

Practitioners of the occult often associate demonic possession with what they call earth-bound entities, spirits of the dead that were too petty and evil in life to move on to the next level of spiritual development. These spirits, according to the occultists, envy the living and torment them with needless fears and evil thoughts. These spirits usually gain access to the living through séances, hypnotism, Ouija board play, magic rituals, and various forms of trance. Usually, they are weak and cowardly and will obey an authoritative command to go away.

Protestant and Catholic exorcists do agree that the revival of interest in the occult has caused a slight increase in the incidence of possession. Martin Ebon, author of many books on parapsychology and the occult, cites several cases of possession caused by using the Ouija board or other experiments with the occult. In his introduction to *The Satan Trap: Dangers of the Occult* (Doubleday, 1976), editor Ebon cautions that "the peddlers of the occult ignore one basic thing: people who are emotionally unstable are their most willing and vulnerable victims. . . . It is precisely for this reason that the promises of 'spiritual development,' the 'instructions in meditation,' or 'self-hypnosis' [must] be tempered with caution, with an understanding of negative as well as positive potential. . . . Certainly, toying with witchcraft and Satanism, possession and exorcism has the same dangers as the drug culture: those who are already delicately balanced emotionally are the first to flock to assorted cults and are therefore most likely to become overinvolved, victims of self-delusion."

Stigmata

Stigmata (singular form—stigma) are the reproduction on a living person's body of the wounds or scars corresponding to those of the crucified Christ. These wounds appear on the hands and feet, near the heart, and sometimes on the head, shoulders, or back. Some people believe that the appearance of these wounds is a sign of mystical participation in the suffering of Christ. In cases where the stigmatized person is not pious, the stigmatization is believed to be caused by the devil.

The attribution of religious significance to wounds and scars predates Christianity. In many primitive rites, wounds and scars are deliberately inflicted as part of the religious ritual. The stigmata of Christ, however, allegedly appear spontaneously on the bodies of extremely devout people.

Medieval Christianity placed great emphasis on compassion for the suffering of Christ. Through contemplation of that suffering, medieval mystics rose to an ecstatic state of identification with Christ that is called participation. In the late twelfth and early thirteenth centuries, some mystics deliberately wounded themselves in the manner they believed Christ had been wounded.

The first reported case of true stigmatization—in which the wounds allegedly appeared spontaneously—was that of St. Francis of Assisi, who died in 1226. His stigmatization, however, is not as well authenticated as many of the other events of his life. The stigmata are said to have taken the form of wounds in his hands and feet and in his side. The stigmata first appeared two years before his death and are said to have been present on his body when he died. The wounds were also said to have had actual nails in them. Many contemporaries of St. Francis of Assisi, including the bishop of Olmütz, were skeptical of his stigmatization.

The Catholic Church does not require its members to believe in the stigmatization of St. Francis or any other stigmatization. In fact, as of 1967, according to the *New Catholic Encyclopedia,* no reliable list of stigmatized persons exists. The Church rejects the belief held by some Catholics that stigmatization is a sign God has granted as a mark of piety.

According to *The Columbia Encyclopedia,* since the time of St. Francis of Assisi, about 240 Roman Catholic women and 60 men have allegedly received stigmata, and the existence of many of these stigmata has been fully attested. Physicians who investigated some of the 29 cases of stigmatization in the nineteenth century were, according to the encyclopedia, "convinced of their objective reality and the honesty of the stigmatized." Stigmatization has also been reported by Muslim ascetics whose wounds are said to correspond to those Mohammed received when he led the fight to spread Islam.

In many cases that have been studied, evidence points to a natural explanation. The stigmatic may inflict the wounds on himself while in a state of religious ecstasy and not remember the event afterward. Or a psychosomatically caused physiological process may produce the appearance of wounds in the tissues. It is thought that one notable twentieth-century case, that of Theresa Neuman (of Konnersreuth, Upper Palatinate, Germany), may have such a physiological explanation. Unfortunately, however, her case did not receive the proper medical examination to support a solid conclusion.

It has been found that the location of the wounds of the stigmatic are related to his beliefs. It is not known whether Christ was wounded on the right or left side. After the cult of the Sacred Heart, which stresses veneration of the heart of Christ as a symbol of His love for man, originated in the Catholic Church in the seventeenth century, more stigmatics tended to have wounds on the left side. Wounds have been found, in some cases, to correspond to wounds in the image of Christ Crucified before which the stigmatic prays.

For additional information, see James Hastings, ed., *Encyclopedia of Religion and Ethics.*

STRANGE
PERSONS

Carlos Castaneda

Carlos Castaneda is the adopted name of an anthropologist and author who won fame and fortune between 1968 and 1974 with four books about Don Juan, a Yaqui sorcerer, or *brujo*.

In his best-selling volumes Castaneda told how he met Don Juan, the old Indian shaman, became his apprentice, experimented with three kinds of drugs, and learned how to perceive with his entire body, not just with his eyes and mind.

His apprenticeship, which lasted a decade, helped him earn a doctorate in anthropology, made him $1,000,000, and turned him into a cult hero of the young. His books, which have been praised as classics and denounced as frauds are: *The Teachings of Don Juan: A Yaqui Way of Knowledge,* 1968; *A Separate Reality: Further Conversations with Don Juan,* 1971; *Journey to Ixtlan: The Lessons of Don Juan,* 1972; and *Tales of Power,* 1974.

A secretive man whose real name is not yet known, Castaneda was born in São Paulo, Brazil, on Christmas Day, 1935. He learned to speak Portuguese, Italian, Spanish, and English. In 1951 he moved to the United States, and eight years later he formally changed his name to Castaneda.

In 1960, when he was a graduate student in anthropology at the University of California in Los Angeles, he went to Arizona to study the use of medicinal plants by the Indians of the Southwest. There, he says, in a dusty border town, the twenty-five-year-old student met the sixty-nine-year-old Indian who had moved from Mexico to Arizona. The youth was so in awe of the wisdom of the white-haired man that he began visiting him regularly.

A year later Don Juan took Castaneda into his confidence, revealing that he was a *brujo*—a medicine man, healer of souls, witch, sorcerer. In June 1961 Castaneda became the sorcerer's apprentice. He listened as the old man talked, took notes, and let himself be introduced to the use of peyote, mushrooms, and jimsonweed.

Under the influence of these hallucinogens and with the guidance of his master, Castaneda felt his consciousness change, had strange visions, heard terrifying sounds, felt the ground shake, thought he was flying, talked to a coyote, and sensed that his thoughts existed outside himself. He was never sure whether any of this "really" happened.

Some critics denounced his books as more fiction than fact. Castaneda, a very private person, did little to clear up the controversy that developed. A researcher spent hours interviewing Castaneda for a cover story about himself, which *Time* published on March 5, 1973, and he told her contradictory things: "I have not lied or contrived. . . . Oh, I am a bullshitter." It is unlikely that Castaneda was ever as naïve or as silly as the student he writes about.

Castaneda was defended by another anthropologist, Paul Riesman of Carleton College, who called his books "among the best that the science of anthropology has produced." His first book was hailed by *Publishers Weekly* as a "classic" and by *The New York Times* as "an extraordinary spiritual and psychological document."

Literal truth or not, the Don Juan books are among the world's best descriptions of the shaman's view of reality.

Edgar Cayce

Edgar Cayce (1877-1945) was a rural Kentucky healer and seer whose trances yielded diagnoses and prescriptions for patients, as well as glimpses into the past and future.

Cayce, who was born on a farm at Hopkinsville, Kentucky, never received any education beyond the ninth grade. At the age of seven, he had his first psychic experience when a voice came to him in the woods, saying, "Your prayers have been heard. What would you ask of me?" He replied, "I'd like to be able to help other people, especially sick children."

His first patient was himself. After being hit by a baseball, he instructed his mother, from a semitrance state, to make a poultice of certain medicines. The wound disappeared within a day. Thereafter Cayce practiced successfully on his friends, family and himself, going into a semitrance condition in which he was able to suggest remedies. Once, after losing his voice for a period of time, he underwent hypnosis. While in the trance, Cayce diagnosed his own condition as paralysis of the vocal cords caused by nerve strain and instructed his body to send blood to the affected area. The condition cleared up, and he was again able to speak normally.

Through medicines prescribed in a trance, Cayce apparently cured his wife of tuberculosis and frequent hemorrhages and restored sight to his son's eyes after an accident, despite the protests of doctors who insisted that one eye should be re-

Edgar Cayce, clairvoyant and healer.

moved. In trances, while lying on a couch in his home, Cayce seemed able to diagnose conditions in patients hundreds of miles away, even describing the patient's physical surroundings in minute detail. He successfully cured a variety of diseases, including many that were considered hopeless.

Cayce, an avid Bible reader with a lively sense of humor, refused to become rich with his powers. He worked unsparingly until his death in 1945. His remedies were often homespun, sometimes outlandish, including vegetables, grape juice, cola syrup, and certain exercises.

Beyond medical diagnosis and prescriptions, Cayce described people's previous lives, spoke Homeric Greek, and answered abstruse anatomical questions. He is said to have predicted the

1929 stock market crash and World War II. He further prophesied that between 1958 and 1998 there would be enormous eruptions and earth changes in the Western Hemisphere, as well as a change in the physical aspect of the west coast of America. He said a polar shift was taking place and that ice caps at the poles would melt, resulting in a change in the world's climate. He predicted that by 1998 most of Los Angeles, San Francisco, and New York would be destroyed by natural causes.

Later in his life Cayce became interested in occult literature and, through answering metaphysical questions while in a trance state, developed a complex occult philosophy. According to Martin Gardner (*Fads and Fallacies,* Dover, 1957), "It seems to be a confusing hodge-podge of Christianity, astrology, Pyramidology, theosophy and other occult traditions." He believed in the extinct civilization of Atlantis and described its use of "terrible crystals," which drew force from the stars with the help of psychic power. Atlantis was destroyed, he said, through a calamitous excess of such energy.

One of Cayce's greatest supporters was Dr. Wesley Ketchum, a reputable doctor of homeopathic medicine, who sought Cayce's advice in more than 100 cases. The association started when Cayce's advice miraculously cured an apparently hopelessly demented young patient of Dr. Ketchum's.

Although Cayce apparently tried to get qualified physicians to treat his patients, he met a great deal of opposition from the medical profession (see Jeffrey Mishlove, *The Roots of Consciousness,* Random House/Bookworks, 1975). Ketchum, however, did examine Cayce's records and made a favorable report to the American Society of Clinical Research at Boston, in 1910. Ketchum told the group, in part: "The cases I have used him in have, in the main, been the rounds before coming to my attention, and in six important cases which had been diagnosed as strictly surgical he stated that no such condition existed, and outlined treatment which was followed with gratifying results in every case."

The Association for Research and Enlightenment, founded in 1931, in Virginia Beach, Virginia, and led by Cayce's sons, has files of more than 9,000 of Cayce's readings. The organization has tried to foster scientific investigation of Cayce's work. ARE also popularizes Cayce's healing, publishing material about him and sponsoring meditative healing groups (see Sally Hammond, *We Are All Healers,* Harper and Row, 1973).

Although interest in Cayce is growing, very little objective serious material is available on him. According to the librarian at the Parapsychology Foundation in New York City, this is because Cayce was unknown for a long time, and later researchers are reluctant to criticize him because of his popularity and the lack of hard data.

Martin Gardner, in *Fads and Fallacies,* states that there is no question of the genuineness of Cayce's trances or of his sincerity. He describes him as a kind, gentle man who was surprised and baffled by his own ability and was fearful it might be a source of evil but was convinced until his death that his gift came from God.

Although Cayce cultists, such as his friend Thomas Sugrue, who in 1943 wrote *There Is a River* as a tribute to Cayce, maintain he could not have possessed the information he gave in his trances, Gardner believes it is more likely he picked up the knowledge from reading and contacts with friends although he may have consciously forgotten it. Gardner also indicates that many of Cayce's earlier readings were given with the assistances of osteopaths and homeopaths and that this association had an important influence on his readings. For instance, he often diagnosed spinal lesions as the causes of pain and prescribed spinal manipulations. Also, many of the remedies Cayce prescribed were borrowed from homeopathy and naturopathy. He also points out that although many thousands of people believed they were cured by Cayce, many of his initial diagnoses were off the mark. In one instance, which is recorded in Sugrue's tribute to Cayce, Dr. J. B. Rhine was not impressed with Cayce's abilities when his reading for Rhine's daughter failed to fit the facts.

For more information, see J. Stearn, *Edgar Cayce, the Sleeping Prophet* (Doubleday, 1967); J. Glass, *They Foresaw the Future* (Putnam, 1969); and H. Holzer, *Predictions: Fact or Fallacy?* (Hawthorne, 1968).

Aleister Crowley

Aleister Crowley was a British sexual mystic and proponent of black magic.

Crowley was born in England in 1875 into a family of fanatic and very strict sectarians. Because of his rebelliousness, Crowley was believed by his mother to be Antichrist. The boy soon came to agree with her and determined that he was a prophet who would usher in a new era and sweep away the shambles of an outworn Christianity.

Crowley set out to become a magus, an adept in the secret arts of magic. At the age of twenty-one he had a terrifying mystical experience and thereafter believed he had the power to satisfy hitherto-dormant parts of his being.

Sexual exploits assumed a major role in Crowley's career. He was described by associates as a satyr, and throughout his life he had numerous sexual liaisons with both men and women, though he was reportedly devoid of natural affection. He propounded the theory that sexual aberrations were acts of sex magic, in a version of Tantrism, an Indian cult. Attracted by the figure of the Scarlet Woman, Mother of Harlots, in the Book of Revelation, he recruited a succession of ugly, masochistic women to play the role for him throughout his life. He married three times.

As he grew older, he became more and more "Satanic" and acquired a taste for physical sadism. Among his numerous eccentricities was the habit of defecating on carpets; his excretions, he claimed, were sacred.

In a search for greater enlightenment and adventure, Crowley traveled extensively, living at times in New York, Mexico, France, Italy, China, and India, where he developed a skill for mountain climbing in the Himalayas. In Scotland and later in Sicily, he set up households where black magic

Aleister Crowley, sexual mystic and proponent of black magic.

was practiced and demons were conjured up. He also traveled on the "astral plane," claiming to be the reincarnation of the sixteenth-century magician Edward Kelley.

Crowley was introduced to mescaline in 1910 and devised a series of public performances (using the hallucinogen) in which religious ecstasies were said to be produced. The use of this drug and others eventually contributed to a twenty-year period of drug and alcohol addiction, leading to his death in 1947.

In 1898 Crowley joined the Hermetic Order of the Golden Dawn and was given the name Brother Perturabo. The group broke up soon after, and Crowley gradually built up his own Order of the Silver Star. In the 1920s he became the head of the German Ordo Templi Orientis (OTO), which also practiced sex magic.

Crowley was a prolific writer of poems, novels, essays, and accounts of his occult philosophy and experiences. Much of his output was pornographic. His central work was *The Book of the Law,* which he claimed had been dictated to him in Cairo in 1904 by a spirit named Aiwass, later identified as his genius and as the solar-phallic energy supposedly worshiped by the ancient pagans.

The book expounded Crowley's creed, "Do what thou wilt," or "Do what you have to do." It foretold an era in the near future in which man would be godlike, gradually realizing all his powers. Rituals, whether Christian or occult, would be discarded in favor of total cosmic union.

Crowley's literary works have more or less faded into obscurity, and his organizational efforts did not prove to be lasting. His theories and practices, however, have had an influence on current-day Satanists.

Crowley was also, as it transpired, a prophet of certain attitudes and values common to the counterculture of the West, in his assertion of the redeeming power of sex in attaining personal fulfillment, his rejection of old rituals and taboos, his use of drugs, and his desire for boundless spiritual union with the universe.

For more information, see J. Symonds, *The Great Beast: The Life of Aleister Crowley* (Ray Publishers, 1952) and C. Wilson, *The Occult* (Vintage Books, 1973).

Dalai Lama

Dalai Lama is the title used in the West for the Gyalwa Rinpoche, the head of the Yellow Hat Order (Dge-lugs-pa), the most important Buddhist monastic order in Tibet.

"Lama," the European adaptation of the Tibetan *bla-ma*, means "superior one." First used to translate the Sanskrit term *guru* (spiritual leader or guide), it was extended to refer to any Tibetan Buddhist priest or monk. Because Buddhist monasteries have traditionally played a dominant role in Tibetan political and religious life, there have been many important lamas, some believed to be reincarnations of previous lamas.

Until recently the Gyalwa Rinpoche was the religious and temporal ruler of Tibet. The Chinese occupied Tibet in 1950, and in 1959, following an unsuccessful revolt, the Gyalwa Rinpoche was forced to flee.

The first Gyalwa Rinpoche was Dge-'dun-grub-pa (1391–1475). The current and fourteenth Gyalwa Rinpoche, Bstan-'

Dalai Lama, Tibetan Buddhist leader in exile in India, prays to the rhythm of a small drum.

dzin-rgya-mtsho, was born in 1935 of Tibetan parentage in the Chinese province of Tsinghai and was enthroned in 1940.

The Gyalwa Rinpoche is believed to be an incarnation of Avalokitesvara, a Bodhisattva, which, in Mahayana Buddhism, is a saintly or spiritual being that will eventually become a Buddha. In the interim, a bodhisattva is reincarnated when he dies in order to be of immediate and practical help to his people. The bodhisattva Avalokitesvara, who is traditionally depicted with two pairs of arms, is believed to postpone intentionally becoming a Buddha out of compassion for his people.

The process of selecting a new Gyalwa Rinpoche is elaborate and can take several years. The Gyalwa Rinpoche is believed to be reincarnated as a newborn child soon after his death. Occasionally the dying ruler says where he will be reborn. The right child must have the shape and size of ears traditionally ascribed to the Gyalwa Rinpoche and the marks that can be interpreted as traces of a second pair of arms. The newly incarnated ruler should also be able to recall his previous lives by the time he is a few years old.

Soon after the ruler's death, disguised search parties made up of priests and laymen, selected to represent a cross section of the Tibetan people, go out to look for the reborn Gyalwa Rinpoche. Some investigate reports of remarkable children; others go to areas specified by oracles or by omens as the place to look. One oracle that is consulted is Lhamo Latso, a mountain lake, where, shortly before his death, the first Gyalwa Rinpoche had a vision of the goddess Pandan Lhamo. She told him that she would look after his future incarnations and is the guardian spirit of Lhamo Latso.

When the thirteenth Gyalwa Rinpoche died, the regent went to Lhamo Latso, where he saw a house; he described the house, the countryside, and even the color of the family's dog. A disguised search party went in search of the house. When they found the house, it is said, one of the children there identified the abbot who headed the party and also conversed in the official court language. No one else in the family knew the language. Out of a variety of objects, the child recognized those which had belonged to the last Gyalwa Rinpoche, convincing the party that they had succeeded in their search.

Next, the regent consulted the oracle of Nechung, another deity that promised to watch over the reincarnations of the Gyalwa Rinpoche. He, too, confirmed the conclusion of the search party. However, because the backers of a rival Gyalwa Rinpoche were suspicious of the Nechung oracle's honesty, a test was conducted: The oracle was asked to answer questions which could not be seen since they were sealed in scrolls. The oracle passed the test. Then, in a special ceremony, the boy's name was selected from a lottery, and he was accepted as the Gyalwa Rinpoche.

Occasionally, the process of finding the Gyalwa Rinpoche is more difficult and complicated because the voice may be reborn in one child, the body in another, and the mind in still another. The child with the Gyalwa Rinpoche's mind is the chosen one.

Occasionally, fraudulent claims are made to influence the selection of the new Gyalwa Rinpoche. For instance, in one case a family coached a boy to be able to remember his supposed previous lives. The fraud was discovered but was not held against the boy, who eventually became an important religious leader. In another case a prominent family attempted to fake an omen by forcing the horses of the deceased Gyalwa Rinpoche to stampede toward their stable.

For more information, see Sir Charles Bell, *The Religion of Tibet* (Oxford, 1931) and Thubeten Jigme Norbu and Colin M. Turnbull, *Tibet* (Clarendon Press, 1968).

Nostradamus

Nostradamus was a popular French physician and astrologer of the sixteenth century who appeared to have correctly predicted many events far in the future.

Born in Provence in 1503 of Jewish descent, Michel de Nostredame (later called Nostradamus) received his medical degree from Montpellier in 1529, after courageously fighting a plague epidemic when the local physicians had fled. He settled in Agen, married, and became the father of two children, but plague killed his whole family. His second marriage in 1547 to a wealthy widow gave him the financial independence to devote himself to astrology.

The first edition of his prophecies, called *Centuries,* appeared in 1555, in the form of oracular, rhymed quatrains. The book was such a success that Nostradamus was invited by Catherine de' Medici, the queen consort, to cast the horoscopes of her children. Upon his accession to the throne in 1560, Charles IX appointed Nostradamus court physician. Thereafter several more books of prophecies were published. Nostradamus died in 1566.

Nostradamus' prophecies covered events that are due to occur all the way to the fourth millennium A.D. Because of their frequently vague quality, however, they continue to generate controversy. Opponents dub him a charlatan; defenders marvel at his insight, crediting him with the prediction of the French Revolution, World War II, and other events, as well as with the invention of the periscope, submarine, airplane, balloon, and other devices.

Among his seemingly clearest predictions was one that stated: "The blood of the just requires London to be burned with fire in sixty-six." The great fire of London occurred in 1666.

Before Elizabeth I became queen of England, Nostradamus wrote: "The rejected one shall accede to the throne/Her enemies shall be found to be conspirators/Her time shall triumph as never before/At 70 she shall surely die, in the third year of the century." This roughly conforms to what later happened, including Elizabeth's death in 1603 in her seventieth year.

The prophecy "An old man with the title of chief will arise, of doddering sense . . . the country divided, conceded to gendarmes" has been interpreted to refer to Marshal Henri Pétain and his regime in the half of France given over to Vichy "gendarmes" during World War II.

While Nostradamus' verses were often vague about the years in which the predicted events were to occur, some of his prose predictions were more precise, making them more vulnerable to disproof. For example, he cited 1732 as the climax of a series of natural calamities that would nearly wipe out mankind and 1792 as the climax of a violent religious persecution. Neither prediction was borne out.

Since Nostradamus' specific predictions did not go much beyond the end of the eighteenth century, it would probably be pointless to try to pin down those concerning current events. It is interesting to note, however, that he foresaw the emergence of a new Arab empire.

Anecdotes about Nostradamus, perhaps apocryphal, abound: While traveling in Italy, Nostradamus saw a young monk, who had only recently worked as a poor swineherd, walking toward him. Nostradamus knelt in the dust and said, "I kneel before your Holiness." The monk ultimately became Pope Sixtus V. . . . Nostradamus was once asked by a noble host to foretell the future of two pigs. "You will eat the black one," the seer said, "and a wolf will eat the white one." Though the nobleman ordered his cook to prepare the white pig for dinner, a wolf stole into the kitchen and devoured it. The cook substituted the black one, which the nobleman consumed, confident that he had thwarted the prophecy until the cook explained what had transpired. . . . Nearly fifty years after the death of Nostradamus, the authorities of Salon decided to remove his coffin to a place of greater importance in the church. When the casket was opened a small metal plate engraved with the date of his exhumation was found on the corpse's breastbone. Apparently Nostradamus had foreseen even this event.

Given the large number of predictions and their ambiguity, some of them were bound to be confirmed in some way. Nostradamus claimed that he could have given more exact dates and other details, were it not for fear of being accused of witchcraft. The controversy will probably never be resolved.

For additional information, see L. McCann, *Nostradamus— The Man Who Saw Through Time* (Creative Age, 1941) and C. A. Ward, *Oracles of Nostradamus* (Modern Library, 1940).

Emanuel Swedenborg

Emanuel Swedenborg (1688-1772) was a Swedish philosopher, scientist, mystic, prophet, and visionary. Through his claim of having attained communication with the dead and with higher planes of being, he had a strong influence on modern occultism, spiritualism, and psychology.

Swedenborg was born in Stockholm into a religious background. His father served as court chaplain, was a professor and dean at Uppsala University, and in 1702 became the bishop of Skara. The family was ennobled by Queen Ulrica Eleanora in 1719.

Swedenborg was graduated from the University of Uppsala in 1709 and embarked on a series of travels throughout Europe. In 1716 he was appointed assessor extraordinary in the Swedish College of Mines, a position he held for more than thirty years. Shortly thereafter he became a member of the Swedish Diet, where he was noted for fiscal reform, liquor legislation, and economic policies.

Although Swedenborg's early studies at Uppsala had been in mathematics and mining, his travels broadened his perspective. He began to master diverse languages—nine by the time of his death—developed an interest in philosophy, and

Emanuel Swedenborg, philosopher and visionary.

then branched out into several scientific fields. By 1743 he had written substantial treatises in psychology, physiology, neurobiology, cosmology, zoology, chemistry, physics, geology, astronomy, and mineralogy. In the 1880s, the Swedish Royal Academy of Sciences translated from the Latin his four-volume work *The Brain* and discovered that much of his work was well in advance of his time. He had developed a version of the modern neuron theory and recognized the functions of the pituitary gland 200 years before endocrinology became a field of study. His scholarly contributions included discoveries in metallurgy, algebra, geology, crystallography, and blood circulation. He also made practical contributions, including drafts for inventions of a flying machine, an airtight stove, a submarine, a mercury air pump, and a mechanical carriage.

When Swedenborg was fifty-seven years old, he began to have unusual experiences that involved him with religion until his death at the age of eighty-four. He became clairvoyant and had strange visions. In one instance he described a fire which occurred about 300 miles away. He also startlingly predicted the day of his own death. In 1743 he maintained that God had given him a mission to interpret the Bible from a spiritual viewpoint. In order to accomplish this, Swedenborg said, God had allowed him to witness the world of afterlife, where he saw the social organization of heaven, hell, and the realm where spirits go immediately upon death.

In his book *Heaven and Hell*, Swedenborg described the afterlife and its inhabitants in detail. He said there was no single ruler of hell called the devil, although the individual inhabitants of hell might have an influence on people. He stated that everything in the physical world corresponded with everything in the spiritual world. He also stated that after death people gravitate to the realm closest to their dominant inclination on earth—the good go to heaven, and the bad to hell. But no one is "sentenced, he merely moves toward the place with which he has the greatest affinity." Swedenborg also wrote that the Second Coming of Christ would not take place in physical form.

He saw his own mission as a partial fulfillment of the Second Coming. He believed through his teachings he would bring about the New Jerusalem or New Church. However, he never attempted to form his own sect and remained a Lutheran until his death. Nonetheless, a dozen years after his death the Church of the New Jerusalem—also called Swedenborgian—was founded. Today the church has about 100,000 members in many countries. The educational arm of the Swedenborgian movement, the Swedenborg Foundation, was established in 1849.

Swedenborg's work has inspired many influential people, including Honoré de Balzac, Abraham Lincoln, Ralph Waldo Emerson, Carl Jung, and Helen Keller, whose *My Religion* is a testimony to the man. Swedenborg's writings have been translated into thirty languages. Sweden honored his memory with burial in the national cathedral in Uppsala. Swedenborg's major books include *Apocalypse Explained, Apocalypse Revealed, Divine Love and Wisdom, Four Doctrines, True Christian Religion, Economy of the Animal Kingdom,* and *The Animal Kingdom.*

For more information, see James Hastings, *Encyclopedia of*

Religion and Ethics and these publications of the Swedenborg Foundation: *The Church of the New Jerusalem, Chart of Swedenborg's Life and Works,* and *Real Religion.*

STRANGE
OBJECTS

The Tunguska Explosion

On June 30, 1908, a huge explosion occurred in the basin of the Podkamennaya Tunguska River in central Siberia at 7:17 A.M. local time. Scientists are still debating the cause of the explosion.

According to eyewitness accounts collected by E. L. Krinov, a Soviet scientist who is the leading authority on the explosion, the following events occurred that morning. Over a huge area of central Siberia about 931 miles in diameter, ranging from the banks of the Yenisei River in the west to the inhabited points along the Vitim and Mukhtuia rivers in the east, witnesses saw an object fall in a cloudless sky. Krinov states that the object crossed the sky in a matter of a few seconds, moving from the southeast to the northwest. It was so blindingly bright it made even the sun appear dark. A thick trail of dust in the form of a gigantic column was seen along the path of the object. Witnesses at nearby points saw fire and a cloud of "smoke" over the location of the fall. According to David W. Hughes ("Tunguska Revisited," *Nature,* February 26, 1976), the explosion took the form of "a vertical column of fire and threw incandescent matter up to a height of 20 km." When the object disappeared, a deafening detonation was heard as far away as 1,000 kilometers from the place of the fall. Thunder, crackling, and rumbling followed. Ground tremors which shook buildings, broke windowpanes, and displaced household objects were felt over an area almost equal to that over which the fall of the light was observed. The concussion wave, as it spread from the place of the fall, threw many witnesses to the ground. The effect was especially strong at the Vanovera trading station, some thirty-seven miles from the site of the fall, where a person sitting on the porch of a house was thrown several meters. Just prior to this, he said, he felt heat radiating from the area of the fall. At a distance of some twenty-five miles to the southeast, a tent of Evenkians, nomadic reindeer herders of the region, was lifted into the air together with the people inside. The night following the explosion was unusually bright in European Russia, western Siberia, and the rest of Europe as well. Apparently, even as far south as the Caucasus, it was possible to read newspapers without artificial light at midnight. The following nights were also unusually bright.

In an area with a radius of eighteen to twenty-five miles

around the location of the fall, trees were uprooted and piled in concentric rings with their crowns pointing radially outward from the place of the fall. On an inspection nineteen years later, traces of fire were found over an area of eleven miles radius.

The explosion air wave, according to microbarograph measurements, traveled around the world twice. Seismographs around the world registered an earthquake. Instruments at Irkutsk registered magnetic disturbances of a kind that later would be associated with the atmospheric tests of nuclear weapons. Two weeks later the atmosphere in California was found to be less transparent than usual. This phenomenon was attributed to the addition of several million tons of dust by the object as it traveled to earth. This dust was responsible for the bright nights.

Recently Ari Ben-Menahem of the Adolpho Bloch Geophysical Observatory at Rehovot, Israel, using techniques developed to analyze nuclear weapons tests, analyzed the seismographic records of the explosion in order to reconstruct some of its features. He believes that the main explosion took place five miles above the ground. He has calculated the energy of the explosion to have been five (plus or minus one) times 10^{23} ergs—the equivalent of 12.5 (plus or minus 2.5) megatons of TNT, the size of a powerful thermonuclear explosion.

The most popular explanation for the explosion, put forth in the early 1930s by Fred Lawrence Whipple and I. S. Astapovich, is that it was the result of a small comet's striking the earth. A comet consists of a nucleus and a tail. According to Whipple's theory, the nucleus is made up of dust and rocks loosely connected by frozen water, methane, and ammonia. The tail consists of dust and gas. Whipple's theory states that the energy of the explosion was created when the comet was slowed down by the resistance of the earth's atmosphere. The brightness of the nights after the explosion would have been caused by the dust from the comet's tail. Small globules of magnetite and silicate, which could have been formed from the dust of the comet, have been found at the site. Whipple believes that the comet and the earth were traveling at opposite directions and collided at a velocity of thirty-seven miles per second. The diameter of the comet, according to Whipple's calculations, was about forty-four yards, too small to have been seen before the collision. It is calculated that the earth collides with a comet of this size on an average of once every 2,000 years.

Various other colorful explanations have been put forth, but none has any considerable support. In 1960 J. N. Hung, R. Palmer, and Sir William Penney proposed that nuclear fission, like that in an atomic bomb, caused the explosion. A mass of some fissionable material—like deuterium or tritium—which was traveling through space in a state just bordering on an explosive chain reaction, finally exploded when it entered the atmosphere. The authors of the theory, however, do not explain how the mass could have got into a state bordering on a nuclear chain reaction and have stayed in that state while it traveled through space.

In 1965 Clyde Cowan, C. R. Atluri, and W. F. Libby proposed that the explosion occurred when a large body of antimatter was annihilated in the atmosphere. Antimatter is a substance that is destroyed when it comes into contact with matter, which is also destroyed. Because matter and energy are equivalent, the destruction of both matter and antimatter is accompanied by the production of energy that would account for the explosion. There are some problems with this theory. First, no large body of antimatter has yet been detected. Secondly, if such a large body were to approach the atmosphere, it is expected that it would be annihilated as soon as it made its first contact with matter. The resulting explosion would occur too high above the ground to account for the Tunguska explosion.

In 1973 A. A. Jackson IV and Michael P. Ryan, Jr., proposed that a black hole (see Black Hole) shot through the earth, causing the explosion. According to this theory, the black hole would have exited in the mid-Atlantic. However, no severe shock or blast waves were recorded in that area.

In 1976, in their book *The Fire Came By* (Doubleday), John Baxter and Thomas Atkins speculated that the explosion was caused by the atomic drive of a disabled spaceship. As evidence they cite eyewitness accounts of a "cylindrical object" crossing the sky and of a change of direction, a maneuver, of the object just before the explosion.

Prehistoric Nuclear Reactor

A prehistoric nuclear reaction, caused by natural forces, occurred 1,700,000 years ago in the subtropical region of present-day Gabon.

In 1972 French scientists found evidence that natural forces had built a water-cooled nuclear reactor that had operated intermittently at Oklo, Gabon, in West Africa for as long as 1,000,000 years. The report was made by Dr. F. Perrin, former chairman of the Commissariat à l'Energie Atomique (CEA) (see *New Scientist,* November 9, 1972).

A nuclear chain reaction occurs when neutrons created by the breakup of uranium bombard other uranium atoms, thereby producing more neutrons. If there are insufficient "moderators" to gobble up some of the excess neutrons, an atomic explosion results. If there is an excess of moderators, the process dies out quickly.

The key evidence that made the French researchers adopt the natural reactor hypothesis was a puzzling reduction in a

Prehistoric natural nuclear reactions occurred in zones 1–6 in this uranium mine at Oklo, Gabon; part of zone 2 will be preserved.

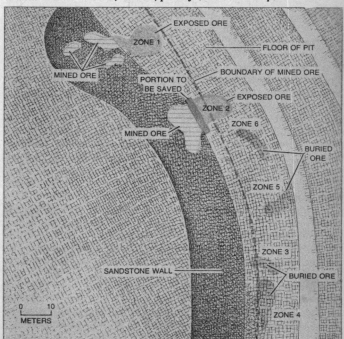

certain isotope of uranium. Normally, uranium contains 0.72 percent of the isotope U-235. The deposits at Oklo contain less of this isotope. On the basis of this discovery, the scientists concluded: "The only possible explanation . . . seems to be the occurrence of a spontaneous nuclear reaction thousands of millions of years ago."

Other indications found in the area supported the conclusion. Some of the material in the Oklo uranium deposits actually had a higher incidence of U-235 than is normal. Possibly, just as in man-made reactors, the chain reaction had produced some plutonium which had decayed back into uranium. This "new" uranium was "younger" and thus richer in U-235 than primordial uranium. An Oklo sample of uranium showed the presence of four rare elements—neodymium, samarium, europium, and cerium—with proportions of isotopes previously found only in man-made reactors.

Certain conditions theoretically must be present for the occurrence of an atomic chain reaction: The concentration of uranium must be high; a moderator and coolant are necessary; and the region must be relatively free of neutron-absorbing substances which could inhibit a chain reaction. Geological study of the Oklo region as it presumably existed in the Pre-cambrian era showed that these conditions had been satisfied. According to the official report, "nature had . . . painstakingly constructed her own heterogeneous, enriched uranium nuclear reactor. . . . The indications are that once ignition occurred the reaction continued until water permeating the layers of sandstone and uranium turned to steam. It then halted to allow cooling, only to break out again in another sector. Like some giant witch's cauldron the whole Oklo site simmered and spluttered for nigh a million years." The size of the reactor is estimated at about five meters in radius.

According to J. L. Lancelot and other researchers (*Earth and Planetary Science Letters,* Vol. 25, March 1975), the most plausible estimate of the age of the reactor is 1.78 billion years. The estimate was based on determination of the uranium-lead and rubidium-strontium ratios of the surrounding terrain. The figure is consistent with an estimate based on the total uranium content of the ore and the ratio between uranium 238 and uranium 235 isotopes.

The discovery of the Oklo reaction raised the question of whether it was a unique or widespread phenomenon. The answer has important economic implications because it bears on the world uranium supply. Lancelot and others believe that propitious conditions for the start of a nuclear reactor have existed elsewhere. However, the reactions could only have taken place in former geologic epochs (according to *New Scientist*, November 9, 1972) because, owing to continual radioactive decay, "no such fantastic combination of circumstances can ever occur on our planet again."

For additional information, see *The New York Times* (June 21, 1976, p. 16).

The Antikythera Mechanism

The Antikythera mechanism is a metal object, discovered in the wreck of a 2,000-year-old ship, which apparently contains gears and constitutes some sort of instrument or mechanism.

In 1900 a party of Greek sponge divers discovered the wreck of an ancient ship off the small island of Antikythera, which lies between Greece and Crete. Underwater archaeological expeditions dispatched to the area recovered some pottery, statues, and corroded items, which dated the wreck back approximately 2,000 years ago. In 1902 Valerios Stais, an archaeologist at the National Museum in Athens, examined some of the objects and came upon a metal object which became known as the Antikythera mechanism. Closer study revealed that the object was a box with gauges on the outside and a complex assembly of gears inside, including at least twenty gear wheels. All the surfaces of the device were covered with Greek inscriptions.

Before the discovery of the mechanism, no comparable object or device had ever been found or described. Heretofore established knowledge of Hellenistic technology had denied the possibility that such a device could have been constructed during the period.

On the basis of the amphoras, pottery, and objects found in the wreck, researchers are reasonably certain the wreck occurred in 65 B.C., plus or minus fifteen years. A study of the letters in the inscriptions shows that they stem from the first century B.C., certainly no later than the birth of Christ. This date is also consistent with the language used and the nature of astronomical references in the inscriptions. For example, the most extensive inscription is part of an astronomical calendar strikingly similar to one known to be written in 77 B.C.

Currently it is thought most likely that the device was an

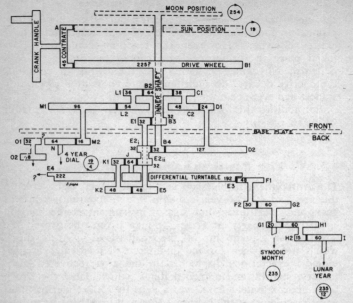

A diagram of the gear trains of the Antikythera mechanism. Numbers refer to number of teeth in each gear wheel, while alphanumerics (e.g., B2) merely identify each wheel.

astronomical computer which mechanized cyclic relations of the solar system and the stars. It is possible that it was set in a statue and used as an exhibition piece. It may have been actuated by waterpower. The greater part of the restoration and reconstruction work that led to this conclusion has been conducted by Derek J. de Solla Price of Yale University (see *Scientific American*, April 1974).

Starting in the early 1950s, Price began restoration of the device, which was covered with layers of encrustation and badly corroded. The next step was a translation of the inscriptions, most of which are illegible. The sun is mentioned several times, Venus once, and the ecliptic is named. One inscription, "76 years, 19 years," refers to the so-called Calippic cycle of 76 years and the Metonic cycle of four times 19 years (235 lunar months). The following line includes the number 223—a reference to the eclipse cycle of 223 lunar months.

On the basis of an X ray and a gamma ray study of the

fragments, done in 1972, Price established many details of the construction and operation of the device. It was apparently constructed with a central axle. When the axle turned, a system of gear trains and shafts was activated, causing pointers to move at various speeds around a set of dials. The dials are difficult to read owing to corrosion. The front one, however, clearly shows the motion of the sun in the zodiac and the risings and settings of important stars and constellations. Price believes that the back dials, which are more complex and less legible, were connected with planets and lunar phenomena. Price states that the front dial is "the only known extensive specimen from antiquity of a scientifically graduated instrument." Price thinks that the device was probably enclosed in a box approximately 12 by 6 by 3 inches and had hinged panels bearing inscriptions on the large faces. There were probably at least thirty gears inside, all made of bronze and probably cut from a single sheet of metal. The power, he says, was transmitted to a large gear that had four spokes mortised into the rim, soldered and fixed in place by rivets. The most "spectacular mechanical feature of the Antikythera mechanism," according to Price, is a differential turntable. Such a mechanism was not encountered again until sixteenth-century Europe.

On the basis of his research, Price has concluded that contrary to previous opinion, a tradition of high technology did indeed exist in Greece around the time of Christ. Previously it was accepted that the Greeks were familiar with the principle of gears but had only relatively crude geared devices. *Scientific American* (April 1974) agreed with Price that discovery of the mechanism might call for a revision of existing estimates of the state of technology in the Hellenistic period.

M. Clagett, author of *Greek Science in Antiquity* (Abelard-Schuman, 1955), states that there was a mutually complementary relationship between the state of Greek astronomy and the sophistication of extant instruments. To support this, he cites Hipparchus, "the greatest observational astronomer in antiquity," who lived in the second century B.C. and achieved success using improved instruments, such as the diopter—a sighting instrument with a gear mechanism.

For additional information, see Derek de Solla Price, *Gears from the Greeks* (Science History Publications, 1975).

The First Magnetic Compass

A hematite bar found in Mexico is believed to be the first magnetic compass.

Found at an archaeological site at San Lorenzo in the state of Veracruz, the bar was used as a compass before 1000 B.C., according to John B. Carlson, in an article in *Science* (September 5, 1975). Previously, the earliest date given for the discovery of the magnetic compass was between the second century B.C. and the first century A.D. in China.

Objects found at the site were radiocarbon-dated from the period between 1400 B.C. and 1000 B.C. Stylistically, they belong to the Early Formative Olmec culture, which was characterized by the building of ceremonial centers, huge basalt heads, and the use of highly polished ore to make various objects.

The magnetic hematite bar is a fragment of a larger piece. It was broken off in ancient times. The bar is rectangular, with a trapezoidal cross section, and is 34 by 9 by 4 millimeters. It is carefully shaped and highly polished. One of the large sides has a carefully made groove, which runs lengthwise down its central axis.

When Carlson tried to use the bar as a compass, he found that it consistently pointed, within half a degree, to 35.5 degrees west of magnetic north. Carlson conducted the experiment with two methods, both of which he believes could have been used by the Olmecs. In the first method he filled a bowl with water and placed the bar on a piece of cork floating in the water; in the second he let the bar float in a bowl of mercury. Hematite will float in mercury, and since the ancient Maya had liquid mercury, Carlson concluded that the Olmecs may have had it as well.

The Turin Shroud

The Turin shroud is a linen cloth purported to be the burial shroud of Christ.

Since 1578 the Turin shroud has been kept in a silver chest on the altar of the Royal Chapel which adjoins the Cathedral of Turin in Italy. In 1452 the shroud came into the possession of the Savoy family, who entrusted its safekeeping to the archbishop of Turin. The shroud first appeared in 1353 in

The facial portion of the Turin shroud, the purported burial cloth of Jesus.

Lirey, France, in the possession of Geoffrey I de Charny, who maintained that the cloth was the "true Shroud of the Lord." Its earlier history cannot be traced. However, people have put forth claims to have possessed the shroud of Christ since as early as A.D. 120.

Like many other purported shrouds of Christ, the Turin shroud has an image on it. Believers state that it is the image of Christ's body which was imprinted on the cloth while the body was in the tomb.

It is generally conceded that images on purported shrouds

of Christ have been painted on the cloths. Those who advocate that this is also the case with the Turin shroud have some historical evidence in their favor. In 1389 Pierre D'Arcis, the bishop of Troyes in France, stated that the image had been painted by an artist who had confessed it to the previous bishop, Henri de Poitiers. Peter Rinaldi, a believer in the authenticity of the Turin shroud, in *It Is the Lord* (Warner, 1973), rejects the testimony of Pierre D'Arcis. He states that the nature of the image is such that it could not have been painted.

Rinaldi cites several reasons for his conviction. He points out that when the shroud was photographed for the first time in 1898, it was discovered that a print of the negative gives a much more vivid image of a man than can be seen on the shroud itself or on an ordinary positive photograph of the shroud. This, Rinaldi argues, shows that the image on the shroud is a negative image—i.e., one in which the brightness values of the body are reversed. Rinaldi believes that it would be difficult for a painter to paint a negative image which would have necessitated a careful altering of all the shadings. Furthermore, Rinaldi states that there are no examples extant of negative images made by fourteenth-century artists.

Advocates of the authenticity of the Turin shroud propose that the negative image on the linen cloth was produced by some kind of reaction between the body chemicals and the linen cloth which had been rubbed with spices, such as aloe, in keeping with the burial customs of the times. Attempts have been made to produce a comparable image by this process, but as even Rinaldi admits, they have not been successful.

In 1973 Michele Cardinal Pellegrino, the archbishop of Turin, announced that the shroud would be subjected to new scientific tests. Such tests—chromotography, for one—can determine the age and composition of the material without destroying any more than a tiny sample of the material. Thus far the results of the tests have not been announced.

However, even if such tests proved that the body image was created by natural processes, it would still be necessary to prove that the body was that of Christ. It does not seem likely that conclusive proof could be found given the fact that the history of the shroud cannot be traced farther back than 1353.

Pyramids

Pyramids are monumental stone structures with a rectangular base and four flat triangular sides which rise to a point. The largest and most famous pyramids are found in Egypt and Mexico.

The only notable Egyptian pyramids, those for which pyramids are famous, were built in a short period (about 2800 B.C. to 2500 B.C.) early in Egyptian history. Of the thirty-five major Egyptian pyramids, almost all are found at the edge of the plateau of the Libyan Desert, west of the Nile, stretching from the apex of the delta south to Faiyum. The pyramids are located in groups. The most famous group, that at Giza, includes the pyramids of Khufu and Khafre and of their successor Menkure. The largest group, that at Saqqara, consists of twelve pyramids, including two of the earliest, the step pyramids built by Zoser and Hadjefa. Five pyramids are found at both Abusir and Dahshur and others at Zawiyet el Aryan, Abu Roash, Lisht, Illahun, and Howara.

The first pyramidlike structure, Zoser's step pyramid, which was the ancestor of the true pyramids, was begun during the Third Dynasty about 2800 B.C. The first attempt to build a true pyramid, at Meidum, began soon after, or perhaps during, the construction of Zoser's step pyramid. However, it was never completed because its outer casing stones began to slip off during construction. When this happened, the pyramid at Dahshur was already under construction. The cautious builders reduced its angle of elevation halfway to the top in order to prevent a repetition of the Meidum disaster. Consequently, the pyramid at Dahshur is sometimes called the Bent Pyramid. The lesson learned in the construction of these two pyramids paved the way for the perfection of the pyramids at Giza.

The three giant pyramids of Giza, built between 2700 B.C. and 2600 B.C. in the Fourth Dynasty were the last of the great pyramids. The pyramid of Khufu (called Cheops by the Greeks) at Giza is called the Great Pyramid. It is the largest of the three pyramids at Giza and, with the exception of the partly ruined structure at Cholula, Mexico, the largest pyramid in the world. And with the exception of the Great Wall of China, it was the largest ancient structure. The base covers 230 square meters, and it is about 150 meters high. The

The Great Pyramid at Giza with the Sphinx in the foreground.

pyramid is constructed of 6,500,000 tons of limestone. It contains 2,300,000 blocks that weigh approximately 2½ tons apiece. It is so oriented that each of its four sides faces one of the cardinal points. Its angle of elevation is approximately fifty-two degrees. The ratio of its height to the circumference of its base is equal to one-half pi—to an accuracy of better than 1 in 1,000.

While the pyramids are almost completely solid rock, they do have small passageways bored into their north sides. These passageways lead to small chambers in the solid rock that underlies the building site. It is believed that the pharaohs were buried in these chambers, but the point is debated. The chambers were looted within a few centuries of the construction of the pyramids.

Not only have they been looted, but the pyramids have been used as sources of stone ever since they were built. Fortunately, however, the losses have not been great in proportion to the total amount of stone in the pyramids. In AD 1215 the eccentric Caliph Malek al Aziz Othman ordered all the pyramids taken down. He assembled a huge work force which started to disassemble the smallest of the Giza pyramids. After eight months of intensive effort he gave up in frustration, having made only the slightest impression on the appearance of the pyramids.

Throughout history and especially during the Middle Ages and the Renaissance, the Great Pyramid was associated with many cults, primarily in the Rosicrucian and other occult traditions. The pyramids have been variously interpreted as displays of royal power, vaults and archives, models of Noah's Ark, astronomical observatories, phallic symbols, Masonic halls, and nuclear reactors. However, it was not until 1859 that a modern cult of pyramidology was born (see Martin Gardner, *Fads and Fallacies,* Dover, 1957). On the basis of the measurements of Colonel Howard Vyse, who had blasted his way into the Khufu and Menkure pyramids in the 1830s, John Taylor published *The Great Pyramid: Why Was It Built and Who Built It?* He maintained that Noah, under divine guidance, had built the pyramid. Although Taylor himself had never visited the pyramid, he found in its structure a myriad of mathematical truths that he argued surpassed the knowledge of ancient Egypt. He cited the occurrence of pi in the structure and stated that the basic measuring unit employed had been the biblical "cubit" used by Noah in the construction of the ark, by Abraham in the building of the tabernacle, and by Solomon in his temples. He supported these purported truths with scores of passages from the Bible.

Taylor's ideas were boosted by Charles Piazzi Smyth, the astronomer royal of Scotland, who became convinced there were greater truths to be found in the pyramid than Taylor suspected. His book *Our Inheritance in the Great Pyramid*, first published in 1864, became a great popular success, comparable to Donnelly's book on Atlantis (see Atlantis). After its publication, he spent four years at the pyramid measuring with specially made, extremely accurate instruments. Smyth claimed among other things (see L. Sprague de Camp and Catherine C. de Camp, *Citadels of Mystery*, Ballantine, 1973) that the sides of the Great Pyramid were perfect equilateral triangles and the perimeter of the base was 36,524 "pyramid inches," or 100 times the number of inches that there are days in the year. This pyramid inch was 1/25 of the width of a casing stone, none other than the biblical cubit. Smyth also claimed that the height of the pyramid was 1/270,000 of the circumference of the earth and one-billionth of the distance to the sun. Going even further, Smyth elaborated on a theory of Robert Menzies, another Scotsman, that the measurements of the internal passageways symbolized great events in the outline of history, including the coming of a great miracle in 1881.

Both Gardner and the De Camps point out that given enough measurements, anyone can come up with apparently cosmic results. The De Camps argue that Smyth's "pyramid inch" was imaginary because the original height and mass of the pyramid are not known owing to its state of dilapidation.

Therefore, no one can state for certain what ratios these measurements bear to the size of the earth or of the solar system. Nevertheless, despite such obvious facts and the failure of Smyth's prediction, the cult of pyramidology has continued. Recently great powers have been attributed to pyramids; they include rejuvenation, healing, purification of water, enrichment of foods, sharpening of razor blades (see Pyramid Power), improvement of sex life, and so on (see Bill Schul and Ed Pettit, *The Secret Power of Pyramids*, Fawcett, 1975).

According to the De Camps, "the pyramids are wonderful enough without bedizening them with such occult absurdities." Kurt Mendelssohn, in *The Riddle of the Pyramids* (Praeger, 1975), states that pyramid building was a milestone in human history because it was the first application of large-scale technology and involved the use of tools and methods already known but whose potentialities had not been previously recognized. The Egyptians also had unlimited manpower and infinite patience.

According to the De Camps, most of the stone used was quarried from local outcrops and could have been dragged directly to the site on sleds. The lavish use of levers, ropes, and ramps would have facilitated the movement of the stones onto the sleds. If, as a painting on the tomb of Lord Dehutihotep indicates, 172 men were strong enough to move a sixty-ton statue, about 8 men could have dragged a two-and-a-half-ton pyramid block across level ground. The sides of the base could have been marked off into a square by the use of cords. The problem of placing the blocks on top of each other could have been easily solved by raising a mound of earth on each side of the pyramid with ramps for dragging up the stones. When the pyramid had been completed and the earth mounds removed, the workmen could have trimmed away any irregularities remaining in the stone facing.

Mendelssohn explains how two of the key problems—manpower and organization—involved in the construction of the pyramids were resolved. The pyramids did not mark a high point in Egyptian arts and sciences. In fact, as they were perfected, the general level of Egyptian culture declined. The pyramids, which were uniform and standardized, did not require the art of specialists that had been involved in the construction of temples and other buildings. However, the pyramids were a great administrative success. Because specialists were not needed, the building could be controlled by bureaucrats. The age of pyramids was a time when various regional groups were united under a centralized government. The building of the pyramids was made possible by this centralization and, simultaneously, was a great force in its development and preservation.

The work, Mendelssohn maintains, was not done by slaves, as many have speculated. During three months of each year the Nile flooded the fields of the Nile Valley, and no agricultural work could be done. Many people were left idle, and before the age of the pyramids, local groups formed raiding parties and attacked each other. The building of the pyramids gave these people something constructive to do during the flood season. Workers came from every village in Egypt during the flood season. They were organized into teams, each of which had a high sense of team spirit. Their names, such as Vigorous Gang and Enduring Gang are inscribed on the stones of the pyramids. The workers must have sensed a common identification with a project that involved all Egypt, not just a region.

Facilities were set up to house, feed, and take care of the other needs of the workers. This would have been done by the central bureaucracy—which probably developed into a powerful "pyramid establishment"—that had a vested interest in building more and more pyramids. The pyramids needed fewer workers as they neared completion. It would have been too costly to disband the work force as one pyramid was finished and to reorganize it when the next pyramid was to be built. Consequently more than one pyramid was under construction at the same time. Pyramid building had its own momentum and strengthened the central government of Egypt. In a sense, it was its own purpose—nothing else in Egypt was so expensive or involved so many people, estimated at 150,000 seasonal workers who returned each year. For this reason, Mendelssohn believes, speculation about the religious significance of the pyramids is misleading because the Egyptians could have found cheaper ways to satisfy their religious needs.

Perhaps, the only "mystifying secret" of the pyramids that cannot be easily explained is the presence of one-half pi in the ratio of the height of the Great Pyramid to its base circumference. Although many have speculated that this indicates the ancient Egyptians knew the true value of pi, other explanations are possible. It may have been a by-product of construction. Gardner notes that if Herodotus was correct in stating that the pyramid was built so that the area of each face would be equal to the area of a square whose side is equal to the height of the pyramid, then the ratio of height to twice the base would, surprisingly enough, automatically equal the accurate value of pi. Another explanation, offered by Mendelssohn, states that the Egyptians may have used a drum whose diameter was the basic unit of length. If they followed a formula that for every four units of height the base must be the length covered in one roll of the drum, then the ratio of the height to the base circumference could be one-half pi. All the builder would have had to know was the ratio of four to one.

Pyramid Power

Pyramid power is the faddish name for a claim that certain precise pyramid shapes will sharpen razor blades and dehydrate food placed inside them.

The claim was recently promoted by Sheila Ostrander and Lynn Shroeder in *Psychic Discoveries Behind the Iron Curtain* (Prentice-Hall, 1970; Bantam, 1971). They describe experiments by a Czechoslovakian radio engineer, Karel Drbal, who prescribes a pyramid with a base-to-height ratio of 1.5708, or one-half pi, the constant ratio of the diameter to the circumference of a circle. A razor blade or a food item placed on a platform at one-third the height of the pyramid will be affected within two weeks. Drbal maintains that the pyramid must precisely face magnetic north. Other advocates of pyramid power say the pyramid should be oriented on true north. Drbal also maintains that the razor blades must face east-west if the pyramid is to work. Some advocates say much better results are obtained if the material to be worked on is placed as close to the top of the pyramid as possible.

Advocates of pyramid power emphasize the importance of precise measurement and orientation. Yet the inherent inaccuracy of their measurement and construction methods and their disagreement about orientation, combined with their universal claim of positive results, make it unlikely that either their theses or their claims are valid.

The base/height ratio of the Great Pyramid of Khufu serves as a model for advocates of pyramid power. The ratio in the Great Pyramid is within 0.052 percent of 1.5708; but most of the pyramids now marketed vary considerably from this precision, and most homemade cardboard pyramids will vary from the ideal by as much as 5 percent.

Peter Tompkins, in *Secrets of the Great Pyramids* (Harper & Row, 1971), argues that the Great Pyramid was really constructed to meet an ideal of one-half *phi* (0.809017) times the base length equals the slant height. The Great Pyramid varies 0.15 percent from that ideal. An ideal pyramid using both the *pi* and *phi* ratios is mathematically impossible.

Most razor blade experiments used to demonstrate the power of pyramids have relied on subjective tests of dullness. In experiments by Dale Simmons, a Toronto engineer, photomicrographs of the blades before and after the experiments showed no appreciable improvement in the quality of the edges of three dulled blades—one left in the open air and two placed in different pyramids. All three blades were alike, in that areas of wear which had been jagged were slightly rounded off owing to minute erosion and the normal tendency of many metals to return to a state of equilibrium after undergoing the stress and tension of use.

Another fault of most pyramid experiments is that while an object is often left outside a pyramid as a control, an object is seldom placed in a different-shaped container. Simmons ran two tests of flower dehydration using two pyramids and a cube of similar volume. After seven days the flowers enclosed in the pyramids and the cube were in a similar condition compared to the flowers left in the open air.

These and other experiments, along with a discussion of pyramid measurements, are reported in *New Horizons,* Vol. 1, No. 2, available at the New Horizons Research Foundation, 10 North Sherbourne Street, Toronto, Ontario, Canada.

The Baghdad Battery

The Baghdad battery is an artifact discovered near Baghdad, reportedly among the ruins of a 2,000-year-old village, that resembles a modern chemical battery cell used to produce electricity.

In 1936 William Koenig, a German amateur archaeologist living in Iraq, was shown an object that strongly resembled a battery cell. He was told that the object had recently been unearthed at Khujut Rabu'a, the site of an ancient village near Baghdad.

The object consisted of an earthenware vase, in which was cemented a metal cylinder about four inches high. The cylinder was made of a sheet of copper soldered together with an alloy of 60 percent tin, similar to the solder in use today. A copper disk, insulated with asphaltum, was attached to the bottom of the cylinder. The top was closed by an asphaltum stopper, through which projected an iron rod, which had been eroded in a way that was consistent with its possible use as an electrode.

An American engineer, Willard F. M. Gray, learning of this find, constructed a working model of the cell in 1940. He filled the model with copper sulfate as an electrolyte and found that it did indeed produce current. It is not known what electrolyte could have been used in the original model, but acetic or citric acid would have been available.

Koenig learned that similar objects, possibly deriving from Ctesiphon, another ancient site near Baghdad, were in the possession of the Berlin Museum. They consisted of three large vases, one containing ten copper cylinders, another containing ten metal rods, and the last containing asphaltum stoppers.

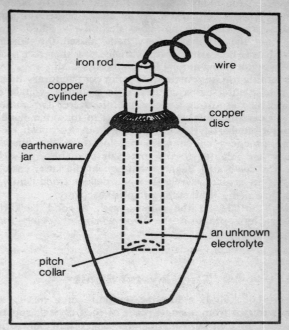

An artist's conception of the interior of the Baghdad battery.

While Ctesiphon continued to be inhabited until the eighth century A.D., the village at Khujut Rabu'a is believed to have flourished in the Parthian period, which ended during the third century A.D.

Koenig speculated that the cells had been used in a process of electroplating gold onto ornamental vessels. He claimed that evidence of electroplating was present on copper vases dating back to the year 2500 B.C. which had been unearthed in Iraq. When these vases were lightly tapped, a thin bluish patina separated from the surface; this would be consonant with an electroplated layer of gold.

It is altogether possible that the technology needed to manufacture and use a cell producing direct current could have existed in the Near East 2,000 years ago, given the long history of advances in metallurgy and chemistry that preceded the period.

However, too many details of the story remain obscure to permit a positive conclusion. As far as can be determined, the artifacts involved have not been definitively dated. Koenig wrote that the original battery had "passed through many hands" before he learned of its existence. It is therefore possible that it was not found among Parthian ruins at all.

According to Gray, metalworkers in contemporary Baghdad use metal-plating baths connected to primitive voltaic cells. Perhaps they are using a technique discovered two millennia ago and carefully guarded ever since. On the other hand, the technique could have been derived from European electroplating practices which were developed in the nineteenth century and adapted to the materials available in the Near East. The celebrated Baghdad battery, in the latter case, may be a recent artifact, carelessly discarded or fraudulently presented to Koenig as an archaeological discovery.

Gray's article on the subject with a good background bibliography appeared in the *Electrochemical Society Journal* of September 1963.

The Crystal Skull

The crystal skull is a life-size sculpture of a human skull, finely wrought from a single piece of rock crystal, apparently unearthed in Central America. Its age, origin, and original function are unknown.

The skull was allegedly discovered in 1927 by Anna Mitchell-Hedges, the adopted daughter of the British explorer and adventurer Frederick A. Mitchell-Hedges. Though the discovery was made at the ruined Mayan city Lubaantun, in Belize (then British Honduras), it is superior in technique to similar Indian artifacts, a fact that immediately raised questions about its origins.

Made of clear, transparent quartz with beautiful internal veins and bubbles, the skull was apparently carved without metal age tools, for no scratches or tool marks were observed under a microscope. The surface is smoothly polished, and may have been worked by rubbing down the original quartz block with sand. If so, it would have taken as much as 150 years of constant effort by several generations of artisans to complete the work.

The lower jaw is separate and movable, and the zygomatic arches (leading back from the eye sockets to the bottom of

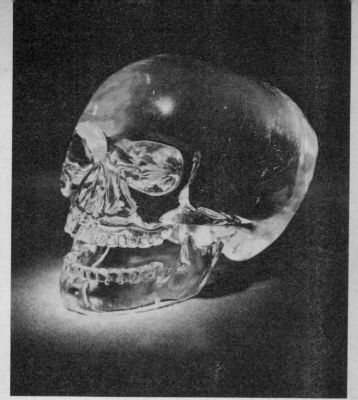

The crystal skull, unearthed in Mayan ruins and credited with occult powers.

the skull) have been hollowed out and serve to channel light beams, making the sockets flicker with light. A prism is carved into the base of the skull. The entire object is about five inches high, seven inches long, and five inches wide, and it weighs eleven pounds seven ounces. Various anatomical features suggest that the skull was modeled from a woman.

Skulls of clay, wood, bone, and shell were in use in all the Indian civilizations of the Americas as ritual objects connected with beliefs about death and rebirth. However, the Mitchell-Hedges skull is the only life-size articulated crystal skull, and the overall workmanship and attention to realistic detail are far superior to that of the other extant crystal skulls.

Ever since the skull's discovery, various supernatural

phenomena have been attributed to it by its discoverer and by others who have been in contact with it. Miss Mitchell-Hedges claimed that the 300 Indians who were working on the dig with her fell to their knees and kissed the ground when the object was uncovered and that they prayed and wept for two weeks thereafter.

Frank Dorland, an art restorer who conducted various physical experiments with the skull for six years, claimed that a halo or aura once surrounded it for several minutes; that high-pitched, silvery, bell-like sounds would at times fill his house, where the skull was kept; that strange veils, lights, and images of skulls, faces, mountains, and other objects would appear inside the skull at times, while at other times it would become totally transparent; and that a characteristic odor was sometimes emitted. Both he, Mitchell-Hedges, and other observers attributed to the skull the power to affect people's moods and thoughts.

The problem of the skull's origin is made difficult by the impossibility of dating it by current methods. There is, however, little reason to doubt that it was of Central American Indian manufacture, assuming the honesty of the Mitchell-Hedges family. Skulls were a common artistic motif of the region. The center of the Aztec calendar was a featureless face, skulls of victims of Aztec human sacrifice were sometimes encrusted with turquoise and obsidian, and the Mixtecs used the skull motif in their goldwork. Since the skull was uncovered in what appears to be a temple complex, it may well have been used in religious rituals.

As for the occult properties, they were not in evidence during the year the skull was on exhibit at the Museum of the American Indian in New York City in the early 1970s. However, as it revolved on its pedestal in the museum, it did produce brilliant visual effects.

For more information, see R. Garvin, *The Crystal Skull* (Doubleday, 1973) and J. Soustelle, *Daily Life of the Aztec* (Macmillan, 1961).

The Piri Reis Map

The Piri Reis map is a sixteenth-century map of the world which shows South America and Africa in correct relative longitude, purportedly a remarkable feat for a map of such antiquity.

The map, which dates from 1513, was discovered in 1929 in the Topkapi Palace in Istanbul, Turkey, when the palace's former harem section was under renovation. The map was signed by Piri Ibn Haji Memmed, a Turkish admiral (*reis* means admiral).

Piri was probably of Greek origin. In 1523 he presented an atlas of the Aegean and Mediterranean to Suleiman the Magnificent; parts of this atlas are in the Berlin Museum. He was beheaded in 1554 or 1555 for having accepted a bribe to lift the siege of Gibraltar.

The Piri Reis map is drawn on gazelle hide and has several inscriptions. One inscription reads: " . . . it is reported thus that a Genoese infidel, his name was Colombo, he it was who discovered these places. For instance, a book fell into the hands of said Colombo, and he found it said in this book that at the end of the Western sea . . . there were coasts and islands and all kinds of metal and also precious stones. . . . " This reference to Columbus attracted immediate attention.

Besides the facts that the map was one of the earliest known of America and that it showed South America and Africa in correct relative longitude, it had other remarkable features. An inscription by Piri Reis states that he had used about twenty sources, including some from the time of Alexander the Great. Some believed that the map also rendered the coast of Antarctica with extreme accuracy. The United States government took great interest and asked the Turkish government to conduct a search for other possible maps by Piri Reis and for the "lost map of Columbus," but no further material was found.

Since its discovery the Piri Reis map has spurred considerable, often fanciful, speculation on its significance.

Captain Arlington H. Mallary, an expert on old maps, was one of the first to conclude that the map showed regions in Queen Maud Land in Antarctica which are now concealed under ice. An unknown source at the U.S. Air Force Base at Westover, Massachusetts, is reported to have stated that

The map of Piri Reis.

details showing the contours of Antarctica agree "with the results of the seismic profile made across the top of the ice-cap by the Swedish-British-Norwegian Antarctic Expedition of 1949. This indicates that the coastline had been mapped before it was covered by the ice-cap. The ice-cap in this region is now about a mile thick."

C. H. Hapgood, archaeologist, science historian, cartographer, and professor at Keene State College in New Hampshire, proposed in his book *Maps of the Ancient Sea Kings* (Chilton, 1966) that the Piri Reis map was derived from prototypes of pre-Hellenic times, that it is based on sophisticated knowledge of spherical trigonometry, and that it displayed exact knowledge of coastal features throughout most of the world. The prototypes, Hapgood postulated, were composite maps made by Greek geographers of the school of Alexandria. These, he stated, were more accurate than medieval maps and were "evidence of a decline of science from remote antiquity to classical times." John K. Wright, former director of the American Geographical Society, who wrote the introduction to Hapgood's book, admitted that "It ain't necessarily *not* so."

R. Charroux, in *One Hundred Thousand Years of Man's Unknown History* (Berkley, 1963), concludes that the map shows Antarctic mountain ranges that were not described until 1952 and gives their exact altitudes.

Louis Pauwels and Jacques Bergier, in *The Morning of the Magicians* (Avon, 1960), note what they consider the remarkable features of the map and suggest it may have been traced from observations made on board a flying machine.

However, L. S. Henwood, an astronomer and amateur historian in Toronto, Ontario, believes that there is no need to attribute the map to aerial observation by spacemen or to ancient sea kings, as Hapgood does (see "An Explanation of the Piri Reis Map," *New Horizons,* July 1974). Henwood states that it is known that the map contains nothing that is not explicable in terms of the geographical knowledge available in 1513 and that its peculiarities are compatible with the conventions and practices of mapmakers of the time. He also maintains that there is no solid evidence Piri Reis used extremely ancient and accurate maps or that the map shows a part of the Antarctic coastline. Henwood bases his argument on a close analysis of the map in relation to the history of European and Arab mapmaking. In style, he notes, it corresponds very well with old sea charts or portolans, of which the earliest known date to about A.D. 1280. He argues that the coast purported by many to be part of Antarctica is a bad match for Antarctica but reasonably close to that of South America. As far as Hapgood's assertion that the map shows sophisticated knowledge of spherical trigonometry, Henwood indicates maps accompanying Claudius Ptolemy's *Geographics* (A.D. 160) which show a spherical earth, had been preserved by the Muslims through the Dark Ages and were available in 1513. He also asserts that the notion that high-altitude photography would be necessary for maps of high accuracy is "ridiculous." He points out that nineteenth-century maps, drawn before photography of any kind was in practical use, were accurate and that high-altitude photography "has generally confirmed the shapes and dimensions established by traditional methods of surveying, which are principally exercises in applied trigonometry." He concludes that Piri Reis, in fact, used the charts of contemporary sea captains, who, because their lives often depended on their accuracy, "possessed extremely sophisticated maps."

Fibonacci Numbers

Fibonacci numbers are a mathematical sequence, the terms and ratios of which correspond to a surprising variety of natural and artistic phenomena.

The sequence was named for its thirteenth-century discoverer, Leonardo of Pisa, called Fibonacci. In one section of his celebrated treatise *Liber Abaci,* Fibonacci posited a mathematical problem: If a pair of rabbits is isolated, "how many rabbits will be born in the course of one year, it being assumed that every month a pair of rabbits produces another pair, and that rabbits begin to bear young two months after their own birth?"

In arriving at the solution, we may prepare three lists. One records the total number of rabbit pairs at the end of each month, another records the number of fertile pairs, and a third records the number of immature pairs. The three lists turn out to be identical (except that the list of immature pairs starts with 0, and the list of total pairs lacks the first number in the sequence, 1). The list of total pairs for each month reads, 1, 2, 3, 5, 8, 13, 21, 34, 55, 89, 144, 233, and 377. The last figure in the list gives the solution to the problem—376 pairs will be born over twelve months (we must subtract the first pair, which were already born).

The full Fibonacci sequence is derived from the list of mature pairs: 1, 1, 2, 3, 5, 8, 13, 21, etc. This sequence of numbers has the mathematical property that each term (starting with the second) equals the sum of the previous two terms. Using this formula, we can extend the sequence to infinity.

The sequence has another interesting mathematical property. This can be seen by comparing each term with the previous term as a ratio. Starting with the first two terms, the ratio is 1–1, or simply 1. The second ratio is 2–1, or 2. The third ratio is 3–2, or 1.5; the fourth is 5–3, or about 1.67; the fifth is 8–5, or 1.6. The next few ratios are 1.625, about 1.615, about 1.619, about 1.618.

It was discovered in the eighteenth century that these

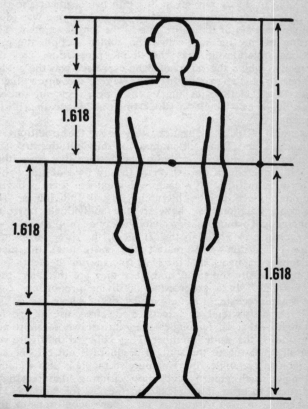

The modular human body, devised by the architect Le Corbusier, divides the body at neck, navel, and knee into golden sections.

ratios converge on an irrational number called phi, the first terms of which are 1.618034. (More precisely, phi is ½ the square root of 5, plus ½.) This means that as we go higher in the Fibonacci sequence, each number is about 1.618034 times as large as the preceding number.

This very number, phi, had already played an important role in Western civilization. It was known as the golden number, and it expressed a ratio which the ancient Greeks called the divine proportion.

The Greek geometers, using straight edges and compasses, were able to divide any given line into two segments, so that the ratio of the longer segment to the shorter one was identical to the ratio of the entire line to the longer segment. The division of the line was called the golden section, the proportional relationship was the divine proportion, and the number in which the ratio could be expressed was the golden number or golden mean. In other words, the entire line is about 1.618034 times as long as the longer segment, and the longer segment is about 1.618034 times as long as the shorter segment.

Classical Greek civilization, especially the traditions of Pythagoras and Plato, attempted to unify all the arts and sciences according to harmonic relationships that were, they thought, inherent in the universe. In any field of study—for example, human society—each individual was seen as having a unique place in the hierarchy of all individuals. The hierarchal relationships between the individuals mirrored mathematical principles, especially the divine proportion.

According to Plato, in the *Timaeus*, the three terms in a divine proportion—the greatest (the entire line), the mean (the longer segment), and the least (the shorter segment)—are "all by necessity the same, and since they are the same, they are but one." In a progression of divine proportions each part is a microcosm, or minute model, of the whole.

Greek artists and architects made free use of golden rectangles—that is, rectangles the ratio of whose short and long sides is the golden number. They believed the figure was naturally pleasing to the soul. If a square is cut off one end of a golden rectangle, the remaining rectangle is also a golden rectangle. Such golden rectangles within golden rectangles were used to draw floor plans and facades for temples. The Parthenon, on the Acropolis in Athens, conforms to this formula.

Greek vases and figure sculptures were also constructed

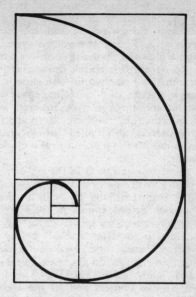

A golden spiral derived from a series of diminishing golden rectangles.

according to the divine proportion. For example, the navel on a statue would divide a body's height into two golden segments. Then the upper segment would be divided at the neck into two more such segments. Finally, the eyes would similarly divide the head.

Since the Renaissance the European fine arts tradition has also made frequent, deliberate use of the divine proportion in the shapes of canvases, the dimensions of figures, and other details. Composers have also used the divine proportion in their musical scores. In this case, time replaces space as the dimension being divided. As far as is known, the musical use of the divine proportion was nondeliberate until the twentieth century. This lends support to the belief that the proportion is naturally pleasing.

In the nineteenth century it was found that a high proportion of thousands of common rectangular objects, such as playing cards, windows, book covers, and writing pads, approximated golden rectangles. Since that time commercial designers have deliberately made use of golden dimensions in designing packages, store windows, and advertising.

A related geometric figure, the golden spiral, is another medium through which the divine proportion may be seen in many objects. To obtain this spiral, draw a series of golden rectangles of diminishing size within one another. This drawing will also show a series of diminishing squares. Now draw a series of circular arcs through these squares, with the sides of the squares as radii. The resulting curve approximates the golden spiral, which is also called the logarithmic spiral. (The precise equation for the golden spiral includes the golden number as a factor.)

The golden spiral can be found in the art of many cultures and in many places in the natural world. Several varieties of common sea life, from plankton to snails to the chambered nautilus, demonstrate golden spirals in their growth patterns or shells. The undersides of ocean waves form golden spirals, leading shipbuilders to construct anchors in the same shape. Most natural horns, fangs, tusks, beaks, and claws also approximate golden spirals, as do the vast spiral arms of the Milky Way and many other galaxies. The golden spiral appears in the tails of comets and in the webs of certain spiders.

Golden spirals can also be found in the distribution of seeds on the heads of many species of flowers, in the arrangement of scales on pineapples and of bracts (tabs) on pinecones. These and other botanical examples, it has been discovered, are expressive in still another way of the divine proportion, as manifested in the Fibonacci sequence.

On the head of a typical sunflower, for example, the number of seed spirals very often falls into this pattern: 89 spirals radiating steeply clockwise, 55 moving counterclockwise, and 34 moving less steeply clockwise. These are three adjacent numbers in the Fibonacci sequence. The largest known sunflower had 144, 89, and 55 spirals.

With many plant species, especially numbers of the family Asteraceae (sunflowers, daisies, etc.), the number of petals on each flower is usually a Fibonacci number, such as 5, 13, 55, or even 377, as with the ice plant. The bracts on a pinecone arrange themselves in two sets of spirals from the branch outward—one set of spirals reads clockwise; the other reads counterclockwise. In a survey of more than 4,000 cones from ten pine species, it was found that more than 98 percent contained a Fibonacci number of spirals in each direction. Furthermore, the two numbers were adjacent, or adjacent but one, in the Fibonacci sequence—e.g., 8 spirals one way, 13 the other, or 8 spirals one way, 21 the other. The scales of pineapples exhibit an even more invariant adherence to Fibonacci phenomena: Not one exception was found in a sample test of 2,000 pineapples.

Fibonacci numbers also occur frequently in phyllotaxy, the arrangement of leaves on a stem. On many types of trees the leaves will grow on each stem in a pattern that includes two Fibonacci numbers. Starting with the first leaf, one may count leaves up the stem until one reaches a leaf directly above the first. Depending on the species, this will be the second, third, fifth, eighth, or thirteenth leaf. In addition, it will take one, two, three, or five spiral turns around the stem to reach this leaf.

These discoveries in botany, zoology, and astronomy would not have surprised the ancient Greeks, convinced as they were of the geometric harmony of the universe. In fact, some of the data described in this article were used in a modern theory of "dynamic symmetry," developed by the American scholar Jay Hambridge. This theory attributed the dynamic power of Greek art to its use of the "whirling squares," of the divine proportion.

Perhaps there will still be found some underlying growth principle that will connect all the natural examples of golden phenomena and point to still other manifestations not yet discovered. Perhaps human beings have unconsciously perceived such a principle in these natural phenomena and have used it as a standard in judging works of art.

On the other hand, we may well be dealing with coincidence. It has been noted that there are only a limited number of possible orderly designs available to artists. A certain amount of repetition of these designs is inevitable.

Besides, many great works of art have no apparent relation to the divine proportion. And many examples only approximate the ideal. Finally, the taste for the divine proportion may have come to seem natural only after long use by the Greeks and their imitators.

In nature as well, we find that some of the cited phenomena are only occasional or approximate manifestations of the golden spiral or Fibonacci sequence. In any case, these examples involve only limited numbers of phenomena. Specific theories have been advanced in various fields to explain some of the specific instances, such as in phyllotaxy (leaf arrangement). These theories do not have any universal application.

Even if a universal explanation is never found, the study of Fibonacci and golden phenomena may be seen as a noble exercise in the search for unities and mathematical relationships. After all, the search was a basic characteristic of Greek philosophy, and it still animates modern science.

For further information, see Jay Hambridge, *The Elements of Dynamic Symmetry* (Peter Smith, 1926); V. E. Hoggatt, *Fibonacci and Lucas Numbers* (Houghton Mifflin, 1969); and Peter S. Stevens, *Patterns in Nature* (Little, Brown, 1974).

STRANGE
CREATURES

Loch Ness Monster

The Loch Ness Monster (Nessiteras rhombopteryx) is a hypothetical marine creature inhabiting Loch Ness in Scotland.

Loch Ness, the largest freshwater lake (in volume) in Great Britain and the third largest in Europe, lies in Great Glen, the major geological fault that traverses Scotland. The lake, lying 52 feet above sea level, is only 24 miles long and about 1 mile wide, but it reaches a depth of more than 600 feet. The water temperature hovers around 42 degrees F all year and, because of suspended peat particles, is so murky that maximum underwater visibility is limited to a few feet. The waters, which are unpolluted and support a great quantity of life, are fished for salmon and trout.

The local populace has been sacrificing animals to the creature or creatures believed to inhabit the lake since time immemorial, but no bodies of such animals or of people who have drowned in the lake have ever been found. Until 1933, when a major roadway was built along the lake's western shore, much of the lake was obscured by the surrounding vegetation.

Nicholas Witchell, in his book The *Loch Ness Story* (Penguin Books, 1975), states that more than 4,000 people believe they have seen an unknown animal in Loch Ness. Of these 4,000 reports Witchell believes a substantial quantity— 15 to 20 percent—"defy any attempt to dismiss them in terms of known animals and objects, hoaxes or fraudulent witnesses."

On the basis of such eyewitness reports and alleged photographs, a consistent picture of the Loch Ness Monster emerges: a dark gray or brownish black creature with a long, slender neck, topped by a small head; a heavy body; a long powerful tail; and four diamond-shaped paddles or fins. Varying numbers of humps—from one to three—have also been reported, as have bony, angular protuberances from the head. The size of the creature seems to range from fifteen to twenty feet, suggesting to those who have studied the "Nessie" question the presence of a herd of animals. Approximately 90 percent of the sightings have taken place when the lake is calm. The creature swims rapidly, both with and against prevailing winds, and submerges and surfaces, creating a definite wake as it moves.

Although international interest in the Loch Ness Monster ignited in the early 1930s, the history of such a supposed creature can be traced back to 565 A.D., when St. Columba, the Irish poet who brought the Christian religion to Scotland, warded off a beast from a swimmer. An account entitled "Of the Driving Away of a Certain Water Monster by Virtue of the Prayer of the Holy Man" is related in a biography of St. Columba, written a century after his death.

Legends have always abounded in the Scottish Highlands. One legend tells of a water horse or kelpie whose favorite haunts were the lonely lochs. The kelpie was believed to be an evil spirit, which lured weary travelers to their deaths. Witchell suggests that this belief and its association with the kelpie caused the historical reluctance of Highlanders to discuss any real experiences prior to the 1930s with creatures believed to inhabit Loch Ness.

Sporadic written accounts of sightings of mysterious creatures in Loch Ness have cropped up through the centuries. But it was not until May 2, 1933, that the "Loch Ness Monster" was officially born. A chronology of major events in search for the Loch Ness Monster follows:

May 2, 1933: Alan Campbell, the local correspondent of the Inverness *Courier*, described an April sighting by Mr. and Mrs. John Mackay of Drumnadrochit of "an enormous animal rolling and plunging" in Loch Ness. At the instigation of Campbell's editor, the animal was christened the Loch Ness Monster. Upon publication of Campbell's story, previous reports of sightings began to surface. One such previously unnoticed report by a party of anglers had appeared in July 1930 in the *Northern Chronicle* as "A Strange Experience at Loch Ness."

July 22, 1933: London businessman George Spicer and his wife saw a large, long-necked creature shoot across the road in jerks and disappear into Loch Ness.

October 1933: With more than twenty water sightings since publication of the Mackay story, "Nessie" (as it was affectionately nicknamed by the press) began to make news in the national papers. *The Scotsman* sent its own correspondent, and the London *Daily Mail* and *Daily Express* began their own inquiries and published special reports. As monster hunters flooded the Loch Ness area, an almost carnivallike atmosphere developed.

October 29, 1933: Not everyone took the "Nessie" search seriously. E. G. Boulenger, the director of the Aquarium at the London Zoo, wrote in the *Observer:* "The case of the Monster in Loch Ness is worthy of our consideration if only because it presents a striking example of mass hallucination. For countless centuries a wealth of weird and eerie legend has centered round this great inland waterway. . . . Any person with the slightest knowledge of human susceptibility should therefore find no difficulty in understanding how the animal, once being said to have been seen by a few persons, should have shortly revealed itself to many more. . . ."

November 13, 1933: Hugh Gray, an employee of the British Aluminium Company, took, from a distance of 200 feet, the first photograph of a large object that had surfaced in Loch Ness. Its publication fanned monster fever to even greater proportions. Although authenticity of the photo was verified, various zoologists were highly skeptical that the object was a living creature and suggested that it was a rotting tree trunk or a decaying mat of vegetation.

December 12, 1933: Malcolm Irvine of Scottish Film Productions took the first film claiming to show "Nessie." The whereabouts of the film are not known today.

December 12, 1933: The *Daily Mail* headline read MONSTER OF LOCH NESS IS NOT A LEGEND BUT A FACT. The *Daily Mail* revealed that M. A. Wetherall, a fellow of the Royal Geographical Society and the Royal Zoological Society, had found a spoor, a footprint in this case, of the monster. However, the spoor turned out to be a hoax—it was actually a faked hippopotamus print—and the whole affair had a detrimental effect on "Nessie's" reputation. Scientists and skeptics were relieved, and the press began to assume a more cautious attitude.

April 21, 1934: The *Daily Mail* published a photograph taken by Lieutenant Colonel Robert Kenneth Wilson, a London gynecologist, of the upraised head and neck of a creature in Loch Ness. No evidence of faking of the film negative was found. The zoological community was genuinely baffled by what came to be known as the "Surgeon's Photograph."

July–August 1934: Under the sponsorship of insurance magnate Sir Edward Mountain, the first serious investigative expedition was conducted. Several clear sightings were made, but the real success was a film taken by Captain James Fraser of Inverness. Zoologists who viewed the film, however, agreed that the animal portrayed was a seal. At about the same time Rupert Gould, a retired naval officer, who had gone to Loch Ness the previous year, published *The Loch Ness Monster and Others,* a collection of forty-seven sighting records, complete with drawings and photographs.

By the end of 1934 the national press had lost interest in "Nessie" and the public mania for monster hunting had died down, but sightings continued over the next twenty years and occasionally were reported in the local press.

April 1957: Constance Whyte published *More Than a Legend,* a serious collation of the evidence existing in support of the monster's authenticity. The book was very successful and became an important turning point in the campaign for serious investigation. Interest in the Loch Ness Monster began to escalate once again as the number of visitors to the Highlands increased.

1960: On April 23, in what was to be a year of great activity at Loch Ness, Tim Dinsdale, an English aeronautical engineer who would become a full-time monster hunter, took fifty feet of good film of the monster and thereby put "Nessie" back in the news. The previous year Dinsdale had constructed a statistical picture of the monster based on reports in Whyte's book and had concluded that the creature was a prehistoric plesiosaur, a theory Whyte had half accepted. In July an expedition of Oxford and Cambridge graduates and undergraduates led by Dr. Denys W. Tucker, a principal scientific officer of the British Museum of Natural History, conducted an ecological study of Loch Ness and concluded that it was capable of supporting a colony of large predatory animals.

March 20, 1962: The Bureau for Investigating the Loch Ness Monster Phenomenon Ltd. was officially incorporated. Its directors were Constance Whyte; Sir Peter Scott, son of the great Antarctic explorer and founder of the Wildfowl Trust; Richard Fitter, council member of the Fauna Preservation Society and nature correspondent of the *Observer;* and David James, Antarctic traveler and Scottish MP. A period of intense activity, including many investigative expeditions, followed.

January 1966: Results of a study by the Royal Air Force's Joint Air Reconnaissance Intelligence Center (JARIC) of Dinsdale's 1960 film were reported. The report rejected the possibility that the object filmed was a boat (as skeptics had suggested) and concluded that "it is probably an animate object." However, Maurice Burton, a professional zoologist, writing in the *New Scientist,* rejected this conclusion. Burton was convinced the creature was an ordinary otter.

September 1966: Dr. Roy Mackal, a professor of biochemistry at the University of Chicago and a newly appointed director of the Loch Ness Investigation Bureau, arrived at Loch Ness, bringing to the investigation his scientific support, as well as financial aid from the United States.

December 19, 1968: The *New Scientist* published a report of sonar echoes of animals in Loch Ness, which had been obtained by a team from the University of Birmingham. The team engineer, Hugh Braithwaite, who concluded that it was unlikely the creatures were fish, wrote, "It is a temptation to suppose they must be the fabulous Loch Ness monsters" now observed for the first time in their underwater activities.

August 7–8, 1972: The Academy of Applied Science team, led by Robert H. Rines, using an underwater stroboscopic camera (developed by MIT's Professor Harold Edgerton) and Raytheon sonar equipment, obtained sonar and photographic images of a large, solid animal. After computer enhancement by NASA, one frame in particular showed a flipperlike appendage attached to a rough-textured robust body. For the first time, photographic and sonar evidence corroborated each other, thereby presenting the most significant discovery to date in the investigations at Loch Ness. The Boston, Massachusetts, Academy of Applied Science had been established in 1963 to support unusual areas of research. The academy's first expedition, in 1970, using high-frequency side-scan sonar, had produced sonar recordings of large moving objects, but no photographs had been obtained.

June 19–20, 1975: The Academy of Applied Science obtained further sonar and photographic evidence of a creature or creatures inhabiting Loch Ness. According to Alan Gillepsie of the California Institute of Technology's Jet Propulsion Laboratory, who performed the computer enhancement on the photographs (*Technology Review,* March/April, 1976):

> . . . One picture showed a body with a long neck and two stubby appendages. . . . The second frame appeared to show a neck and head, with the head closer to the camera than the body . . . the neck was reticulated. The head supported projections. . . . I see no evidence that

they are pictures of a model, toy or whatever. I emphasize: I detect no evidence of a fraud. These objects are not patterns of algae, sediment or gas bubbles.

The conclusion of the academy expedition (*Technology Review*, March/April 1976) was that the photographs and sonar evidence obtained in 1972 and 1975 agree with each other and with past evidence that "there is a species of large aquatic creature in Loch Ness." The team stated further:

> Although we make no claim to being expert zoologists, we can find no combination of phenomena that account for these data as well as the simple explanation that a large creature inhabits the loch. Not even the experts have offered a plausible alternative explanation, in our view. In addition, there have been other investigations which suggest that the loch is capable of supporting a breeding population of such animals, and that physiological adaptation to the cold loch waters is feasible for a wide variety of candidate species.

Sir Peter Scott has given the creature a scientific name— *Nessiteras rhombopteryx* (Ness marvel with diamond-shaped fin)—to make it eligible for legislative protection.

Although the same camera system was used in 1975, several improvements had been made over the 1972 setup. The camera range was increased from ten to thirty feet, and a new triggering system was attached to the camera-strobe system which would allow the camera to begin taking pictures only in the presence of a large object.

June 1976: Another Academy of Applied Science expedition, now also sponsored by *The New York Times*, arrived at Loch Ness to continue the search to identify the Loch Ness Monster.

The most recent evidence, although it was met with a great deal of skepticism when first introduced in London in December 1976, is steadily gaining support and generating enthusiasm for further investigations. Owing to the premature publication of a chapter of a book on Loch Ness and overblown publicity, an Edinburgh conference scheduled to present new evidence was canceled, leading to speculation about the authenticity of the evidence. The photographs, however, were presented in December 1975 in the British House of Commons and published in the spring of 1976 in two highly respectable publications, MIT's *Technology Review* and *MCZ Newsletter*, which is published by Harvard University's Museum of Comparative Zoology. Dr. Alfred W. Crompton, the head of the Harvard zoology museum, termed the evidence "extremely intriguing" and "sufficiently suggestive of a large aquatic animal" to merit further investigations similar to those conducted in 1972 and 1975. Dr. Christopher McGowan, associate curator of the department of vertebrate paleontology at Toronto's Royal Ontario Museum, and Dr. George Zug, curator of reptiles and amphibians at the Smithsonian Institution, have voiced similar support. Zug has stated that he observed bilateral symmetry—matching left and right sides—in the alleged head photograph, suggesting a living creature. The scholarly and often skeptical British journal *Nature* stated that with further discoveries by the Academy of Applied Science the natural history of Loch Ness may even become a respectable line of study."

The critics and skeptics are, however, still much in evidence. In a unanimous, cautious statement, five zoologists and paleontologists from London's Natural History Museum agreed that the 1972 photographs showed a "flipper-like object," but were not convinced the 1975 photos supported the conclusions of the Academy of Applied Science expedition. They suggested that air sacs of swarms of phantom midget larvae could have produced the images. More adamant skeptics have suggested that the pictured objects are the prow or stern of a sunken Viking ship, the flipperlike objects are oars, and the head is a carved dragon of the kind that once embellished Viking vessels.

However, although a considerable number of expert zoologists now accept the existence of large aquatic creatures in Loch Ness, no one can yet identify them or explain how they came to be in Loch Ness.

Despite some problems, the most popular theory on the identity of "Nessie" is that the creature is a plesiosaur, a fish-eating marine dinosaur which became extinct about 70,000,000 years ago. McGowan dismisses this theory because he thinks that water in Loch Ness is too cold. However, the fact that the elasmosaurus, a member of the plesiosaur family, was probably almost identical to the hypothetical description of "Nessie" makes the theory intriguing. If the plesiosaur theory is correct, the discovery would be one of the greatest zoological finds of recent centuries.

McGowan also casts doubt on some of the other possibilities that have been suggested. That it is some kind of mammal—a whale or dolphin or seal—is unlikely because mammals are very active and would have been seen more often and consequently identified. Mammals also would have to surface to breathe, and there have been very few surface sightings. However, it is possible they have nostrils set high on the head which only need to be exposed. Nor could the creature be a sea cow or a manatee because they are vegetarians and generally inhabit warmer waters.

Roy Mackal, in *The Monsters of Loch Ness* (Swallow Press, 1976), has proposed that the creatures are gigantic relatives of the salamander or newt, specifically a primitive aquatic amphibian of a species called the embolomer. The amphibian theory is attractive because such a creature can live in water and on land and breathe through its skin. Alternatively, Mackal has suggested that "Nessie" may be a large, thick-bodied, eellike creature.

There are two possibilities to explain how the creatures got into the lake: Either they were trapped in it many thousand years ago or they entered more recently.

The first possibility would be the more convenient since many potential solutions to the identity of "Nessie" include saltwater creatures. Geological changes following the last ice age raised the Scottish Highlands and isolated Loch Ness from the sea. It is possible that some large seagoing creatures were trapped and that those creatures, over the past several thousand years, gradually adapted to the gradual change to fresh water. This sort of change has occurred previously, notably in the case of several shark species found in freshwater lakes in parts of Africa which once were connected to the sea.

Nicholas Witchell, in *The Loch Ness Story*, suggests several reasons why it is unlikely the creatures entered Loch Ness recently. The fact that the lake lies fifty-two feet above sea level rules out the possibility of an underwater tunnel. Nor does it seem likely that the creatures came via the River Ness (which runs from the northern end of the lake to the sea) because it is extremely shallow.

Of course, the last possibility as to identity is that the creatures are something totally unknown and not related to any extinct or existing species. Or they may indeed be an illusion or a hallucination.

Abominable Snowman

The Abominable Snowman is a creature combining certain traits of both human and ape, said by Sherpa natives to inhabit remote areas of the Himalaya region and regarded by them as objects of religious awe.

Reports about the Abominable Snowman reached Europe as early as the mid-fifteenth century, but it was not until the nineteenth century that the subject began to arouse interest in the West. A British officer, Major L. A. Waddel, related in his 1899 book *Among the Himalayas* his discovery of large footprints in the snows of Sikkim. Since that time there has been gathered much circumstantial evidence testifying to the existence of an ape-man living on the Himalayan slopes near the snow line, including the reports of more than forty Westerners who claimed to have seen the creature or its footprints. Some of these prints may well have been made by other animals.

To the people of the region, the creature, often known locally as the yeti, has religious significance and is feared and protected. Their descriptions of the yeti vary greatly. Many Sherpas say it is a small, squat animal the size of a fourteen-year-old boy, with stiff red or black hair, a monkeylike face, and no tail. The creature sighted by Western observers has generally been larger, but size variation between sexes and among age groups can be expected.

According to Edward Cronin, a zoologist who has worked in the Himalayas, a composite picture could be drawn from Western accounts, showing a stocky, apelike creature five and a half to six feet tall. Short brown or black hair covers all parts of the body, except for the flat, hairless face. Massive teeth (not fangs) fill the large mouth. The head comes to a pointy crown. Long arms dangle from the animal's heavy, rounded shoulders. The yeti has no tail.

Western and Sherpa accounts agree more closely about the yeti's behavior. The animal usually walks on two legs, as do other apes in certain circumstances (for example, in the snow). When faced with danger, the yeti adopts an apelike threatening stance.

Among the photographs of possible yeti footprints, the ones that have provoked the greatest interest were taken by Eric Shipton and Michael Ward during the 1951 British

Sir Edmund Hillary (second from left) and others displaying scalp claimed to be a 200-year-old relic of an Abominable Snowman.

One of the footprints photographed by the Shipton-Ward expedition, possibly made by an Abominable Snowman.

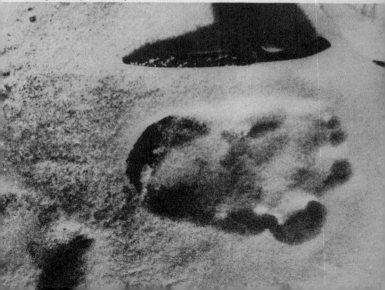

Mount Everest reconnaissance. The clear footprints, made in firm snow and ice, were more than twelve inches long and seven and a half inches wide. The big toe was large and apparently more opposable than the human big toe. The second toe was the longest and relatively thin. There is no prominent arch, and the heel is almost as wide as the front part. Several other footprints that resemble these in shape have been found, though the size varies greatly.

A trail of prints, remarkably similar to those found by Shipton and Ward, were discovered on December 18, 1972, by Cronin and a colleague, Howard Emery, near Kongmaa La Mountain in Nepal. The prints were smaller than Shipton's and might have been made by a young individual of the same species.

Cronin dismisses most of the alternate identifications of the prints. Human and lemur feet make much narrower prints; snow leopards and wolves leave circular prints; eagles have four narrow, radiating toes; and bear prints show an equal-sized, symmetrical arrangement of toes, unlike Shipton's photographed prints and Cronin's own finds.

Cronin's prints strongly suggest bipedal progression—upright walking. Right print followed left in an uninterrupted pattern.

There has been widespread speculation that the Abominable Snowman, along with the Sasquatch of the American Pacific coast and the Mono Grande of the Andes, are survivors of a species of large anthropoids that once roamed the earth. Such an animal might have been the *Gigantopithecus,* a large primate whose remains have been found in southern China, as well as in the Himalayas, and dated to as far back as 9,000,000 years ago and as recently as 500,000 years ago. *Gigantopithecus* might have been forced by the ancestors of modern man into the remote valleys of the Himalayas, where many species exist that are elsewhere extinct (see Sasquatch).

Some observers dismiss the Sherpa accounts as either mythology, bugbears to keep children well behaved, or scape-goats onto which humans can project their own savage tendencies. Others have suggested that bands of bears or langur monkeys seen at a distance may have been mistaken for ape-men, and that yeti tracks are in fact bear paw prints.

There is no justification, however, for a patronizing attitude toward Sherpa lore. Prescientific peoples may be quicker to form fanciful explanations of unusual phenomena, but their eyesight and their knowledge of the typical local wildlife (such as bears and monkeys) are probably reliable.

The lush valley forests of the Himalayas provide a rich variety and quantity of edible plants and support significant populations of large animals. Because they are superimposed on a steep, sloping topography, these forests cover a much wider area than is generally supposed. Because they are nearly impenetrable, they are but poorly explored by natives or foreign naturalists. Furthermore, the dense vegetation could easily conceal a hiding animal.

Cronin suggests that the yeti is not a "snowman" at all but inhabits the lush valleys. The yeti, he maintains, probably emerges onto the snow-covered ridges only in order to pass from one valley to the next.

The large number of sightings in the Himalayas reported by both natives and outsiders may lead to a presumption that the Abominable Snowman does exist. However, until a specimen is caught or carefully photographed, its actual existence remains problematic.

For further information, see Edward J. Cronin, Jr., "The Yeti," *Atlantic Monthly* (November 1975); M. Grumley, *There Are Giants in the Earth* (Doubleday, 1974); R. Izzard, *The Abominable Snowman* (Doubleday, 1955); John Napier, *Bigfoot* (Dutton, 1973); I. T. Sanderson, *Abominable Snowman —Legend Come to Life* (Robert Hale, 1961); and O. Tchernine, *The Snowman and Company* (Robert Hale, 1961).

Sasquatch

Sasquatch, also known as Bigfoot, is the name given to a hypothetical species of primates living in the Pacific Northwest. Reports of sightings of such a creature date from 1840, and all come from a well-defined area that covers the mountains of southern British Columbia and the Cascade ranges of western Washington, western Oregon, and northern California. Much of this area is covered with uninhabited and almost impenetrable forests.

On the basis of sightings and plaster casts of purported footprints, the creature is believed to be between seven and nine feet tall and weigh from 600 to 900 pounds. Sasquatch is described as an apelike creature with thick fur, long arms, and powerful shoulders, which walks upright and leaves large footprints approximately sixteen inches long and six inches wide. According to most reports, the creature does nothing

A frame from the 1967 Patterson film, apparently of a seven-foot-tall female Sasquatch.

extraordinary, nor is it ferocious in any way. It generally stands quietly until it senses that people are watching and then it slips away.

Sasquatch is part of the legends of many of the Indian tribes of the region. It is called Sasquatch ("hairy man") after a legendary tribe of aboriginal giants in the folklore of the Northwest Coast Indians. It is the belief of the Chehalis Indians near Vancouver, British Columbia, that Sasquatch is descended from two bands of giants that were destroyed in battle many years ago. The earliest known recording of Sasquatch, according to Don Hunt and Rene Dahinden (*Sasquatch*, Signet, 1975), is on the totem poles and masks carved by the Pacific Coast Indians of British Columbia, particularly the Kwakiutls. These carvings, they say, suggest a creature that is more human in appearance than animal.

Most of the contemporary sightings date from 1950. In 1957 a Canadian lumberman revealed that he had been kidnapped thirty-three years earlier, near Vancouver Island, by a tribe of hairy apelike creatures. He was held captive for about a week and then escaped but kept the story to himself for fear no one would believe him. Since then the rate of sightings has escalated, and in the past ten years about 300 people have reported seeing Sasquatch.

Currently reports of sightings or footprints are being collected by the Bigfoot Information Center in The Dalles, Oregon, a small town in the heart of the Bigfoot region. The center is run by Peter Byrne, formerly a professional hunter in Nepal, who once searched for the yeti and has now turned his attention to Sasquatch. The center investigates each report, using a network of volunteers. Although many sightings are eventually dismissed as fakes, Byrne believes he has collected the details of ninety-four sightings that are believable. The center has many more reports of tracks, which, in most cases, consist of long tracks of footprints that can be followed for several miles. Byrne has been operating the center for five years, supported by admission fees to a small exhibit and donations from other sources, including the Academy of Applied Sciences, which is currently the chief sponsor of the Loch Ness expedition.

Another major piece of evidence purporting to show Sasquatch is a film taken in 1967 by two amateur Sasquatch hunters in Northern California. The 16mm color film is twenty-eight feet long (about sixty seconds) and, on the whole, of poor quality. It purports to show a large, heavy, upright-walking creature. According to R. Gimlin and R. Patterson who took the film, they were riding on horseback through a dry riverbed when they suddenly came upon a female Bigfoot. The animal caused the horses to bolt, but Gimlin and Patterson managed to shoot the film before the huge animal disappeared into the forest. Byrne, who is 95 percent certain the film is not a fake, asserts in his *The Search for Bigfoot* (Pocket Books, 1975) that most scientists consider the film a hoax without offering convincing arguments for their view. John Napier, a British anthropologist expert in the anatomy of ape and human feet and a veteran of the yeti searches, believes that Sasquatch exists but thinks the film is a hoax. After a thorough study of the film, he felt that, among other things, the animal's foot seemed out of proportion with the rest of the body. Napier also had a British expert on gait, D. W. Grieve, a reader in biomechanics, Royal Free Hospital School of Medicine, examine the film. Grieve's report was inconclusive, largely because there was no certainty about at what speed the film had been shot.

Napier feels that some of the most persuasive evidence is a set of footprints found in 1969, near Bossburg, Washington. The 1,089 prints cover half a mile, and the right ones appear to have been made by a crippled foot. Napier thinks that the prints look very human except that they are seventeen and a half inches long and seven inches wide. He has concluded that "they are not the footprints of modern man" but "could conceivably be the footprints of unknown members of the human family" (*The New York Times,* June 30, 1976). He discounts the possibility of fakery because "It is very difficult to conceive of a hoaxer so subtle, so knowledgeable, and so sick as to fake a footprint of this nature." He also discounts the often-made allegation that so-called Sasquatch prints were made by bears by simply pointing out that the bears of the Pacific Northwest are too small to make a print more than half the size ascribed to the Sasquatch.

There has been some speculation (see *The New York Times,* June 30, 1976) that Sasquatch is a survival of the supposedly extinct form of ape-man known as *Gigantopithecus.* Fossils of *Gigantopithecus* have been found in Asia, and it may have migrated across the Bering land bridge to America long before true humans.

For more information, see John Napier, *Bigfoot* (Berkley Medallion, 1974) and John Green, *The Sasquatch File* (Cheam Publishing, 1973).

PSYCHIC
PHENOMENA

Psychics

An Interview with Ingo Swann, Psychic

Since 1971 Ingo Swann has participated in dozens of major experiments in psychokinesis (PK) and clairvoyance, which he prefers to call remote viewing. In most of these experiments he has made important contributions to the design of the tests. He has insisted on the tightest possible controls so as to avoid any criticism of conscious fraud. He has also insisted that tests be so designed that results can be attributed only to paranormal causes. For example, he refused to try to influence the readings of a seismometer when he discovered that a minor variation in its readings could be attributed to a passing truck.

He has also urged researchers in clairvoyance to use real-life targets rather than meaningless abstract symbols. In the early 1970s he participated in a series of tests at the American Society for Psychical Research. These tests used oddly shaped objects and such arbitrarily chosen items as mirrors and letter openers. After struggling (successfully) to make sense of these items clairvoyantly, Swann decided never again to work with anything but real objects in the real world—geographical sites, for example (see A Clairvoyance Experiment).

Born on September 14, 1933, in Telluride, Colorado, Swann has the fair complexion, blue eyes, and rangy grace of a Westerner of Swedish-German ancestry. He received a bachelor's degree in biology from Westminster College in Salt Lake City in 1955. After three years in Korea as an Army enlistee, he moved to New York City, where he worked for twelve years for the United Nations Secretariat. In his free time he concentrated on developing his skills as a painter.

In the late 1960s he developed an interest in Scientology. The process of Scientology and experiences with paranormal senses in plants and animals led Swann to explore more thoroughly his psychic potentials, abilities he remembered

Ingo Swann.

exercising as a child but which he had repressed. Soon thereafter his life took a dramatic turn for the better. The quality of his painting improved, he began to write extensively, and he started his long in-the-lab training as a serious student of paranormal phenomena.

As both a researcher and a subject in parapsychology, Swann serves as a vital bridge between people too often prejudged as freaks or frauds and the world of science and rational debate. As the following interview demonstrates, Swann's approach to both worlds is marked by amused irony, critical detachment, and a strong determination to advance the boundaries of knowledge.

WA: You've just written a novel.
SWANN: Yes. It's about an ideal fictional psychic who can do all the incredible things fictional psychics are supposed to

do. He lives in a world—about ten years from now—where the hydrogen bomb is obsolete, because technology has developed ways to affect people's minds at a distance, simply turn them into robots. The book is about his struggle with the authorities when he tries to destroy this new technology.

The book is not a fantasy; it's based on real technological possibilities. In fact, we added an appendix to document the science behind the novel. For a fictive work, it's quite an innovation.

WA: What's the name of the book?

SWANN: It's had several titles, but the one that may go now is *Star Fire*. It will be an original Dell paperback and will be on the stands about June 1977. It's taken me three years to write it. It took two years to accumulate the research, to really make sure that I knew what I was talking about.

WA: You say in your autobiography [*To Kiss Earth Goodbye*, Hawthorne, 1975] that a good religion should add to the workableness of life. Has Scientology done that for you?

SWANN: Yes, indeed. Look at what I'm involved with. I used to sit around Lower East Side bars drinking and complaining about the failure of the art world to take notice of me.

WA: When did you get interested in painting?

SWANN: When I was about six. It's been a lifetime interest.

WA: And you learned some of your techniques in the Orient, I understand.

SWANN: I studied calligraphy and composition and one or two other things—symbolism—with a very nice Korean professor in Seoul when I was there. I went three evenings a week with an interpreter. After about ten months of very intensive training, my teacher was suddenly shot down in the street. It turned out he had been a North Korean spy all along. He was a grand old man. It was horrible that he had any politics at all, much less been a spy.

WA: That's a horrible story.

SWANN: It's life.

WA: There are charges that Scientology does not allow much freedom of individual expression. Is this true?

SWANN: That's propaganda in the press. And if anyone cares to ask Scientologists rather than the propagandists about it, I think they'd find better answers. I consider myself extremely free to do or say what I want.

WA: Was it through Scientology that you became aware of past lives?

SWANN: Not particularly. When I was a child, I was commenting on the immediate life before this one—to the embarrassment of everybody. I didn't understand for a long time that you weren't supposed to do that.

WA: You're suggesting that society is very repressive of psychic talents.

SWANN: The history of humanity is characterized mostly by the repressions that humans have inflicted on humans. It occurs at a level where there is a conflict, not with human nature, but with the biases and prejudices of certain systems of viewing the world. History records so many repressions of that type. For example, the trouble that people went through trying to introduce the benefits of vaccination was twice as terrible as anything the parapsychologists have been through. The critics of vaccination invoked religion because they believed it was a sin to inject a foreign substance into the body. In modern scientific thought, it" psychological; it's a sin to inject foreign information into the mainstream of modern psychology.

WA: Parapsychology has been in existence for 100 years. The experimenters have tried hard to meet the demands of established science, particularly in the last few decades. But they've had very little success.

SWANN: No. No. That's not true. They have been successful. The Parapsychology Association has been accepted by the AAAS [American Association for the Advancement of Science] through the intervention of Dr. Margaret Mead. It's been a grudging acceptance, but the fact that it can have professional standing in America's scientific community shows that it is accepted as a discipline.

WA: But the AAAS publication, *Science,* has never published a report which supports the existence of parapsychological phenomena.

SWANN: That's a problem with the editorial policy of *Science,* which is dominated by materialists who would have to drop some of their basic illusions if they accepted the feasibility of nonmaterial mental interactions. They should accept them; physics has. So this is just an internecine fight; it has nothing to do with the facts available on the subject.

WA: Do you think that parapsychologists could do anything to improve their standing in the scientific community?

SWANN: Research such as I have helped establish broadens the concept of what is possible. Parapsychologists, because of the fight they've had with established science, are very

Target objects, concealed in sealed boxes, used in an ESP experiment at the American Society for Psychical Research.

statistically minded. We have two generations of parapsychologists who have been trained in statistical methodology. They can't get out of it too easily.

A very well-known parapsychologist announced recently that parapsychologists should not be interested in any abilities that are displayed too far above chance because

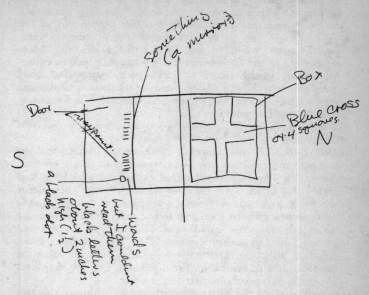

Drawings by Ingo Swann, made after viewing boxes containing the objects. Swann later attributed his failure to detect the American flag to its being shiny, although he was able to detect the mirror in the other box.

present psychology is not prepared to deal with it. That's the kind of people I always get in a hassle with. Most of the things I've been doing—and I've seen other people do—are successful a million times above chance. Take paranormal viewing—viewing target situations out of eyesight—where the psychic vision of the target was just less than a photographic image. Statistics become meaningless there. You only need safeguards that there wasn't fraud of some type.

WA: Do you think parapsychology's position on the fringe of establishment science affects the quality of the work that's done?

SWANN: Creative, competent people are prevented from getting into the field in the first place; that's what affects the quality of the work. Most parapsychologists are there because of devotion to the cause, not because it's a good job or because it has a rewarding financial and cultural future. I think it's a lack of respect and lack of funding and a lack of enjoyment that keeps really creative people out of the field. That's not to say we haven't got creative parapsychologists. We have. But they're in the minority. Most people are in the field because it's a cause. If you're cause-motivated, you're likely to have your vision and your imagination and your discernment a little biased to support your cause. And of course, the best researcher is somebody who can operate with less bias.

WA: How do some parapsychologists come to view the field as a cause?

SWANN: I tend to view extreme adherents to parapsychology and extreme critics as just two opposite ends of a spectrum, the middle of which is a psychic experience at a level that makes it a crisis. They have to do something. They either accept it and try to find an explanation, which makes parapsychologists of them, or they totally reject it because it undermines their mind sets. That makes the devoted critic. You can reassure yourself in a creative or a destructive direction. That's the only thing that accounts for the rabidness of critics, on the one hand, and the rabidness of certain parapsychologists, on the other.

WA: Isn't part of the difficulty with parapsychology the fact that the implications are tremendous? It's not going to upset anyone particularly if there is or isn't argon on Mars, but precognition and telepathy have immense implications for everyone.

SWANN: The difficulty is that we have parapsychology as a science, on the one hand, but on the other, we have expectations that have originated essentially in science fiction. There is nothing going on in parapsychology, that I know of, that even remotely approaches the consequences that have been implied in science fiction. Here is this very small, innocuous ability, and—oh, my God, the next thing he's going to do is explode an atomic warhead with his mind. Not on your life! Maybe in 2090 or something like that, but with the state of the art today—no.

So critics are not actually responding to the work that's going on, but to their fear of what they think the outcome of the work will be. They're dealing in fictions, not facts. That's why critics create a fictional situation to criticize, using selected facts from psychic research to fit their fiction.

WA: Do you find the general public as confused as that?

SWANN: Actually, at the public level there's a very healthy attitude about psychic potential. It's seen more for what it really is. The farmer knows when it's time to plant. Other workers have certain senses about their work. There is a high utilization level of innate intuitive responses, which can really be called psychic because there's no perceptible material input to explain these things.

WA: Have you found that most people have had paranormal experiences?

SWANN: I find that almost everybody has had one to some degree. The people who don't want to believe these things exist, of course, don't query or test very large populations. It might be interesting to get the cooperation of a town in the Midwest to study this. Or get the Census Bureau to add this sort of question to its forms, so we can get a better picture of just how widespread the experience is.

WA: Charges of fraud are commonly made against parapsychology experiments. How can they be dealt with, or can they be dealt with at all?

SWANN: If I ever was encouraged to respond to charges of fraud, then I would charge fraud in return. Because it is fraudulent for critics to use selected data to support their own thesis, and they usually do. The most damaging thing is that they often encroach on civil rights in doing this sort of thing. You cannot persecute or criticize a person because of his political, philosophical, or religious preference. In fact, you may not even mention it. It comes under the title of fair comment. The critics' reports always give the idea of [Harold] Puthoff and [Russell] Targ running a little show all by themselves—completely free agents. But everything they did had to be approved by the Blue Ribbon Panel at SRI [Stanford Research Institute]. Many of them were very suspicious of psychic phenomenon. They monitored every step very carefully. The critics' behavior really inhibits scientific and philosophical debate.

WA: How many so-called psychics really are frauds and hustlers?

SWANN: Of those who present themselves in the realm of psychism and parapsychology, a good number. But I consider this a very small percentage of psychics or gifted people. I think the most successful psychics have never subjected themselves to scrutiny; they have just used their hunches and gut feelings and gone on to form big corporations or write successful books. They hassled through life as best they could without the intervention of parapsychologists or the critics. So parapsychology probably has not had a choice selection of psychics to examine. The psychics that advertise themselves as psychics and want to be tested and proved are the smallest tip of the iceberg. I think it's a very irrelevant one, too.

WA: Couldn't some of the more outstanding of the genuine paranormals get together and establish an organization to weed out . . . ?

SWANN: I'm trying to establish that at the present time. I intend to organize a conference to which I will invite only those subjects who have worked at some length with parapsychologists and who have had papers published about their work. I've been able to find seventeen people who've worked in labs around the world. And I hope they'll agree to come.

WA: You spoke of the best psychics going into business and using their hunches. Do you have hunches?

SWANN: I have hunches, but I usually don't follow them. A first-class precognition has certain attributes, including strangeness. If it doesn't fit into what you're usually doing, you'd better start paying attention. Of course, that's why people don't pay attention. If people could be taught about these characteristics, they could deal with their precognitions more responsibly. It's unfair that we're taught that this is just imagination and to disregard these things.

WA: What other kinds of normal things in the world really depend on the paranormal?

SWANN: Just living. Successfully. We can't even operate at chance level without being a little psychic. Life is so rough that it knocks you down if you don't have a little bit of good prediction going for you. The more psychic you are, the higher you exist above chance expectation.

I'm usually asked why it is that the societal image of man doesn't have a way of even entertaining these possibilities. And the questioner wants to know how he can live with his psychic talents when his society makes it so unpleasant for him. And I usually say, "So what? OK, so it makes you uncomfortable; life is uncomfortable!"

Crime Solving

Crime solving by psychic means has long been standard fare in the Sunday supplements. Almost everyone has heard of the famous European clairvoyants who are reported to work in close cooperation with the police of Belgium, the Netherlands, and other European countries.

The most noted European psychic crime solver is probably Gerard Croiset, said to be the most tested psychic in the world (see J. H. Pollack, *Croiset, The Clairvoyant,* Doubleday, 1964). Born on March 10, 1909, in the Netherlands, Croiset has worked for years in close cooperation with Dr. W. H. C. Tenhaeff, director of the Parapsychological Division of the Psychological Laboratory at the University of Utrecht in Holland. A great deal of Croiset's work for the police and for private citizens is recorded by Tenhaeff and his colleagues, who have also collected an impressive file of affidavits from public officials and private individuals attesting to Croiset's effectiveness. Croiset works without using any props, such as crystal balls or dowsing rods. While he gets many clues through psychometry, he does not need to rely on handling an object or even being in the vicinity of crime to get strong impressions about events. He prefers to work without any knowledge of a case, so that he does not obscure the information that comes to him through ESP. His work is so well documented there can be little doubt of the genuineness of his talents.

Perhaps the most interesting crime-solving psychic in the United States is also Dutch. M. B. Dykshoorn came to the United States in 1970, after a youth spent in the Netherlands and several years of adulthood in Australia. His work is not as well documented as Croiset's, but he has impressive affidavits confirming his effectiveness in Europe, Australia, and North Carolina. Unlike Croiset, Dykshoorn uses a small bent wire like a dowsing rod to assist him in "seeing" what has happened at the scene of a crime. Both Croiset and Dykshoorn become highly excited when working on a case and often dramatically act out the crime from both the victim's and the criminal's standpoint. Neither one accepts pay for police work. (For details about Dykshoorn, see his autobiography, *My Passport Says Clairvoyant,* Hawthorne, 1974, and Dan Greenburg, *Something's There: My Adventures in the Occult,* Doubleday, 1976.)

A notable recent case of psychic detective work involved the disappearance of two little girls from Burnt Hills, New York. Their father, Andrew Tomchik, had picked up his daughters—Lisa, five, and Amy, three—at their mother's house. The Tomchiks were separated, and Andrew Tomchik had limited visitation rights. He often took the girls for drives, but on this occasion he did not bring them back. Mrs. Tomchik spent nearly two years looking for her daughters, first through regular police channels and then with private detectives. In desperation, she finally asked a psychic, Millie Coutant of Saratoga Springs, New York to help. After looking at photos of the children and Mr. Tomchik, Mrs. Coutant said she saw a blue pickup truck with North Carolina license plates. She reported the number on the plates. With the help of Detective Bob Bryan of the New York State Police Bureau of Criminal Investigation, the information was checked out with North Carolina authorities. When the North Carolina police reported that they had found a man with two little girls who drove a blue pickup truck, Mrs. Tomchik and a private investigator immediately went to North Carolina, where officials led them to the two missing Tomchik girls and arranged for the extradition of Andrew Tomchik to New York.

Given the well-documented record of success in psychic crime solving, it seems strange that police forces do not use psychic assistance more often. While it is likely that many cases of psychic crime solving are not reported in the press, there are very compelling reasons for the police to avoid using psychics. First, the unsupported evidence of a psychic would hardly be permitted in court, let alone persuade a jury. Secondly, psychic information is not reliable and could send the police off on time-wasting wild-goose chases. Thirdly, and most important, unreliable psychic information could create serious trouble for an innocent person.

An interesting and disturbing view of a self-proclaimed psychic involved in crime solving was reported by William A. Clark in *The Girl on the Volkswagen Floor* (Harper & Row, 1971), which, considerably changed, was made into the movie *Man on a Swing,* with Joel Grey and Cliff Robertson, in 1975. The "psychic" did reveal otherwise unknown things about the case of a murdered girl near Dayton, Ohio, but it later was disclosed that he was acquainted with the accused murderer and may have had a strange influence on him. The possibility arose that the "psychic" may have been an accessory to the murder. Since paranormal knowledge is not an officially accepted possibility, the person who comes forward with "psychic" information about a criminal case may well become a suspect.

Psychometry

Psychometry literally means "measure of the soul," but the term has come to mean object reading. Recently the word "psychoscopy" has been coined to name the activity. Object reading is the paranormal ability of some sensitives to obtain facts about the history of an object, including the people and events connected with it. This is usually accomplished by touching or handling the object in the belief that inanimate objects act as a kind of recorder of information that can be activated and played back by the human mind.

Psychometry is also used to obtain impressions about the life and experiences of the owner of an object. Dr. Thelma Moss conducted an experiment with her own key chain. The first sensitive she tested, Barry Taff, held the chain and then gave specific pieces of information concerning two of Dr. Moss' women friends. Another psychic described Dr. Moss' home and her young daughter in great detail, while holding the same key ring. Yet another psychic described Dr. Moss' laboratory, and another described a box of jewelry kept in a safe-deposit box.

Dr. Moss believes each of the persons received information which can be attributed to their personalities. Barry Taff is quite interested in women; one psychic was a college student and identified most with Dr. Moss' college-age daughter, etc. All of the different pieces of accurate information were derived from the same key chain. Dr. Moss holds the view that in psychometry and in other psychic revelations the personality characteristics of the psychic often determine the nature of the impressions which they receive.

In 1958 Peter Hurkos reportedly gave this reading from a sealed package that contained a small pottery jar from the ruins of Pompeii, Italy, buried A.D. 79 by the ashes from Vesuvius: "This object blew up—an explosion. There was an explosion—a long time ago. I hear a strange language. It is very old. It had to do also with water. I don't know what it is. I see a dark color. . . . I am sure that the owner of the cylinder is dead." Hurkos' statements are a fair approximation of the contents of the package, even though he did not specifically state it was a jar.

Hurkos can also, supposedly, obtain information about people from their photographs. His best intelligence is ob-

Peter Hurkos, a practitioner of psychometry, in 1964.

tained from a negative film, less from a positive transparency, and very little from a printed reproduction of that photograph. He is even able to deduce future happenings, such as medical problems and accidents that will occur (see A. Pucarich, *Beyond Telepathy*, Doubleday, 1973, and N. L. Browning, *The Psychic World of Peter Hurkos*, Doubleday, 1970).

During psychometry, the psychic seems to experience directly conscious activities which have been associated with the object. But he or she cannot choose what will be experienced or received. One psychic explains, "When I take an object it is mostly silent. But sometimes it behaves like when you listen to a record . . . you listen with a mind 'outside' your ordinary mind, and the hand which holds the object acts like the pickup arm" (see N. O. Jacobson, *Life Without Death?*, Delacorte, 1971).

Astral Projection or Out-of-Body Experience

Out-of-body experience (OOBE) is a specific term for an experience of astral projection. Astral projection, also known as traveling clairvoyance, is based on the assumption that a person has two bodies—an astral, or ethereal, body and a physical body—and that it is possible to live and function consciously outside the physical body.

According to one definition, OOBE is an event in which a person perceives a portion of an environment that could not possibly be perceived from the location of that person's physical body. In such an event the person experiencing OOBE knows at the time that he is not dreaming or fantasizing. Charles T. Tart, professor of psychology at the University of California, states in his introduction to Robert A. Monroe's *Journeys Out of the Body* (Doubleday, 1971) that OOBE is a universal phenomenon in that it has happened to all sorts of people throughout history. Usually OOBE is a once-in-a-lifetime experience that has a profound effect on the experiencer. It is generally a joyful experience.

Belief in OOBE and astral projection is extremely old. "Second body" experiences were accepted in the cultures of Egypt, India, and China and were known to Christian saints and mystics as well. The doctrine of an astral body was fundamental to Kabbalah, which declared that a human possesses a spirit body of roughly the same shape and extent as his earthly body. This spirit body can detach itself from the earthly body and move upward. The Theosophists posit that in addition to the physical body, there are astral, mental, causal, spiritual, and buddhic bodies.

One of the earliest and most famous cases of bilocation—being in one place in spirit while the physical body is elsewhere—is that of Alphonsus Liguori. One day in 1774, while at his monastery at Arienzo, four days' journey from Rome, he fell into a deep sleep that lasted two hours. When he awoke, he stated that he had just returned from the Pope's bedside in Rome and that the Pope had just died. When news of the Pope's death reached Arienzo, the whole thing was attributed to coincidence until the arrival of startling information that people attending the dying Pontiff had seen and talked to Liguori, who had led the prayers for the Pope.

Among the well-known nineteenth-century reports of OOBE is that of playwright August Strindberg, who "projected" himself into his Scandinavian home while lying ill in Paris. In the twentieth century prominent experiences of OOBE occurred to Oliver Fox, an Englishman active in psychic research, and Sylvan Muldoon, who has published books considered classics in OOBE. Uri Geller has reported OOBE experiences, as did the late Indian yogi Swami Pranabananda, who was called "the saint with two bodies."

Sylvan Muldoon had his first OOBE at the age of twelve, when he saw his body lying on a bed while he watched from above. Following the first, he had numerous similar experiences. In *The Phenomenon of Astral Projection* (Weiser, 1972), written with Hereward Carrington, Muldoon listed dozens of OOBEs reported by others and classified the reports according to the circumstances surrounding the event. His classifications included astral projection produced by drugs and anesthetics; astral projections of people undergoing surgery, who were often able to report details of the operation while presumably under anesthesia; and experiences associated with illness or accident or near death. In most instances, transition to the spiritual world seemed easy and pleasant, and the experience in that world was blissful. In reviewing the cases, Muldoon and Carrington concluded that certain similarities stand out in OOBEs: floating or soaring above the physical body; the presence of an "astral cord" uniting the two bodies; physical numbness, or an inability to move; and a feeling of depression just prior to the OOBE.

On the basis of his personal experiences, Muldoon stated that during astral projection the experiencer remains on this planet. He does not travel to a "higher realm"—that is, his experiences are related to life on earth. He is generally alone, not with other spirits, although occasionally he converses with the dead. Muldoon generally saw places well known to him but occasionally was "transported" to distant scenes and lands.

According to Monroe in *Journeys Out of the Body*, thought and action seem to merge in OOBE, and there is no mechanical translation of thought into action. The subject experiences changes in perception; he no longer depends on his senses for information. For example, the experiencer can "see" in all directions at once. During his own OOBE, Monroe was strongly aware of sexual arousal, but it took the form of a far more inclusive feeling than ordinary physical sex. He concluded from this that there is intrinsically an extremely strong attraction between human beings which, in our physical incarnation, takes the form of sex. In OOBE, "sex" becomes the desire to interpenetrate totally with the other and to "equalize the charge" as if the two beings were oppositely charged magnets or electric poles.

In spite of many reports of OOBE throughout history, there is not even preliminary scientific evidence that the phenomenon actually exists. One of the basic objections to the OOBE phenomenon is that the experiences cannot be clearly differentiated from dreaming. Muldoon argues that although there are many similarities between OOBEs and dreams, the OOBE projector maintains "his full waking consciousness." Monroe lists five characteristics of OOBE that he maintains differentiate the phenomenon from dreams: continuity of conscious awareness; intellectual and emotional decision making; the presence of "multivalued perception via sensory input" during OOBE; nonrecurrence of patterns; and development of events in chronological sequence, implying a genuine time lapse. It is noteworthy that primitive people regard dreams as analogous to OOBEs, believing that a sleeping person must be wakened carefully to allow time for the spirit to return to the body. Charles Tart, the University of California professor of psychology, monitored Monroe's physiological functions while he was presumably in an OOBE state and asked him to read a series of concealed numbers. Although the results were inconclusive, Tart believed they indicated that from a physiological viewpoint the OOBE state is similar to that of dreaming.

Muldoon admits that rigorous scientific proof is difficult to obtain because the phenomenon generally cannot be repeated at will. He grants that the studies thus far are scattered and inconclusive but claims the existence of astral projection has been proved in a variety of ways. He cites testimony, since earliest times, from all parts of the world, both among civilized and primitive peoples, and cases in which the astral body seemed to have a "mind of its own and was able to give information the experiencer could not have known at the time." He also cites as evidence instances where material effects were produced. In fact, Muldoon believes that if the OOBE theory were confirmed, it would confirm a number of hitherto-puzzling phenomena, such as apparitions, haunted houses, poltergeists, certain instances of clairvoyance, and déjà vu.

The ghost Philip, as drawn by Andy, one of the members of the Philip group.

The Philip Phenomenon

The Philip phenomenon refers to raps and table motion, similar to those produced in spiritualist séances, attributed to an intentional fantasy—a ghost named Philip—created by a group of eight researchers working at the Toronto Society for Psychical Research.

The Philip group originally hypothesized that a ghost apparition might be a psychic creation of its observers. After a year of trying to produce an apparition by sober meditation on the "ghost," whose fictitious biography and portrait they had created, the group purposely changed its method to that of the Victorian séance. Sitting around a card table, they sang rousing songs and told bawdy jokes in an attempt to produce the apparition. Within a few weeks of the change, raps occurred in or on the séance table, and the table began to move, seemingly by itself. From that time on, the group claims, it has been able to produce the Philip phenomenon on demand, anywhere, in full light, and before strangers, scientists, and skeptics. Only four members of the group, any four, need be present to produce the phenomenon.

The raps are very short and sharp, sometimes almost inaudible but clearly felt under the hands of the person who asks "Philip" a question. "Philip" responds with one rap for yes, two for no, and with scratching noises when "he" doesn't know the answer or doesn't like the question. On occasion, after a particularly good joke, the raps follow each other quickly and move around the table.

Table motion consists mostly of rocking on all four legs. though at times the table tilts on two legs or on one leg and can slide rapidly about the room on one leg or more. The group claims to have fully levitated the table once, but was unable to get an adequate picture of the event. On occasion the table will turn completely over so that its top rests on the floor. In that circumstance, the participants rest their hands on the bottom side of the top; the raps continue to occur as if coming from the side against the floor. The wooden tables used in the experiment stood on a deep pile carpet, which resists table movement caused by ordinary physical pushing or pulling.

The Philip group (left to right): Andy, Al, Iris, Lorne, Sidney, Dorothy, Sue.

The group, which began its experiment in September 1972 and first produced the Philip phenomenon in August 1973, consists of: Iris M. Owen, a former nurse and wife of Dr. A. R. G. Owen, an expert on poltergeist phenomena and a mathematician at the University of Toronto; Margaret "Sue" Sparrow, former chairman of Mensa (a society of people with very high IQs) in Canada and formerly a nurse; Andy H., housewife; Lorne H., Andy's husband and an industrial designer; Al P., a heating engineer and business owner; Bernice M., an accountant; Dorothy O'D., housewife and bookkeeper; and Sidney K., a sociology student. The group's meetings were observed by either Dr. Owen or Dr. Joel Whitton, a psychologist. They meet regularly on Thursday evenings.

The group is presently working with a metal tabletop. Their present aim is to analyze the sound of the raps, and the denser, more uniform metal table is better for this purpose. The top is hung from the ceiling so that the table does not create additional noises or upset the recording machinery as it would if it were free to move about.

The group emphasizes the importance of play in its sessions. The members theorize that a childlike attitude of play, a general expectation that the Philip phenomenon will appear, and a refusal to be astonished or soberly impressed with the phenomenon are essential if the phenomenon is to appear. They constantly remind themselves and observe that "Philip" is wholly imaginary and that there is no real entity causing the phenomenon. The phenomenon has been duplicated by two other Toronto groups working with other imaginary "beings."

A researcher for this book has seen the group create the Philip phenomenon with both the metal top and a wooden table and has participated by asking "Philip" questions and receiving rapping answers. The reporter also saw and felt the table shaking violently and recorded the raps and the sounds of the shaking. One videotape seen by the editor was a recording of a regularly scheduled TV show before a live audience of about fifty people. The table was seen to move extensively during the show.

Another of the videotapes seen by the editor was made in the laboratory of Professor Wilbur Franklin, a physicist at Kent State University in Ohio. Professor Franklin stated that his physical tests of the table motion were inconclusive and offered the hypothesis that the table might be made to rise up and move about by an initial unconscious application of hand pressure followed by very gentle but highly synchronized hand motions by the group. Another observer present at some of these tests, Terry J. Spencer, associate professor of psychology at Kent State, asserts that finger and hand pressure alone was responsible for the table movement.

The Philip phenomenon, if authentic, may explain claims of hauntings, possession and exorcism, communication with other-world persons and the dead, various possible apparitions including UFOs, and a variety of other paranormal events.

Each of the above may not be caused by genuine entities such as ghosts, demons, or extraterrestrials. The various phenomena associated with these events, including psychic phenomena, could be the consequence of unconscious psychic collaboration by believing participants. It may be that people in groups or as individuals can cause and accept psychic phenomena more easily if it is ascribed to another entity, thus relieving them of responsibility for whatever occurs (see Psi-Mediated Instrumental Response).

There are, however, serious questions about the authenticity of the phenomenon. Milbourne Christopher, in his excellent debunking book *ESP, Seers and Psychics* (T. Y. Crowell, 1970), cites experiments in 1853 by the noted British physicist Michael Faraday which show that the table motion can be fully explained by unconscious muscular effort. Faraday placed thin glass rods between two boards the size of the tabletop. The boards were held together, with the rods pressed between them, with several large elastic bands. This device was set on top of the table so that the participants touched the uppermost board, not the table. An indicator attached to the boards displayed the slightest pressure applied to the top board. In each case, when the table moved in a certain direction, the device indicated that the participants had unconsciously applied physical pressure in that direction. (For further details of Faraday's experiments, see Joseph Jastrow, *Error and Eccentricity,* Dover, 1962.) Christopher cites many cases of table tipping as an entertainment and concludes that it is merely an unusual physical phenomenon which can be produced by any group of people without paranormal assistance.

The sounds of the Philip raps on both the wooden and metal tabletops have been recorded and tested for acoustic quality. The envelopes, or profiles, of the Philip raps are unusual in that the intensity builds up slowly and drops off rapidly. Raps produced by other methods show a sharp onset and a slow decay (see *New Horizons,* Vol. 2, Nos. 1 [April 1975] and 2 [June 1976] for details).

Christopher, in an interview, said there were several methods of producing table raps that will fool naïve participants.

These range from surreptitious knuckle cracking and fingernail clicking to such crude methods as light kicks on the legs with a foot. All these methods imply conscious fraud.

It is very difficult, however, to discover any motive for such a fraud on the part of the group as a whole or of particular members. They are hospitable to visiting reporters but do not seek publicity. There is little, if any, potential for profit in the phenomenon. The weekly sessions, now entering their fifth year, are time-consuming, tiring, and boring. None of the members of the group seems gullible or self-deluding; on the contrary, their attitudes outside the sessions convey skepticism, doubt, and critical intelligence.

A full account of the Philip phenomenon may be read in *Conjuring Up Philip,* by Iris M. Owen and Margaret Sparrow (Harper & Row, 1976). A fifteen-minute film of the Philip group at work may be purchased or rented from George Ritter Films Ltd., 2264 Lakeshore Boulevard West, Toronto, Ontario M8V 1A9, Canada. The film is titled *Philip, the Imaginary Ghost.* An excellent critique of the book, *Conjuring Up Philip,* can be read in the *Journal of the American Society for Psychical Research,* Vol. 71, No. 2 (April, 1977).

Automatism

Automatism is any sensory or motor activity carried out by a person while he is in a dissociated state or without any conscious muscular effort or mental direction on his part.

When the pointer of an Ouija board "moves by itself" or when a person writes "automatically," unconscious muscular action is involved. To understand the origin of the various automatisms, the way ordinary physical habits are formed should first be considered. After sufficient repetition, muscular movements occur without conscious attention being necessary. Switching on a light or traveling down a familiar road to home, you don't need to decide which way to turn; you do it automatically. And once a task, such as typing or even walking, becomes established it becomes difficult to perform if you begin to follow it consciously. Thus, in forming a habit, we allow the control of our muscular movements to drop below the level of consciousness. When movement drops out of consciousness, it can do so because the mind allows itself to separate a bit, to dissociate.

The most outstanding instance of the use of the Ouija

board is that made by Mrs. Curran, a St. Louis resident who, in 1913, discovered she could get intelligent responses from it. Only occasionally, if at all, does an Ouija message provide the person operating it with information not previously known to him. In Mrs. Curran's case, the board revealed the personality of Patience Worth, an Englishwoman of the seventeenth century. The language the messages were received in was that of England in the seventeenth century, but no verification has ever been made of the existence of Patience Worth.

The subject of automatic writing has aroused a great deal of controversy in recent years owing to the widespread interest in spiritualism. There are usually two approaches to the subject—the spiritual and the psychological. For many years the Society for Psychical Research has reported cases of automatic writing which it considered to be mediumistic messages or instances of thought transference. Psychologists, however, consider this phenomenon an indication of a splitting or dissociation of the personality.

Some people consider automatic writing to be any script produced involuntarily—and that definition would include common, everyday doodling—performed without the person's being totally aware of the process, even though he is in a waking state (see A. M. Muhl, *Automatic Writing,* Helix, 1963).

Of automatic writing, Louisa E. Rhine writes: "Occasionally, an individual . . . found his hand had indeed written something of which he had no direct awareness. . . . The messages so received, like most of those via the Ouija, may have no particular meaning. They at least have none for parapsychology unless . . . they tell something true that the person holding the pencil did not know" (L. E. Rhine, *PSI: What Is It?,* Harper & Row, 1975).

Other types of automatisms occur. Radiesthesia is the use of a free-swinging pendulum to determine yes or no answers, or the pendulum may be suspended over a chart to read fortunes. Radiesthesia also includes dowsing, the use of a rod to find underground water and another form of motor automatism. There is also the age-old practice of table tipping. In this a group of people are seated around a table with their hands lightly on the top. If the table tips sufficiently to tap a leg on the floor, sometimes an intelligent response is received by using a prearranged code. In this procedure, if movement is obtained, the operators may not be aware that even with their slight contact with the table, they can unconsciously exert sufficient pressure to cause the motion. Rhine feels it could be considered a psychic experience only if it fulfilled the definition of information received without using the normal senses. The automatism in itself is not sufficient.

The most notable case of automatism today is that of Rosemary Brown, a quiet Englishwoman who composes good music, supposedly with the assistance of long-dead masters.

When Mrs. Brown was only seven years old, Franz Liszt dropped by to say hello, even though he had been dead for more than fifty years. She recalls, "He had long white hair and wore a black gown . . . and he told me that when I grew up, he would give me music." One day in 1964, while Rosemary was playing the piano, she suddenly lost control of her hands and found Liszt guiding her fingers over the keys.

Soon not only Liszt but Mozart, Bach, Chopin, Beethoven, Schubert, Debussy, Brahms, Grieg, and Schumann were guiding her compositions. As she explains it, "Liszt controls my hands for a few bars at a time, and then I write the music down. . . . Chopin tells me the notes at the piano and pushes my hands onto the right keys; if it is a song, Schubert tries to sing it—but he hasn't got a very good voice. Beethoven and Bach prefer to have me seated at the table with pencil and paper; then they give me the key, the timing, the left hand and the right hand."

Rosemary and her friends began to attract attention in 1969. Sir George Trevelyan, and music experts George and Mary Firth set up a fund to permit her to devote her full time to composing. Other musicians became interested, and the BBC asked her to make television appearances. Philips Records also recorded a collection of her music entitled *A Musical Séance*. She has written two books: *Unfinished Symphonies* (Morrow, 1971) and *Immortals by My Side* (Regnery, 1975).

Whether or not one believes in communication with the dead, Rosemary remains a musical mystery. All the pieces are characteristic of their alleged composers, and some are almost good enough to have actually been written by a Liszt or Beethoven on an off day. She claims to have had psychic experiences as a child and little musical training. Also, repeated tests suggest that she cannot take down a simple melody by dictation. Who, then, is smuggling those notes into Rosemary's piano? Not many people are willing to believe that she is really in touch with Liszt and his friends, yet even celebrated musical doubters show a grudging respect for Rosemary. "If she is a fake, she is a brilliant one and must have had years of training," said British composer Richard Rodney Bennett.

Perhaps the best way to prove she really is in touch with Liszt is to have Rosemary discover something from the past, such as Liszt's now-vanished manual of piano technique, which he wrote for the Geneva Conservatoire. Unfortunately the spirits that mediums raise always refuse to answer the very questions that would prove their existence. When *Time* magazine posed a choice of twenty musical mysteries for solution, Rosemary replied, "I cannot push a button and call on composers just like that."

The most outspoken faith in Mrs. Brown comes from Sir Donald Tovey, one of England's most respected musicologists. On the liner notes of her album he declared that the composer's communications are real. Sir Donald dictated his liner notes to Rosemary Brown on January 1, 1970. He died in 1940 (see *Time*, July 6, 1970).

On April 14, 1970, CBS carried a segment about Mrs. Brown on its program *Sixty Minutes*. Composers Virgil Thomson and André Previn were interviewed about her music. Previn noted that for a person even to forge this kind of music would require a good deal of technique and knowledge of music notation. He did believe, however, that the quality of the music was fourth-rate compared to that of the famous composers Mrs. Brown relies on. Thomson considered the music reminiscent of the composers to whom it was attributed, but he insisted there was an underlying similarity between the various works, which he believed would indicate they had all been written by the same person.

Mrs. Brown was examined by a psychiatrist from the University of London, who stated she was neither schizophrenic nor neurotic but had probably repressed a desire to write music and had unconsciously picked up a good deal of technique and musical information which she was now expressing (see I. Litvag, *Singer in the Shadows*, Macmillan, 1972).

The automatic use of the hands, an Ouija board or planchette, or any other device is not essential to the phenomenon of automatism. Only the element of dissociation is required to class the behavior as automatism. As shown in Rosemary Brown's case, highly creative elements of the personality

Jane Roberts, through whom a disembodied spirit called Seth purportedly communicates his philosophy.

appear to be able to emerge more clearly in some people if they can dissociate themselves from their creative work. Jane Roberts and Joan Grant are interesting examples of this kind of creativity at work.

In 1963 Jane Roberts and her husband, Robert Butts, began tinkering with an Ouija board, when a personality called "Seth" began to dictate messages. Soon Ms. Roberts outgrew the board and shifted to "voice communicating," with the "Seth" personality purportedly dictating volumes of material through her, including discourses on the nature of reality, perception, ESP, and reincarnation. "Seth," depicting "himself" as a disembodied "energy-essence" personality, outlined a complex transcendent reality. Among spirit communicators, "Seth" is exceptional for his high-mindedness, optimism, and profundity. Ms. Roberts now claims to have been independently inspired to invent a new theory, aspect psychology, to incorporate the psychic effects denied by traditional psychology. Before "Seth's" appearance, Ms. Roberts was a professional writer of short stories and poetry. She grew up in Saratoga Springs and attended Skidmore College

(New York). She continues her writing career in Elmira, New York.

Books by Jane Roberts

Adventures in Consciousness: An Introduction to Aspect Psychology (Prentice-Hall, 1974).

The Coming of Seth (Pocket Books, 1976).

Dialogues of the Soul and Mortal Self in Time (Prentice-Hall, 1975).

The Education of Oversoul Seven (Prentice-Hall, 1973).

The Nature of Personal Reality: A Seth Book (Prentice-Hall, 1974).

The Seth Material (Prentice-Hall, 1970).

Seth Speaks: The Eternal Validity of the Soul (Bantam, 1974).

Joan Grant says that as a child she became aware of the gift of "far memory," an ability to recall previous lives in other times and distant places. Her books have been released and reviewed as historical novels and sometimes praised for vividness and detail. She, however, maintains that the books are memories of her former lives. Her historical novels/reincarnation autobiographies have portrayed her as either male or female figures and depicted her in ancient Egypt, Greece, and Israel, among other places.

Books by Joan Grant

Castle Cloud (Ace, 1971).

Life as Carola (Avon, 1975).

Scarlet Feather (Avon, 1975).

So Moses Was Born (Avon, 1952).

Winged Pharaoh (Berkley, Wehman, 1969).

An Exercise in Levitation

A simple experiment in levitation can be easily performed by a group of five people and one experimenter, using one small straight-backed chair, preferably without arms.

The largest and heaviest person sits on the chair. Two others stand behind him, and two stand on either side, near his knees. Throughout the experiment the seated person remains seated. He should not do anything; he should not cooperate, resist, or become active in any way. The four other participants perform a specific set of movements in a rhythm that they establish. The movements are simple and divided into two

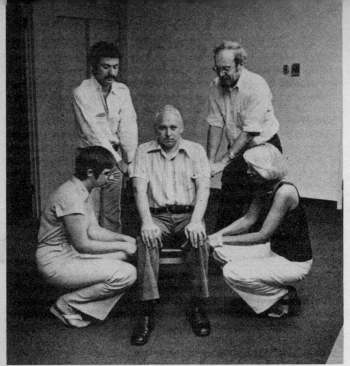

"They are not going to lift me!"

parts. Person 1, at the seated person's right, places his right hand on top of the seated person's head. Person 2, standing at the right rear, then places his right hand on top of Person 1's right hand. Person 3, standing at the left rear, places his right hand on top of Person 2's right hand, and Person 4 standing at the left front, places his right hand on top of all the other hands. There are now four right hands one on top of the other. Then Person 4 places his left hand on top of his own right hand. Person 3 places his left hand on the top of the pile of hands, and Person 2 and Person 1 do the same respectively. These movements should be practiced until they can be performed easily in a rhythmic manner.

Once a rhythm has been established another set of movements is performed. When the experimenter, after the performance of the first of the movements, calls out "Lift," persons 1, 2, 3, and 4 quickly move their hands from the seated person's head, extend the forefingers of each hand palm downward, and place them as follows: Person 1 places his index and middle fingers under the seated person's right knee, Person 2 places his fingers under the right armpit, Person 3 places his fingers under the left armpit, and Person 4 places his fingers under the left knee. These motions should also be practiced until they can be done smoothly. Then, when the experimenter calls out "Lift," the four persons can easily lift the seated person into the air.

Before the experiment the experimenters should have the four persons place their fingers in the designated spots and attempt to lift the person seated in the chair. It will be obvious that it takes an enormous effort to lift the seated person even an inch in the air without the use of the technique described above. A simple physical explanation for this phenomenon might be the better coordination of effort that results from a well-established rhythm.

Uri Geller

Uri Geller is a young Israeli who claims to have psychic powers. He bends spoons, pins, rings, and other things but swears he does not use physical strength—he only uses the power of his mind. He does not know or understand how this is accomplished, and he does not claim he can control it; he accepts the "strange things" he says have always happened around him.

A former model, he is a consummate showman, and his personality onstage is sincere, childlike, and full of wonder at his own accomplishments. He tries to please the audience, and even skeptics have been taken by his charming ways. Yet personal friends sometimes find him childish, arrogant, and difficult to work with. His main goals in life are reported to be money, fame, and women.

His detractors insist that Geller is a trickster, an opportunist out to deceive the rich and the gullible. He has convinced many people of his psychic abilities, and even though he has been caught cheating on several occasions, some scientists believe they have evidence that Geller has exhibited paranormal abilities under laboratory conditions.

Early Life.

Geller was born in Tel Aviv on December 20, 1946. In his autobiography, *My Story* (Warner, 1976), Geller states that

Uri Geller holds a key he claims to have bent without using physical force.

as far back as he can remember he experienced strange events over which he had no control. He believes it all started when he was about three or four years old. One day he heard a loud, high-pitched ringing in his ears. Looking up, he saw a strange silvery mass of light that came closer and closer to him until he was knocked unconscious. When he awoke, he "knew" that something important had happened to him.

At the age of six, he says, he was able to tell his mother exactly how much money she had won or lost at cards. During school, when he wished for recess, he found his wristwatch would run ahead of time. When he was nine years old, silverware began to break in his hands while he was eating, but afraid of being ridiculed, he kept these strange occurrences to himself. About the same time his parents were divorced, and he lived on a kibbutz for about a year until he joined his mother and her new husband on Cyprus, where they ran a hotel for entertainers.

After being wounded while fighting with the Israeli Army in 1967, Geller became an instructor at a resort camp for children. It was here that he met Shipi Shtrang, a twelve-year-old boy who encouraged Geller to perform in front of audiences. Shipi arranged for Geller to perform at his school.

Soon there were other demonstrations at schools and private parties, newspapers in Israel began to write about the shows, and Geller was besieged with contract offers from managers and promoters. Under the guidance of a professional manager, Geller was booked into theaters all over Israel. It was then, says Geller, that he yielded to his manager's urging to spice up his act by adding "tricks" to his routine. With an assistant in the parking lot to usher people to selected seats in the theater, Geller was able "psychically" to read their license plate numbers.

Geller's routine in his shows—in Israel, the United States, Germany, and elsewhere—begins with his claim that the mental energy of his audience is crucial to his success during a performance and that he cannot perform successfully in a hostile environment. During his stage demonstrations he usually starts by asking someone to write a word for a color on a blackboard for the audience to see. Then he asks the volunteer to erase it. He cautions the members of the audience not to whisper the color, and on the count of three they are supposed to think of the color so he can receive the "image." He claims that there is a kind of screen in his mind, "and when I receive something, whatever it is draws itself on that screen." He also guesses which foreign capitals and geometric figures the audience is thinking of, bends metal objects, and makes stopped watches start again. Sometimes he attempts to transmit a message to a member of the audience, and on occasion he has taken volunteers for a car ride while blindfolded, supposedly using the vision of the other passengers to navigate.

Geller Is Discovered.

In August 1971 Dr. Andrija Puharich, an American physician and psychic investigator, who had received a report of Geller's psychic powers, went to Israel to investigate him. Puharich conducted a number of experiments with Geller, experiments which Geller claims were 80 percent successful and which totally convinced Puharich that Geller was a genuine psychic.

During the course of these experiments the strangeness level of Geller's life increased sharply. Hypnotized by Puharich, Geller spoke in a flat, mechanical, computerlike voice. The voice identified itself as "Spectra," a computer aboard a spaceship from a distant planet. The spaceship and the monster computer it contained are under the control of Hoova, one of a team whose members supervise planetary civilizations. Hoova intervenes in the earth's affairs every 6,000 years and, for this intervention, had chosen Uri Geller to help the world and Puharich to help Geller.

Geller soon began to see and photograph UFOs. Objects, such as the tape from a cassette and the cartridge from inside a ball-point pen, began to disappear. When Geller, in a trance, was drawn into a UFO, the cartridge was miraculously restored to its proper place inside the pen.

How much of this was Geller's imagination and how much Puharich's is unclear. In *Uri: A Journal of the Mystery of Uri Geller* (Doubleday, 1974), Puharich reveals that as far back as 1952 he had been contacted, through a medium, by the Nine, the highest minds in the universe. Subsequently, Spectra indicated that Hoova was an employee of the Nine. In the ensuing years Puharich made a great deal of money on medical electronic devices he invented. He also explored the potentials of hallucinogenic mushrooms, brought Dutch psychic Peter Hurkos to America, investigated Brazilian healer Arigo, and wrote two books: *Beyond Telepathy* (Doubleday, 1962) and *The Sacred Mushroom* (Doubleday, 1959). In the Afterword of John Fuller's report of the Arigo investigation (*Arigo: Surgeon of the Rusty Knife*, T. Y. Crowell, 1974), Puharich states that in early 1971, soon after he heard of Arigo's death, he decided that he had failed "Arigo and humanity by not completing my studies of Arigo's healing work. . . . I was sure there would never be another Arigo in my lifetime. But if there was, I would not fail the next time." Within months he had found the newest object of his messianic compulsions. In a letter purportedly written by Puharich in early 1972, five months after he arrived in Israel, he announced that he had again been contacted by the highest minds in the universe and that Geller and he had already begun to save mankind by averting World War III.

Geller, however, seems to want to put some distance between himself and some of Puharich's wilder ideas. Geller speaks of "Spectra" as the "cosmic clown" who is merely playing tricks with us. He uses this idea to explain why a potential messiah can only bend car keys and make tie clips disappear instead of walking on water and feeding multitudes. He expresses considerable doubt that "Spectra" has fully informed him and Puharich of the plans of the Nine. This suggests that Geller may be unconvinced about "the highest

minds in the universe" and may only be humoring Puharich
by pretending to believe in Hoova.

The SRI Tests.

Puharich believed that Geller would never be taken seriously until his talents had been tested by scientists. So after
a promotion and show-business tour of Germany, Geller, at
Puharich's urging, went to the United States in November
1973 to undergo testing at the Stanford Research Institute
(SRI) with Dr. Harold Puthoff and Russell Targ, laser
physicists interested in psychic phenomena (see A Clairvoyance Experiment). (SRI, in Menlo Park, California, is a
private organization without any institutional connection
with nearby Stanford University.) Funding for the Geller
study was provided in part by Judy Skutch of New York and
by former astronaut Dr. Edgar Mitchell, now president of
the Institute of Noetic Sciences in Palo Alto, California.
The investigation was conducted off and on between November 1972 and August 1973 and was designed to test Geller
for telepathy, clairvoyance, and psychokinesis.

The results of the SRI telepathy and clairvoyance investigations were published in the prestigious British scientific
journal *Nature* (October 18, 1974), but with a lengthy
editorial expressing doubt about the experimental design.
The referees of the journal felt the details of the experimental
conditions were "disconcertingly vague," and they were not
convinced that sufficient precautions were taken to safeguard
against the possibility of conscious or unconscious fraud.
Despite its shortcomings, the paper was published "because it
would allow parapsychologists, and all other scientists interested in researching this arguable field, to gauge the quality
of the Stanford research and assess how much it is contributing
to parapsychology."

Remote Perception of Graphic Material.

The first of three tests reported in the SRI paper was
conducted in August 1973. It deals with experiments to
determine Uri's ability to reproduce target pictures chosen
from a dictionary (trials 1–4); targets prepared by someone
outside the experimental group (trials 5–7); pictures from a
target pool which were selected before the experiment (trials
8–10); and targets drawn on a cathode ray tube display by

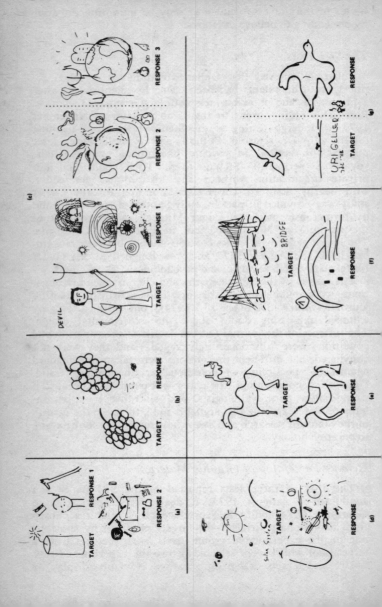

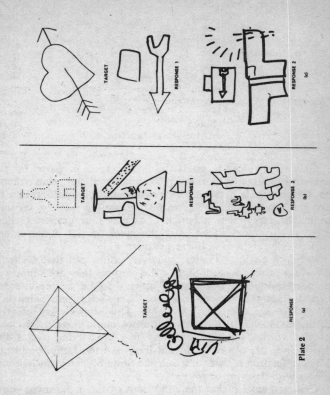

Plate 2

computer laboratory personnel (trials 11–13). This was primarily a telepathy test since the target was known by an experimenter at the time of the trial. Geller was granted the right to refuse to try to guess the target at any time during the tests.

PICTURE DRAWING TEST AT SRI

trial	target	outcome
Pictures chosen from a dictionary:		
1	firecracker	poor
2	grapes	good
3	devil	poor
4	solar system	good

Pictures prepared by an outsider:

5	rabbit	pass
6	tree	pass
7	envelope	pass

Pictures from target pool:

8	camel	good
9	bridge	fair
10	seagull	good

Pictures from the computer laboratory:

11	kite	good
12	church	good
13	arrow through heart	fair

Geller did refuse to guess the three targets prepared by an outside investigator (targets 5–7), but in all ten trials where he did attempt a drawing there was some relation between it and the target picture. The most outstanding was the second trial. The target was a bunch of twenty-four grapes; Geller drew twenty-four grapes, and the stem of the bunch even curled to the right as in the target picture.

A major critic of Geller, however, points out that Geller's drawings often do not look like the pictures they are supposed to correspond to, but instead appear to be a response to verbal clues (Dr. Joseph Hanlon, "Uri Geller and Science," *New Scientist*, October 17, 1974). This shows most clearly in targets 4 and 10. Geller's responses might have been cued by the words "solar system" and "big bird flying over little bird" since his drawings do not look like the target pictures. The implication is that someone like Shipi Shtrang was helping Geller with descriptive words.

Critics maintain that the conditions of the experiment were not adequately controlled. They assert that the room in which Geller was "isolated" was not secure and that Geller's assistant, Shipi Shtrang, could have passed signals to him. Edgar Mitchell is reported to have described the conditions as chaotic and videotapes taken during the tests are reported to show Geller getting up and even walking around, moving from one task to another, and sometimes even leaving the room. Puthoff responds that Shtrang was never "in the target area" but does not deny that Shtrang was constantly about.

An earlier test conducted in November or December 1972 was designed to test Geller's clairvoyance. Geller was successful eight times out of ten at calling the uppermost face of a die which was in a closed metal card-index box. But again, the critics complain that the tests went on for hours in uncontrolled conditions and that besides the ten tests in which Geller got eight hits, there were dozens of other tests which went unrecorded. The critics also claim that Geller was allowed to handle the file box, that it is no problem for a magician to distract observers and sneak a peek inside such a box, that the long hours make it unlikely that the experimenters gave Geller their constant attention, and that Targ is extremely nearsighted in any case.

Hanlon reports that Targ himself described conditions this way: "Deliberately or accidentally, Geller manipulates the experiments to a degree of chaos where he feels comfortable and we feel uncomfortable." Targ has also admitted that "Geller will cheat if he can."

The third test reported in the SRI paper was conducted in August 1973. This test, also one of clairvoyance, involved a pool of 100 target pictures sealed, along with black cardboard, inside envelopes. Each day envelopes were selected at random, and Geller tried to draw the target pictures inside them. The report states that "the drawings resulting from this experiment did not depart significantly from what would be expected by chance." In other words, Geller failed this test.

In their report in *Nature*, Targ and Puthoff also wrote: "Although metal bending by Geller has been observed in our laboratory, we have not been able to combine such observations with adequately controlled experiments to obtain data sufficient to support the paranormal hypothesis."

If Geller did cheat on the tests, he used the techniques of magicians and psychological trickery. Puthoff and Targ believed they had guarded against this possibility by calling in an amateur magician named Arthur Hastings, who is also a student of parapsychology. James "The Amazing" Randi, a professional magician, reports in a privately circulated paper that Hastings denied being present during any of the experiments reported by Puthoff and Targ. Targ himself is also an amateur magician, though there is considerable doubt if this qualifies him to detect the use of sleight-of-hand tricks. Another professional magician, Milbourne Christopher, was brought in after the tests to observe the videotapes and films of the experiment and to suggest procedures for future tests. Apparently, experienced prestidigitators were not fully consulted before and during the experiments.

Harry Houdini stated in *A Magician Among the Spirits* (his exposé of the spiritualists of his day):

> "I have read with keen curiosity the articles by leading scientists on the subject of psychic phenomenon. . . . There is no doubt in my mind that some of these scientists are sincere in their belief but unfortunately it is through this very sincerity that thousands became converts. The fact that they are scientists does not endow them with an especial gift for detecting the particular sort of fraud used by mediums, nor does it bar them from being deceived. . . .

Exposing Geller.

"It takes a magician to catch a magician," says James Randi, and his book *The Magic of Uri Geller* (Ballantine, 1975) is a record of his duplication of all of Geller's tricks, often for the same people Geller had once impressed with his talents. Another attack on Geller's claims appears in an entertaining forty-page booklet entitled *Confessions of a Psychic*. Written by Uriah Fuller, a pseudonym for one of America's most entertaining science writers, the book is a humorous satire on the Geller saga. Uriah, a lazy, second-rate magician, decides he won't have to work as hard and can make more money by touting himself as a psychic. With the help of his assistant, Schleppi Strangelove, Fuller fools Boobharich and the physicists at the Shameford Institute. By the end of the book, Uriah is thinking about starting a new religion. (*Confessions* is available at some magic stores and from Karl Fulves, Box 433, Teaneck, New Jersey 07666.) In "Magic and Paraphysics" (*Technology Review,* June 1976), Martin Gardner, mathematics columnist for *Scientific American*, writes a more sober critique of the Geller phenomenon and related issues.

The basic point of the debunkers' approach to the Geller phenomenon is that the rule of Occam's razor must be applied to Geller's work: One should not assume a more complex hypothesis until all the simpler explanations have failed. The simpler explanations in Geller's case all turn on sleight of hand, misdirection, and psychological forcing. Since we know that these methods can be used to mystify people and since we are not sure that real psychic abilities do exist, we ought to take the simpler explanation, say the critics—Geller is a clever magician.

When Uri Geller arrived on the American scene in 1972, he left a trail of bent and broken silverware behind him, and some prominent people believing in him. Edgar Mitchell, the Apollo 14 astronaut, believed one of his old tie clips materialized in some ice cream that Uri was eating; for a long time he waited for Geller to teleport back to earth a camera he had accidentally left on the moon. Mitchell has since fallen out with Geller and speaks of him harshly.

Many times people who see Geller perform react like eyewitnesses to a car accident: they report totally different stories. Even experienced observers can misreport what has happened. A reporter may write that Geller bent a key without even touching it. More likely, the person means that Geller had held the key, apparently attempting to bend it with his mind, but soon gave up and put the key to one side. Later, when someone examined the key, they found it had bent "by itself," after Geller, distracting his audience with some other piece of business, had surreptitiously bent the key against his chair or replaced it with a previously prepared key.

Guessing Colors.

Geller may find an opportunity to peek quickly while the audience is watching the person writing the color on the blackboard. (Uriah Fuller, the fictional Uri Geller, always picks an attractive woman for this task to make sure all eyes are on her, not on him.) While that method is a bit risky, a signaler in the audience is *almost* foolproof. In fact, David Marks and Richard Kammann, psychologists at the University of Otago in New Zealand, have observed Geller's secretary give distinctive hand signals from her seat in the audience during this part of Geller's routine. An article in the *Journal of the Society for Psychical Research* (December 1974) reported that Geller had been exposed in front of an audience in Israel for reading hand signals from an accomplice.

Guessing Foreign Capitals.

The instructions, according to Uriah Fuller, go something like this: "Write the name of a city that is the capital of a large foreign country. Not London, that's too easy." The natural reaction would be to write Paris or Rome.

The point is that not many people will remember the exact instructions and do not recognize that they have been psychologically manipulated. People do not like to believe that such manipulation is possible, but if it weren't, a great deal of ordinary magic would also be impossible.

Sending Telepathic Messages to Someone in the Audience.

Again psychological forcing and misdirection can be applied in the instructions: "I am going to draw a simple geometric shape—not a square, that's too simple—and I am going to draw another simple geometric shape inside the first one." Most people would respond by drawing a circle and a triangle, either one inside the other. After all, how many simple geometric shapes are there? Also, even if Geller guesses wrong, he can't lose; the audience concludes that the person selected doesn't have any psychic abilities. If Geller guesses right, the audience is highly impressed.

Reproducing a Drawing "Hidden" in a Sealed Envelope.

In a test conducted by David Marks and Richard Kammann at the University of Otago in New Zealand, forty-eight students were asked to study three envelopes under normal indoor lighting to see if they could get a sense of the envelopes' contents. Divided into four groups, the students were given five, ten, twenty, or fifty seconds to examine the envelopes. Each envelope contained a target drawing which Kammann and Marks had earlier presented to Geller under similar conditions. The drawings presented to the students were folded and placed in the envelopes in exactly the same manner as those used to test Geller. Geller's response to the original tests were faithfully reproduced, and his entry was marked "student #49." Six judges were then asked to rate the drawings. Geller was rated well above the average student, but in comparison with the best students' drawings, his feat is unremarkable. Geller's work looks simple, especially when one considers the amount of practice he has had and the unlimited amount of time he takes to produce a drawing, compared to first attempts by naive students who received a maximum of only fifty seconds to examine the envelope.

On casual inspection of the envelopes, the lines of the drawings were not apparent, but held up to the light, the drawings did become faintly visible. The key to the study was that the drawings were folded so as to distort or omit important elements of the picture or to add an extraneous element—

one of the pictures was drawn on paper with a lined border around it; folded, that border added confusing lines to the picture. Looking through the envelopes, the students overlooked the added lines, left out the fold-hidden sun above a flower, and faithfully reproduced a black blob that, unfolded, became the edge of a shaded-in goblet. Geller, using his "psychic" talents, reported the same distorted and partial images as the students. This strongly suggests that he, too, merely looked through the envelopes.

Fixing Broken Watches.

Kammann and Marks also interviewed jewelers and found that more than half the watches brought in for repair are not really broken; they are just suffering from gummed-up oil and dust. They argue that holding the watch in the hand raises the temperature and thins the oil.

After a few slight movements this starts the watch ticking again. This seems rather too simple an explanation, but in an experiment with seven jewelers, Marks and Kammann found that 60 watches out of 106 did begin to tick again—a success rate of 57 percent. Since this was not a controlled experiment and the jewelers might have been lying, psychology students were tested for their success rate. They attained a rate of 68.9 percent in thirty-two attempts.

There is an interesting similarity here. Just as few people would normally notice the faint lines that can be seen through an envelope, few people have ever attempted to "repair" a watch by merely holding it. But these experiments illustrate that it can be done. (The two psychologists revealed their research on Geller in a paper presented to the Psychonomic Society meeting in Denver, Colorado, November 6, 1975.)

Bending Metal Objects.

Many times Geller has had the opportunity to examine test materials beforehand, and his critics claim that a fork or spoon can be prepared by bending it back and forth until it is on the verge of breaking from metal fatigue. Then, with the slightest bit of pressure, the fork or spoon will seem to "melt" and crack in two.

For spikes and nails, spoons and keys, sleight of hand— replacing the straight nail with a bent one, surreptitiously— is an excellent means of producing results. It is also possible to bend a key by pressing it against a wall, chair frame, or tabletop while no one is looking.

The fact that the objects never seem to bend when someone is looking directly at them is termed the shyness effect by John Taylor, professor of mathematics at King's College, University of London. In his book *Superminds: A Scientist Looks at the Paranormal* (Viking, 1975), Taylor notes that the shyness effect is usually related to the presence of skeptics and others who have a poor relationship with the psychic.

Responding to the claims of hundreds of schoolchildren that they could bend silverware just as Geller did, Taylor tested a number of them. Taylor put metal bars inside glass tubes and sealed corks into the ends of the tubes. To overcome the shyness effect, he let the children take the tubes home. When the tubes were returned, many of the metal bars were bent.

Randi maintains that in some cases where the bars were bent, the seals on the tubes were loosened or showed other signs of tampering (see *New Scientist,* October 16, 1975). Randi and other investigators attribute the shyness effect to the necessity of privacy if the bars are to be bent without anyone's seeing physical force applied.

One of the strongest cases of possible cheating by Geller was observed by Sandy McCrae, a sound recorder for Thames Television in England. He reported actually seeing Geller bend a large kitchen spoon by hand. It seems that film magazines contain ten minutes of film, but a standard sound tape runs twenty minutes. While the cameramen were busy reloading the film, Geller attempted to divert everyone else's attention by referring them back to a fork he had just broken. But McCrae, who was not busy reloading his equipment, did not turn to the broken fork and said he saw Geller bend the spoon by hand. Geller then called attention to the bent spoon, and the filming resumed. Support for McCrae's story comes from the facts that McCrae was a strong believer in Geller before this incident and that Geller and his associates were obsessively interested in how long it took to reload a film magazine.

Finding the Filled Film Can.

One of Geller's standard feats is finding an object that has been placed into one of ten light aluminum 35mm film cans.

On the *Merv Griffin Show*, Uri performed this trick success-fully but some people thought they saw him jar the table so that he could tell which can was the heaviest. When he appeared on Johnny Carson's show, he was not allowed near the cans, and there is a possibility that the Carson people coated the bottom of the cans with a skidproof material to prevent them from sliding. The result—Uri was not able to find the filled can.

On the *AM America* show, the staff used heavier film cans that could not be jarred. But on the day of the show Geller was at the studio before 5:50 A.M., when the staff members arrived (the show didn't start until 7 A.M.). The person in charge of filling the cans was aware that Geller had watched her fill the cans and tape them. At the last minute she called magician Felix Greenfield for advice. He told her to retape the cans when Geller wasn't around. She did this, and Geller failed again.

A Special Test.

In October 1973 Eldon Byrd, an engineer and an experi-menter in the area of plant sensitivity, tested Geller in a lab in Maryland. The test material was nitinol wire, a special alloy of nickel and titanium. The crystalline structure of this alloy gives the wire a very unusual property: No matter how it is bent, it will return to its original shape when heated to about 210 degrees F. In order permanently to change the shape of the wire, it must be constrained in the desired shape and heated to a temperature of 932 degrees F. Geller did succeed in bending a nitinol wire so that it would not return to the expected shape when heated.

A great deal of the impact of this test depends on statements that the material was a "special new" alloy (*National En-quirer*, July 20, 1976), was "not generally available to the public" and was "produced in very small quantities at the Naval Ordnance Laboratory" (Eldon Byrd in *The Geller Papers*, Charles Panati, ed., Houghton Mifflin, 1976). If these statements are true, a sleight-of-hand substitution of wires by Geller would seem to be ruled out.

In fact, however, nitinol wire had been available from the Edmund Scientific Company in Barrington, New Jersey, since May 1971. It was sold in a $5 kit of six wires. For another $1 the buyer could get a booklet by the National Aeronautics and Space Administration describing the properties of nitinol.

Shortly thereafter a New York magician had devised a trick using the wire, and for a time the trick was marketed by Davenport's, a major trick manufacturer in London, England. Given the availability of the alloy and the knowledge of its uses in some circles of magicians, it is not unlikely that Geller, probably knowing in advance that he would be tested with nitinol, could have obtained some, prepared it before going to Maryland, and substituted it for the wire Byrd gave him.

Conclusion.

With the application of Occam's razor—the simplest answer is the most likely—to Geller's talents, it becomes obvious that the events surrounding Geller can be explained by normal methods of magic and psychology. There is no reason to postulate a paranormal power that would require a complete reevaluation of the relationship between mind and matter.

But to be fair, if the reports of observers who say Geller is a genuine psychic cannot be trusted, why should any faith be placed in the observations of those who say he is a cheater? Except in a few cases where he has been caught cheating, most of the evidence against Geller is merely circumstantial.

Until scientists gain Geller's cooperation in a foolproof test under rigorously controlled conditions, the question will remain open. That is probably the reason why Geller has refused to submit to any rigorous testing before and since the SRI tests. As long as no definitive test is made, Geller need not fear losing the confidence of those who believe in his powers. Thus, what should be a scientific issue remains merely a debate between the believers and the skeptics. Geller has a responsibility to the public to help resolve this issue. If he does not, that fact and the preponderance of other evidence must result in a verdict against him.

Psychic Doings

Poltergeist

Poltergeist is a term used to describe unexplained noises, the movement of objects, the breaking of dishes, and similar phenomena. In parapsychological terminology, poltergeist activity is defined as recurrent spontaneous psychokinesis (RSPK).

The word "poltergeist" comes from the German for noisy spirit. It was already current in the Reformation era, when Martin Luther referred to the poltergeist as a noisy type of demon. However, it was only toward the latter half of the seventeenth century that the study of ghosts and poltergeists began to be viewed in a scientific spirit and detailed descriptions became available. According to British/Canadian author A. R. G. Owen, poltergeists were first recognized as a specific entity by Mrs. Catherine Crowe, whose 1848 book *The Night-Side of Nature* is still considered a classic of poltergeist literature. Hereward Carrington, a well-known writer on the occult, published *Historic Poltergeists* in 1935, listing approximately 400 recorded cases.

A. R. G. Owen, in his comprehensive and carefully documented book *Can We Explain the Poltergeist?*, describes in detail a number of the more prominent cases, including those he believes to be fakes and thirty-six he considers genuine. Among the latter, one of the most recent—and striking—is a poltergeist incident which broke out in Sauchie, Scotland, in 1960. Owen did not personally observe the alleged poltergeist activity but arrived at Sauchie shortly afterward and interviewed a number of witnesses. They included a minister, several physicians, and a teacher, and Owen was impressed by their character and stature in the community. The case centered on an eleven-year-old girl, Virginia Campbell, who had come to Scotland to live at the home of an elder brother after a secluded early childhood in Ireland. One day, when Virginia was home from school, having tea with her brother and his wife, a sideboard moved out five inches from the wall and then moved back again. Virginia was sitting in an armchair next to the sideboard but was not touching it. At school doors opened and closed, and the lid of Virginia's desk rose by itself. A "thunking" noise, like a bouncing ball, was heard in the bedroom while Virginia was in bed. As with all other manifestations, it ceased entirely when the girl went to sleep. Owen notes that the events in the case and the attendant circumstances appear to rule out natural causes, fraud, and mass hallucination.

The Sauchie case, he says, "must be regarded as establishing beyond all reasonable doubt the objective reality of some poltergeist phenomena."

In 1958 W. G. Roll and J. G. Pratt investigated poltergeist activity in the Seaford, New York, home of Mr. and Mrs. James Herrmann and their two children, Lucille, age thirteen, and James, Jr., age twelve. The tops of bottles opened, objects fell off shelves, and containers came tumbling down to the floor. Roll and Pratt first searched for normal explanations for the events, such as bad plumbing, sonic booms, and underground river currents, but to no avail. After analyzing a total of sixty-seven incidents reported by the Herrmanns, it became apparent that the great majority occurred when Jimmy was present and awake. The poltergeist activity had ceased almost entirely by the time the two investigators arrived on the scene. However, they did witness one incident: There was a loud noise, and a bleach bottle in the basement blew its cap under circumstances that seemed to rule out trickery on Jimmy's part. However, as the author's note in their article (*Journal of Parapsychology*, June 1958), the family declined their request to submit to a lie-detector test.

One of the strongest cases parapsychologists feel they have as evidence of poltergeist phenomena occurred in Miami in 1967. The events took place at a wholesale firm dealing in souvenirs and involved objects falling off shelves and breaking. When Roll and Pratt were called in to investigate, it became apparent that the focus of the activity was a nineteen-year-old Cuban refugee named Julio since most of the disturbances occurred during working hours when he was present and ceased entirely when he left the firm. Roll and Pratt report that there was no evidence to indicate an object was ever pushed, thrown, or moved by trick devices or that any other fraudulent means were used. The Miami case is noteworthy for having been the first in which an investigator was able to impose experimental control on poltergeist movements: Target objects were placed in areas of high activity, and their movements were subsequently traced.

Julio was tested in the laboratory for psychokinetic ability, but the results were not significant. His personality, as revealed by psychological studies, showed some of the traits considered typical in poltergeist cases. He was angry, had problems at home with his stepmother, and was suspected of robbing the warehouse. (See W. G. Roll and J. T. Pratt, "The Miami Disturbances," *Journal of the American Society for Psychic Research,* October 1971.)

One of the most dramatic poltergeist occurrences ever witnessed by Roll took place in Olive Hill, Kentucky, where the focus seemed to be twelve-year-old Roger Callihan. As Roger entered the kitchen of his home, he turned toward Roll and at that moment the kitchen table jumped into the air, rotated about forty-five degrees and came to rest on the backs of chairs standing alongside. Previously, Roger had predicted a number of poltergeist occurrences, and they happened suspiciously close to him. However, as Roll stated in his report, the kitchen-table incident convinced him that the Olive Hill case had real parapsychological significance (see *Research in Parapsychology 1974,* Scarecrow, 1975).

A bizarre series of poltergeist events was reported by a German investigator, Professor Hans Bender (*Zeitschrift für Parapsychologie und Grenzebiete der Psychologie,* LL:104, 1968; see also W. G. Roll, *The Poltergeist,* Doubleday, 1972). In November 1967 a Bavarian law office located in the town of Rosenheim was plagued by inexplicable occurrences: Light bulbs unscrewed themselves from their sockets; telephone calls "that were never made" showed up on the bill; noises were heard. Finally, when light bulbs began to explode, Bender was called in to investigate. It became evident that these strange occurrences took place only during hours when a nineteen-year-old employee named Annemarie was present. According to Bender, when she walked through the hall, light bulbs exploded, ceiling lamps swung, a 400-pound filing cabinet slid away from the wall, and paintings on the wall rotated. After Annemarie left her position with the firm, the events ceased.

In the majority of the alleged poltergeist occurrences that have been reported through the centuries there is either insufficient evidence to form objective judgments or fraud of some kind has been proved or can be reasonably assumed. After these have been eliminated, however, there is still a hard core of "genuine" cases which seem to defy conventional explanations. Various theories have been advanced, some of a parapsychological nature, and some within the bounds of known laws and principles of natural science. A notable example of the latter is the hypothesis that typical poltergeist phenomena may be explained by the sounds and vibrations made by the movement of underground currents of water. A. R. G. Owen points out, however, that while "natural" causes such as hallucinations, vibrations caused by underground water, or structural instability of buildings can account for some known cases, they do not apply to all the genuine poltergeist phenomena observed.

Psychologists are in agreement with parapsychologists on one key point: The poltergeist incident characteristically centers on an emotionally disturbed person, often an adolescent. Within the framework of conventional psychology, the poltergeist phenomenon is seen as a species of adolescent prank, consciously or unconsciously intended to get attention or to "get even" with parents, employers, or other adults. Parapsychologists tend to agree that the incidents are often triggered by a resentful adolescent, but they postulate that the actual noises and movements of objects are carried out through forces as yet unknown to conventional science.

Premonitions and the Sinking of the *Titanic*

People have long reported receiving premonitory messages, not fairly clear ones as in precognition, but vague feelings or even hallucinations that, when tied into facts that become known later, begin to seem more than coincidental. A young girl thinks she sees her friend for an instant; minutes later she learns that friend was in an accident and has been asking to see her. A young mother rushes to her infant. The child was in danger of choking. Even though no sounds were heard, the mother "knew" she had to help her child.

In 1912, when the SS *Titanic* hit an iceberg and sank to the bottom of the Atlantic Ocean with more than 1,500 passengers, many people came forward and reported their dreams, intuitions, and premonitions concerning the disaster. Some brought canceled tickets, and others were able to cite supporting testimony of those in whom they had confided their precognitions of disaster. The nineteen authenticated paranormal experiences associated with the *Titanic* sinking ranged from "feelings" to specific dreams.

One woman in New York awoke from a vivid dream that night and told her husband, "I just saw Mother in a crowded lifeboat rocking in the ocean swell. The boat was so crowded with people that it looked as if it might be swamped any minute." The next morning she was horrified to find her mother's name on the passenger list. Her mother had intended to surprise the family with an unexpected visit and had not told her daughter about her voyage on the *Titanic*. Luckily she survived the disaster and eventually reached New York.

One of the strangest instances of apparent precognition surrounding the *Titanic* is the novel *Futility*. Written by Morgan Robertson in 1898, it recounts the voyage of the ship *Titan,* an "unsinkable" vessel that collided with an iceberg and sank. There are many details of the novel that seem to foreshadow the sinking of the *Titanic:* the name of the ship, the myth of unsinkability, the collision with an iceberg, the sinking in the month of April, too few lifeboats, the number of passengers, the speed at impact with the iceberg, the displacement tonnage of the liner, the length of the ship, and the number of propellers.

While Dr. Ian Stevenson agrees that the ten points of correspondence strongly suggest foreknowledge, he doubts that informed inference can be excluded as a source of Robertson's story. At the end of the nineteenth century confidence in engineering skill ran high. Stevenson believes a thoughtful person with an awareness of man's growing and excessive confidence in marine engineering might be able to make additional inferences about the ships of the future. A

	Titan	Titanic	Percent of Difference
Number of passengers	3,000	2,207	26.5
Number of lifeboats	24	20	17.6
Speed at impact with the iceberg	25 knots	23 knots	8.0
Displacement tonnage of the liner	75,000	66,000	12.0
Length of the ship	800 feet	882.5 feet	9.4
Number of propellers	3	3	0

large ship would probably have great power and speed, and the name *Titan* has connoted power and size for 3,000 years. Overconfidence in engineering capabilities could result in too few lifeboats and racing through areas of the Atlantic where icebergs are common. Since icebergs drift south in the spring, April is a likely month for collision. Each of the other facts regarding the two ships could also be attributed to inference. The number of passengers is the single point where inference might lead to a very wide disparity—and, indeed it does.

While people have been acting on their hunches and intuition from the beginning, it is only within the last few years that scientific efforts have been made to collect prophetic dreams and other precognitive experiences. This is necessary if precognition is ever to rise above the level of interesting and eerie stories which cannot be proved.

One combination of spontaneous premonition and scientific control is found in the work of Dr. Hans Bender, at the Institute for Border Areas of Psychology at Freiburg University in West Germany. One of his more celebrated cases involved the actress Chrystine Mylius. She began to notice that her dreams were coming true with startling regularity and in 1954 began sending reports to Dr. Bender. In 1958 she dreamed of two films that would be produced. The dreams were filed at Bender's lab over a period of several weeks. In 1959 a writer published a book which subsequently became a film. The story matched a dream Mylius had placed on file in Bender's laboratory more than a year before. Even more incredibly, the film crew that was to shoot this film was at the same time working on another film the plot of which matched the second of Mylius' dreams.

Bureaus to record premonitions in advance of events have been established in the United States, Canada, and Britain. So far a great deal of interesting material has been filed, but there has not been a great number of premonitions applied to a single case, as in the *Titanic* disaster. The bureaus have been successful in bringing to light a number of people who seem to have a gift for precognition and might be investigated in an attempt to shed more light on the subject.

If you have premonitions you would like recorded, write to:
Central Premonition Registry, Box 482, Times Square Station, New York, New York 10036.
Toronto Society for Psychical Research, P.O. Box 427, Station F, Toronto, Ontario M4Y 2L8, Canada.

British Premonitions Bureau, T.V. Times, 247 Tottenham Court Road, London w1POAU, England.

For further information, see A. MacKenzie, *Riddle of the Future* (Taplinger, 1974); M. Ebon, *Prophecy in Our Time* (Wilshire Book Co., 1968); W. O. Stevens, *The Mystery of Dreams* (Dodd, Mead, 1949); and I. Stevenson, "A Review and Analysis of Paranormal Experiences Connected with the Sinking of the *Titanic*," *Journal of the American Society for Psychical Research* (October 1960). For a laboratory experiment in precognition, see A Clairvoyance Experiment.

Dermal Vision

Dermal vision, or paroptic vision, is the supposed ability to "see" with the skin. If dermal vision can be established as fact, it would suggest that the skin contains photoreceptors or receptors that are sensitive to electrostatic differentials. Alternatively, dermal vision may be a psychic phenomenon.

Kuda Bux in 1938 claiming to read a newspaper through the blindfolds. Photograph was taken during a press conference in New York to provide advance publicity for Bux's show-business tour of the United States.

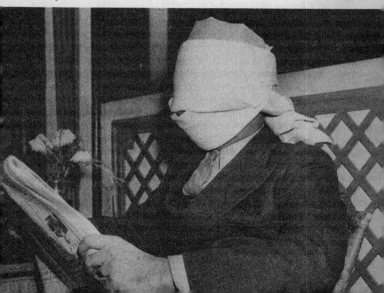

The most famous exponent of dermal vision in recent years was Kuda Bux, a Pakistani performer who specialized in reading or riding a bike or driving a car while blindfolded. Magicians, however, have ready explanations for the techniques of these tricks, and Bux is generally regarded today as a very able magician.

In the 1960s eyeless vision became a major subject for experimentation in the Soviet Union. A young woman, Rosa Kuleshova, told her doctor in 1962 that she could see with her fingers. Tests showed she could correctly name the colors of sheets of paper, describe photographs, and name objects held before her while blindfolded. Unfortunately Rosa and some other subjects inspired by her example were caught cheating. In 1964, however, a Bulgarian psychic researcher, Dr. G. Lozanov, tested sixty children who had been blind from birth to exclude any possibility of fraud. In more than 400 tests he found that most of the children could be trained to "see" something with their skin (see S. Ostrander and L. Schroeder, *The ESP Papers,* Bantam, 1976).

A new interest in paroptic vision arose in the United States in the late 1960s. R. P. Youtz and Caroll B. Nash conducted tests on fingertip vision. Both became convinced that subjects could detect color differences by minor temperature variations. Black, for example, is slightly warmer than other colors since it reflects heat more efficiently. This temperature sense, however, could not be considered vision.

Nash later designed a box which fitted over the entire head, resting on the shoulders, to exclude any possibility of peeking. (The use of a head box had been proposed by Martin Gardner in "Dermal-optical Perception: a Peek down the Nose," *Science,* February 11, 1966.) Nash then tested subjects' ability to distinguish red and black. There were three types of targets: uncovered, covered with a sheet of cellophane .03 millimeter thick, and covered with a sheet of glass 3 millimeters thick. Of the sixty subjects tested with uncovered red and black sheets of paper, fifty-nine scored above chance; out of fifty-two tested with cellophane-covered targets, thirty-six scored above chance. Only twenty-five subjects out of forty-three scored above chance when tested with glass-covered targets (see Nash, "Cutaneous Perception of Color with a Head Box," *Journal of the American Society for Psychical Research,* January 1971).

The results were interpreted to indicate dermal perception, rather than clairvoyance, because there would be little reason to expect such a marked difference in results if psi were involved. There are, however, some indications that different modes of psi are used to perceive reflective and nonreflective targets.

For further details, see A. Ivanov, "Soviet Experiments in Eyeless Vision," *International Journal of Parapsychology* (Winter 1964); Milbourne Christopher, *Mediums, Mystics and the Occult* (T. Y. Crowell, 1975) and *ESP, Seers and Psychics* (T. Y. Crowell, 1970); S. Ostrander and L. Schroeder, *Psychic Discoveries Behind the Iron Curtain* (Bantam, 1971); and Yvonne Duplessis, *The Paranormal Perception of Color* (Parapsychology Foundation, 1975).

Healing Energy

A healing energy trick is sometimes dishonestly used to demonstrate the presence of psychic energy in the palms of the hands.

At a meeting neighbors are asked to touch their hands together, palm to palm. The leader asks if there is any special feeling in the hands. If the meeting has attracted some believers in psychic healing, there will probably be some assent to the idea that there is a special feeling in the hands. The leader then asks everyone to take deep breaths while continuing to touch palms. After several breaths, everyone, even skeptics, will agree that there *is* a strange tingling or prickling sensation or a coolness in their hands, especially in the knuckles or the fingertips or thumbs. This tingling is supposed to be a mark of healing energy in the hands.

Deep breathing washes carbon dioxide out of the blood. This changes the ionic balance of the body fluids in a way that alters the excitability of the nerves. That change in excitability produces the tingling sensation. There is no new energy drawn into the body with the deep breaths.

Plant Sensitivity

Plant sensitivity is the phenomenon of "primary perception" in plants, alleged by polygraph expert Cleve Backster.

Cleve Backster explains the phenomenon of primary perception as a still-undefined sensory system or perception capability with "extrasensory perception," but in Backster's view, there is nothing "extra" about it. It is, according to

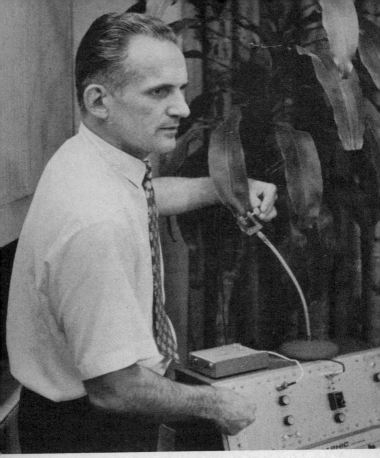

Cleve Backster, experimenter in plant sensitivity.

Backster, a basic primary capability of the specialized senses of higher organisms.

Before Backster's work, throughout history, in fact, humans have felt a strong sense of communication with trees and other plants. The German poet Rainer Maria Rilke expressed this communication beautifully in his poetry, and Algernon Blackwood assumed it for his eerie stories "The Willows" and "The Man Whom the Trees Loved."

The first investigation of plant response to external stimuli was conducted by Charles Darwin with the Venus's-flytrap

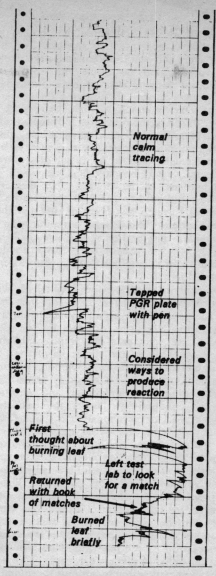

Normal
calm
tracing

Tapped
PGR plate
with pen

Considered
ways to
produce
reaction

First
thought about
burning leaf

Left test
lab to look
for a match

Returned
with book
of matches

Burned
leaf
briefly

Polygraph tracing from Backster's first test of plant sensitivity.

(Dionaea muscipela). He discovered that both body weight and moisture had to be present in an object for the plant to respond completely and that the Venus's-flytrap could discriminate among various kinds of objects. He also discovered that the plant showed fatigue after stimulation and needed a period of time for recovery. In studying the power of movement in plants, Darwin concluded that the root tip of a plant had the power to direct the movements of the adjoining parts. In the early 1900s the Indian scientist Sir Jagadis Chandra Bose showed that plants possess a nervous system capable of being stimulated by electric fields and thus parallel many of the bioelectrical and physiological responses present in animals and humans. In the 1920s Luther Burbank demonstrated that he could modify and fit a plant into a pattern he had in his mind through a process of directed thought (see Marcel Vogel's article, "Man-Plant Communication," in Edgar Mitchell's *Psychic Exploration: A Challenge for Science,* G. Putnam, 1974). His use of only "love" to develop the spineless cactus from its original spiny ancestors demonstrated such a modification.

Backster's experimentation (the results of which were published in the Winter 1968 issue of the *International Journal of Parapsychology*) began by accident in 1966. On February 2, 1966. Backster decided to test a *Dracaena massangeana* to see whether a polygraph could measure the rate at which water rose from the roots of the plant to the leaves. In a human subject, a polygraph, or lie detector, measures three functions simultaneously: rate of breathing, changes in blood pressure and pulse, and variations in the skin's electrical conductivity. It was the last, the galvanic skin response (GSR) or psychogalvanic reflex (PGR) of the plant leaf, that Backster hoped to measure. There was no reaction to the water, but a minute later there appeared on the polygraph tracing a contour, which Backster reported was "similar to a reaction pattern of a human subject experiencing an emotional stimulation of short duration." Then, with the PGR electrodes still attached on each side of the leaf, Backster began to think about burning the leaves of the plant to see whether that would produce a reaction. He claimed that his *thought* of burning the leaves was enough to trigger a reaction by the plant, indicating the existence of a perception capability in plant life.

To test the plant perception hypothesis thoroughly, Backster, working at the Backster Research Foundation in New York

City, ran several experiments using live brine shrimp (*Artemia salina*) and automated equipment. He wired three philodendrons, each in a separate room, to polygraphs. In another room, Backster placed equipment that automatically killed shrimp on a random basis by dumping them into boiling water. He discovered that five to seven seconds after every occasion when shrimp were killed, the polygraph recording needle jumped violently while attached to the plant. Even shielding the plant in a Faraday screen and a lead container had no effect; the plant was still able to respond to the deaths. The results led Backster to consider whether it is possible that cell life, when it dies, broadcasts a signal to other living cells.

Backster then expanded his experimentation to include fresh fruit, vegetables, mold cultures, and cell life. In each case, his results supported his primary perception hypothesis. He also claimed to have obtained a sort of "heartbeat" recording from an *unfertilized* egg. In testing a yogurt culture, Backster maintained that it showed electrical changes when he fed drops of milk to another culture. On the basis of all his experiments, Backster hypothesizes the existence of an unknown signal which links all living things.

Attempts by other researchers to replicate Backster's experimental results have proved both positive and negative.

Marcel Vogel, a senior research chemist at the IBM Advanced Systems Development Division Laboratory in Los Gatos, California, began human-and-plant communication experimentation in 1969, after reading about Backster's work. He claims that he has confirmed all of Backster's results (see Vogel's article "Man-Plant Communication" in Edgar D. Mitchell's *Psychic Exploration: A Challenge for Science*, Putnam, 1974). Vogel, however, puts a different interpretation on the cause of those effects: "My own view is that human beings are the causative agency in man-plant communication by sensitizing, or 'charging,' the plant to be receptive of thoughts and emotions." He maintains that in order to establish any link between humans and the plant, the experimenter must first release an initial charge of thought energy to the plant, which then isolates the plant from any secondary influences which might be present in the room or laboratory. The experimenter must maintain a high level of emotional control—the higher the control, the more precise the results become. "The experimenter may then," Vogel states, "focus his mind to get a response to (a) the act of damaging another plant, (b) the destruction of another life form, and (c) the release of a thought form of love and other emotions, healing, symbols, and visual imagery."

Portions of Backster's experiments have been replicated by Robert Brier at the Institute of Parapsychology in North Carolina; by Dr. Aristide H. Esser, a psychiatrist and head of the research laboratory at Rockland State Hospital in Orangeburg, New York; and by Douglas Dean of the Newark College of Engineering. Both Esser and Douglas have reported on their experiments in *Medical World News* (No. 17, 1969).

More recently, Kenneth A. Horowitz, Donald C. Lewis, and Edgar L. Gasteiger, of the Section of Neurobiology and Behavior, Division of Biological Sciences and Department of Physical Biology of the New York State Veterinary College at Cornell University (see *Science*, Vol. 189, February 25, 1975), repeated Backster's brine shrimp experiment and found "no relationship between brine shrimp killing and electrical 'responsiveness' of the philodendron." They state that they duplicated Backster's conditions and, in some cases, used more stringent controls. They had undertaken the experiment because they thought the scientific community had unjustly disregarded Backster's work. The experimenters concluded, on the basis of their results: "While the hypothesis will remain as an intriguing speculation, one should note that only the limited published data of Backster support it."

Backster has challenged the attempts of scientists to reproduce his experiments because, he claims, their procedures were not precisely identical to his. He discounts the significance of his own failure to attempt to replicate the results of the shrimp experiment. He states that his new experiments have yielded further evidence—i.e., that yogurt has emotions, too.

Dr. Clifford L. Slayman, a Yale University expert in detecting and interpreting electrical activity in people and animals for medical purposes, said it was extremely difficult to eliminate electrical fluctuations in such experiments because of outside sources. He has suggested that Backster's fluctuations could have been the result of several aspects of the experiment's design. For instance, Backster sandwiched the plant leaf between layers of gauze, which had been soaked in salt water, and two flat metal electrodes. According to Slayman, the mechanical pressure, the salt water, and the drying of the gauze all could have caused large fluctuations in the measured electrical activity of the plant.

For additional information, see P. Tompkins and C. Bird,

The Secret Life of Plants (Harper & Row, 1973) and C. Panati, *Supersenses: Our Potential for Parasensory Experience* (Quadrangle, 1974).

Reincarnation

Reincarnation is the belief that some aspect of a deceased person is reborn into another living human being. Unlike possession, in which a person's mind, body, and soul are *taken over* by another personality, the primary personality is not displaced in reincarnation. The current personality might cling to his previous life emotionally, but there is never an attempt to attend to the "unfinished business" of the first life.

Dr. Ian Stevenson is the world's foremost investigator in this area of survival research. He has written many articles and books on reincarnation and investigated more than 1,040 cases suggestive of reincarnation. Most of the 1,300 claims received by Dr. Stevenson came from Southeast Asia and the Middle East. Relatively few cases originate in Europe, the United States or Canada, except among the Tlingit Indians of Alaska. Dr. Stevenson cites cultural differences as the reason for the low incidence of reported cases in these areas.

Most of the cases involve young children, between the ages of one and four, who claim to be someone who has previously died. They are able to remember events and identify family members from their previous lives, and occasionally they have character traits, physical features, or scars similar to those of the deceased. Their memories of the previous life are strongest in childhood and tend to fade at adolescence.

The following cases are taken from Dr. Stevenson's books *Twenty Cases Suggestive of Reincarnation* (University Press of Virginia, 1974), and *Cases of the Reincarnation Type, Vol. 1* (University Press of Virginia, 1975).

The Case of Prakash.

When Prakash was four and a half years old, he began to wake in the middle of the night and run out of his house in Chhatta, India. He claimed that his name was Nirmal and he lived in the nearby town of Kosi Kalan. He insisted that he be taken to his "real" home. After repeatedly insisting that he was Nirmal, Prakash forced his family to investigate his story. Prakash's family discovered that a ten-year-old boy named Nirmal had died in Kosi Kalan in April 1950, sixteen months before Prakash's birth in 1951. On his deathbed, Nirmal had pointed in the direction of Chhatta, the town where Prakash was born, and said he was going to his mother.

Although the towns were only six miles apart, the families did not know one another. Yet when Prakash was brought to Kosi Kalan, he was able to recognize Nirmal's relatives and state their relationships and also to identify personal objects.

The Case of Jasbir.

This is the only case of "exchange incarnation" in Stevenson's files. Usually an average of five years elapses between the death of the previous personality and the birth of the current personality.

Jasbir was ill with smallpox at the age of three and a half. It appeared that he was dead, but just before the funeral, he revived, although he remained weak and unable to speak for several weeks. When he was fully recovered, he claimed to be a Brahmin and refused to eat the food of his father's lower caste. His family asked a Brahmin woman to cook his meals for him, and for a time they humored Jasbir by allowing him to eat first, which is the right of a person of a higher caste. On a visit to a nearby village the Brahmin woman connected Jasbir's story with that of a young Brahmin man who had died during the time Jasbir was seriously ill. Stevenson believes that while Jasbir was close to death, a personality "exchange" took place with the recently deceased Brahmin.

Although he had never visited the deceased's town, Jasbir was able to describe the parts of town where his family lived and was able to recognize family members.

The Case of Gopal.

One evening, when he was two and a half years old, Gopal Gupta became outraged at being asked to remove a glass from the table. He said he had servants for such things and proceeded to throw a temper tantrum. Gopal said he was a Sharma (a subcaste of Brahmins) and not of the lower caste of his father, the Banias. He also claimed he owned a company that was concerned with medicines, Sukh Sharcharak, and said he had a wife with whom he quarreled constantly, a father, and two brothers, one of whom had shot him, in the town of Mathura. When he was on business in Mathura five years later, Gopal's father sought verification for his son's story and learned that there was a similarity between Gopal's story and the life of Shaktipal Sharma. Sharma had a wife he had always quarreled with, a father and two brothers in Mathura, and was once an executive with the pharmaceutical concern, Sukh Sharcharak. Sharma died in May 1948 after being shot by his brother. Gopal was born on August 26, 1956.

Gopal was able to identify Sharma's wife, but only after they had met twice and she had revealed her identity to his father. Stevenson cites Gopal's mother's cravings for citrus juices while she was pregnant with Gopal's and Sharma's fondness for citrus fruit as additional evidence favoring the reincarnation hypothesis in this case.

The primary difficulty in researching these cases lies in the unreliability of the witnesses' memories. The statements made by the reincarnates are not usually written down before attempts at verification of their stories are made, and often many years elapse between the time of the first claim and the actual confrontation with the alleged "former" parents and relatives. Other problems lie in the areas of translation from the original language and the fact that the information is often obtained second- or thirdhand.

Some researchers have used hypnosis to regress subjects back to a "previous life." One of the most famous cases of hypnotic regression was that of Bridey Murphy (Morey Bernstein, *The Search for Bridey Murphy,* Doubleday, 1956), but many researchers doubt the validity of this technique. It appears that the "previous" personality evoked during hypnotically induced regressions include the subject's current personality, his expectations of what the hypnotist wants, his fantasies of what his previous life might have been, and borrowings from the lives of former acquaintances.

In his book *Twenty Cases Suggestive of Reincarnation,* Stevenson also states that it is impossible to know whether a subject is describing a previous life or if telepathy or clairvoyance with a discarnate personality is responsible in cases of regression. That is why he believes the most promising evidence for reincarnation will come from the spontaneous cases, especially those in which behavior and physical similarities are present in addition to information about the deceased.

While Stevenson admits the weaknesses of many of the

cases presented in his books and believes that fraud, crypt-omnesia, or ESP with a discarnate personality might account for some portion of the information in each of the stories, he does not believe that all the information can be accounted for in this manner. He has not yet found the perfect case, but Stevenson believes it will contain correspondence between the behavioral aspects of the deceased and those of the living personality, a correspondence of skills, and even a corre-spondence between wounds of the deceased and birthmarks of the current personality. He believes that in the main, the cases do provide evidence of the survival of bodily death.

In her book *Reincarnation and Science* (Sterling, 1973) Ruth Reyna states that Stevenson's books are the most reveal-ing documents of chicanery and naïveté ever published on the subject of reincarnation—chicanery on the part of the claimant's relatives and naïveté on the part of the investigator. She cites the following points as suspect: (1) All the cases arise from primitive or underdeveloped areas; (2) the first reports of reincarnation are obtained when a child is between the ages of one and four; (3) all the cases were reported by parents or relatives of the subject; and (4) the details were filled in mainly by adults or someone other than the child.

Reyna cites the psychological compulsion of a parent to prize his offspring and the wish to have him be different from or better than other children as the reason why so many cases of reincarnation appear in underdeveloped countries. In these areas there is little chance for individual improvement owing to the lack of educational opportunity and depressed economic conditions. One of the few avenues open to distinc-tion is to hold one's child up as a reincarnate. Note that the children usually claim to have belonged to a *higher* caste in their previous lives.

What about the evidence and the instances where a child recognized his former parents? Reyna believes that the recognitions that occurred were either due to suggestion from a knowing adult or a result of subtle gestures and verbal clues, such as "Which of these two women is your grandmother?"

In some instances where the child was believed to be the reincarnation of a beloved relative who said he would return, Reyna believes parental influence was responsible for molding the personality and behavioral patterns of the child. Young children are easily manipulated and can be maneuvered into believing they were once someone else. She notes that all of the cases involved young children, whose memories of the past life faded at adolescence. Reyna believes that if the child's claims had been genuine, the memories would have increased with age.

Survival After Death Projects

Dr. Ian Stevenson, a leading researcher in the question of survival of bodily death, has two ongoing research projects designed to demonstrate the reality of life after death either as a spiritual being or through reincarnation.

In the combination lock test for survival, Dr. Stevenson is registering certain types of combination locks whose combinations have been secretly set by a man or woman. The assumption is that this person, after death, will attempt to communicate that combination to a friend or relative through a medium, dreams, or other methods. The project involves complex instructions to those who set the locks.

Dr. Stevenson wants to limit the project to those he considers qualified to participate, and he requires prior correspondence and acceptance into the program before he will accept any lock for registration. Participants must also be prepared to follow the rules and instructions of the project.

In another project a person sixty-five or older fills out a form identifying his or her characteristics and experiences during this life. This provides a basic check for genuine correspondence in cases of reincarnation or communication with the dead. Again, prior correspondence and acceptance into the program is required. This project is only for people sixty-five or older.

If you believe you may qualify to participate, write:

> Dr. Ian Stevenson
> Division of Parapsychology
> Department of Psychiatry
> University of Virginia School of Medicine
> Charlottesville, Virginia 22901

For further details on the lock project, see Stevenson's articles in the *Journal of the Society for Psychical Research* (July 1968 and April 1976).

Spiritualism

Spiritualism (or spiritism) is the belief that the human personality survives death, and that the spirit may communicate with the living through a medium or a psychic.

Believers in spiritualism hold that communication from the spirit world may manifest itself through mental phenomena, such as clairvoyance and telepathy or speech through a medium, or through physical phenomena, such as levitation, table tipping, noises and rappings, automatic writing, and apports—the movement or sudden appearance of objects.

Modern spiritualism had its beginning with the Fox sisters, Kate and Maggie, in 1848. These two young girls from a farm in upstate New York first gained local attention through mysterious rappings happening in their presence, which presumably formed a code for communicating with spirits. Under the tutelage of their older sister Leah, the Fox girls toured the country and received a great deal of publicity and fame. A number of eminent people, including newspaper pioneer Horace Greeley, concluded that the girls' accomplishments were genuine. However, this was questioned by other authorities, and after a family quarrel Maggie revealed that their claim to communicate with spirits had been a fraud and that the rappings were actually produced by the girls through cracking the joints in their feet. This confession, later retracted, failed to dampen the enthusiasm of numerous followers.

Another famous nineteenth-century medium whose popularity was not seriously diminished by repeated charges of fraud was Florence Cook. No less a personage than Sir William Crookes, eminent scientist and inventor of the Crookes vacuum tube, was convinced that Florence Cook had genuine psychic powers.

The greatest medium of all time was Eusapia Palladino. She was born in southern Italy in 1854 and early in life showed abilities that aroused the interest of spiritualist circles. She was examined by the famous criminologist and psychologist Cesare Lombroso and convinced him of her supernatural abilities. She was celebrated throughout Europe, traveled widely, but was frequently accused of deception. The results of several scientific investigations were inconclusive. Finally, after a suspicious performance at Cambridge, the Society for Psychical Research classified her as a fraudulent medium.

"Perhaps the most remarkable and convincing medium who has so far appeared"—this is how British author Colin Wilson describes Daniel Douglas Home (*The Occult,* Vintage, 1971). Home was born in Scotland in 1833. A committee from Harvard University, which included the poet William Cullen Bryant, testified that during a Home séance the table at which they had been sitting had pushed them backward and floated several inches off the ground, the floor had vibrated as if cannons were being fired, and the table had risen up on two legs like a rearing horse. According to Wilson, what is so convincing about Home is the sheer volume of evidence: In the course of his career, hundreds of witnesses—perhaps thousands—vouched for the phenomena. His powers were so strong that he never asked for the lights to be lowered.

Toward the end of the last century spiritualism waned, largely as a result of mounting exposés of fraud, but it enjoyed a new vogue after World War I and is extremely popular today.

The history of spiritualism certainly provides enough ammunition for skeptics, since instances of proved or probable fraud are legion. C. E. M. Hansel, a severe critic of spiritualism and extrasensory phenomena, points out that famous mediums such as Eusapia Palladino and Margery Crandon mystified investigators but were confounded as soon as professional magicians were present, presumably because they were familiar with the tricks of the trade. Margery Crandon, in fact, was unmasked by the legendary magician Houdini. Houdini, once a believer who attempted to communicate with his departed mother, later turned into a crusader against mediums and in his book *A Magician Among Spirits* exposed many of the favorite devices and tricks used by mediums during séances.

The tricks used by contemporary spiritualists are described by M. Lamar Keene in the book *The Psychic Mafia* (St. Martin's, 1976). Once a thriving medium himself, Keene obtained information about his gullible clients from chance remarks, eavesdropping with electronic equipment, use of two-way mirrors, pilfering of handbags during séances, and collusion with other spirtualists. Chiffon gauze in a darkened séance room gave the illusion of flowing "ectoplasm" (a physical emanation from a medium). According to Keene, such deception is common, and "modern spiritualism has been riddled with fakery, humbug and deceit."

Nevertheless, no amount of proved fraud can conclusively rule out the possibility that genuine communication with the spirit world can at times take place. The ultimate source of a medium's powers may be a need to communicate fundamental realities. The noted psychologist C. G. Jung, after studying a wide range of spiritualistic literature, concluded that spiritualism may have certain parallels with psychotherapy. In *The Structure and Dynamics of the Psyche* (*Collected Works*, Vol. 8, Pantheon, 1960), he wrote: "In spiritualism we have a spontaneous attempt of the unconscious to become conscious in a collective form."

DIVINATION

Entrail Reading

Entrail reading, or divination by studying the appearance of the internal organs, most commonly the liver, of ritually killed animals was one of the most common forms of divination in ancient times and in primitive societies.

The ancient art of divination by the study of sheep livers was fully developed by 2000 B.C. in Mesopotamia and continued in use there until about 200 B.C. The Mesopotamians left writings on the subject as well as terra-cotta models of livers. The ancient Greeks also practiced liver divination.

The most famous entrail readers were the haruspices, Etruscan priests who practiced the art for the Romans. The Etruscans had ruled Rome until approximately 500 B.C. The haruspices practiced their art until the fall of the Roman civilization.

The art of the haruspices, called haruspimancy or haruspication, was elaborate and esoteric. Using an involved system, the Etruscans could read messages in the surface of the liver. They also studied the folds in the liver, the veins, and other features. Signs could also be found in the spleens, lungs, and hearts of sheep.

The Romans believed that certain strange occurrences or omens, called prodigies, indicated that the gods were displeased by the conduct of humans. When a prodigy occurred, sheep were sacrificed and the haruspices would examine the livers to determine the will of the gods. The haruspices also began to make predictions of the future based on these examinations. The Roman Senate sometimes used one haruspex to check on another to make certain he was truthfully telling all he read in a liver. Generals often made haruspices part of their staffs to help make major decisions.

At various times haruspices were regarded with a great deal of skepticism. However, during the Roman Empire, the haruspices were organized into a college and received a salary from the state. The college existed until the fifth century A.D.

Etruscan models of livers and knowledge of Etruscan religious practices provide clues to the origin and practice of entrail reading.

One simple Etruscan model shows wrinkles caused by the pressure of surrounding organs. Modern anatomists generally ignore these wrinkles because they have no functional sig-

Concave face of an Etruscan bronze model of a sheep's liver, found in Piacenza and dating from about the third or second century B.C.

nificance. The ancient Assyrians, however, attached great importance to two of the wrinkles. One was particularly important because it indicated whether there was a divine presence in the liver. The Etruscan model features these two wrinkles, indicating the influence of Mesopotamian entrail reading on the practices of the Etruscan haruspices.

A much more detailed bronze model, found in Piacenza and dating to about the third or second century B.C., provides more clues. The model liver is divided into parts that correspond to descriptions of relationships between different elements in Etruscan religious thought. The Etruscans divided the sky into sixteen parts and assigned each division to a god. The concave face of the liver model contains sixteen roughly rectangular compartments, each containing the name of a god and forming a continuing border around the periphery. These divisions are comparable to the sixteen divisions of the sky. Those bordering the left lobe of the liver correspond to the western sky; those bordering the right lobe represent the eastern sky. Within the border the left lobe has six trapezoids which form a wheel. In each trapezoid the name of gods are written, forty in all. To the right of the wheel are the names of two more gods, neither of which is completely enclosed by lines. The right lobe, which contains the gallbladder, is a rectangular grid. The rectangles contain the names of thirteen gods. Three more names, not completely enclosed by lines, also appear.

The convex face of the model is divided into halves, one for the sun-god and the other for the moon-god. This division corresponds to the Etruscan division of all things into two classes, those similar to the sun and those similar to the moon—making the convex face a simple model of a dualistic universe.

Knowledge of the religious thought of the ancient Romans, ancient Hindus, and the Etruscans helps explain the meaning of the wheel and the grid. To these peoples, the difference between the round and the square was analogous to the difference between the mundane and celestial worlds. Using their complex division of the world mirrored on the surface of the liver, the Etruscans read messages similarly to the way a palmist reads a palm.

Entrail reading, as practiced by the Etruscans, was integrally related to their pagan religion. When this religion was replaced by Christianity, entrail reading disappeared along with the religious beliefs that supported it.

For more information, see *Pausanias' Description of Greece,* Vol 4, translation and commentary by T. G. Frazer (Biblo and Tannen, 1965) and Georges Dumezil, *Archaic Roman Religion*, Vol. 2 (University of Chicago Press, 1970).

I Ching

The *I Ching,* the Book of Changes, is an ancient Chinese text, which has profoundly influenced Chinese minds for more than 3,000 years and is considered one of the five classics of Confucianism.

Originally, the *I Ching* was simply a source of oracles that gave yes-or-no answers to questions, similar to the oracular stage of religion in other primitive societies. It gradually acquired ethical meaning and ultimately became a compendium of Chinese wisdom.

The philosophical assumptions of the *I Ching* are: Everything changes; immutables laws—the laws of Tao—lie behind change; change involves transformation between the yang, the masculine principle, and the yin, the feminine principle; and the study of the *I Ching* gives a comprehensive view of experience and can shape one's actions in harmony with the ultimate Tao (the "correct" way or "heaven's way"), which lies at the heart of all existence.

The present system of the *I Ching* consists of sixty-four hexagrams, or symbols, made up of six lines. Each hexagram is a combination of two of eight basic trigrams—symbols consisting of three lines—which represent "images of all that happens on earth and in heaven." The basic concept is transition; the eight trigrams represent tendencies in movement. The lines that make up each trigram are either solid, representing yang, or broken, representing yin.

According to certain principles, the hexagrams transmute and pass into each other. Certain lines, considered "strong" lines, change into their opposites, creating a new situation. The hexagrams can be used not only as oracles, but also as guides to action because every situation involves a right course of action and a wrong one. When one consults the

The flag of South Korea uses the circular monad, representing yin and yang, and four basic trigrams from the I Ching *(clockwise from upper left):* Ch'ien, *the Creative, strong, air;* K'an, *the Abysmal, danger, water;* Li, *the Clinging, light-giving, fire; and* K'un, *the Receptive, yielding, earth.*

I Ching, coins are thrown or special stalks are counted in a certain way to determine which hexagram applies. The text first explains each line of the hexagram separately and then gives an overall interpretation. The text is often cryptic, giving the user considerable leeway in interpreting the meaning.

Four men are cited in Chinese literature as the authors of the *I Ching:* Fu-hsi (c. 3000 B.C.), a legendary figure representing the dawn of civilization; King Wen Wang (c. 1150 B.C.) and his son Duke Kau; and Confucius (551 to 479 B.C.). Fu-hsi is credited with constructing the trigrams from markings on the back of a tortoise. Although some commentaries are attributed to Confucius, he claimed he had acted only as a compiler and editor. One legend states that King Wen Wang elaborated the system to sixty-four hexagrams and that his son added commentaries.

During the Ch'in and Han dynasties (221 B.C. to A.D. 220), the *I Ching* was debased by emphasis on magic and sorcery. The great scholar Wang Pi (A.D. 226 to 249) cleared away these accretions and restored the *I Ching* as a book of wisdom.

Richard Wilhelm, the scholar responsible for the modern translation and interpretation of the *I Ching,* evaluated the book as "unquestionably one of the most important books in the world's literature." Although its impact on Chinese culture has been enormous, Wilhelm pointed out that its effect was not always wholesome because at times it hindered the growth of free inquiry into reality, thereby curbing the development of Chinese science.

C. G. Jung, Hermann Hesse, and other modern Western thinkers have devoted a great deal of serious study to the *I Ching.* Jung noted that although the West had tended to ignore the book, considering it a collection of abstruse and impractical magic spells, it is actually uncommonly significant for exploring the unconscious and for enhancing self-knowledge. Although the Chinese never valued science highly or believed in causality as the basic principle of nature, the West much later, Jung stated, came to the realization that the so-called laws of science are merely statistical truths. Jung asserted that the Chinese mind, as reflected in the *I Ching,* is concerned with the "chance" aspects of events and that the hexagrams represent the principle of coincidence as opposed to that of causality.

For additional information; see W. Wilhelm and C. F. Baynes, *The I Ching or Book of Changes* (Princeton University Press, 1950) and R. Wilhelm, *Eight Lectures on the I Ching* (Princeton University Press, 1960).

Astrology

Astrology is the practice or technique of divining events and studying personalities through patterns derived from astronomy in the belief that heavenly bodies influence human affairs.

While modern astrology is an extraordinarily complex topic, with a number of diverse methods and a variety of purposes, most astrologers agree that the horoscope—also called the birth chart or natal chart—is the basic tool of the trade. The uses of this instrument and the methods by which it is devised from the crux of most astrological distinctions.

The horoscope, in general terms, is a symbolic representation of the sky for any given moment, usually the time and place of an individual's birth. The yearly orbit of the earth around the sun is called the ecliptic. However, because astrology is largely geocentric (based on an earthbound perspective), the astrological ecliptic usually refers to the sun's apparent yearly orbit around the earth. Within a latitude of about seven degrees north and seven degrees south of the ecliptic can be found a "belt" consisting of twelve constellations of stars, which collectively are called the zodiac (Greek for "carved figures"). In ancient times each constellation was plotted, named, and attributed mythical qualities, which eventually led to the twelve signs of the zodiac.

All the planets of the solar system also pass through the zodiac belt, so that at any given time the positions of the sun, moon, and planets (astrologers refer to all as planets) can be calculated in relation to where they appear in the zodiac; this is the horoscope.

Modern Astrology: Popular.

By far the most common manifestations of popular, or mass, astrology are the horoscope columns appearing in newspapers and magazines. These are based on the sun sign, the sign of the zodiac in which the sun appeared upon one's birth. The individual locates the sign covering his month and day of birth in the columns. These are usually listed as: Aries

(March 21–April 19); Taurus (April 20–May 20); Gemini (May 21–June 21); Cancer (June 22–July 22); Leo (July 23–August 22); Virgo (August 23–September 22); Libra (September 23–October 22); Scorpio (October 23–November 21); Sagittarius (November 22–December 21); Capricorn (December 22–January 19); Aquarius (January 20–February 18); and Pisces (February 19–March 20).

The beginning and ending dates for each sign are not always agreed on because the sun can pass from one constellation to another at hours other than midnight. People born at these points are said to be on the "cusp" of the two signs and in sun sign astrology are usually thought to share attributes of both.

The astrological columnist constructs horoscopes for each day using some arbitrary time (say, noon) to determine planetary positions. Then he figures how these positions relate to the traditional associations given each sign, including the characteristics of the sign, the planet which is said to rule it, the house with which it is associated, and other variables.

Then the astrologer, using traditional formulas, makes very general statements about what he considers good or bad indications for each sign.

This method can be extended to weekly, monthly, and even yearly periods because the planetary positions are calculated well in advance in a book called an ephemeris. The astrologer takes his data from the ephemeris, projects the influence of the moving planets on a sun sign for a long period, and prepares his statement in accordance with these movements.

Modern Astrology: Serious.

For most professional astrologers, the sun sign projections are considered, at best, woefully overgeneral and, at worst, outright charlatanry. Sun sign astrology divides the population into twelve rigid types and makes predictions based on a small number of factors. The serious or systematic—sometimes called scientific, although this can be misleading—astrologer casts horoscopes for individual clients based on the exact time and place of birth. With this added information, he is able to calculate the degree of the zodiac which crossed the eastern horizon at the birth moment, called the ascendant or rising sign, and the exact position of the moon at birth. He can also calculate the position approximately ninety degrees from the ascendant to the north, called the medium coeli (MC) or mid-heaven, and another significant birth chart division, the twelve houses.

The astrologer finds the ascendant and mid-heaven in another publication, the table of houses. Once the ascendant degree and sign are located, the houses can be placed within the zodiac circle, counterclockwise from the line of the horizon, with the ascendant as the cusp of the first house. Although many methods of house division are used, the most popular is the equal house method, with each house using thirty degrees around the circle of the zodiac. This makes for simplicity because the houses are made to correspond with the zodiac signs, each of which also occupies thirty degrees. Its accuracy, however, is disputed by some astrologers.

Nature of the Signs.

Generally speaking, the zodiac signs symbolically represent abstract, universal qualities, while the houses relate to everyday activity.

The signs are divided into distinct groups of four, three, and two. Each sign is said to partake of the nature of the symbolic four elements—fire, earth, air, and water.

Fire signs—Aries, Leo, and Sagittarius—indicate intensity, emotionality, and activity.

Earth signs—Taurus, Virgo, and Capricorn—symbolize stability, concreteness, practicality, and collectivity.

Air signs—Gemini, Libra, and Aquarius—connote adaptability, intellectuality, transcendence, and abstraction.

Water signs—Cancer, Scorpio, and Pisces—symbolize empathy, emotionality, universality, and sensuality.

The threefold division called modes may be considered the way in which a sign utilizes its energy.

Cardinal, which includes Aries, Libra, Cancer, and Capricorn, refers to the initiating and generating of power.

Fixed refers to concretizing and focalizing energy in structures and includes Taurus, Leo, Scorpio, and Aquarius.

Mutable means the distribution of energy by flexibility and adaptation and includes Gemini, Virgo, Sagittarius, and Pisces.

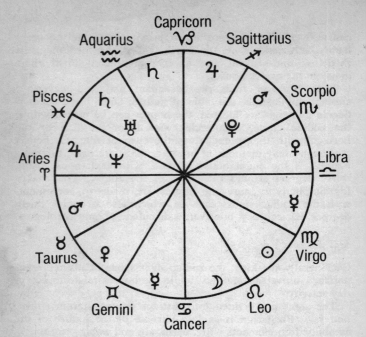

The archetypical zodiac showing the planetary rulers of each sign.

The twofold division is traditionally called Male/Female and refers to an active-passive or positive-negative polarity. The air and fire signs are considered male, and the earth and water signs female.

Character of Each Sign.

In popular sun sign astrology practically the entire personality of the individual is determined by the sign occupied by the sun. In serious astrology, however, this is only one factor, albeit important, among many. Systematic astrologers, nonetheless, do assign symbolic characteristics to each sign, and when a particular sign is prominent on a birth chart, the "native" is said to display these qualities. Signs are also traditionally associated with anatomy, another example of the astrological tenet "as above [meaning the heavens], so below" [meaning the earth].

Aries (the ram): assertiveness, urgency, headstrong, courage, immediacy, aggressiveness, self-willed. The head.

Taurus (the bull): permanency, possessiveness, stubbornness, practicality, luxury. The throat.

Gemini (the twins): communication, versatility, duality, changeability, restlessness. Shoulders, arms, lungs.

Cancer (the crab): home and family, sensitivity, protectiveness, emotionality. Chest, breast, stomach.

Leo (the lion): self-expression, impressiveness, creativity, confidence, authority. Heart and spine.

Virgo (the virgin): critical, analytical, discriminating, meticulous, fussy. Intestines, solar plexus, spleen.

Libra (the scales): idealism, justice, balance, harmony, aesthetics, easygoing. Kidneys and liver.

Scorpio (the scorpion): sexuality, intensity, passion, secretive, purposeful, jealousy. Sex organs.

Sagittarius (the archer): expansiveness, optimism, philosophical, broad-minded, versatility. Thighs, pelvis.

Capricorn (the goat): calculating, ambitious, status quo, stability, disciplined. Skeleton, joints.

Aquarius (the water bearer): humanism, independence, intellectuality, idealism, unconventionality. Legs, ankles.

Pisces (the fishes): impressionability, devotion, self-sacrifice, dreaminess, compassion, emotionalism. Feet, lymphatic system.

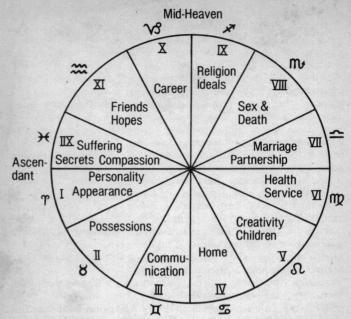

The areas of life associated with each astrological house. While the signs of the zodiac move around the circle, the positions of the houses remain the same.

The Houses.

Like the signs, the houses also have cyclic referents, although they refer to everyday affairs. The first, fourth, seventh, and tenth are called angular or active, which means they have an initiating, activating nature. The second, fifth, eighth, and eleventh houses are known as succedent or reactive and are said to expand or focus the processes of the active houses. The third, sixth, ninth, and twelfth cadent or resultant houses are described as universalizing and harmonizing. These three distinctions are roughly analogous to the sign modes of Cardinal, Fixed, and Mutable.

Symbolic Meanings of the Houses

First: personality, health, appearance, outward behavior.
Second: possessions and one's attitude toward them; worldly resources.
Third: communications, writing, education, short journeys.
Fourth: the home, security, parents.
Fifth: children, creativity, pleasure, speculation, love affairs, casual relationships, pets.

Table of Planetary Dignities

Planet	Exaltation	Detriment	Fall
Sun	Aries	Aquarius	Libra
Moon	Taurus	Capricorn	Scorpio
Mercury	Gemini	Sagittarius, Pisces	Sagittarius
Venus	Pisces	Scorpio, Aries	Virgo
Mars	Capricorn	Libra, Taurus	Cancer
Jupiter	Cancer	Gemini, Virgo	Capricorn
Saturn	Libra	Leo, Cancer	Aries
Uranus	Scorpio	Leo	Taurus
Neptune	Leo	Virgo	Aquarius
Pluto	Aquarius	Libra	Leo

Sixth: health, employment, service to others.
Seventh: marriage, partnerships, contracts, open enemies.
Eighth: death, legacies, business, sex, the occult, crime.
Ninth: deep study, philosophy, higher education, long journeys, morals.
Tenth: aspirations, position, honors, status, profession, the father, responsibility.
Eleventh: friends, social life, hopes, objectives, intellectual pleasures.
Twelfth: seclusion, confinement, hidden enemies, fate, obstacles, self-sacrifice.

The Planets.

The position of the ten heavenly bodies of the solar system, or planets, in the birth chart is a focal point in systematic astrology. Planets are said to have four fundamental relationships to the zodiac signs. Rulership (control) and exaltation (affinity) are considered positive, while detriment and fall (both indicating disharmony) are negative.

Planetary Meanings.

Sun: power, vitality, will, personality.
Moon: instincts, the mother, emotions, fluctuations, responses.
Mercury: communication, intellect, interchange, association.
Venus: harmony, art, beauty, affection, partnership, possessions.
Mars: energy, force, will, desire, aggressiveness, initiative.
Jupiter: expansion, success, beneficence, prosperity, higher principle, generosity.
Saturn: restriction, limitation, discipline, sorrow, hardship, endurance.

The last three planets are sometimes referred to as Trans-Saturnian. Because they take so long to circle through the zodiac (more than an average lifetime) and stay in one sign for so long, they are often said to have a generational rather than an individual influence.

Uranus: change, disruption, revolution, eccentricity, inventiveness.
Neptune: imagination, impressionability, psychic ability, dreaminess, the illusory, spirituality.
Pluto: renewal, regeneration, elimination, eruptions, compulsions.

Because the earth moves at a different speed from that of all the other planets, it sometimes seems as though a planet will reverse its direction in the sky and, perhaps, even move backwards into a preceding sign before starting forward again. Planets in this process in a birth chart are called retrograde. Some astrologers believe that this condition inhibits or turns inward the normal planetary qualities.

Chart Interpretation.

This phase of astrology is so complex that it is usually determined by the intuitions and insights of the individual astrologer. The twelve houses are each said to be ruled by the sign which appears on each cusp, with each sign in turn being ruled by a planet. The position of the planets in houses/signs

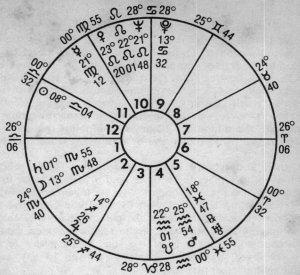

President Carter's natal horoscope suggests a man of confidence and ambition, compassion and idealism. It also suggests that he will be bitterly disappointed if the country does not live up to his high expectations. The horoscope is cast for Plains, Georgia (84° W24/32° N02), at 7 A.M. CST, October 1, 1924.

is supposed to determine the focus of the energy represented by the particular house/sign.

The angles between planets, called aspects, are also important. These involve certain circular distances which are traditionally considered good (well aspected, beneficed) or bad (afflicted, maleficed). There are many different angles, according to astrological persuasion, but the most important are:

Benefics: conjunction (0 degrees); trine (120 degrees); sextile (60 degrees).

Malefics: opposition (180 degrees); square (90 degrees); quincunx (150 degrees).

Since planets are rarely found in exact aspect, an orb, or a few degrees of difference, is usually allowed.

In addition to planets, aspects can be made to many abstract points on the chart. Foremost is the ascendant, which represents self-awareness and individualization. Another significant abstraction is the mid-heaven, representing the individual's social integration and career. Planets in aspect to either are especially significant. The line extending from the ascendant to its opposite point on the circle (the descendant) divides the chart in half on an east/west basis, while a similar line from the mid-heaven to its opposite (the imum coeli, or IC) divides it north/south. The two divisions together result in four quadrants. Aspects to these points can be important, as well as aspects to the points bisecting each quadrant, the midpoints. Planetary midpoints (points exactly between two planets) can also be significant when the planets are in aspect.

Other abstractions include nodes, the places where a planet's orbit crosses the ecliptic, and planetary parts, formed by adding one planet's longitude to the ascendant's longitude and subtracting a second planet's longitude from the total. The most popular part, called the part of fortune, is obtained by summing the longitudes of the moon and ascendant and subtracting the longitude of the sun. When nodes or parts are employed, particular attention is given to any aspects made to important planets.

Another means of interpretation is called progressing the birth chart. The idea is that as one grows older, one will have progressed along the path of life's development. This development will be indicated by the progressed chart. Progressions are based on the formula that one day equals one year; thus, a progressed chart for a thirty-five-year-old will be based upon planetary movements thirty-five days from birth. Progressed planets and abstractions are usually superimposed upon the natal chart, and aspects between both progressed and natal planets are noted.

Transits, the daily motion of the planets, form the basis of popular sun astrology and are also essential in systematic work. Significant aspects of transiting planets to natal and progressed planets are sought, and predictions based on certain standard indications can be made. For instance, if a transiting Saturn (traditionally malefic) is found to be moving toward opposition with an important natal planet in the seventh house, marital discord could be brewing.

Astrologers make a point of considering the pattern of the chart as a whole, rather than as a collection of parts. Therefore, particular attention is paid to unusual formations between planets. An example is the T-Square, formed by an opposition between two planets with a third planet in between, squaring both. Some formations, like the T-Square, are considered obstacles, while others are thought of as beneficial. A key interpretive tool is preponderance of any sort—by element (e.g., too many fire signs), mode (e.g., too few mutables), clustering (e.g., too many planets in a house/sign/quadrant), by isolation (e.g., no planets in a quadrant/hemisphere), by aspect (e.g., too many squares), or by any other feature that predominates.

Astrological Viewpoints.

Most of the foregoing would be considered natal astrology because the focus is on the birth chart. Although the origins of astrology appear to coincide with the advent of civilization and it was practiced by ancient Mesopotamians, Sumerians, and Chaldeans, the earliest surviving natal horoscope has been dated only as far back as about 668 B.C. Before then astrology was generally connected with royalty and aristocracy and was mainly used to forecast large-scale events like weather conditions, wars, or the decisions of rulers. This type of astrology is called political or mundane and is now employed to produce horoscopes for inanimate objects, nations, animals, corporations, political figures, or even the world. The key is to find a suitable symbolic birth moment—in many cases, the time of signing a contract, treaty, or declaration.

A type of modern astrology rapidly gaining popularity is horary astrology, sometimes referred to as the *I Ching* of astrology. In this method, answers are sought for given questions by casting a chart for the exact time the question was formulated. The chart is then interpreted for possible indications of an answer.

Since popular astrology has always been concerned with astrological compatibility in relationships, systematic astrologers have developed this in the technique called synastry. Here two birth charts are compared for anyone engaged in or about to engage in partnership, marriage, business, or parenthood. Certain key indicators are looked for. For example, the aspect of the man's Mars to the woman's Venus is said to indicate degree of sexual attraction.

As with any developed discipline, there are many perspectives in serious astrology, although it is surprising how much of modern astrology still conforms to the myths and assumptions of Claudius Ptolemy (flourished about 130 A.D.) and his *Tetrabiblos*, called the "greatest astrological textbook."

Perhaps the widest diversity involves house division, with several other techniques, including the Placidus, Regiomontanus, and Campanus systems, competing with the equal house approach.

The other disputes involve the constellations that the zodiac signs were named after. Within the zodiacal belt intrude two additional constellations not considered part of the zodiac, Ophiuchus (the whale) and Cetus (the serpent bearer). Some have argued that there should be a total of fourteen signs. The other constellation dispute is known as the Tropical vs. Sidereal Zodiac Controversy. The combined pull of the sun and moon leads to a slow retrograding of the poles known as the precession of the equinoxes. Since ancient times the poles have shifted one sign backward. The sidereal zodiac astrologers employ a different framework to allow for this change. Most astrologers use the tropical zodiac, maintaining that the correspondence between the signs and the true constellations is purely symbolic.

There are some systems of astrology which employ as-yet-undiscovered planets, said to be beyond the orbit of Neptune. Alfred Witte, a nineteenth-century German astrologer, calculated eight "transneptunian" planets, not including Pluto, which had not yet been discovered. These extra planets—Cupid, Hades, Kronos, Apollo, Admetus, Vulcanus, and Poseidon—are employed in the school now known as Uranian Astrology, which also employs charts and house divisions that differ from more traditional approaches.

Non-Western.

All the above approaches, whatever their distinctions, are Western. Although astrology throughout the world can be traced to Mesopotamia and the dawn of civilization, the flow of ideas to the East resulted in different perspectives. The myths and religions of each culture affected Oriental astrology, including the Nile cult in Egypt, Taoism in China, and the karma/reincarnation beliefs of India. Indian astrologers also use the sidereal, rather than tropical, zodiac and Chinese and Japanese zodiacs use different signs from those of Westerners: all animals, including the snake, cock, hare, tiger, and rat.

Science and Astrology.

Astrology, with all its variables, does not lend itself well to the controls of science. Moreover, many astrologers view their study as mystical, aesthetic, or philosophical and thus are not concerned with the rigors of science. Some astrologers, however, point to the field of cosmobiology as substantiation. They cite, for instance, the work of Northwestern's Dr. Frank Brown, who demonstrated a direct effect of the moon (independent of tides) on oysters, and radio engineer John H. Nelson of RCA, who showed a correspondence between atmospheric magnetic disturbance, solar flares, and conjunctions and aspects of major planets. More direct evidence for planetary influence can be seen in the statistical studies of Sorbonne-educated psychologist Michel Gauquelin, who has shown high statistical correlations between certain planetary positions in the birth charts of people in certain professions. In spite of these studies, there is no scientific evidence that astrology has any validity.

Michel Gauquelin

Michel Gauquelin is a French psychologist whose attempts to test statistically the assertions of astrology have led to some unusual and unexpected correlations and to his theory of planetary heredity. Michel Gauquelin is *not* an astrologer.

In the 1950s he began to subject to statistical scrutiny certain postulates of astrology, including the assertion that the astrological malefics Saturn and Mars are likely to transit a birth chart sun upon death; the importance of the planet Mars in certain house positions in criminals; the birth chart appearance at mid-heaven of the great benefic Jupiter in successful people, regardless of profession. Using probability theory and large samples, he found no statistically significant relationships in any of these cases. In another test he had professional astrologers try to sort out the birth charts of criminals and peaceful citizens and found their results were no better than chance. These and other experiments led him to the conclusion that "every attempt, whether of astrologers or scientists, to produce evidence of the validity of astrological laws has been in vain."

Nonetheless, on the road to his critique of astrology, he came upon some unusual and unanticipated correlations. A sample of birth charts of 576 members of the French Academy of Medicine showed a significant tendency for great physicians to have either Mars or Saturn rising or culminating at birth. Astrologically, "rising," or ascension, refers to the intersection of the planet with the eastern horizon; "culmination" signifies the uppermost point the planet reaches in the sky. This finding—made in 1950—was followed by comparisons with a random sample of ordinary individuals and a second sample of 508 eminent physicians. The random sample showed no significant Mars-Saturn clustering, but the physicians fell into the same pattern as the first group.

In the mid-1950s Gauquelin collected the birthdates of "every famous Frenchmen we were able to find," as well as samples from Italy, Germany, Belgium, and the Netherlands. In all, he assembled 25,000 cases. The Mars-Saturn pattern was found to predominate among doctors and scientists. Other relationships were found as well. Athletes and military men were discovered to have statistically significant clusterings of Mars rising or culminating. Jupiter was shown in the same positions for military men, politicians, actors, and journalists, and the moon in the same positions for writers and politicians. In addition, statistically significant *negative* associations occurred (i.e., nonappearances): Mars—painters, musicians, writers; Jupiter—scientists, physicians; Saturn—painters, writers; moon—athletes.

The sample of 25,000 yielded no other astronomical oddities; no significant relationships were found for the signs of the zodiac or for Mercury, Venus, Uranus, Neptune, Pluto or the sun. Gauquelin has emphasized that the relationships he did discern do not fit traditional astrological lore. The rising and culminating planets were clustered in the equivalents of astrological houses twelve and nine, not one (personality) or ten (profession), as astrologers might expect.

Nonetheless, the results were startling enough. Gauquelin's attempts at explanation led him to the theory of planetary heredity, which states that children have predispositions to be born when certain planets are rising or culminating. He has speculated that the fetus somehow "senses" the appearance of the relevant planet and, through hormonal secretions, can "influence" the mother's uterine contractions. As evidence for his theory of planetary heredity, Gauquelin has found a relationship between planetary positions of parents and children. After assembling birth data on more than 30,000 parents and their children, he found a high statistical correlation with the moon, Venus, Mars, Jupiter and Saturn. If a child has one of these planets rising or culminating, the pattern is likely to be the same in the birth charts of one of his parents. The frequency is even higher when both parents have similar planetary positions. No relationships were found for tiny Mercury or distant Uranus, Neptune, and Pluto. Unnatural births—requiring drugs or surgery—did not follow this pattern of planetary heredity.

Gauquelin's research has come under a great deal of scrutiny by other scientists. The engineer and science writer Lawrence Jerome has been particularly critical, charging that Gauquelin has trumped up his statistical odds by employing binomial probability, which requires one of only two possible outcomes (see Bart Bok and Lawrence Jerome, eds., *Objections to Astrology*, Prometheus Books, 1975). Jerome asserts that Gauquelin lumps his statistics together for all twelve sectors (houses) in which a planet can appear and thus, by the binary method, achieves high probability. Instead, according to Je-

Planets and Vocations

Profession	Number of Births	Observed R/C*	Expected R/C*	Chance Probability
Mars:				
Scientists/ Physicians	3305	666	566	1 in 500,000
Athletes	1485	327	253	1 in 5,000,000
Military Men	3142	634	536	1 in 1,000,000
Musicians	703	94	120	1 in 100
Painters	1345	188	299	1 in 300
Writers	826	117	142	1 in 40
Jupiter:				
Military Men	3142	644	526	1 in 5,000,000
Politicians	993	208	164	1 in 5,000
Actors	1270	252	211	1 in 500
Journalists	824	168	137	1 in 200
Scientists/ Physicians	3305	497	546	1 in 50
Saturn:				
Scientists/ Physicians	3305	632	540	1 in 100,000
Painters	1345	178	217	1 in 250
Writers	826	108	136	1 in 130
Moon:				
Politicians	858	173	143	1 in 200
Writers	826	180	138	1 in 15,000
Athletes	1485	211	248	1 in 250

*At rise or culmination of planet. (Adapted from Gauquelin, *Cosmic Clocks*, Regnery, 1967.)

rome, Gauquelin should list the total number divided by twelve for each sector, which should bring his probabilities "well within chance level."

Gauquelin's work has actually employed many different divisions, including twelve, twenty-four, and thirty-six sectors, with no effect on results. For each sector, he compared the "theoretical frequency" of the planet in that sector (found by correcting for astronomical artifacts, like planetary speeds, and demographic artifacts, like time of day for most births) with the actually planetary positions of his many samples. His results for the Mars-athlete connection were repeated with a sample of 535 sportsmen in an experiment by the Belgian Committee for Investigations into Phenomena that Are Reputedly Paranormal—a group of scientists generally hostile to nonnatural explanations. According to Gauquelin, the committee has run repeated controls to disprove his experiments but has been unsuccessful.

For additional information, see Michel Gauquelin, *Cosmic Clocks* (Regnery, 1967) and *Scientific Basis of Astrology* (Stein and Day, 1969).

Tarot Fortune-Telling

Tarot fortune-telling is a form of cartomancy, divination by the use of cards, using a seventy-eight-card deck which is divided into twenty-two special picture cards and fifty-six cards similar to modern playing cards.

The tarot deck of seventy-eight cards is known to have been used for games and fortune-telling since at least A.D. 1400. Although elaborate speculations trace the cards to ancient Egypt, India, the Kabbalah, and elsewhere, their true origins and the reasoning behind their symbols are unknown. The origin of the word "tarot" is also uncertain.

The fifty-six Minor Arcana cards are roughly equivalent to present-day playing cards. They are divided into four suits, each running ace through ten and through four face cards: page (jack), knight, queen, king. A popular theory for the origin of the four suits relates them to the classes of medieval Europe: swords (modern spades) for the nobility and knights; cups (hearts) for the clergy; pentacles or coins (diamonds) for merchants and craftsmen; and wands or batons (clubs) for peasants and laborers.

The twenty-two Major Arcana cards each bear a title and a

The first two tarot cards (on the left) are from the traditional deck; the third (on the right) is from a deck designed by Fergus Hall.

symbolic picture. Most of them are straightforward symbols of universal abstract ideas: the Emperor, the Lovers, Justice, the Wheel of Fortune, etc. Still others, while not universal in concept, do relate easily to most human traditions: the Fool, the High Priestess, the Chariot, the Hermit.

Two cards, however, seem at first glance opaque and alien to Western traditions. The twelfth card, the Hanged Man, portrays a man with his hands tied behind his back, hanging upside down from a gibbet. His eyes are open, and he stares intently at the ground inches from his face. He bears a look of quiet satisfaction. The sixteenth card, the Tower, shows a brick tower rising straight up from the ground. The roof of the tower is being blown off by a lightning stroke, and two people are apparently falling from the tower. This card has sometimes been called the Tower of Babel, but it is also known as the House of God.

The divinatory meanings of all the cards draw on a variety of traditions from Christian to Jungian to theosophical. The most elaborate relates the Major Arcana to the twenty-two letters of the Hebrew alphabet in order (except for the un-numbered card, the Fool, which is linked with the Hebrew letter *shin*) and to the rich esoteric tradition of the Kabbalah.

Recent versions of the cards include the deck devised by the occult scholar Arthur Edward Waite. Using an idealistic, romantic style, Waite created special pictures for every card, including the pip cards of the Minor Arcana. He placed the Fool first, as it probably was in classical tarot decks, but he exchanged the positions of Strength and Justice, traditionally XI and VIII respectively.

Other modern designs include Oswald Wirth's (*Les Tarot des Imagiers du Moyen Age*), which uses the Kabbalah order. Paul Foster Case's design (*The Tarot: A Key to the Wisdom of the Ages*) is similar to Waite's in appearance and uses the traditional numbering; C. C. Zain's (*The Sacred Tarot*) is rich in symbolism but departs widely from the traditional deck; and Aleister Crowley's (*The Book of Thoth*) is a complete departure from the usual tarot deck. The most modern deck, designed in a surrealistic style by Fergus Hall for use in the James Bond movie *Live and Let Die*, uses the traditional images with minor, vaguely mocking elaborations.

Beliefs that the tarot cards represent a secret body of knowledge or a "key to the Mysteries" have no more valid basis than similar fad beliefs in the power of numbers, the "science" of astrology, or any other divination method.

Each card has so many potential meanings and is subject to so many changes of meaning, depending on the position of other cards, that an intelligent and insightful diviner can arrive at almost any interpretation. Nevertheless, in the hands of a skillful reader, a tarot reading can seem remarkably relevant and accurate; the simplest and least sophisticated interpretation often seems to be uncannily appropriate.

Occult theory would explain a successful tarot reading as a conjunction of the forces of the questioner and the circumstances to influence the order of the cards as the questioner shuffles them. Parapsychology might theorize that the cards are, in part, manipulated psychically by the questioner and also serve the diviner as a blank field on which telepathic and clairvoyant images can form.

More acceptable to modern psychology is the opinion that the cards serve as a suggestive screen which provokes the reader's imagination and against which the reader can project a pattern of intuitions and feelings that might otherwise be repressed.

Tarot, like any divination method, is always a dangerous alternative to clear rational analysis and careful, prudent planning. People who are indecisive, overly suggestible, or easily influenced would be well advised to avoid any divinatory scheme or consultation. But for the strong-willed and decisive, the tarot deck may be able to suggest opportunities or dangers that would otherwise be overlooked.

For further details, see Stuart R. Kaplan, *Tarot Classic* (Grosset & Dunlap, 1972) and Doris Doane and King Keyer, *How to Read Tarot Cards* (Funk & Wagnall, 1967).

Palms, Crystals, Tea Leaves, and Ouija Boards

Palmistry.

Palmistry, an oversimplified term, includes studying the entire hand from wrist to fingertips. Other terms for it include chirognomy and chriomancy. Mention of the art can be found in Indian and Chinese writings 3,000 years old, while the earliest Western reference is said to have been made by Aristotle. Historically, palmistry has been associated with astrology, as evidenced by the astrological symbolism used in naming sections of the hand.

The left hand is supposed to indicate inherited character-istics, while the right reveals individuality and fulfillment of potential (in left-handers, this is reversed). Analysis usually begins with size and shape, with several classification schemes available. Most systems include the elemental hand—thick, broad, associated with solid, earthy, manual labor—and the sensitive type—slender, flexible, associated with emotionality.

The analysis then proceeds to the fingers, all named after a Greco-Roman god. Astrological symbolism is followed here, with the dominant index finger, for instance, named after the god-king Jupiter. Each segment of the finger, or phalanx, also has special associations, as do the fingertips. After the fingers, analysis shifts to the fleshy areas around the palm, called mounts, which also have astrological references. The mount of Venus is located at the base of the thumb and is associated with sexuality and physical energies. Opposite it is the mount of the moon, with associations ranging from creativity to instability, depending on development. The other mounts, located at the base of the fingers, derive their names and symbolism from the fingers.

The palmist then interprets the most popular aspect of the art—the lines of the palm, all of which have standard names signifying some facet of existence. The most significant are:

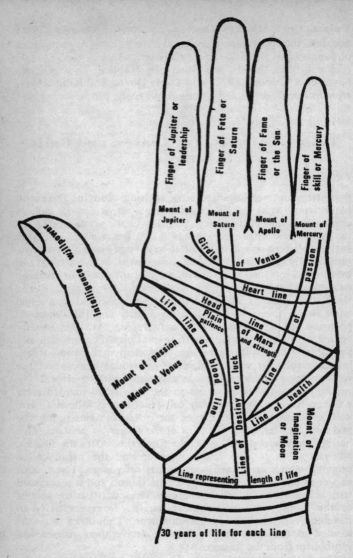

A drawing of the meaningful elements in reading palms.

the life line (curving down toward the wrist), indicating physical vitality; the head line (horizontal, immediately above the origin of the life line), referring to mental capacities; the heart line (parallel with and above the head line) associated with emotions, love, and sexiness; the fate line (vertical, down the center of the palm), indicating destiny. The palmist looks for definition, breaks, continuity, adjacency to other lines, and shapes like chains, stars, triangles, etc., each with a special meaning. The interpretation can also be extended to the rascettes, or bracelet lines of the wrist, also with separate significations.

That palmistry is not all subjective interpretation is supported by certain modern research. A German psychologist, Julius Spier, spent much of his life studying children's hands while developing his theories of psycho-chirology. Renowned psychiatrist Carl Jung wrote the preface to Spier's book *Hands of Children,* strengthening its legitimacy. Biologists have discovered relationships between inherited disorders and palm abnormalities. A broad, Y-shaped palm or the presence of a "simian" line (the heart and head lines running as one, a traditional palmist sign of "degeneracy") have been linked with chromosome damage, heart defects, Down's syndrome (mongolism), and retardation.

Ouija Boards.

The Ouija board and its cousin, the planchette, are automatic writing devices. The simpler planchette is a triangular plate mounted on tiny wheels with a pencil attached. Several people place their fingertips on it and wait for messages to be written.

The more elaborate Ouija board (derived from the French *oui* and German *ja,* both meaning yes) consists of a flat piece of polished wood emblazoned with the words "yes" and "no," the entire alphabet and numbers from 0 to 9. Users place their fingers lightly on a small heart-shaped device attached to felt-tipped legs, which moves across the board to spell messages and answer questions. Before the twentieth century it was assumed that the messages (often startling, embarrassing, or obscene) were caused by disembodied spirits. With modern psychology, however, the answers were sought in repressed, subconscious material in participants' minds. Nonetheless, some Ouija experiments seem to elicit materials not connected with psychological processes, such as data about

Ouija board and heart-shaped device that spells messages and answers questions.

distant events. This may indicate a link with telepathic capacities or other paranormal possibilities.

Ouija boards rank high with the parlor-room psychic set, and the Parker Brothers game company is now the registered owner of the "Ouija" trademark.

Crystal Gazing.

The word "crystal" derives from the Greek, meaning "clear ice" or "frozen water," and for centuries it was believed that rock crystal was water rendered into stone. In occult symbolism the crystal has been connected with serenity, poise, and sharpening of the intellect and thus was chosen for crystallomancy, or divination through the medium of crystal gazing. One nineteenth-century source states that the favorite mineral used by the "ancient seers" was beryl (a silicate of beryllium), which crystallizes into six-sided prisms. The emerald is one type, but aquamarine, a pale water-green variety, was the ancient favorite, possibly because of the astrological connection between that color and the moon, with its astrological associations with intuition.

Two persons consult a Ouija board.

Crystal gazing is part of the art of scrying, which also includes gazing at blobs of ink, pools of water, mirrors, or any transparent or reflecting object. Scrying dates from antiquity and can be found throughout the world. Divination usually involves concentrating on the surface until "clouding" occurs, at which time images and symbols are supposed to appear. Some observers have attributed the effects to auto-hypnosis or unconscious material, but cases of apparent precognition have also been recorded. So-called crystal balls, composed of clear glass, are less expensive and therefore more often used.

Teacup Reading.

Also known as tasseography, it remains one of the most popular parlor-room varieties of divination. Coffee grounds can be substituted, but the lack of leaves lessens the symbolism. China tea or any high grade with a minimum of tea dust supposedly brings the best results. The tea should be brewed in a pot without a strainer.

An undecorated (preferably, white) cup with a very wide rim, slanting sides, and a fairly large bottom is employed. The individual whose fortune is being read drinks the brew, leaving some at the bottom. The reader then grasps the cup handle with his left hand and slowly moves it from left to right three times, distributing the leaves.

Time is represented by different sections of the cup: rim—present or immediate future; sides—future; bottom—distant future. Another time significator is the handle, which represents the home or environment of the subject. Close proximity to the handle indicates a closely occurring event. Shapes taken by the leaves, stems, and tea dust are considered symbols and assigned various meanings, general and specific. General examples include: numbers—time; letters—people; dots—journeys; stars or triangles—good fortune; circles—success; squares—protection; clear shapes—luck; vague shapes—indecision, obstacles. Among specific symbols are: bear—misfortune; cage—marriage proposal; fruit—ambitions attained; key—enlightenment; ladder, wheel—advancement; spider—secretiveness.

Naturally, it takes a bit of practice to recognize the symbols. The imagination and intuition of the reader are essential parts of any reading.

For more information, see Walter B. Gibson and Litzka R. Gibson, *Complete Illustrated Book of the Psychic Sciences* (Doubleday, 1966); John Melville, *Crystal Gazing and Clairvoyance* (Weiser, 1974); Theodore Besterman, *Crystal Gazing* (University Books, 1965); Richard Cavendish, *The Black Arts* (Putnam, 1967); and Richard Cavendish, *Encyclopedia of the Unexplained* (McGraw-Hill, 1974).

UNIDENTIFIED
FLYING
OBJECTS

Extraterrestrial Intelligence

Extraterrestrial intelligence is defined as life forms capable of technological development that may exist in other bodies in the universe.

It is natural for humans to assume that life on other planets, intelligent or not, might resemble life on earth, at least concerning the most basic chemical processes. Even with the exclusion of other possible forms of life, there is good reason to believe that such life does indeed exist on innumerable planets in our galaxy alone.

While there is no planet in our solar system believed to have the necessary conditions to support life, the Milky Way galaxy (the group of stars of which our sun is a member) is believed to have billions of stars with planets of their own. A certain unknown proportion of these planets might have earthlike conditions.

Scientists have not yet been able to reconstruct the process by which life originated on earth. Therefore, it is not yet possible to determine the probability of the same process' occurring on other planets similar to earth. There are three lines of evidence, however, which suggest that the probability is high. The first is that recent experiments have duplicated in laboratories those conditions believed to have existed on earth at the time life originated. It was found that under these conditions considerable amounts of amino acids, sugars, and nitrogenous bases are produced by spontaneous chemical reactions. Proteins and nucleic acids, which are the chief constituents of life as we know it, are built up from just such spontaneously occurring chemicals.

Secondly, spectral analysis indicates the presence of molecules of organic compounds even in the vast, nearly empty reaches of interstellar space. If such compounds do indeed permeate the galaxy, their combination and evolution may be common.

The third line of evidence concerns the interval that elapsed from the time life was possible on earth to the time it actually appeared. Life on earth probably became possible about 4 billion years ago, when the surface of the earth cooled enough to solidify. Traces of bacteria and algae have been found in rock samples formed from 2.7 to 3.5 billion years ago. Thus, it only took a few hundred million years for life to appear—a short time in astronomical terms and an indication that the process may well have been repeated elsewhere.

By similar reasoning, however, it would seem that highly intelligent life may not be very common, since man did not appear until life had existed on earth for 3 billion years. On the other hand, higher intelligence can be viewed as a kind of evolutionary adaptation, and natural history is full of examples of one adaptation evolving in different organisms (for example, the adaptation of flying has evolved among many insects, bats, and birds). Intelligence is such an advantageous adaptation (or so we like to believe) that it may well have evolved in very different kinds of life organisms in different parts of the universe. Astronomers Carl Sagan and Francis Drake have estimated that about 1,000,000 planets in our galaxy alone possess technology at a level at least as high as ours.

Despite the abundance of high civilizations that may exist, a meaningful dialogue with any of them may well be a long way off.

According to current understanding, information cannot be transmitted at a speed greater than the speed of light. A signal sent from earth would take 300 years to reach a planet of a close neighboring star 300 light-years distant (a light-year is the distance that light travels in a year). If such a signal were detected by intelligent beings and they responded, their response would reach us 600 years after the original signal had been transmitted.

Since 1960 several major attempts have been made with radio telescopes to detect signals from other worlds. No intelligent signals, whether aimed at us or simply overheard by us, have been found.

For additional information, see Walter Sullivan, *We Are Not Alone* (McGraw-Hill, 1964); A. G. W. Cameron, ed., *Interstellar Communication* (Houghton Mifflin, 1963); and Carl Sagan, *Communication with Extraterrestrial Intelligence* (MIT Press, 1973).

A Brief History of UFOs

In 1896 and 1897 the United States was swept by a wave of eyewitness reports of mysterious airships, passing through the skies over cities and farms. Some of the ships were seen landing or were found on the ground with pilot and crew, all of whom usually appeared to be ordinary human beings.

At that period many Americans were eagerly awaiting the advent of successful lighter-than-air flying craft, and the reported shapes of the mysterious airships accorded well with the cigar-shaped dirigibles that the public knew might soon be launched. Consequently newspapers often interpreted the sightings as the products of fevered imaginations. But today UFO followers usually consider this nineteenth-century wave to have been the first mass manifestation of the modern UFO phenomenon.

Nearly half a century passed before the next major UFO wave, although individual cases and small local rashes of sightings were reported from time to time. During World War II, Allied pilots reported that strange balls of light and disklike objects often appeared near their planes while they flew over Germany and Japan. They believed that these "foo-fighters," as they were called, might be secret Axis psychological weapons, but German and Japanese pilots, it later was disclosed, had seen similar objects. Then, from 1946 to 1948, unidentified cigar-shaped flying objects were observed over Scandinavia and Western Europe, stimulating U.S. fears about possible Soviet secret weapons.

At the same time, a wave of "flying saucer" sightings hit the United States. In June 1947 Idaho businessman Kenneth Arnold saw nine undulating disks flying in formation near his private plane over Washington State. Arnold said the motion of each disk resembled "a saucer skipping over water." The term "flying saucer" derives from this incident. By the end of the year, 850 similar reports had been recorded all over the country, and the Air Force began an organized investigation to determine whether national security was threatened.

Since that year reports of flying objects, nocturnal lights, humanoid visitations, in fact, the full range of UFO activities, have never ceased in the United States. The incidence of sightings has varied, with extensive waves occurring in 1952, 1957, 1965–67, and 1973–74. Private UFO study groups, ranging from prestigious scientific bodies to quasi-religious saucer cults, proliferated.

A succession of Air Force UFO investigation projects were organized, including Sign, Grudge, and Blue Book, which was dissolved in 1969. But the Air Force never appeared to pursue the matter with persistence and thoroughness.

UFOs have also been sighted in great numbers in other countries across the globe, with active waves recorded, for example, in France in 1954 and in Spain in 1968, 1969, and 1974.

Typical examples of the untypical event that constitutes a UFO sighting follow.

From Daylight Disks to Dwarfs

Primary References: Charles Bowen ed., *The Humanoids* (Regnery, 1969), referred to as *Humanoids*
J. Allen Hynek and Jacques Vallee, *The Edge of Reality* (Regnery, 1975), referred to as *Edge*
J. Allen Hynek, *The UFO Experience* (Ballantine, 1972), referred to as *Experience*
Jacques Vallee, *Passport to Magonia* (Regnery, 1969), referred to as *Magonia*

In *Experience,* astronomer J. Allen Hynek constructed a classification system for understanding UFO sightings. Owing to the highly diverse nature of UFO reports, Hynek's categories are not necessarily mutually exclusive. Therefore, daylight disks might very well be nocturnal lights when seen at night; a daylight disk or nocturnal light which lands can become a close encounter, possibly leaving physical traces or being spotted by radar. Although the categories are indistinct, they are useful for an analytical grasp of this confusing phenomenon. The examples we have chosen come from a variety of respected sources.

Nocturnal Lights.

"The typical Nocturnal Light is a bright light, generally not a point source, of indeterminate linear size and of varying color but most usually yellowish orange, although no color of the spectrum has been consistently absent, which follows a path not ascribable to a balloon, aircraft, or other natural object and which often gives the appearance of intelligent action." *(Experience.)*
January 14, 1966, 5:55 P.M., *Weston, Massachusetts*
A scientist associated with MIT and three other witnesses observed an intense white light which hovered over the horizon for about ten minutes. The light was surrounded by peripheral colors of red and green, which the scientist could not attribute to "any known type of lamp." It traveled about thirty degrees

in altitude, stopped and hovered again, apparently in concert with a passing airliner. Highest speed was about one degree per second. (*Experience.*)

November 26, 1968, 5:40 P.M., Bismarck, North Dakota

Three airport tower operators on duty, plus several other witnesses, spied two bright points of light perform quick maneuvers, direction changes, and, finally, a rapid disappearance. Initially, one light headed south, the other north, but the southbound light suddenly executed a 180-degree turn and joined the other. The two then flew off together in formation. The tower operators, one of whom had twenty-seven years' experience, could not identify the lights as airplanes, satellites, or other "normal" phenomena. (*Experience.*)

Daylight Disks.

"The object (often objects in pairs) is variously described as oval, disc-shaped, 'a stunted dill pickle,' and ellipsoid. It generally is shiny or glowing (but almost never described as having distinct point source lights), yellowish, white, or metallic. It exhibits in most cases what we would anthropomorphically describe as 'purposeful' directed motion, with the ability to accelerate extremely rapidly. No loud sounds or roars seem to be associated with the Daylight Discs; sometimes there is a faint swishing sound." (*Experience.*)

August 15, 1950, 11:30 A.M., Great Falls, Montana

In this "classic" case, two observers saw thin pointlike lights in a bright sky for about one minute. One of the witnesses, Nicholas Mariana, an amateur photographer, filmed the objects. Because the movie incorporated many reference objects (like a water tower), fake photography has been almost precluded. The motion of the points could not be ascribed to aircraft, balloons, or natural phenomena. (*Experience*; M. L. Baker, and "Observational Evidence of Anomalistic Phenomena," *Journal of Astronautical Sciences,* 1968.) UFO investigator Klass asserts that this sighting was due to two Air Force jets landing at a nearby base.

October 21, 1967, 8:45 A.M., Blytheville AFB, Arkansas

Two tower operators and an airman were on duty at the alert pad at the end of the runway when they spotted "two oblong-shaped devices having the appearance of a table platter." With clear weather and excellent visibility, the objects were viewed for about thirty seconds. The observers could not determine their nature. *(Experience.)*

July 4, 1975, 12:05 A.M., 10 P.M., Parsippany and Caldwell, New Jersey

A huge cigar-shaped object, about sixty to eighty feet long, was observed moving slowly and gracefully parallel to the ground some seventy-five feet in the air, by a college student, Mr. Cahill, and his friend, Miss Tiger, who were returning home from the movies, in Parsippany, New Jersey, on July 4, 1975, at 12:05 A.M. The witnesses heard no sound but observed a light unlike any they had ever seen, bright enough to illuminate the surrounding area, yet with no glare. On closer observation, they noted a particular pattern of blue-green, red, and white lights coming from different parts of the object. A bright white light emitting from the front and bottom appeared to sweep the ground for a while. After moving about and hovering for several minutes, the object suddenly "whizzed off" into the sky in less than a second.

At 10 P.M. on July 4 private pilot Jim Quodomine and his fiancée were approached by another couple, at nearby Caldwell Field, who pointed out a UFO similar to the one seen by Cahill and Tiger. The object was visible as a large white light in the distance, so Quodomine and his fiancée took off in pursuit. They came to within 4 or 5 miles of the object at an altitude of 3,000 feet and confirmed the other witnesses' description. The pilot tried to approach the UFO at 100 miles per hour, whereupon the object changed brightness, moved away rapidly, and disappeared in seconds. (NICAP's *UFO Investigator*, September 1975.)

Radar-Visual.

"The Radar operator observes a blip on his screen that, he avers, is definite, is akin to the type of blip given by a large aircraft, is not the result of malfunction, and does not resemble weather phenomena. . . . Reversals of motion and sharp turns, not abrupt 90-degree turns, are characteristic of Radar-Visual cases." *(Experience.)*

August 13–14, 1956, 10 P.M.–3:30 A.M., Lakenheath, England

This case involved two separate ground radar operators, a military pilot, and a tower operator. Even the conservative Condon Report conceded that "the probability that at least one genuine UFO was involved appears to be fairly high."

This case is striking in the overlap of observations from many reliable sources, including four separate radar sightings prior to Lakenheath at nearby Bentwaters GCA (ground control approach). Both the pilot of a C-47 aircraft flying over the station at 4,000-feet altitude and the control tower at Bentwaters reported a "bright light" traveling at "terrific speed" from east to west.

Bentwaters contacted Lakenheath RATCC (radar air traffic control center), which picked up a UFO on radar. A second radar sighting of the UFO was made at Lakenheath GCA. The Royal Air Force dispatched a Venom night fighter to investigate the UFO over Lakenheath. The pilot visually sighted a "bright white light" and locked it on his radar fire-control system. When he got to within about a half mile of the object, it disappeared. Lakenheath RATCC informed him that the UFO had made a quick circle and was now behind the Venom. Seeing it, the pilot attempted many evasive maneuvers but was unable to shake it. The Venom returned to base. A second Venom was dispatched but experienced engine malfunction and had to return before sighting the UFO. After the chase Lakenheath radar reported that the object made a few more sharp moves, then traveled north at 600 mph, finally leaving radar range. (*Experience* and G. D. Thayer, "UFO Encounter II," *Astronautics and Aeronautics,* September 1971.)

July 17, 1957, 4:10 P.M., Louisiana, Texas, Oklahoma

Another classic, which the Condon Report described as "unusual, intriguing and puzzling" and listed as "unidentified." An RB-47 out of Forbes Air Force Base in Topeka, Kansas, sighted an intense bluish white light over Louisiana. A radar signal, which may have originated from the UFO, was then picked up on the plane's electronic countermeasures (ECM) tracking equipment by radar operator Frank B. McClure. The RB-47 increased speed to the allowable maximum, but the relative bearing of the UFO remained constant. When the plane flew over East Texas, radar picked up the UFO at Duncanville, Texas. Near Dallas the RB-47 began chasing the UFO, but both ground radar and the RB-47 lost the signal. At that point the UFO disappeared from sight as well. It soon reappeared visually and on radar. When the RB-47 closed in on the object, it rapidly dropped 5,000 feet, and all contact again ceased. Running low on fuel, the plane headed north to base. The UFO was once again sighted and picked up on radar, this time on the RB-47's tail. The object followed the RB-47 all the way from Fort Worth, Texas, to near Oklahoma City, Oklahoma, where contact was lost. The UFO had been spotted for a total distance of 700 miles, covering four states over a period of 1.5 hours. Highly unusual aspects of this case include simultaneous appearances/disappearances, and rapidity of maneuvers beyond the crew's experience. (James McDonald, "UFO Encounter I," *Astronautics and Aeronautics,* July 1971 and *Experience.*) Philip Klass proposed an explanation for this case in *UFOs Explained* (Random House, 1974). He suggests that the disappearing and reappearing visible objects may have included a variety of natural objects. The radar signal picked up by the RB-47, which the crew suspected had come from the UFO, had all the essential characteristics of signals used by air defense radar installations deployed in the area at that time, according to Klass.

Object sighted by Mr. and Mrs. Paul Trent of McMinnville, Oregon. NICAP considers this photo the best recording of a UFO; it could not be explained by the chief photographic expert of the Condon Committee. Klass, however, believes the picture is a hoax.

Close Encounters I: Simple.

"Close Encounter" types, according to Hynek, involve close-range sightings, generally at less than 500 feet. The first kind (simple) is characterized by "brilliant luminescence, relatively small size (of the order of tens rather than hundreds of feet), generally oval shape—sometimes capped with a dome—absence of conventional wings, or other protuberances, and ability to hover and to accelerate very rapidly to high speeds. . . . UFO trajectories are largely vertical when speeds are high—takeoffs at 45 degrees or greater seem to be the rule. There is little tendency for the UFO to 'cruise about the country' except locally." *(Experience.)*

April 17, 1966, 5:05 A.M., Portage County, Ohio

Considered the "wildest UFO chase on record," this case involved an object that was continuously followed by a police car for more than 70 miles across two states at speeds up to 150 mph. Two members of the Portage County, Ohio, sheriff's office, Deputy Sheriff Dale F. Spaur and Deputy Wilbur Neff, spotted the UFO in a wooded area. The object, said to be shaped like an ice-cream cone about 25 to 35 feet in diameter and highly illuminated, moved toward the police and hovered about 100 feet over their car. The two officers chased it and were joined by another patrol car, driven by Officer Wayne Huston, about 40 miles east near East Palestine, Ohio. The two patrol cars then followed the object 30 miles farther to Conway, Pennsylvania, where they finally stopped near the parked Pennsylvania patrol car of Officer Frank Panzanella. All four policemen saw the thing rapidly rise up to about 3,500 feet, stop, then continue up until it disappeared. *(Experience.)*

June 4, 1974, 9:05 P.M., Woodcliff Lake, New Jersey

Robert J. LeDonne, editor of the Special Events Unit of ABC News, sighted a "brilliant oval of lights" in the southeastern sky. Around treetop level the object had one rear red light and a string of bright yellow lights revolving around the craft. There was no engine sound; this ruled out a helicopter. The object was seen to "dip abruptly, then return to its normal altitude." After being seen for two to three minutes, the UFO disappeared behind a treetop. When LeDonne notified the police, he was told that a local patrol car had recently reported a UFO in the same area. *(Edge.)*

Close Encounters II: Physical Effects.

Hynek describes these sightings as "similar to the first kind except that physical effects on both animate and inanimate material are noted. Vegetation is often reported as having been pressed down, burned, or scorched; tree branches are reported broken; animals are frightened, sometimes to the extent of physically injuring themselves in their fright. Inanimate objects, most often vehicles, are reported as becoming momentarily disabled, their engines killed, radios stopped, and headlights dimmed or extinguished." *(Experience.)*

November 2–3, 1957, 11 P.M., Levelland, Texas

While these episodes in the vicinity of Levelland, in the Texas Panhandle, were typical of many that have been reported over the years, the concentration of sightings, independently reported, was startling. Ten incidents involving twelve witnesses occurred within two and a half hours.

The first incident took place at about 11 P.M. Pedro Saucedo and Joe Salaz were driving a truck 4 miles west of Levelland, when a brilliantly illuminated 200-foot-long torpedo-shaped object passed over the car at about 600 to 800 mph. The truck's headlights and engine went dead during the overpass, and the passengers felt an intense heat. After the object passed, the truck functioned normally.

Saucedo phoned in a report to the Levelland police. An hour later another caller reported that his car engine and headlights had failed as he approached a luminous 200-foot-long egg-shaped vehicle parked in the road. When he got out of his car, the object rose up about 200 feet and disappeared. He could then restart his engine. In the course of the night several more reports were called in, matching the second call closely in their descriptions of the size and shape of the object and the mechanical malfunctions of the witnesses' cars.

The police sent out patrol cars to investigate. A sheriff and his deputy saw an oval-shaped brilliant light crossing the highway a few hundred yards away; two patrolmen following a few miles behind saw a similar flash in the direction of the sheriff's car. By morning seven cases of sightings with accompanying automobile malfunctions and three sightings without physical effects became known to the police. Several additional UFO incidents were reported that day and the next in that area of Texas and neighboring New Mexico.

October 26, 1958, 10:30 P.M., Loch Raven Dam, Maryland

Two men were driving toward a bridge across the Loch Raven Reservoir near Baltimore when they saw a brilliantly lighted UFO which was described as "a large, flat sort of egg-shaped object hanging between 100 to 150 feet off the top of the superstructure of the bridge over the lake." When they drove to within 80 feet of the bridge, the car's dashlights, headlights, and engine failed, and the ignition refused to start. They watched the object for thirty to forty-five seconds, saw a brilliant flash of light, and heard a loud noise. Then the thing began a rapid vertical ascent and was gone in about five to ten seconds. Subsequently, several other witnesses asserted they had seen a strange light in the vicinity of the bridge. (Vallee, *Challenge to Science*, Regnery, 1966.)

September 1, 1974, 10 A.M., Saskatchewan, Canada

A thirty-six-year-old farmer, Edwin Fuhr, was harvesting his crop when he spotted a metal dome about 50 feet away. He got off the swather, approached to within 15 feet, and saw that the object was spinning and moving the grass beneath it. He returned to the swather, climbed up on the seat and saw four more metal domes, all the same size, and all spinning clockwise like the first one. They all were hovering about one foot off the ground in a rough semicircle.

After several minutes they rapidly ascended to about 200 feet in a step formation, then emitted a dark-gray vapor from ports in their bases. This was accompanied by a strong downward gust of wind. The objects, described as 5 feet high and 11 feet at the base, then formed a straight line and quickly ascended until they could no longer be seen.

After that, five rings of flattened, matted grass were found. There was no burning, exhaust, or odors, but the grass was flattened in a clockwise direction, just as the UFOs had spun. An investigator from the Royal Canadian Mounted Police arrived at the scene the next day, and photos were taken. The rings were isolated, with no footprints or machine tracks nearby. In an interview the RCMP investigator said that the grass "was undisturbed except for the circles and whatever was in there. It came out of the air and departed the same way."

For several days before and after the sighting, other strange effects occurred in the vicinity: they included cattle bellowing and breaking fences, dogs barking, and television interference.

Two days later a sixth ring was found, and two weeks later, a seventh. *(Edge.)*

Close Encounters III: Occupants.

These sightings are distinguished by the presence of occupants, which come in many colors, shapes, and sizes, including dwarfs with "large heads, spindly feet, and, generally, a head that sits squat on the shoulders without much evidence of neck. . . . The larger humanoids are reported to be of human size or a little larger and are generally very well formed. Sometimes they have been termed beautiful. The small ones generally are described as about three and a half feet tall." *(Experience.)*

April 24, 1964, 5:45 P.M., Socorro, New Mexico

Another widely reported UFO classic. Lonnie Zamora, a Socorro policeman, was chasing a speeder when he heard a roar and saw a bluish white flame descending about three-fourths of a mile to the southeast. The sound stopped, and he did not see the object again until he drove up a steep hill. Then about 150 to 200 yards south he saw a shiny, white, aluminumlike object, egg-shaped with two "legs" supporting it on the ground. Next to it were two figures, below average height, in white coveralls. They appeared "normal in shape." One turned and "seemed startled" at the officer's presence.

Zamora left his car and was beginning to approach the object when he heard a bang and saw that the coveralled figures had disappeared. Another roar, with a flame under the object, accompanied the slow lifting of the UFO off the ground. Before it left, Zamora noticed a large red insignia on the craft. He saw the UFO heading toward the southeast, moving very rapidly in a straight line about ten to fifteen feet off the ground. It rose and cleared a nearby mountain, then disappeared. It traveled in the air without flames, smoke, or noise.

Zamora later returned to the site with state police, FBI and Air Force witnesses and saw bent and burned brush in several places. The state police and Air Force witnesses measured the distance between four indentations in the sand, a half inch to two inches deep. The four indentations (possible landing-pod marks) formed a quadrilateral whose diagonals intersected at a right angle. The midpoints of its sides defined a circle, whose center (which under certain conditions would

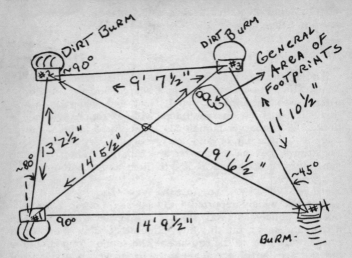

The original sketch of the marks left in the earth by the Socorro UFO. It was drawn by Air Force Captain Richard T. Holder according to measurements made by him, an FBI agent, an Air Force sergeant, Socorro policemen, and others immediately after the sighting.

be directly under the vehicle's center of gravity) coincided with the chief fire scar. Klass labels this sighting a hoax designed to create some tourist trade for Socorro. (W. T. Powers, "The Landing at Socorro," in *Humanoids; Experience;* and *Magonia.*)

August 21, 1955, Evening, Kelly-Hopkinsville, Kentucky

Called the "granddaddy of all occupant sightings," this bizarre tale began when a member of the Sutton family saw a light land in a gully near his family's farmhouse. A few minutes later a small, "glowing" figure was seen approaching the house. About three to three and a half feet tall, the creature had a roundish head, large elephantine ears, a slitlike mouth, huge eyes, and long arms ending in clawlike hands. In characteristic Kentucky fashion, several shots were fired by the Suttons, and the creature scurried off.

However, other creatures appeared, near the window, on the roof, and on trees. One playfully tapped a Sutton on the head with a clawed hand. A creature in a tree was shot

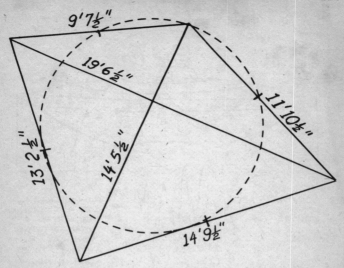

When the same sketch is redrawn to scale, the measurements prove to be accurate to within two inches. The diagonals are revealed to be perpendicular, and arcs drawn through the midpoints of the four sides describe a circle.

directly, but it floated to the ground and ran away. After hours of this, the entire family of eleven rushed into their cars and drove to the police, who returned with them but found nothing. Once the police departed, the creatures reappeared to continue their antics but left before dawn. (*Experience; Magonia; Humanoids.*)

November 2, 1967, 9:30 P.M., Ririe, Idaho

Two Navajo Indians, Willie Begay and Guy Tossie, were driving on Highway 26 near Ririe, Idaho. Suddenly, they later reported, there was a blinding flash of light, and a small UFO appeared in the air right before their car. It was shaped like two saucers rim to rim. The vehicle was five to eight feet in diameter and about two feet thick, with a transparent dome on top. Two occupants were visible within.

The witnesses' car was brought to a stop. Green and orange lights flashed through holes which moved around the perimeter of the vehicle. The dome was unhinged, and a

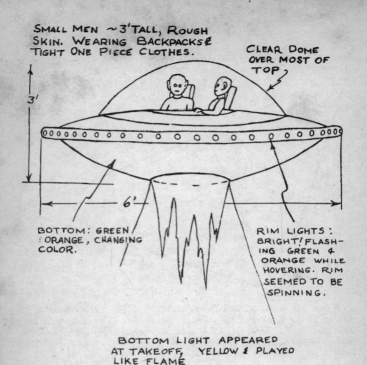

SMALL MEN ~3' TALL, ROUGH SKIN. WEARING BACKPACKS & TIGHT ONE PIECE CLOTHES.

CLEAR DOME OVER MOST OF TOP

3'

6'

BOTTOM: GREEN & ORANGE, CHANGING COLOR.

RIM LIGHTS: BRIGHT! FLASHING GREEN & ORANGE WHILE HOVERING. RIM SEEMED TO BE SPINNING.

BOTTOM LIGHT APPEARED AT TAKEOFF, YELLOW & PLAYED LIKE FLAME

Sketch of the Ririe, Idaho, UFO by investigator C. R. Ricks after the descriptions of Begay and Tossie.

three-and-a-half-foot-high occupant floated to the car, opened it, and entered. Rough, scarred skin covered its face, which had high ears, round eyes, a slit for a mouth, and no nose. It wore coveralls and a high backpack.

The car moved, or was towed, into a field. Begay jumped out and ran to a nearby farmhouse, pursued by one of the occupants. The other occupant remained in the car and tried to talk to Tossie in a warbling, unintelligible voice. When the first occupant returned, the two reentered the UFO, which rose in a zigzag pattern. A flaming yellow light was emitted from the bottom of the vehicle, which turned very bright and moved rapidly off.

Begay returned after fifteen minutes, with Willard Hammon, a farmer, and Hammon's son. The two Indians went with Hammon to the local police to report the incident. The Indians admitted they had been drinking beer, but according to the investigator, witnesses agreed they were not drunk.

About eleven-thirty the same night a similar incident reportedly occurred at another highway near Ririe. A truck was stopped by a small UFO descending in front of it. A small man got out of the UFO and tried to enter the truck. The driver told UFO investigator C. Reed Ricks that he managed to evade the occupant and drove away. (Shelly, Idaho *Pioneer*, December 7, 1967; *UFO Investigator*, September/October 1969.)

January, 1975, North Bergen, New Jersey

George O'Barski, a teetotaling liquor store owner, was driving through North Hudson Park in North Bergen, New Jersey, around 3 A.M. on a mild night in January, listening to his car radio. The radio had begun to show static interference and a fading signal when O'Barski heard a droning hum to his left. A large, bright object flew past, stopped, and hovered a few feet over the park lawn.

The vehicle was circular, about thirty feet across, flat on the bottom, with vertical sides and a convex roof, which rose to a maximum of about eight feet from the bottom of the craft. Ten or twelve oblong, vertical windows were spaced equally all around the UFO. A light shining through the windows illuminated the area.

A landing ladder descended, a door opened, and eight to eleven three-and-a-half-foot-tall figures descended, dressed in helmets and jump suits. They appeared to scoop up samples

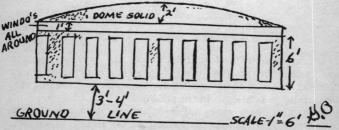

Sketch of the UFO observed by George O'Barski in North Hudson Park, New Jersey. The sketch was made by O'Barski.

of soil and put them in bags, then returned to the UFO, which ascended rapidly out of view.

The next day O'Barski returned to the park and found a series of holes in the ground, four or five inches wide and six inches deep.

Several other UFO sightings occurred in the same area that month, two of them agreeing closely with much of O'Barski's testimony. Evidence indicates that these two sightings occurred the same night as O'Barski's sighting, but this has not been conclusively established.

William Pawlowski was on doorman duty at the Stonehenge, an apartment building across the street from North Hudson Park. At 2:30 or 3 A.M. on January 12 he saw a series of eight to fifteen bright round lights, attached to a dark, round object hovering over the park. Pawlowski telephoned a tenant; while he was speaking, he heard a high-pitched sound and saw the plate-glass lobby window crack near the floor, with a nick of glass gouged out from the street side. The lights soon disappeared. Pawlowski calculated that any projectile or force that could pass over the street wall and hit near the bottom of the window would have had to originate several feet above the level of the park. Pawlowski and O'Barski independently located the site of the hovering UFO at precisely the same spot, according to UFO investigators Ted Bloecher, Budd Hopkins, and Jerry Stoehrer.

The third major incident involved the Wamsley family, all five members of which reported seeing a domed UFO with oblong windows, emitting a hum, pass near their house at 9:30 P.M., probably on January 11, and disappear near Pawlowski's building. (*Village Voice*, March 1, 1976; "The Stonehenge Incidents," Proceedings of the Center for UFO Studies Conference, April 30–May 2, 1976.)

Five Classic Abduction Cases

These examples of "Close Encounters III" are among the most bizarre in the literature. They all have attracted much attention. Most of the witnesses appear to have suffered emotional traumas as a result of the episodes.

In each of these cases UFO occupants were reported to have forcibly abducted, or seemed to be trying to abduct, a witness or witnesses. We relate the versions given by the abductees, which by their nature can have no certain outside verification. (Besides the previously mentioned sources, data on some of these cases were taken from David Jacobs, *The UFO Controversy in America,* Indiana University Press, 1975; referred to as *Controversy*.)

September 1961, near midnight, Whitfield, New Hampshire

This startling case involved an interracial New Hampshire couple, Betty and Barney Hill. While driving home along Route 3 through the White Mountains of New Hampshire, they spotted a light in the sky moving erratically. It followed them for several miles. Barney stopped the car to look at the object through binoculars. He saw a disk-shaped craft about sixty-five feet across, with a red light on one side and a double row of windows. Frightened, the couple drove off. Then they heard beeping sounds and felt the car vibrating. They became drowsy, then alert again, and found themselves still driving, but thirty-five miles south of where they had been originally. They also noticed that it was two hours later.

The Hills remained silent about the sighting, telling only a few relatives, but the puzzling memory gap caused Barney to have nervous disorders, including an ulcer. Betty had frightening dreams of being aboard a spaceship. Barney began psychiatric treatment, finally being sent to well-known Boston psychiatrist Dr. Benjamin Simon in December 1963. Two months later Dr. Simon began to unravel the mystery by placing the Hills under deep hypnosis. They were hypnotized separately, but their two accounts did not materially disagree.

Under hypnosis, they recalled that when the beeping ceased, they found themselves on an unknown road, where they were stopped by a group of humanoids and dragged up a ramp into the landed craft. The abductors were small, under five feet, with grayish skin, large, slanted eyes, almost no noses, and slitlike mouths. Their heads were triangular, with large craniums tapering down to the chins. The beings communicated by making strange sounds, which somehow were translated into English in the couple's thoughts.

The Hills were taken into separate "examination rooms" in the spacecraft. Both were placed on "operating tables" in a brightly lit room. Barney's groin was examined, and his false teeth were inspected. Betty had a long needle inserted into her navel, said to be a "pregnancy test." She also had samples of hair and toenail taken, but the examiner seemed perplexed when her natural teeth, unlike Barney's, could not be removed. The couple was told that they would forget the experience and were returned to their car.

It should be noted that many psychiatrists do not accept hypnotic regression as a reliable method of obtaining factual evidence. (*Experience; Edge; Humanoids.*)

October 11, 1973, 9 A.M., Pascagoula, Mississippi

Calvin Parker (nineteen years old) and Charles Hickson (forty-two) of Gautier, Mississippi, were fishing in the Pascagoula River when they heard a buzzing sound. They saw an egg-shaped object with glowing blue lights, about ten feet wide and eight feet high. As it hovered a few feet off the ground close by, a door opened and several humanoids "floated" down. They were described as about five feet tall, with light gray, wrinkled skin, bullet-shaped heads, no necks or eyes, slitlike mouths, clawlike hands, and conical appendages where ears and noses would have been in humans.

Two of the creatures grabbed Hickson and "floated" him into the UFO, where he was taken into a brightly lit room. A third occupant grabbed Parker, who fainted. Hickson was held while an object resembling an eye, apparently not attached to anything, moved over his body in an apparent examination. The humanoids then left him suspended in midair, unable to move anything but his eyes. About twenty minutes after the craft had been first seen, they floated Hickson outside, where he joined the hysterical Parker. The UFO then flew straight up and disappeared.

The two men reported the incident to the sheriff and were left alone in a sound-monitored room. Their "private" conversation did not indicate a hoax, and the pair also passed lie-detector tests. Hypnosis was attempted, but it was found to be too traumatic. (*Edge; Controversy.*)

Snowflake, Arizona, daytime, November 5, 1975

Travis Walton, twenty-three, was riding in a truck with six other members of a private lumbering crew when they spotted a saucerlike object in the air about thirty yards off the road. They stopped the truck, and Walton walked over to the object, which emitted a "high-pitched, buzzing" sound and started to move. Walton crouched down by a log. Then a beam came out of the bottom of the saucer, hit him, and knocked him about ten feet, according to one witness. Walton said he "felt a kind of electric shock [which] knocked me

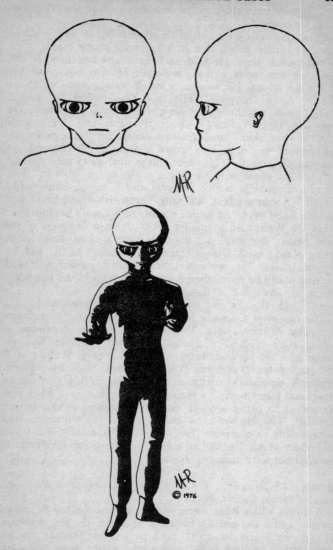

Artist's rendering of the humanoids described by Travis Walton as having abducted him.

out." The others were terrified and drove off in the truck "as fast as we could."

A five-day search by a sheriff's posse failed to find Walton. Relatives finally found him in a highway phone booth, after he had called them. He said he believed he had been in the UFO for the entire period, although he was conscious for only a few hours. He awoke in an all-metal room, which he took to be a "hospital." His shirt was pulled up, and a "thing," not attached anywhere, lay across his chest. He then saw three "aliens"—about five feet tall, bald, with "chalky white skin," small features except for big brown eyes, and dressed in "orangeish-brown coveralls." Frightened, he knocked the object off his chest and pushed away the "aliens," who left the room without saying anything. A "human" then entered, dressed in a blue uniform and a "clear, bubble-type helmet." About six feet tall, with "brownish-blond hair" and "golden-hazel eyes," he smiled silently at Walton's babbling.

He led Walton to a smaller room down a hallway, where three other "humans" put over his face a clear, soft, form-fitting plastic mask with a black ball attached to it, "like an oxygen mask," but without tubes. Walton passed out, and the next thing he remembered was waking up in the roadway, where he "saw this craft disappear straight up."

Although Walton and the witnesses were awarded $5,000 by the *National Enquirer* for their account of the experience (see The Million-Dollar Prize), UFO experts continue to debate their credibility. Philip Klass has documentary evidence of a secret lie-detector test which Travis Walton took and *failed* on November 15, five days after his return. Walton's defenders attribute the failure to his continuing emotional upset over the incident. Klass believes a hoax was concocted to bring a quick end to a government lumbering contract. The lumber crew chief, one of the witnesses, had been unable to complete the contract satisfactorily, but stood to collect about $2,000 in withheld Forest Service funds if the contract were canceled. It was.

October 15–16, 1957, 1 A.M., Near San Francisco de Sales, state of Minos Gerais, Brazil

Antonio Villas Boas, twenty-three, an uneducated Brazilian farmer, often worked on his farm at night. On the evenings of October 5 and 14, 1957, both he and his brother saw an inexplicable "bright light" overhead, at one time near the home and at the other over a field.

On October 15 Boas was alone plowing the field with his tractor at about 1 A.M. when he saw a "luminous egg-shaped object flying toward me at terrific speed." The craft, about thirty-five feet long and twenty-three feet wide, hovered directly above him for a while, then landed in front of him. As three metal "legs" emerged beneath the machine to support it, Boas' tractor lights and engine went dead. He was grabbed by four helmeted occupants, who dragged him up a ladder into the craft.

He was taken into several rooms lighted by fluorescent white lights and having "silvery polished metal walls." One room was furnished with a "strangely shaped" table and several backless swivel chairs, all made of "white metal." His five captors were dressed in gray, tight-fitting overalls. With their helmets, they were about the same height as Boas (five feet four inches). The helmets, which prevented him from seeing any features but their "blue" eyes, had "three round silvery tubes" which emerged into the uniform. Although Boas did not detect any "lumps" or protuberances indicating a breathing apparatus, the uniforms seemed self-enclosed from gloves to boots to helmets.

Boas was brought to a small room furnished only by a large "couch" covered with a thick gray material. The occupants then applied thick rubber tubes attached to a flask to Boas' chin and extracted blood. This operation left scars that could be seen for some time after the incident. The occupants, who seemed unable either to communicate with or to understand Boas, "talked" with each other via strange barking noises.

To prepare him for the next stage of their experiments, he was forcibly stripped naked and sponged with a liquid. Then a "woman" entered the room, also completely nude. Her hair was fair, reaching halfway down her neck; her skin was white; her eyes were large and blue, slanting outward. She reached only up to his shoulders and had thin lips, a small nose and ears, a thin waist, "high and well-separated breasts," wide hips, large thighs, normal fingers, feet, and nails. Most unusual was her triangular face, with very high, wide cheeks which narrowed sharply to a pointed chin. Also unusual was the blood-red color of her armpits and pubic hair. Nonetheless, Boas described her body as "much more beautiful than that of any woman I have ever known before."

They engaged in intercourse, which he described as "a normal act. . . . she behaved just as any woman would."

Before leaving she pointed to her stomach, then to Boas, and then toward the sky, which he took as a reference to their future extraterrestrial infant. "What they wanted of me [was] a good stallion to improve their own stock," he asserted.

He was then given back his clothes and taken on a guided tour of the craft. Finally, he was allowed to disembark, and he watched the UFO rise, and shoot off "like a bullet" until it was out of sight. Boas, who had been aboard for more than four hours, reported his story to a Brazilian journalist and gave a signed deposition before Dr. Olavo Fontes of Rio de Janeiro a few months after the event. He was thoroughly interrogated by Dr. Fontes and the journalist, but his story remained unchanged. Dr. Fontes' medical analysis revealed possible radiation poisoning, as well as the scars on Boas' chin. (*Humanoids.*)

September 4, 1964, night, Cisco Grove, California

Three men had been bow-and-arrow hunting in the mountains when they became separated. One of them, Don Shrum, was unable to find his way back to camp before nightfall. He saw odd lights in the distance which came in his direction and hovered without making a sound. Perturbed, Mr. Shrum climbed about twelve feet up a twenty-five-to-thirty-foot tree. He noted a flash, and a dark object descending. Soon he saw a "dome-shaped affair" on or near the ground about 450 yards away.

He then noticed two creatures, about five and one half feet tall, dressed in a silvery-gray material. He could see no facial features. They stood at the base of the tree and watched him as a third entity joined them. This one moved more clumsily than the others and was dark gray or black with two glowing reddish orange "eyes" about three inches in diameter. It, too, had no neck, but had a "mouth" which extended completely across the face and seemed to "drop" open, making a rectangular hole in the face. Shrum thought that this third creature was a "robot."

Throughout the night the first two entities attempted to climb the tree by boosting each other up but failed. Periodically, the third one would issue from its mouth a puff of white smoke which would render Shrum unconscious for several seconds. He attempted several defensive measures, including firing three arrows at the "robot." These produced sparks when they hit, suggesting metal. Shrum also threw down his canteen (which they examined), his bow, and some coins. He also set fire to his cap, oversuit, and jacket, and threw them at the beings, which momentarily backed off.

Around dawn a second "robot" joined the first and faced him. Sparks and a glow appeared between their chests, and a cloud of gas issued from them and engulfed Shrum. He blacked out, and when he awakened, he found the things were gone. He was nauseated and exhausted. One of his companions located him. Returning to camp, he was told one of the other men had also seen the craft the night before. Shrum reported the incident to the Air Force. (*Humanoids.*)

Physical Traces of UFOs

Observers of close-encounter UFO incidents often report finding physical traces after the departure of the UFO, most often in the form of changes in soil or vegetation, sometimes in the form of damage to property. Occasionally, residues or artifacts seem to have been left behind by the objects. At times, similar traces or residues have been found without any accompanying UFO sightings.

Traces have been reported from all over the world and as far back as the earliest UFO sightings, with several examples dating from the nineteenth century and a handful from even earlier. Many of these traces have been observed and

J. Allen Hynek, founder of CUFOS and former UFO skeptic.

recorded by law officers and UFO investigators after the incident was over. Some witnesses have also displayed skin burns and other physical injuries, attributed to the UFO encounter, which were at times treated by medical personnel.

A total of 831 physical trace cases were compiled by UFO investigator Ted Phillips in a 1975 study published by the Center for UFO Studies (CUFOS). In 561 of these cases a UFO was observed in connection with traces; 154 other cases involved similar effects with no known connection to an UFO sighting. In the remaining 116 cases, details were too sketchy to characterize the incident. Even this lengthy list is not complete, especially concerning incidents in Communist countries, and new cases are being added all the time.

As always in the UFO field, the unexpectedness of each incident and the lack of coordinated, well-funded investigations makes analysis difficult. However, some similarities among trace reports enable us to discuss certain common categories.

1. The most common physical traces are circular or ringlike depressions in soil, snow, or vegetation, presumably showing the imprint of saucer-shaped craft. Within the circle the flattened grass is frequently found swirled clockwise or counterclockwise or facing outward like the spokes of a wheel. The diameter of these circles can vary from a few feet to more than a hundred. Broken and even uprooted trees are often found in the vicinity.

Smaller but deeper indentations are frequently in evidence within the circle, possibly indicating where landing pods touched down. These indentations are usually arranged in some sort of symmetrical pattern, triangular or quadrilateral. Sometimes these marks are found alone, with no circle. "Footprints" of various shapes, usually smaller than human prints, are sometimes found near the circles or indentations.

2. The soil within the circles or around independent indentations often displays unusual characteristics. Frequently vegetation dies and does not grow back, even for a period of years. Sometimes the area becomes impervious to water. Radiation levels a few times higher than in the surrounding area have been recorded. Soil analysis at the Wallingford, Kentucky, site of a 1951 saucer visitation showed levels of

chromium, iron, and manganese not usually found in the clay soil of the area.

A more detailed analysis was made of soil from an eight-foot ring apparently left by a glowing, rumbling object near Delphos, Kansas, on November 2, 1971. The tests, conducted by Utah State and Northwestern universities and by private agricultural laboratories, found (according to the CUFOS study):

> Soil from the ring, compared to the control sample from the ground nearby: does not absorb water, is more acidic and higher in soluble salts; contains five to ten times more calcium than the control and somewhat more minerals (magnesium, potassium); produces less seed growth than the control, and is coated with a hydrocarbon. . . . The coating of soil particles is of a material of low atomic weight, with globules of higher atomic weight imbedded in it. Unique icicle-shaped crystals 0.1 to 0.05 microns long were found, as was a previously uncatalogued crystalline structure of low atomic weight.

3. Various heat effects are commonly noticed in the soil and throughout the impact area. In milder cases, grass withers, tree trunks are scorched, snow melts, and the earth is dehydrated, blackened, or covered with ash. In the Ethiopian case discussed below, tin roofs and metal pots melted. Gravel and grass have often been calcined (burned at very high temperatures without fusing), and rock samples have been fused and melted.

In Tucumán, Argentina, in January 1963, an egg-shaped object was seen descending toward a spot where two scorched rings were later found. Within the rings, grass roots were scorched down to four inches below the ground. They appeared to have been desiccated without combustion by a temperature of more than 2,000 degrees Centigrade, according to local scientists. Soil within a depression in a Griffin, Georgia, field measured 200 to 300 degrees Fahrenheit several hours after an egg-shaped object had been seen there on September 10, 1973.

4. Surprisingly little damage has been reported to property, considering the vast number of UFO cases and the apparent power and speed of the craft. Among the reported property

damage episodes, a garage roof was said to have been blown off in one case, a truck burned out in another. More seriously, a private plane was dented and scratched in flight near Mexico City on May 3, 1975, by one of three saucer-shaped objects dogging the plane.

One frightening example of possible hostility occurred at the village of Saladare, in Ethiopia, on August 7, 1970. A red glowing object zoomed through the village, hovered, and zoomed back, destroying several stone houses and the half-meter-thick wall of a stone bridge, uprooting trees, burning grass, and melting asphalt without any visible fire. The sky was cloudless, making lightning an unlikely explanation for the event.

5. A large variety of residues have been found at sites of UFO landings or flyovers. These residues include liquids, solids, powders, crystals, and flakes in nearly all colors of the spectrum.

Descriptions of oil, grease, tar, or an oily black substance are among the most common residue reports. Yellow stains, dust, or powder also seem to be present in many cases. A green liquid has been observed at times, and three witnesses reported that a UFO in the air at a southwestern Indiana site spewed out "a cascade of greenish-phosphorescent material which shimmered as it came down" during an October 10, 1966, incident. Gray, silver, and white powders have also been reported. A hot "silver rain" fell from a UFO over Campinas, Brazil, on December 19, 1954. A local chemist found the substance to be a mixture of pure tin, 88.9 percent, and oxygen, 11.1 percent.

A substance dubbed angel's hair has intrigued UFO enthusiasts for years. It is described as a fibrous weblike substance found on the ground, trees, and other surface features over areas far too large to be accounted for by spiders. The substance tends to disintegrate rapidly, although samples have been preserved long enough for analysis in some cases. In about half the reported cases the material was seen descending from a UFO or was seen in the immediate area of an UFO sighting.

As far back as September 21, 1741, large quantities of a similar material fell for a period of hours over Bradley, England. More recently, reports of angel's hair have come from Australia, New Zealand, France, Italy, and the United States.

A housewife in Sudbury, Massachusetts, collected samples of the material, which fell within a 1,500-foot circumference on October 22, 1973, while a glowing silvery globe passed overhead. Three other witnesses watched the sticky substance fall. Samples were examined by various public and private laboratories in Massachusetts, one of which determined that the substance contained the same amino acid as does spider web. However, according to the NICAP investigator of the case, experts disagreed about the possibility of such a large quantity of spider web's suddenly appearing in one place. Experts also disagreed about a theory that the glowing silvery ball seen in the sky could have been a congealed mass of spider web.

A detailed analysis of such material which fell near Houston, Texas, on November 6, 1968, during a UFO sighting found that the substance "would not dissolve in water, alcohol, or sulfuric acid. . . . Microscopic and tactile examination indicates the substance is fibrous, elastic, relatively strong, somewhat sticky, and white in color," according to the Houston *Post*. The University of Manitoba conducted an infrared spectroscope analysis of white fibrous material which fell on a farm in Manitoba from the sides of a UFO on September 18, 1968. The material was found to be celluloselike and unstable, with a uniform fiber diameter of one two-hundredth millimeter.

Reports of "white filaments," cotton, or wool falling from the heavens may well be placed in the angel's hair category, though a fall of white filament over a wide area at Caldwell, New Jersey, was identified as ordinary nylon filament, like fish line.

Among the other residues reported have been "silvery needles" (Michigan, 1971), metal fragments of various colors, "plastic-looking strips" which turned papery (North Dakota, 1969), and "a metal foil" (Indiana, 1967).

6. Far less often, witnesses have reported finding what appeared to be artifacts at UFO sites. Strange printed messages were reportedly left by UFO occupants in two undetailed cases, one in Weeki-Wachee, Florida, in 1965, the other in Mexico City the same year. A disk-shaped UFO was seen to explode near the seashore at Ubatuba, Brazil, on September 7, 1957; a fragment that fell to the beach proved to be nearly 100 percent pure magnesium. A stainless-steel alloy disk, twenty inches in diameter, with holes in the

center and around the edges, was found at a 1965 Pennsylvania landing site; a peculiar flat orange-red stone with purple pits was found after a 1972 Indiana UFO visitation.

7. External physical injuries to humans or animals may also be considered traces. Skin burns have been most common. A lone witness at Falcon Lake, Manitoba, was treated for first-degree abdominal burns after being knocked to the ground by a blast of hot air when, he said, he tried to peer through an opening into a landed UFO on May 20, 1967. Temporary blindness has been reported in a few cases. A truck driver on a road near Jackson, Missouri, was partially blinded for several days by a flash or ball of light apparently emanating from a spinning, top-shaped UFO. The frames of his eyeglasses were melted and twisted. His wife, who was riding next to him, failed to see the UFO.

These physical traces no more constitute "proof" that UFOs are anomalous phenomena than any other type of UFO report. One might even say that the extraterrestrial hypothesis is weakened by the paucity of obviously alien artifacts or debris. But the evidence of physical matter remaining in one place for a period of time, available for investigation by people other than the actual witnesses, at least suggests that the UFOs involved, whatever their nature, were neither optical illusions nor figments of the imagination.

However, mundane explanations for many of the traces can be suggested. Lightning or meteorites could bring physical or chemical changes to localized areas. Debris dropped from conventional aircraft or discarded by passersby, human or animal, might account for the presence of matter foreign to the immediate vicinity. Severe local air pollution could conceivably take the form of colored "rain" or dust.

If traces are indeed connected with UFOs, the question arises whether the materials involved originated within the UFO or merely represent local matter metamorphosed in some way through contact with the UFO. For example, it has been suggested that angel's hair is an unstable cellulose compound formed from carbon, hydrogen, and oxygen present in the air combined by electrical discharges or microwave radiation from the UFO. The glowing effect noted at some landing sites has been tentatively explained as a result of slow oxidation of phosphorus which had been released from phosphates in the soil by the intense heat of the UFO encounter.

If the mystery of UFOs is to be even partially solved, the traces they have left behind must be far more thoroughly studied. UFO investigators and organizations must provide greater follow-through on the most interesting cases. If not, we are left with only oil slicks and a lot of withered grass.

Further details can be found in Ted Philips, *Physical Traces Associated with UFO Sightings* (Center for UFO Studies, 1975); *UFO Investigator* (periodical), NICAP (March and June 1974); *Official UFO* (commercial periodical) (July 1976).

Ten UFOlogical Principles

The case studies we have presented are based, for the most part, on eyewitness accounts. Philip Klass has created a list of ten "UFOlogical Principles" that illuminate the dangers of accepting these accounts at face value even when the witnesses have been carefully questioned by sophisticated researchers.

Though Klass is a confirmed UFO skeptic, the more competent of the "believing" UFO investigators would have no trouble endorsing at least some of these cautionary statements.

Principle 1: "Basically honest and intelligent persons who are suddenly exposed to a brief, unexpected event, especially one that involves an unfamiliar object, may be grossly inaccurate in trying to describe precisely what they have seen."

Principle 2: "Despite the intrinsic limitations of human perception when exposed to brief, unexpected and unusual events, some details recalled by the observer may be reasonably accurate. The problem facing the UFO investigator is to try to distinguish between those details that are accurate and those that are grossly inaccurate. This may be impossible until the true identity of the UFO can be determined, so that in some cases this poses an insoluble problem."

Principle 3: "If a person observing an unusual or unfamiliar object concludes that it is probably a spaceship from another world, he can readily adduce that the object is reacting to his presence or actions when in reality there is absolutely no cause-effect relationship."

Principle 4: "Newspapers that give great prominence to a UFO report when it is first received subsequently devote little if any space or time to reporting a prosaic explanation for the case when all the facts are uncovered."

Principle 5: "No human observer, including experienced flight crews, can accurately estimate either the distance/altitude or the size of an unfamiliar object in the sky, unless it is in very close proximity to a familiar object whose altitude or size is known."

Principle 6: "Once news media coverage leads the public to believe that UFOs may be in the vicinity, there are numerous natural and man-made objects which, especially when seen at night, can take on unusual characteristics in the minds of hopeful viewers. Their UFO reports in turn add to the mass excitement which encourages still more observers to watch for UFOs. This situation feeds upon itself until such time as the news media lose interest in the subjects, and then the 'flap' quickly runs out of steam."

Principle 7: "In attempting to determine whether a UFO report is a hoax, an investigator should rely on physical evidence, or the lack of it where evidence should exist, and should not depend on character endorsements of the principals involved."

Principle 8: "The inability of even experienced investigators to fully and positively explain a UFO report for lack of sufficient information, even after a rigorous effort, does not really provide evidence to support the hypothesis that spaceships from other worlds are visiting Earth."

Principle 9: "Whenever a light is sighted in the night skies that is believed to be a UFO and this is reported to a radar operator, who is asked to search his scope for an unknown target, almost invariably an 'unknown' target will be found. Conversely, if an unusual target is spotted on a radarscope at night that is suspected of being a UFO, and an observer is dispatched or asked to search for a light in the night sky, almost invariably a visual sighting will be made."

Principle 10: "Many UFO cases seem puzzling and unexplainable simply because case investigators have failed to devote a sufficiently rigorous effort to the investigation."

(From *UFOs Explained*, by Philip J. Klass. Copyright © 1974 by Philip J. Klass. Reprinted by permission of Random House, Inc.)

UFOs—What's Going On?

A useful definition of a UFO is something reportedly seen in the sky by a reputable person or persons, which astronomers, meteorologists, and other experts cannot identify on the basis of current generally accepted knowledge. It is conceivable, as skeptics claim, that all UFOs could be identified as known phenomena if enough data were noted by the observers. Indeed, some of the numerous theories that have been advanced to explain the objects involve no important changes in our scientific view of the world.

Some students of UFOs, however, have suggested explanations that, if true, would require changes of theory in physics, astronomy, biology, psychology, and other fields. We present an outline of several UFO theories, some widely held, some the whimsy of a few. They are arranged in roughly ascending order of their challenge to current science.

1. Puzzling UFO reports are hoaxes. Undoubtedly some reports of UFO sightings, contacts, and photographs are deliberately false, as has been demonstrated or admitted in some cases. However, the number of people who report seeing UFOs is so large (11 percent of the American population, according to a 1974 Gallup Poll), that one would have to posit that millions of people throughout the world have chosen to tell whopping lies for no apparent reason and at the risk of being publicly ridiculed. Since the number of people claiming to have had extended contact or interaction with UFO occupants is much smaller, the possibility of hoaxes in these cases is correspondingly greater.

2. Apparent UFOs are really airplanes, helicopters, weather balloons, or artificial earth satellites, misidentified by observers. A large proportion of reported UFOs turn out on further investigation to fit into this category. However, experienced civilian and military pilots have frequently reported very close encounters with objects whose shape, position, and movements were unlike those of any known craft.

A 1964 Air Force hoax project, which released a series of flares attached to parachutes over a populated area of Florida, found that nearly all of eighty chance observers accurately described the movements of the lights and more or less correctly identified the cause as flares. None of the witnesses had prior knowledge of the objects or had been expecting to see them. This result tends to confirm the reliability of the general public in reporting aerial phenomena.

On the other hand, the shape and behavior of UFOs over the years have changed, from the slow-moving "airships" of the 1890s to the saucers of recent years. This may indicate that observers often see what they expect to see.

3. Most UFO sightings, especially at night, are misapprehended heavenly bodies. In fact, pilots have been known to take risky evasive maneuvers in order to avoid collision with what turned out to be the moon. Planets or stars, especially when seen from moving vehicles, over winding or rolling roads, may well appear to be moving erratically or to be changing in color or brightness. But many sightings occur in daylight at close range.

4. Atmospheric phenomena, such as swamp gas or the reflection and refraction of light in clouds and temperature inversions, are the probable origin of most visual and radar sightings. The erratic movements of the brilliantly luminescent objects involved in many UFO reports might well be accounted for by the little-known phenomenon of ball lightning, which might also account for radio interference and the failure of automobile electrical systems so often noted in connection with UFO sightings.

5. UFO observers are hallucinating victims of personal psychological stress; multiple witness cases represent mass hysteria; UFO sighting waves represent mass suggestion and are a result of social stress. Apart from the arrogant presuppositions of this line of thought, it must be noted that at least a sizable minority of sightings are reported by reputable individuals, with no history of mental disorder, whose testimony on other matters would be accepted in a court of law.

6. In the late 1940s and early 1950s, when the first great wave of modern UFOs occurred, it was widely believed that the objects were secret Soviet or U.S. craft. Since that time, several former prominent Air Force personnel, on both sides of the UFO controversy, have publicly revealed inside accounts of the government's handling of the controversy. These accounts provide no evidence whatsoever for this theory. If either nation had perfected such advanced aerial technology, we may reasonably assume that it would have used that ability in the political and military crises

that have since occurred or in the space race. There has never been any evidence of such use.

7. UFOs represent a secret technology developed in seclusion by private individuals in possession of advanced scientific knowledge. Given the worldwide scope of the sightings, such a private group would have to be so numerous and have resources so great that it could hardly remain undetected for three decades.

8. The most popular explanation of UFOs is that they are vehicles built and manned by intelligent creatures residing on other planets, probably beyond our solar system. Some UFOlogists prefer to avoid speculation along these lines until UFOs are definitely shown to be an anomalous phenomenon, but the subject inevitably appeals to the modern imagination.

In any case, this hypothesis has appeared more plausible to some in recent years in light of the growing belief among astronomers, biologists, and chemists that intelligent life exists elsewhere in the universe. But most astronomers continue to maintain that the great distances between stars and the theoretical limits on the speed that matter may travel make actual visits between solars systems highly unlikely, especially in view of the possibilities of radio communication. And, they ask, if "manned" probes have been sent to earth, would the probes take the form of literally thousands of visits over decades, usually to remote rural areas, in a bewildering variety of vehicles, with no more effect than jamming auto ignitions and frightening dogs?

Defenders of the extraterrestrial hypothesis respond that a race different from our own and possibly more intelligent than our own may have technologies beyond our power to conceive, just as the twentieth-century technologies of television, space exploration, or atomic energy would have been beyond the imaginative capacities of earlier humans. As for the peculiar behavior of the UFOs, their hypothetical occupants may have motivations we cannot comprehend or may simply be trying to divert our attention from their genuine purpose. Also, certain consistencies in appearance and behavior may exist among UFOs but could be obscured by inaccurate, incomplete, and false reports. In fact, some UFO experts say, serious UFO reports from many countries do show some consistencies.

But, the skeptics retort, why would a technologically

advanced society bother to launch such a time- and resource-consuming effort to explore our planet, one of so many possible targets? Perhaps, it is said in reply, the human race is at a crucial technological and social juncture, and the UFO occupants wish to influence or at least study our choice of paths.

9. The worldwide spates of UFO sightings represent a religious phenomenon, akin to the revelations that launched the world's current religions. In seeing UFOs, observers may be using long-dormant psychic powers programmed into the human brain as a social survival mechanism. These revelations might help, or hinder, an adjustment of values and myths to changes in people's relation to earth and the universe.

10. Since sightings are occasionally reported from around the world of small humanoids seen in or near UFOs, who appear to resemble the elves and trolls of folklore on all continents, it has been suggested that a race of such humanoids has evolved independently on earth and has by now developed an advanced technology. If so, these elves are very clever at hiding.

11. UFOs are thought forms projected by extraterrestrials or by supremely talented human psychics. But would thought forms leave physical traces, as many UFO reports claim?

12. UFOs are visitors from the future or the past, or from a different space-time continuum, or from a universe parallel to our own, or from a dimension of which our universe is a mere cross section. There is no lack of such speculation on the fringes of science, by those with and without an understanding of advanced physics.

Perhaps, with more systematic observation, most UFOs will be explained by a combination of several of the above theories and cease to be *un*identified flying objects. Perhaps the phenomenon is in truth even more bizarre; perhaps it is totally commonplace. And perhaps a residue of UFOs will always remain, to stimulate wonder and delight the curious.

A Who's Who of the UFO Controversy

1. *Prominent Individuals*—an alphabetical sampling.
Adamski, George, late handyman and popular writer. Adamski was, perhaps, the most famous of the early

"contactees," people who claimed to bring messages of peace and brotherhood from space beings. His books include *Behind the Flying Saucer Mystery* (Paperback Library, 1967). Adamski is generally considered a hoaxer and cultist.

Beckman, Fred, colleague of J. Allen Hynek's at the University of Chicago. Beckman specializes in analyzing purported UFO photographs.

Bowen, Charles, editor of the London-based *Flying Saucer Review.* The *FSR,* the most respected UFO magazine, reports investigations and analyses of sightings. Its address is: 21 Cecil Court, Charing Cross Road, London W.C. 2, England. Bowen edited *The Humanoids* (Regnery, 1974).

Condon, Dr. Edward U., late University of Colorado physicist. Condon headed the 1966 Air Force-sponsored study at the University of Colorado. He was highly skeptical about UFOs, concluding that they were not worth intensive study.

Cruttwell, Reverend Norman E. The Reverend Mr. Cruttwell documented a classic series of about sixty sightings over New Guinea in the late 1960s, reporting them in an article, "Flying Saucers over Papua," which appeared in *Flying Saucer Review,* Special Issue No. 4 (August 1971).

Fowler, Raymond, MUFON (Mutual UFO Network) director for investigations. Fowler has specialized in New England cases. He investigated a classic sighting in Beverly, Massachusetts, that the Condon Report could not explain. He wrote *UFOs, Interplanetary Visitors* (Exposition, 1974).

Fuller, John, journalist. Fuller has reported on several aspects of the UFO controversy, including the Condon Report. He has also written books on some classic cases, including *The Interrupted Journey* (Dial, 1966) and *Incident at Exeter* (Putnam, 1966).

Hynek, Dr. J. Allen, director of the Center for UFO Studies, chairman of the Department of Astronomy at Northwestern University, and director of the Lindeheimer Astronomical Research Center at Northwestern.

Hynek served as the astronomical consultant for various Air Force UFO investigation projects between 1948 and 1968, including Project Blue Book, the most famous of these efforts. His job was to evaluate possible conventional astronomical explanations for UFO reports.

Beginning as a skeptic, Hynek emerged after the mid-1960s as an advocate of serious scientific investigation of all aspects of the UFO phenomenon. He has criticized the methodology used by Blue Book and by the Condon Committee (see U.S. Government below). He is probably the best-known establishment scientist to argue for the possibility of the extraterrestrial hypothesis. His 1972 book *The UFO Experience: A Scientific Inquiry* (Regnery) may be the most cogent argument for that possibility. He also wrote, with Jacques Vallee, *The Edge of Reality*.

Jacobs, David M., assistant professor of history, Temple University. Jacobs has written a definitive history of the public debate, *The UFO Controversy in America* (Indiana Univ. Press, 1975).

Keyhoe, Donald E., former Marine Corps officer and aviation writer. Keyhoe has been writing popular books and articles on UFOs since 1950, many with the theme that the Air Force has been covering up evidence that UFOs are of extraterrestrial origin. Keyhoe helped found and lead NICAP (see below) for thirteen years and lobbied continually in Congress and the media in the 1950s and 1960s against the Air Force policy of silence and skepticism. His latest book is *Aliens from Space* (Doubleday, 1973).

Klass, Philip J., senior editor, *Aviation Week and Space Technology*. An outspoken skeptic, he has lectured and written extensively on the subject, explaining UFOs as meteors, weather balloons, airplanes, hoaxes, atmospheric flukes, and the like. He has summarized his position in two Random House books, *UFOS—Identified* (1968) and *UFOs Explained* (1974).

Lorenzen, Coral and Jim, founders in 1952 of APRO (see below). The Lorenzens have authored many books, including *UFOs over the Americas* (Signet, 1968) and *UFOs: The Whole Story* (Signet, 1969).

McDonald, Dr. James E., late atmospheric physicist at the University of Arizona. McDonald was one of the first respected scientists to advocate in public that UFOs were genuinely anomalous phenomena. He investigated several of the classic UFO cases and served as an inspiration for students of UFOs. After 1965 McDonald embarked on a nationwide lecture tour, exposing government attempts to conceal or downplay UFO evidence. In articles and speeches he disputed Menzel, Klass, and other UFO critics. He was found dead in 1971, apparently a suicide. Some of his UFO colleagues attribute the tragedy to public harassment and ridicule.

Menzel, Donald H., retired Harvard astronomer. Menzel is one of the foremost and persistent skeptics about UFOs, attributing most of them to temperature inversions or mirages. He wrote *Flying Saucers* (Harvard University Press, 1953) and, with Lyle G. Boyd, *The World of Flying Saucers* (Doubleday, 1963).

Michel, Aimé, noted French UFO researcher. He wrote *Flying Saucers and the Straight Line Mystery* (Criterion, 1958), among other works.

Phillips, Ted, a field investigator associated with MUFON (Mutual UFO Network). He specializes in physical traces associated with UFO sightings, such as ground markings, and has catalogued cases in twenty-four countries. CUFOS (see below) published his book *Physical Traces Associated with UFO Sightings* in 1975.

Poher, Claude, director of scientific instruments, French National Center for Space Studies. Poher studied the correlation between 1954 sightings and perturbations in the earth's magnetic field.

Robertson, H. P., Nobel Prize-winning physicist at the California Institute of Technology. Robertson headed a 1953 panel, convened by the Central Intelligence Agency, which hinted that UFOs were unworthy of scientific study and advised the military to debunk and downplay concern over UFOs for reasons of public morale.

Ruppelt, Captain Edward J., the first director of the Air Force's Project Blue Book. Ruppelt coined the term "UFO." After leaving Blue Book, Ruppelt criticized its practices as inadequate in his book *Report on Unidentified Flying Objects* (Doubleday, 1956).

Sagan, Dr. Carl, director of the Center for Planetary Studies, Cornell University, and of the Center for Radiophysics and Space Research, Ithaca, New York. While Sagan has been a leader in speculation about extraterrestrial life, he has publicly debunked the belief that UFOs may be a manifestation of such life. Among his publications was the paper "Physics and Psychology of UFOs" written with L. G. Boyd and published in *Proceedings of the AAAS* [American Association for the Advancement of Science] *Symposium,* Boston, 1969.

Saunders, Dr. David, psychologist, fired from the Condon study after leaking a controversial memorandum. His book (with Roger Harkins) *UFOs? Yes!* (Signet, 1968) recounts Saunders' version of the internal intrigues of the Condon Committee.

Vallee, Dr. Jacques, computer scientist at the Computer Laboratory at Stanford University. Vallee helped found a private UFO research group in France in 1961 and has extensively studied the international UFO scene. His prolific writings include comparisons between humanoid sightings and legendary creatures like elves and parallels among psychic phenomena, religious myths, and UFOs. His *Passport to Magonia* (Regnery, 1969) discusses these comparisons and includes an extensive catalogue of close-encounter UFO sightings. Also of interest is his *Invisible College* (Dutton, 1975).

2. *Major UFO Organizations (U.S.)*

APRO—Aerial Phenomena Research Organization. International Director: James Lorenzen; Secretary-Treasurer: Coral Lorenzen; Research Director: Dr. James A. Harder. Address: 3910 East Kleindale Road, Tucson, Arizona 85712.

The Lorenzens formed APRO in 1952: it is the longest-lived UFO organization. It sponsors conferences, does some field investigation, and publishes UFO news in its monthly *APRO Bulletin.* It also maintains extensive files of local UFO publications and other data.

CUFOS—Center for UFO Studies. Director: J. Allen Hynek. Address: P.O. Box 11, Northfield, Illinois 60093.

CUFOS serves as a clearinghouse for worldwide data on UFOs. It maintains a toll-free UFO central hot line available to law enforcement officials throughout the country to report sightings. When a major case is reported, the center has a string of affiliated researchers who can arrive on the scene quickly.

The group was set up by professional scientists and has begun supporting and disseminating systematic UFO research.

GSW—Ground Saucer Watch. Director: William H. Spaulding. Address: 13238 North Seventh Drive, Phoenix, Arizona 85029.

GSW follows a technically oriented approach to UFO study, with consultants in various fields, including astronomy, engineering, photography, and computer science. The group holds annual conferences.

MUFON—Mutual UFO Network. International Director: Walter H. Andrus, Jr.; Deputy Director: John F. Schuessler. Address: 103 Oldtowne Road, Seguin, Texas 78155.

MUFON was founded in 1969 and has become probably the most vigorous UFO membership organization. A claimed 1,000 investigators throughout the world (concentrated in North America) exchange and report information on sightings and conduct specialized surveys on aspects of the UFO phenomenon. Sighting reports are passed on to CUFOS for compilation and analysis.

MUFON holds an annual symposium and publishes *Skylook,* a monthly bulletin, as well as various books and papers.

NICAP—National Investigations Committee on Aerial Phenomena. Board Chairman and President: John L. Acuff. The board of governors includes prominent political and retired military men, including Senator Barry Goldwater. Address: 3535 University Boulevard West, Kensington, Maryland 20795.

Founded in 1956, NICAP waged a public battle with the Air Force for a more open and extensive study of UFOs and encouraged Congress to investigate. It continues to serve as a sighting clearinghouse and publishes a monthly bulletin, *UFO Investigator.*

PSI—Project Starlight International. Director: Ray Stanford. Address: P.O. Box 5310, Austin, Texas 78763.

PSI specializes in instrumented UFO observation and research. It maintains a battery of equipment at a site near Austin designed to monitor UFO activity and to attempt to communicate with UFOs. PSI publishes the *Journal of Instrumented UFO Research.*

UFO Research Center: Ontario. Chairmen: Henry McKay. Address: P.O. Box 427, Station F, Toronto, Ontario, Canada M4Y2L8.

A standing committee of the Toronto Society for Psychical Research, the center was established in 1975 as a serious research and educational group, concentrating on UFO phenomena reported in Canada. A bimonthly newsletter is published.

UFO Subcommittee, AIAA—American Institute of Aeronautics and Astronautics. Chairman: Joachim P. Kuettner.

The subcommittee, set up in 1967, has published

periodic reports for the consideration of AIAA members. It maintains an open-minded attitude concerning the need for wide scientific study.

Several subcommittee reports have appeared in *Astronautics and Aeronautics,* an official AIAA journal. These include: "UFO, An Appraisal of the Problem," November 1970; "UFO Encounter I: Sample Case," July 1971; "UFO Encounter II," September 1971; "UFO Reports from AIAA Member," May 1974.

3. *U.S. Government Involvement*

The Air Force started its investigations in 1947 with Project Sign. In 1949 the name was changed to Project Grudge and in 1951 to Project Blue Book, which was finally terminated in 1969.

Hynek has charged that the Blue Book project had very poor priority, seen by both the rapid turnover and relatively low rank of the directors. Hynek and others have regarded Blue Book as something between an inept PR outfit and an outright cover-up. Although files on more than 12,000 cases were amassed, no systematic classification, cross-referencing, or computerization of data was attempted. Although statistical ploys (such as dropping words such as "possible" or "probable" before classifications) were used to increase the number of cases considered "solved," there was still a sizable residue of "unidentified" objects.

The CIA got into the act in 1953, after a massive UFO sighting wave a few months before, by sponsoring the five-day Robertson Panel to study the matter. The panel included engineers, physicists, meteorologists, and an astronomer. The panel, which has been criticized for trying to draw conclusions about a complex problem in only five days, asserted that UFOs were no threat to national defense, that there existed no evidence that UFOs required a revision of current scientific concepts, and that national security agencies should take steps to strip UFOs of their "special status" and "aura of mystery" in the eyes of the public. The panel warned that UFO scares could be used to weaken the nation during a national security crisis.

The Air Force-sponsored Condon Committee, based at the University of Colorado from 1966 to 1968, owed its origins to another UFO sighting wave. Its controversial report resulted in the termination of Blue Book. The conclusions of the Condon study, which were sanctioned by the

National Academy of Sciences as methodologically sound (though other scientists disagreed), were that UFO studies were not really worthy of further scientific effort or funding. However, some sections of the report, written by various specialists, seemed less conclusive and included cases for which no conventional explanations could be supplied.

The federal government announced in 1976 that the records of the Air Force's investigations of UFO sightings, compiled between 1947 and 1969, had been opened for public scrutiny. However, names of witnesses who had requested confidentiality were deleted from the public copies. Inquiries should be addressed to: Modern Military Branch (NNMM), National Archives and Records Service, Eighth Street and Pennsylvania Avenue NW, Washington, D.C. 20408.

The Zeta Reticuli Controversy

The Zeta Reticuli controversy concerns a star map which Betty Hill claims she saw in the spaceship which, according to their account, she and her husband, Barney, were taken aboard in September, 1961. Mrs. Hill drew a version of the map under posthypnotic suggestion in 1964.

According to Mrs. Hill, the original map in the spaceship seemed three-dimensional, although the map material was flat and thin. She said there were many more stars on it than she could remember and that she drew only those stars that were connected to the others. According to Mrs. Hill, the lines on the map were described by her humanoid captor as "trade routes." The points which they connected were "places visited occasionally," while dotted lines indicated "expeditions" to other stars.

In 1969 Marjorie Fish, a schoolteacher and amateur astronomer, began to study the possibility that the view shown on the map might correspond to a pattern of stars that already existed. Ms. Fish hung beads of appropriate size and color from the ceiling of a room in her house in Ohio. Each bead represented a star near our solar system. One bead represented our sun. Looking at the beads from various angles, Fish tried to find a pattern of stars like the one on the map which would fulfill the following criteria:

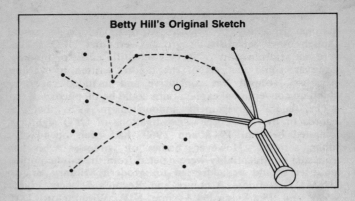

Betty Hill's Original Sketch

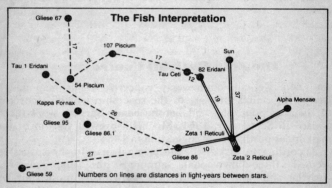

The Fish Interpretation

Gliese 67

107 Piscium

Tau 1 Eridani

54 Piscium

Tau Ceti

82 Eridani

Sun

Kappa Fornax

Gliese 95

Gliese 86.1

Alpha Mensae

Zeta 1 Reticuli

Zeta 2 Reticuli

Gliese 86

Gliese 59

Numbers on lines are distances in light-years between stars.

17 12 17 12 19 37 14 26 10 27

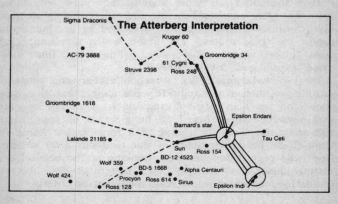

The Atterberg Interpretation

Sigma Draconis

Kruger 60

AC-79 3888

Groombridge 34

Struve 2398

61 Cygni

Ross 248

Groombridge 1618

Epsilon Eridani

Barnard's star

Lalande 21185

Sun

Tau Ceti

Ross 154

Wolf 359

BD-12 4523

BD-5 1668

Alpha Centauri

Wolf 424

Procyon

Ross 614

Sirius

Ross 128

Epsilon Indi

1. The sun had to be part of the pattern with connecting lines.

2. No solar types of star in the same general area of space could be bypassed.

3. The pattern had to be relatively close to the solar system or other solar types of star would be bypassed.

4. The pattern of lines must be logical—that is, a line should not run out to a star 100 light-years away and then come back to a star only 30 light-years off in the same direction.

5. Large, young main-sequence stars (younger versions of our sun) would not be stops along the lines because they are unlikely to have planets or life.

6. Stars not in the main sequence (white dwarfs, giants, and supergiants) would not be visited because they would not sustain planetary life and because they are dangerous since their heat and radiation output are variable.

7. The map's lines should not bypass stars of one type and then stop at a star of a similar type.

8. The base star should be one or both of the two large circles shown on the map with the large number of lines radiating from them.

9. One or both of these base stars must be able to sustain life.

10. Because the two base stars are shown as much larger than other points on the map, they must be either bigger or brighter than the other stars or closer to the viewer.

Fish did find such a pattern. The base stars were identified as the double-star system called Zeta Reticuli, thirty-seven light-years from the sun and one of only two double-star systems which are thought to be able to sustain life. This finding, if valid, would lend credibility to Mrs. Hill's account of her abduction experience.

The controversy surrounding Fish's discovery turns on the question of the mathematical odds of finding such a pattern among the many stars that are within about fifty light-years of the sun. Charles W. Atterberg, an astronomer, found another similar pattern in which all the stars depicted are within 18.2 light-years of the sun, while the Fish map includes stars that are 53 light-years distant. Critics of the Fish map, including astronomer Carl Sagan, argue that if, with a little study, Atterberg could find another combination that fits the Hill map pattern, this proves their contention that given the many stars to work with and the many possible viewing angles, astronomers could come up with several possible candidates for any pattern.

Fish, however, rejects the Atterberg map because it fails to satisfy her seventh and tenth criteria and comes close to failing on the ninth. She points out that Atterberg's base stars, Epsil on Eridani and Epsilon Indi, only just made the list of those stars which could sustain life. Fish also says that Atterberg's map utilizes some red dwarf stars to make the pattern but bypasses an equal number of stars of the same type, thus violating criterion seven. Finally, the two base stars are not the largest or brightest on the Atterberg map, nor are they the closest. The sun and 61 Cygni are much closer to the viewer.

The entire controversy, along with a fascinating speculation on planning a life-hunt trip through the stars, can be read in a beautifully illustrated pamphlet from *Astronomy* magazine, 757 North Broadway, Suite 204, Milwaukee, Wisconsin 53202.

The Million-Dollar Prize

One million dollars will be awarded the person who brings to the *National Enquirer,* the sensationalist weekly tabloid, convincing proof that a UFO comes "from outer space and is not a natural phenomenon." Previously the newspaper had offered $100,000 for such proof.

UFO reports will be screened by Jim Lorenzen of APRO and Jim Acuff of NICAP. The cases which offer the best proof will be passed on to a panel of "scientists and educators." If the panel agrees unanimously that the evidence presented is convincing, their recommendation to pay the award will be passed on to two highly reputable and well-known judges who will determine whether the decision of the panel is valid. If they agree that it is, the *National Enquirer* will pay $1,000,000 to the person or persons who obtained the evidence.

In the meanwhile, until such evidence is found, the tabloid will pay $10,000 each year to the person or persons who offer "the most scientifically valuable evidence on UFOs" even though it falls short of convincing proof.

In 1975 a smaller award of $5,000 was divided among

Travis Walton and six witnesses of his abduction by a UFO (see Five Classic Abduction Cases).

In 1975 an even smaller award went to two airline pilots, an air traffic controller, and an airport security guard in San Antonio, Texas. On the night of October 23 they all saw a reddish sphere—"about as large as our first space capsules," said the controller, who was about a mile from the UFO. One pilot from a distance of 1,500 feet described it as "huge." The two pilots had the object in view between their planes when it suddenly accelerated downward and vanished. Philip Klass has not fully investigated this case but notes that witnesses' statements appear contradictory on the size and the location of the UFO.

In 1974 Captain Lawrence Coyne and three members of his helicopter crew shared a small award. On October 18, 1973, while flying low near Mansfield, Ohio, at night, their craft was closely approached by a large object which stopped suddenly just before hitting the helicopter. When it sped away, the helicopter rose rapidly in the air, though Captain Coyne reported that he had been descending rapidly to avoid a collision with the object. Philip Klass argues that the object was probably a fireball from the Orionid meteor shower which so startled the pilot and copilot that they were unaware that they had pulled up their helicopter to avoid a collision with the ground.

In 1973 an award was made to Durel Johnson, a farmer near Delphos, Kansas. On November 2, 1971, his sixteen-year-old son saw a UFO land and ran into the farmhouse to report it to his parents. All three saw it leaving as they came out of the house. The UFO left physical traces (see Physical Traces of UFOs). Philip Klass suspects a hoax designed to collect the *National Enquirer*'s "convincing proof" award ($50,000 at the time) and speculates that the traces were no more than marks and organic changes left in the ground by an animal feeding or drinking trough that may once have occupied that spot.

The *National Enquirer* can be contacted at Lantana, Florida 33464, or by telephone at (305) 586-1111.

Men in Black

UFO investigators have frequently been told by reluctant witnesses that they had already been contacted, shortly after the sighting, by unknown men, who had confiscated photographs or other evidence or had warned the witnesses to remain silent. These strange "men in black," or MIBs as they are called by UFOlogists, are said to carry police or military credentials and have all the appearance of stereotypical federal agents. They turn up before the witness has reported the episode to the police, sometimes even before the witness has related the experience to anyone.

On the evening of September 3, 1965, Sheriff Robert Goode and a colleague, while driving on a highway near Damon, Texas, saw a huge UFO flying nearby. The light it emanated seemed to heal an open wound that Goode had received on his arm that day from a pet alligator. When he returned to town and entered a restaurant, he was approached by one or two strange men, who described the UFO in detail and advised Goode not to say anything about his experience.

To date, attempts to pin down a genuine MIB story and verify it through multiple witnesses have been unsuccessful. This elusiveness, the suggestion of a vast conspiracy contained in the MIB stories, and the stereotypical elements lend a high probability to the theory that the story is a classic case of rumor with no basis in fact.

LEGENDS
AND
MYTHS

The Lost Dutchman Mine

The Lost Dutchman Mine, according to legend, is a fabulously rich deposit of gold in some unknown location in the Superstition Mountains of Arizona. In 1931 the mine received national publicity, and since then it has captured the imagination of many.

The Superstition Mountains, in places, exceed an altitude of 6,000 feet and cover an area of 240 square miles. There are no known mines in the area, and geological exploration by the United States Bureau of Mines and private companies indicates that there is little chance of finding minerals in the eastern part of the Superstition Mountains, where the Lost Dutchman Mine is said to be located. Today most of the area is a National Wilderness Area.

The local Indians have no superstitions about the Superstition Mountains, and the name came about as a result of a misunderstanding. The Pima Indians called a mountain in the area by a name that described its physical shape, "Crooked Mountain," but this name could also be translated as "Mountain-with-Something-Wrong-with-It." The whites assumed that the Pima had some taboo about the mountain and called it Superstition Mountain. The latter name was extended to all the surrounding highlands.

The Dutchman of the story was really a German named Jacob Waltz. He allegedly either discovered the mine or learned the secret of its existence from others. There are few documentable facts about Waltz's life, beyond a homestead claim in Phoenix in the 1870s and his death in 1891. One other document relating to him exists, and it casts doubt on the supposition that he owned a rich mine: In 1878, he made a contract with an Andrew Starar that Starar would support and take care of him and, in return, receive the homestead upon his death. The rest is legend. Several people who knew Waltz, who was a prospector, claimed to have seen sacks of gold ore which he told them he had obtained from a mine in the Superstition Mountains.

Until 1931 the story of Jacob Waltz's alleged mine was known only to locals, some of whom actually undertook unsuccessful searches for it. In that year a prospector, Adolph

Ruth, disappeared in the Superstitions. Since the area is extremely dry and Ruth disappeared in June, it is likely that the prospector died of thirst or heat. Months later his

An old miner's symbol in the Superstition Mountains says, in substance, "A mine can be found in the direction indicated, around a bend, within a triangle of trees, rocks or cactus." Weaver's Needle, in the background, was near site where Adolph Ruth's skeleton was found.

skeleton was found. The press made a great deal of the fact that the skull was found three-quarters of a mile from other parts of the skeleton and had two holes in it. Both these findings are most plausibly explained as the work of scavengers in the area—vultures, ravens, coyotes, and peccaries—which frequently dismember bodies and spread the remains of their meals across wide areas. The holes in the skull may have been caused by its being bitten or dropped by a scavenger.

Stories of the supposed mystery of Adolph Ruth's death sparked the public's interest in the Lost Dutchman Mine. A great many writers have told colorful and fanciful tales of the mine, most notably Sims Ely, author of *The Lost Dutchman* (William Morrow, 1953). The origins of some of these false stories are interesting to trace. For example, almost all accounts of the Lost Dutchman Mine say that it was owned and worked at one time by a certain Peralta family. This family is said to have received a grant of land, including much of New Mexico and Arizona, from the Spanish Crown in 1748. Supposedly the Superstition Mountains were part of this grant and the Peraltas discovered the mine there. Jacob Waltz and his partner, Jacob Weiser, learned of the mine from descendants of the Peraltas, according to some versions of the story.

The name Peralta is a common one among early residents of the Southwest, but according to records, there never was a Peralta family that received such a grant. The grant was a fiction invented by James Addison Reavis, the megalomaniac "Baron of Arizona," in the 1880s. The "baron" was a horsecar trolley driver from St. Louis who forged documents which included the Peralta grant along with evidence that his wife was heir to the Peralta property. He used them to claim vast amounts of land in Arizona and New Mexico but was convicted of fraud by the federal courts in 1896. *The Baron of Arizona,* a movie starring Vincent Price, was loosely based on his life. Nevertheless, the story of the Peralta grant is recounted as fact by a reference work (*History of Arizona and New Mexico* by Hubert H. Bancroft, 1889), from which many accounts of the Lost Dutchman Mine have been drawn.

For more information, see Gary Jeannings, *The Treasure of the Superstition Mountains* (Norton, 1973) and Harry Sinclair Drago, *Lost Bonanzas* (Dodd, Mead, 1966).

Phantom Hitchhikers

The phantom hitchhiker is a character in a folk legend, popular since the 1940s, who hitches a ride, then disappears and turns out to be either a ghost, a prophet, or Jesus Christ.

The vanishing hitchhiker motif first appeared as a widespread American folk story in the 1940s. According to reports from all parts of the country, basically similar in detail, a young beautiful woman, dressed in white, hitches a ride with a male driver and asks to be taken to a particular address. During the ride she disappears. The puzzled driver proceeds anyway to the address, where he is told that the young woman has died some time before, often at the very spot where she was first seen by the driver.

In many versions of this story it transpires that the girl has often attempted to return to the given address.

At times she is said to leave a scarf or some other possession in the car, and at other times she borrows a sweater from the driver, who later finds it draped over her tombstone.

Other stories from the same period tell of a nun, or a Gypsy, or an old man, who prophesizes such events as the death of Hitler or even the end of World War II.

Similar stories have cropped up occasionally since the 1940s. A popular new version appearing in the 1970s concerns a beautiful young male hippie, dressed in white, who talks about religion and asks the driver if he believes in the Second Coming. The hippie then vanishes, leaving his seat belt buckled. It is implied that the hitchhiker is Jesus Christ.

According to folklorists, the two stories are essentially the same, with superficial details changed in ways appropriate to the period. It is considered the most widely told ghost story in America, with antecedents going back to the nineteenth century. Among the possible origins of the motif were stories brought to America by immigrant groups.

In a Chinese version of the story a young man finds a girl by the road, crying and claiming to be lost. He accompanies her to her house, where she disappears. Her father informs the young man that the girl is dead and has often tried to return home.

An Armenian tale has the young man riding a horse past a cemetery at night. A weeping young woman asks his help in reaching town. The man holds her in front of him on his horse, but when they reach the town at dawn, he discovers that she is dead. Her family is waiting to carry her to the graveyard once again to be buried, as they do every year on the anniversary of her death.

For more information, see Louis C. Jones, *Things That Go Bump in the Night* (Hill and Wang, 1959).

Ten Lost Tribes of Israel

The ten lost tribes of Israel are the legendary remnants of the Israelites conquered by the Assyrians. They are reported to be living in various faraway locales or to be the ancestors of various modern peoples.

The twelve tribes of Israel, the localized clans claiming descent from the twelve sons of Jacob, were said by the Bible to have conquered Canaan in the time of Joshua. They later formed two kingdoms, Judah in the south and Israel in the north. Israel was conquered by the Assyrians in 721 B.C., and the ten tribes that composed the kingdom were taken into exile. The two remaining tribes, Judah and Benjamin, survived, according to tradition, and became the ancestors of the modern Jews. The ten northern tribes disappeared from history.

Ever since, Jews and others have speculated about the fate of the ten *lost* tribes. The Book of Chronicles (probably written about the fourth century B.C.) said that three of the tribes were still in existence at that time, living in the various cities of Assyria to which they had been brought at the time of their defeat.

A legend soon arose that the lost tribes had formed a kingdom, located safely on the other side of the river of crashing stones called Sambatyon. Six days a week the Sambatyon roared, but on the Sabbath, when Jews are not allowed to travel, it rested.

Josephus, the first century A.D. Jewish historian, located the Sambatyon in Syria; the Roman historian Pliny said it was in Judea (in the south of modern Israel). Later Jewish, Christian, and Muslim literature elaborated on the theme.

A ninth-century adventurer, Eldad ha-Dani (i.e., Dan, one of the lost tribes), appeared in Spain and North Africa, claiming to have visited the kingdom of the ten tribes, which he located in "Cush" (probably Ethiopia or Sudan). Over the centuries the Sambatyon has been sought by travelers in India, Africa, China, Japan, and Spain. Beleaguered Jews dreamed that a Jewish king would lead his troops across the Sambatyon to their rescue and usher in the time of the Messiah.

The lost tribes legend took other forms as well. At one time or another a host of religious or ethnic groups, from the British to the Japanese, were thought to be descendants of the ten tribes, often because of superficial similarities between some of their religious practices and those of the Jews. Exotic Jewish communities, like the Falasha, the black Jews of Ethiopia, were also cited as candidates.

The early Mormons believed that the ten tribes had migrated to America, to become the ancestors of some or all of the Indians. Much earlier, a seventeenth-century Dutch Jew, Manasseh ben Israel, had written that since Jews (Indians) were already living in the New World, the biblical prophecy of their dispersion throughout the entire world was near completion. His tract helped convince Britain's Puritan leaders to readmit the Jews, who had been expelled from the country in 1290, in order to complete the prophecy and bring universal salvation.

In all likelihood the ten tribes simply lost their independent identities after their kingdom was destroyed. Some of their exiled members may have assimilated into Assyrian society, as one may infer from Assyrian records, which routinely mention Israelite names among those of other subjects. Others may have merged with later Jewish exiles, who went to Babylonia in 590 B.C. after the destruction of the southern kingdom of Judah. When the Persian Emperor Cyrus allowed these exiles to return in 537 B.C., some of those returning may have been from the ten northern tribes.

The Assyrians probably exiled only a minority of the people of the northern kingdom, singling out the leading strata. Both the Bible and Assyrian inscriptions limit the number of exiles to a few tens of thousands. The rest remained in Israel alongside foreign groups brought in by the Assyrians.

After the rebuilding of the Temple in Jerusalem in the fifth century B.C., the Jews (as they now came to be called) and their coreligionists in Samaria to the north resumed various religious disputes that had raged long before. The

Jews, who eventually prevailed over the Samaritans (i.e., people from Samaria), may have used the story of the ten lost tribes to deny legitimacy to the Samaritans.

About 500 Samaritans remain today, all living in Israel. They continue to maintain their separate identity and distinctive rites and may well have the strongest claim to being the descendants of the ten lost tribes.

For more information, see Robert Wauchope, *Lost Tribes and Sunken Continents* (University of Chicago Press, 1962) and *Encyclopedia Judaica* (Jerusalem, 1971).

Lycanthropy

Lycanthropy is a condition in which people change into animals, which many cultures around the world believe in. The belief dates back into antiquity. Usually the most dangerous animal in the area—tigers in southern Asia and Japan, the hyena or leopard in Africa, the cat in England, and the bear and wolf in Europe and northern Asia—is connected with the belief.

In Greek mythology, Lycaon was a legendary king of Arcadia. He tried to trick Zeus, the king of the gods, into eating human flesh and was changed into a wolf as punishment. This myth was apparently associated with an ancient Greek cult which held annual rites at Mount Lycaeus in Arcadia. The priests were said to prepare a sacrifice which included human flesh. Whoever tasted it was supposed to turn into a wolf. In Rome superstition held that magic spells could transform a man into a wolf.

The werewolf superstition prevalent in sixteenth-century Europe usually involved transformation of a human into a wolf under the influence of the full moon, nightly skirmishes in the woods, attacks on animals and people to eat their flesh, and retransformation into human form. Folklore often mixed werewolves and vampires, witches, fear of the dead and darkness, and animal worship (totemism). People who were werewolves were thought to become vampires upon death, while vampires were said to be the offspring of witches and werewolves. Other legends include gatherings of werewolves at witches' Sabbats, and the ability of witches to transform themselves into werewolves and other animals. Natural disasters, such as storms and plagues, were attributed to werewolves, vampires, witches. The increase in witchcraft trials in the sixteenth century was accompanied by a similar increase in trials for lycanthropy.

Transformation could either be voluntary—by spells, magic belts, or special ointments—or involuntary—by the moon's influence. In the latter case the condition was supposed to result from defective heredity or from the bite of another werewolf. It was believed that wounds inflicted on the wolf form would show in the re-formed human.

In Western Europe a possible genesis of the myth is shown in the custom of the ancient Norse warriors of dressing themselves in skins of slain bears to look fierce. From this, the powers of the beast were attributed to the warriors, and the legend grew. "Beserker," which meant "man in a bear shirt," eventually evolved to "berserk," to mean afflicted with the madness of a beast.

For further information, see Sabine Baring-Gould, *The Book of Werewolves* (Smith, Elder, 1865); Bernhardt Hurwood, *Vampires, Werewolves and Ghouls* (Ace Books, 1973); and C. T. Stewart, *Origin of Werewolf Superstitions* (University of Missouri Social Studies, Series II, 1906).

Vampires

A vampire, in popular superstition, is a bloodsucking creature believed to be the restless soul of a heretic, criminal, or suicide, who leaves his burial place to drink the blood of humans.

The belief in vampires dates back to antiquity. The ancient Mesopotamians feared that corpses that were not properly buried would rise from the grave to attack the living and suck their blood. The word "vampire" is of Magyar origin and possibly means "witch" or "devil." The popular Western horror tales dealing with vampires are derived from Slavic folklore, although similar depictions are found in Greek and Chinese folklore.

The vampire legend is often associated with fear of the dead and fear of the night. Those who have not led "normal" lives—witches, suicides, illegitimates, the excommunicated —were thought to be prime candidates for vampirism upon death, for it was felt that the earth would not accept the unfit.

The Slavic superstitions hold that the corpse thirsts for blood and leaves the grave at night to drain the blood from victims, first relatives, then others. All victims in turn become vampires. The creature must return to his grave before dawn or it becomes helpless. When the grave of a suspected vampire is opened, it will be found undecayed and with bloodstained lips. A stake must be thrust through its heart to end its predations. Other defenses include certain herbs, charms, and sacred symbols.

Another aspect of the superstition is that vampires can have sex with the living. Vampires were also often associated with plagues and epidemics, especially with those in south-eastern Europe in the late seventeenth and early eighteenth centuries.

Occultists have explained vampirism by reference to the twin astral body of each person which should leave its physical counterpart at death. In the case of vampires the astral body becomes trapped in the dead physical body and seeks blood (life fluid) to nourish it.

Irish novelist Bram Stoker created the popular "Dracula" vampire figure in 1897, basing it on the deeds of the infamous Prince Vlad "The Impaler," a fifteenth-century Romanian figure. He was not a vampire but did delight in impaling victims upon stakes.

For additional information, see Bernhardt Hurwood, *Vampires, Werewolves and Ghouls* (Ace Books, 1973); Raymond T. McNally and Radu Florescu, *In Search of Dracula* (New Graphic Society, 1972); and Montague Summers, *The Vampire in Europe* (University Books, 1966).

Atlantis

Atlantis is a legendary, utopian "lost continent" allegedly swallowed up by the sea.

Atlantis, the glittering world which has captured the imagination of countless generations, was first mentioned by Plato (died 347 B.C.) in his dialogue *Critias*. Atlantis, which he described as larger than Libya and Asia combined, was supposedly situated in the Atlantic Ocean in front of the strait called the Pillars of Heracles. It was a stepping-stone to other islands from which it was possible to pass to the continent that surrounded the Atlantic. A great empire had existed on Atlantis 9,000 years before Plato's time. The state was utopian, well ordered, and highly civilized. Its rulers were great kings descended from the gods. The cities

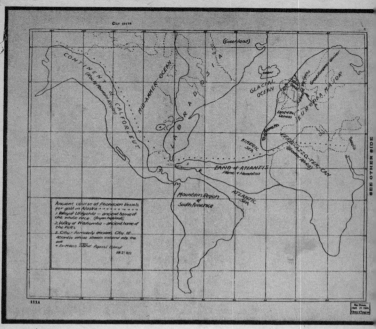

Map of Atlantis drawn by Professor Walter Martin, author of Astrasophy and a new contributor to the Atlantis myth.

were arranged in perfect concentric plans with a wealth of majestic buildings adorned with statues. The island had a profusion of gold and other metals. However, before its destruction, corruption through excessive luxury and a decline in morals set in. The island sank into the sea in the midst of violent earthquakes and floods. Plato said that the sea in the area was impassable because of a mud shoal created by the subsidence of Atlantis.

Plato's contemporaries were generally noncommittal on the subject. Plato's pupil, Aristotle, considered Atlantis pure fable. However, since Plato's time speculation about Atlantis has never faltered. Thousands of books and articles have been written about it.

Of these thousands of works on Atlantis the most ingenuous and eloquent was that of Ignatius Donnelly, a Minnesota reformer (see Martin Gardner, *Fads and Fallacies,* Dover, 1952). In *Atlantis* (Harper & Row, 1882), Donnelly argued

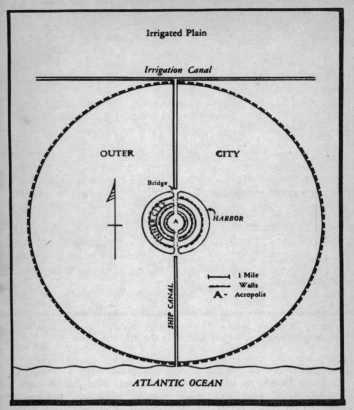

The city of Atlantis, as described by Plato.

that the biblical paradise once existed on a vast continent in the Atlantic Ocean where the world's first civilization developed. Atlantis had a superior culture, a religion of sun worship, and advanced scientific knowledge. Its colonizers spread out to populate America, Europe, and Asia, and its kings and queens became the gods and goddesses of the ancient religions. Then, about 13,000 years ago, the entire continent was submerged in a volcanic cataclysm. As support for this argument, Donnelly assembled a mass of questionable geological, archaeological, and legendary material. His chief evidence were similarities—embalming, a 365-day calendar, the building of pyramids, for instance—

between the Egyptian and Mexican Indian cultures. Consequently, Donnelly argued, there must have been an earlier culture situated on a continent between the Egyptian and early American cultures. Donnelly's book enjoyed an enormous vogue and surpassed all others on the topic in popularity and influence.

Skeptics argue that it would have taken an enormously long time for underwater traces of such a continent to disappear and that such traces should be readily detectable. L. Sprague de Camp, in *Citadels of Mystery* (Ballantine, 1973), argues that geological evidence indicates that whole continents cannot disappear overnight and that it would take thousands or millions of years for a continent to disappear. He also points out that certain kinds of rock, especially granite, are always found in continents and there is no granite in the middle of the North Atlantic and Pacific oceans, where many people speculate that Atlantis once existed. Search for traces in the Atlantic conclusively proved that no continent like Atlantis could have existed in the Pleistocene period (2,500,000 to 10,000 years ago) or thereafter.

The most recent and most interesting theory on the probable site of Atlantis stems from archaeological discoveries on the Greek island of Thera (Santorini). Excavations on Thera and research in the area have shown that a high civilization existed on the island but was destroyed by an enormous volcanic eruption in 1400 B.C. Coincidentally, attention has focused on a geographical paradox in Plato: Although he placed Atlantis in the Atlantic, he said it was ruled by Poseidon and Heracles, both distinctly associated with the Aegean, not the Atlantic. Thus, scholars posit that there could have been an Aegean island that disappeared and it could have been Thera. Egyptian writings contemporaneous with the Thera explosion tell of prolonged darkness, floods, and thunder. It has been shown that the Thera explosion far exceeded the infamous Krakatoa eruption of 1883 and could have caused the phenomena the Egyptians described.

The Thera theory, however, runs into problems. Plato's description of the island made it too large to fit into the Aegean. Also, Plato's dating of Atlantis to earlier than 9000 B.C. does not coincide with the Thera data. Supporters of the Thera hypothesis argue that Plato may have got his data from unreliable Egyptian hieroglyphics. As further support, a Greek scholar superimposed a Plato-based design of

Atlantis on the ruins of Thera, and they matched. He drew a vertical profile of Thera, based on hydrographic charts, which confirmed a pattern of alternating water and land that Plato attributed to the structure of Atlantis (see also Edgar Cayce and Bimini Blocks).

For more information, see L. Sprague de Camp and W. Ley, *Lands Beyond* (Rinehart, 1952); P. Friedlander, *Plato* (Harper, 1958); and "Volcano That Shaped the Western World," *Saturday Review* (November 5, 1966).

Lemuria and Mu

Lemuria and Mu are two names for a hypothetical lost continent, located either in the South Pacific or the Indian Ocean and believed by some mystics to be the birthplace of the human race.

Lemuria was the name proposed by the nineteenth-century British zoologist Philip L. Sclater for a supposed

The supposed Pacific "lost continent" of Mu or Lemuria, as imagined by the cultist writer James Churchward.

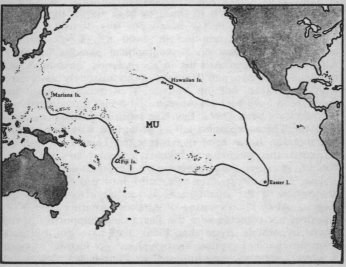

continent in the present-day Indian Ocean, linking the coastal areas of Africa, India, and Malaya. The theory, taken up by the leading German naturalist and Darwinist Ernst Haeckel, was an attempt to explain similarities in the geological and biological environments of these areas, in particular the presence of lemurs (a member of the primate order, along with apes and humans).

Prominent scientists, including Alfred Russel Wallace and Thomas Henry Huxley, lent their support to the theory, at least for a while. Among the evidence supporting the theory was a fact that of thirty-five fossil species indigenous to Natal, on the east coast of South Africa, twenty-two could be found in South India. The Lemuria hypothesis was soon adopted by various romantics and occultists, perennially susceptible to stories of lost continents.

Madame Blavatsky, founder of the Theosophical Society, wrote in 1888 that Lemuria had been the home of the third of the six races of humans which, she asserted, had thus far inhabited the earth. She placed the continent in the Pacific and claimed that the South Pacific islands were remnants of Lemuria.

The Scottish mythologist Lewis Spence posited that Lemuria was ruled by a white race, as evidenced by tales of white gods who brought civilization to the Incas, Aztecs, and Mayas. This racist theme and the Pacific locale were taken up by some of the believers in the lost continent of Mu, popularized by the retired British colonel James Churchward in a series of books published in the 1920s and 1930s.

Churchward claimed to have been initiated into the secret of Mu by the high priest of a temple in India, who showed him secret ancient tablets and taught him the language in which to decipher them. The tablets told of the creation of earth and of the first humans, inhabitants of a gigantic continent, Mu, that stretched from Fiji to Hawaii. Mu was destroyed by earthquakes 12,000 years ago, and its 64,000,000 inhabitants were killed.

Various races existed on Mu, Churchward wrote, but the white race ruled. The legendary Atlantis and ancient Egypt were colonies of Mu. Another colony ruled Central Asia; its descendants were the Aryans, the supposed ancestors of all modern Caucasian races.

The name Lemuria is still used by geologists for a continent or subcontinent that may have linked Africa and Asia during the Jurassic period (190,000,000 to 136,000,000 years ago), long before humans appeared on earth. But a lost continent in the Pacific is considered geologically untenable.

Churchward's Indian tablets, on which the Mu theory primarily rests, have never been seen by anyone else. The legends of Lemuria and Mu may be understood in the context of the discredited racial interpretation of history popular in Europe in the late nineteenth and early twentieth centuries.

For additional information, see H. S. Santesson, *Understanding Mu* (Warner, 1970); L. S. Sprague de Camp and W. Ley, *Lands Beyond* (Rinehart, 1952); and D. Cohen, *Lost Worlds* (Belmont Tower, 1969).

HOAXES
AND
FORGERIES

Protocols of Zion

The Protocols of Zion is a forged document of about 25,000 words purporting to be a plan by Jewish leaders to obtain world domination.

The Protocols of the Learned Elders of Zion, the full title, appeared in Russia early in the twentieth century. By the beginning of World War II the book had been translated into most of the major languages of the world and had attained a total circulation greater than any other modern literary work up to that time.

Protocols was first published in an abbreviated version in an August 1903 edition of the Kishinev, Ukraine, newspaper. A longer version, the basis of all subsequent editions, appeared in 1905 as an appendix to *The Great in the Little,* a book written by the religious mystic Sergei Nilus warning that the Antichrist would soon arrive.

Nilus maintained that *Protocols* was a translation of the French text of a speech, delivered by an unnamed Jewish leader to a secret conclave of 300 prominent Jews, supposedly held several years before. In a 1917 edition of *The Great in the Little,* Nilus claimed that the leader in question had been Theodor Herzl, the founder of the modern Zionist movement, and said the conclave had been held in Basel, Switzerland, in 1897, at the time of the founding congress of the World Zionist Organization.

Protocols is an outline for a world takeover and rule by Jews, with the help of Freemasons. According to *Protocols,* Jews already had a monopoly of gold and controlled the world press. They had also managed to weaken Gentile governments by fostering liberalism and class strife; this power would be further sapped by the deliberate spread of immorality and economic crisis, with the help of Gentile allies of the Jews among atheists, speculators, and members of political parties. If European governments resisted Jewish rule, their capital cities would be sabotaged by the blowing up of their subway systems, or they would be subdued by the use of an American, Chinese, or Japanese military force. Once in power, the Jews would use police and press control to suppress all opposition. Appropriate fiscal and financial measures would then be taken to ensure universal prosperity.

Protocols remained unnoticed for several years. Then, during the Russian Civil War of 1918–20, anti-Semitic factions among those opposing the Bolsheviks distributed copies of the work throughout Russia, in effect attributing Russia's troubles to a Jewish plot. In the ensuing pogroms, more than 100,000 Jews were killed. The distributors also showed copies to Western government officials, in the hope of falsely portraying the Bolshevik coup as a part of a Jewish conspiracy that was also aimed at Western Europe.

The forgery was soon exposed by the London *Times* in 1921. Nevertheless, its promoters claimed that *Protocols*, even if fabricated, somehow reflected the actual course of historical events.

In the United States the industrialist Henry Ford became convinced that *Protocols* was genuine. He printed it in his newspaper *The Dearborn Independent* in 1920 as part of a series of articles, which he then published as a book, *The International Jew*. Ford discovered his error in 1927 and apologized to American Jewish leaders. *Protocols* again received wide distribution in the United States in 1938, when Father Charles E. Coughlin printed it in his weekly, *Social Justice*.

It was in Germany, however, that *Protocols* was most widely accepted. The book was used extensively by the Nazis for propaganda purposes and was sent by them to many countries. The subsequent murder of millions of Jews was justified, in part, as an attempt to thwart their subversive plans.

The first Arabic translation of *Protocols* was published in Damascus in 1921 and was distributed throughout the Middle East, helping incite Arab opposition to Jewish immigration to Palestine. Several new Arabic editions appeared in the 1960s, especially in Kuwait and Lebanon. In 1968 the Islamic Institute for Research and Publication in Beirut, Lebanon, printed 200,000 copies of *Protocols* in French and 100,000 copies in other languages, for distribution in Africa, Asia, and Latin America. The work's authenticity was publicly endorsed by the late Egyptian president Gamal Abdel Nasser. Copies were routinely given to foreign visitors by King Faisal of Saudi Arabia until his assassination in 1975 and by the Libyan leader Muammar el-Qaddafi. In 1973 General Idi Amin, president of Uganda, urged all Africans to read the book in order "to understand the danger

of Zionism," and his government was still promoting it
in 1976.

New editions of *Protocols* have appeared in the 1970s i
Argentina, Brazil, and Italy, among other countries.

Philip Graves, a London *Times* correspondent, demonstrated in 1921 that most of the material in *Protocols* had
been plagiarized from a French political satire of 1864,
Dialogue in Hell Between Machiavelli and Montesquieu,
by Maurice Joly. That work, which made no reference to
Jews at all, was a discussion of how a democratic state could
be subverted and was probably written as a satire of the Second Empire, the regime then in power in France. Joly was
fined and jailed for insulting the government.

Graves had been given a copy of the *Dialogue* by a
Russian émigré, who had obtained it from a former officer
of the czarist secret police. Many passages of the book
paralleled *Protocols* almost word for word, using identical,
extravagant metaphors.

Other Russian émigrés helped further expose the fraud.
One of them, Count Alexandre du Chayla, revealed in 1921
that Nilus himself had admitted to him in 1909 that
Protocols may have been fraudulent and that it had been sen
to Russia by General Pyotr Rachkovsky, who was then
commander of the Russian secret police in Paris.

Conclusive evidence about the origins of *Protocols* was
produced at the 1934 trial of two Swiss Nazis, who had
distributed the work and had been charged under a law
against salacious literature. The historian Vladimir Burtsev
and others testified that several czarist officials, including
Rachkovsky and an assistant who claimed authorship, had
freely admitted that the work was a fraud. *Protocols* had
been printed only through the influence of Nilus at court, over
the opposition of the Moscow censorship committee. Even
Czar Nicholas II, who was unfriendly to his Jewish subjects
had the work withdrawn at one time as a fraud.

Burtsev also uncovered a second source for some details o
Protocols in an 1868 German novel, *Biarritz,* by Herman
Goedsche. The novel depicted a conclave of Jewish leader
planning for world domination. It was translated into Russia
in 1872.

For more information, see *Universal Jewish Encyclo
pedia* (New York, 1941); Norman Rufus Colin Cohn
Warrant for Genocide (Eyre & Spottiswood, 1967); and

Arnold Forster and Benjamin Epstein, *The New Anti-Semitism* (Random House, 1974).

The Vinland Map

The Vinland Map is a forgery which, when discovered in 1957, was believed to be the earliest map to include any part of the Americas.

In 1957 Laurence Witten, a respected New Haven, Connecticut, rare book dealer, approached Alexander O. Vietor, curator of maps at the Yale University Library, and Thomas E. Marston, a collector of medieval manuscripts, with a book he had just obtained in Europe. The book, newly bound, contained a manuscript, partly on parchment, about a church mission to the Tartars during the Middle Ages, "The Tartar Relation." Bound with it was a parchment map of the world, including the Western—i.e., Atlantic—Ocean, Iceland, Greenland, and an island labeled "Vinlanda Insula," which evidently was Vinland. Words to the effect of "discovered by Bjarni and Leif in company" were inscribed above the island.

Independently Marston purchased via mail from a London bookdealer's catalogue a fragment of *Speculum Historiale*, a medieval history. A comparison of the handwriting in it and Witten's book revealed a great deal of similarity. Marston arranged the three documents together and discovered that all the wormholes matched, as did the size of the sheets of paper and the parchment.

Eight years later, on October 11, 1965, Yale University Press published the results of the study of the map in *The Vinland Map and the Tartar Relation*. In the foreword, Vietor stated that about the year 1440 an unknown scribe copied the map and the text from earlier originals into the *Speculum Historiale*. The documents were presumably prepared in connection with a conference of religious scholars known to have taken place at Basel about 1440. Vietor asserted that the Vinland Map "contains the earliest known and indisputable cartographic representation of any part of the Americas, and includes a delineation of Greenland so strikingly accurate it may have well derived from experience." Analysis of the materials—vellum, paper, and ink—had found them compatible with a date in the 1440s. Vietor stated that all

internal and physical evidence indicated that the map w
part of the manuscript from the beginning and that althoug
the map contained material previously unknown, the m
terial was compatible with known historical data. All th
editors affirmed without reservation the genuineness of th
manuscript. They included: R. A. Skelton, superintende
of the Map Room, British Museum; Dr. T. E. Marsto
curator of medieval and renaissance literature, Yale Un
versity Library; and G. D. Painter, assistant keeper
charge of incunabula, British Museum.

In 1975 the documents were submitted to a new test f
the age of inks. The results showed that the inks in th
Speculum and "The Tartar Relation" were authentic fifteent
century materials, but the ink of the Vinland Map was four
to contain anatase, a derivative of titanium oxide not di
covered until the 1920s. This finding has been genera
accepted as proof that the Vinland Map is a modern forgery.

At the very outset the map was viewed with suspici
because the wormholes of the map and the manuscri
without the *Speculum* did not match and the binding w
of a later vintage. But the amazing coincidence of the di
covery of the *Speculum Historiale* allayed doubts for a tim

However, even before the forgery was unveiled, vario
scholars expressed doubts of the map's authenticity. Ma
of the doubts were voiced at a November 1966 conferen
organized by the Department of American Studies of th
Smithsonian Institution. Although Witten impressed th
participants with his frankness, his refusal to reveal whe
he had purchased the map—for $3,500—troubled man
Witten claimed it was common for booksellers to promi
anonymity to clients for tax and legal considerations.

One of the strongest skeptics was Professor Arman
Cortesao of Coimbra, Portugal, the only holder of an e
dowed chair in the history of cartography of the worl
Although he valued the map's potential importance, n
only because of its relevance to the discovery of Ameri
but as the first map to represent Japan, he refused to acce
it as genuine until he learned where it had been obtained.
also insisted that a forgery of the map would have present
no great difficulties. He indicated that an unscrupulo
scholar, with the aid of an expert in the falsification of o
documents, could have concocted the map and attached
to "The Tartar Relation," after separating it from th
Speculum, with the hope of selling it for a large amount

money. There might even have been a blank sheet of parchment in the manuscript which could have been used for the map. The wormholes could have been made easily while all three were together. Then, after the *Speculum* was detached, he could have rebound "The Tartar Relation" and the map.

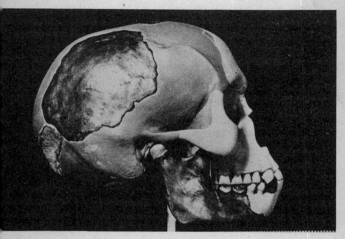

Right lateral view of a reconstruction of the Piltdown skull.

Piltdown Man

The Piltdown man was postulated from a group of fossils of primitive man, dramatically discovered in England in 1912, but later proved fraudulent.

Charles Dawson stunned the world of paleontology with the announcement in 1912 that he had discovered fossil remains that he said belonged to a Briton having a heavy jaw and a high forehead and which predated Neanderthal man. The British journal *Nature* called the find "the most important discovery of its kind hitherto made in England."

The story began in 1908, when Dawson, a lawyer and collector of bones and fossils, found an old skull fragment in a gravel pit on Piltdown Common near Lewes, England. He continued to search the area for more fossils and attempted to identify the soil layer. In 1912, Dawson submitted the skull to Arthur Smith Woodward, a distinguished geologist at the British Museum. Woodward concluded the fossil came from the Tertiary period (65,000,000 to 2,500,000 years ago). Woodward and Dawson, along with Pierre Teilhard de Chardin, undertook further excavation of the area. They discovered fragments of a brain case, half a jawbone with molars, and an isolated canine tooth, as well as nasal bones. In another part of the site they unearthed a piece of frontal bone, a fragment of occipital, and another molar tooth, all of which they attributed to another individual of the same species (Piltdown II). The jawbone looked distinctly simian and seemed to be stained with chromate a protective coating. Further search yielded some primitive flints and a large petrified object that resembled a cudgel. The discovery of fossil remains of animals supported an early Pleistocene dating of the site.

Woodward tried to fit the skull and other fossils of Piltdown I together but had difficulty. The reconstructed skull resembled a cross between a human and a chimpanzee. Woodward named it *Eoanthropus dawsoni*—Dawson's "dawn man." Anthropologists were not comfortable with the Piltdown man, but several attempts at reconstructions to reconcile the apelike jaw and *Homo sapiens*-like cranium produced no advances. Several scientists finally agreed to consider it an aberration, an error of nature, a blind alley of evolution. It was, however, considered authentic and placed in the British Museum.

Doubts, however, steadily increased and in 1949, Alvan Theopilus Marston, the discoverer of the 500,000-year-old "Swanscombe fossil," urged Kenneth P. Oakley, a researcher at the British Museum, to date the fragments using the fluorine analysis method he had developed. Tests conducted by Oakley and his associates, in 1953–54, showed that the jawbone, stained and abraded to give it an ancient appearance, actually belonged to a modern orangutang. The cranium was found to be a genuine *Homo sapiens* fossil, but not very ancient. It was found that the animal remains were of widely scattered origin and that the relics had been tampered with to make them appear to be contemporary with the fossils. Since the jawbone, which was stained with chromate, had been found in Woodward's presence, it could not have been treated after the excavation without his knowledge. Therefore, it seems likely that the chromate had been applied before the jaw was found in the gravel. Although the results of the tests were open to some question, the only plausible explanation for the presence of the chromate was forgery. Carbon 14 tests conducted in 1959 confirmed these conclusions.

The public announcement (November 1953) of the forgery caused a furor. In debates held on the matter in the House of Commons, the government was asked to explain how it was possible for eminent scholars and museum experts to have been so badly fooled for such a long time.

The questions surrounding the hoax have been heatedly debated ever since its discovery. The intricacy of the hoax was baffling. Where had the jawbone which corresponded with the cranium come from? Who was expert enough to have applied the chromate? Why had the forger gone to all the trouble?

Dawson, certainly a possible culprit, was generally accepted as an honorable man and considered sufficiently skilled to have undertaken the delicate operations required. Possibly Dawson was responsible, although not deliberately, through an honest mistake on his part. The perpetrator could have been someone who wanted to gain fame or immortality, or he could have been a fanatical opponent of the theory of evolution who hoped the hoax would ridicule prehistoric research.

R. Millar, in *The Piltdown Men* (St. Martin's, 1972), examined all these and other possibilities and concluded that the most likely culprit was Grafton Elliot Smith, an Australian anatomist, who was one of the researchers involved in the examination of the Piltdown skull. Millar eliminated Woodward because he was too honest and Teilhard de Chardin because he lacked the necessary anatomical knowledge. First, Millar states that the discovery of an extremely primitive man as far west as Britain would have confirmed Smith's pet theory of westward cultural migration. Secondly, Millar argues that because at the time of the "planting" of the fossils Smith was stuck in a backwater job in Cairo, he may have perpetrated the hoax to move into a more prominent position in England. However, Millar admits that his conclusions are far from decisive.

For additional information, see J. S. Weiner, *The Piltdown Forgery* (Oxford University Press, 1955) and H. Wendt, *In Search of Adam* (Houghton Mifflin, 1956).

The Bermuda Triangle

The Bermuda Triangle is an area in the Atlantic Ocean in which, according to legend, numerous ships and planes have disappeared mysteriously.

There is no agreement on the precise boundaries of the Bermuda Triangle. The Coast Guard defines it as an area roughly bounded by a line from Miami to Bermuda to San Juan in Puerto Rico. Charles Berlitz, in his sensationalist best-seller *The Bermuda Triangle,* places the eastern point of the triangle nearly 500 miles farther east at about 55° West longitude. Lawrence David Kusche in his debunking book *The Bermuda Triangle Mystery—Solved* takes the Coast Guard definition and then expands the area with a line running from Norfolk, Virginia, to 60° West longitude, then south to Barbados, northwest around Jamaica to the western tip of Cuba, and northeast to the tip of Cape Sable in southern Florida.

The legend, similar to many others that have developed among sailors about busy or dangerous sea lanes, is of very recent origin. It did not put in a public appearance until the mid-1960s, when Vincent H. Gaddis gave the legend its name with an article in *Argosy* magazine, "The Deadly Bermuda Triangle." A *National Geographic* news bulletin entitled "Bermuda Triangle Adds to Baffling Sea Lore" received wide attention and did nothing to clear up the confusion that was beginning to develop in the public's mind. Ivan T. Sanderson, founder of the Society for the Investigation of the Unexplained, wrote several magazine articles and book chapters on the subject between 1968 and 1973, accepting most of the data at face value because they supported his theory of "vile vortices," supposed geomagnetic anomalies regularly spaced around the world. The first full book on the subject was published in 1973. By then even the *Encyclopaedia Britannica* could treat the legend as virtual reality in its latest, fifteenth edition.

The best-known part of the legend is probably the story of the "Lost Patrol," a training flight of five Navy Avenger torpedo bombers whose pilots are supposed to have become mysteriously disoriented in the triangle and then to have suddenly disappeared in the midst of a radio transmission.

A Martin Mariner sent out to search for the missing planes is also supposed to have disappeared.

A common account of the incident quotes the flight leader as saying, "We don't know which way is west. Everything is wrong. . . . Strange. . . . We can't be sure of any direction —even the ocean doesn't look as it should." Examination of the record of a radio conversation between the ground and other planes and the "Lost Patrol" finds no such statement (Kusche, and R. J. Durant in *Pursuit*, Vol. 8, No. 3, July 1975, p. 77; *Pursuit* is published by the Society for the Investigation of the Unexplained). Most accounts leave out the facts that four of the five pilots were students and that the instructor was unfamiliar with the area. Most accounts also leave out the fact that the flight was in intermittent radio contact with the ground or other planes until shortly before the pilots were ready to "ditch" their planes for lack of fuel. Above all, when the legendary account ends with the phrase "vanished without a trace," they forget to mention that tests have shown that this type of plane will sink in sixty seconds. Nor do they mention how easy it is to lose even large objects in more than 1,000,000 square miles of ocean with rapid currents and changeable weather, especially at night. As for the Martin Mariner, it did not vanish mysteriously; it was seen to explode in midair.

The Bermuda Triangle legend and its ready acceptance as possible fact can be blamed on careless, incomplete, and slanted research by people with axes to grind or money to make. It can also be blamed on writing that is either deliberately misleading or dangerously imaginative. When an author states that the *Gloria Colita* was from the British West Indies and was found abandoned in the Gulf of Mexico, he wants the reader to believe the voyage was begun in the triangle. In fact, the *Gloria Colita*'s *home port* was in the Indies, but it had just *sailed from Mobile* for Cuba with a load of lumber. When an author writes that the *Marine Sulphur Queen*, a large tanker, vanished mysteriously, he wants the reader to believe that no good explanation exists for the disappearance. In fact, the *Queen* was carrying a highly explosive cargo for which it was not originally designed and was later found unseaworthy in a court of law. When a writer tells a reader that the disappearance of a plane or a ship "remains unexplained to this day," he wants the reader to believe that some unknown mysterious force must be involved. But unexplained or unsolved only means that there was insufficient information about the accident to decide on a probable cause.

Finally, if there were really forces operating in the triangle that made it a particularly dangerous place, insurance companies would be the first to charge more for insurance for ships plying the area regularly. Jay Edelson, marine manager at DeWitt, Stern, Gutmann and Company, stated, in an interview, that neither he nor his firm had any specific or unusual policy with respect to the Bermuda Triangle. They do not charge higher rates or impose special restrictions. The season of the year and weather conditions, said Mr. Edelson, play a greater role in evaluating risk than any particular geographic area. In general, travel on inland waterways would pose greater risks, he said, because of the danger of collision and theft. Albert Jackson, ocean marine manager at Kemper Associates, echoed the statements of Mr. Edelson, but added that given the known storm problems of the area, he would exercise greater caution before insuring small craft for travel in the triangle.

A Catalogue of "Losses" "in" "The Bermuda Triangle" Adapted from *The Bermuda Triangle Mystery Solved* by Lawrence David Kusche.

SHIPS

Year	Name (Type)	Fate	Possible Explanation	Season[1]	In Triangle?
1840	*Rosalia* (large ?)	Deserted	Really named *Rossini*, ran aground, passengers and crew rescued	4	Yes
1854	*Bella* (?)	Broke up (?)	Overloaded	3	No
1866	*Lotta*	Vanished	No data available*	—	—
1868	*Viego*	Vanished	No data available*	—	—
1872	*Mary Celeste* (brigantine)	Deserted	Unsolved	1	No
1880	*Atlanta* (sailing trainer)	Vanished	Sudden storm	1	No (?)
1881	derelict	Deserted	Supposedly found by the *Ellen Austin*; no record of a ship named *Ellen Austin*	—	—

SHIPS (cont.)

Year	Name (Type)	Fate	Possible Explanation	Season[1]	In Triangle?
1884	Miramon	Vanished	No data available*	—	—
1902	Freya (bark)	Capsized	Seaquake. Ship was sailing out of Manzanillo, Mexico, not Cuba	2	No
1909	Spray (yawl)	Vanished	One-man crew, J. Slocum, was elderly; Spray may have been unseaworthy	2	?
1918	Cyclops	Vanished	Storm off Norfolk	3	Yes
1921	Carroll A. Deering (schooner) et al.	Sank and vanished	Several small ships at about the same time; storms, or (?) unsolved	1	Yes
1925	Raifuku Maru (freighter)	Sank	Heavy storm in North Atlantic	3	No
1925	Cotopaxi (freighter)	Vanished	Gale	1	Yes
1926	Suduffco (freighter)	Vanished	Gale	3	Yes (?)
1931	Stavenger (?)	Vanished	No record of such a loss	(2)	(?)
1932	John & Mary (schooner)	Deserted	Engine exploded off New Jersey; ship abandoned, drifted into triangle. Crew found	3	No
1935	La Dahama (yacht)	Deserted	Crew rescued by Rex five days before ship was found deserted by Aztec	4	No
1940	Gloria Colita (schooner)	Deserted	Storms in Gulf of Mexico	1	No
1941	Nereus, Proteus (freighters)	Vanished	Probably torpedoed by Germans	1,2	?

SHIPS (cont.)

Year	Name (Type)	Fate	Possible Explanation	Season[1]	In Triangle?
1944	*Rubicon* (freighter)	Deserted	Broke moorings in Havana during hurricane	2	Yes
1946	*City Belle* (sloop)	Deserted	Heavy seas; crew later found	1	Yes
1948	Al Snider, a noted jockey	Lost	Rowed away from cabin cruiser in boat with two friends to fish; high winds came up	2	Yes
1950	*Sandra* (freighter)	Vanished	Storms	4	Yes
1954	*Southern Districts* (freighter)	Vanished	Unseaworthy, caught in heavy seas	1	Yes
1955	*Connemara IV* (yacht)	Deserted	Hurricane Ione	2	Yes
1958	*Revonoc* (yacht)	Vanished	Gale	1	Yes
1963	*Marine Sulphur Queen* (tanker)	Vanished	Ship later declared unseaworthy	1	Yes (?)
1963	*Sno' Boy* (charter fishing boat)	Vanished	Overloaded, swamped	4	Yes
1967	*Witchcraft* (cabin cruiser)	Vanished	Swamped in heavy seas	1	Yes
1968	*Scorpion* (nuclear submarine)	Sank	Unsolved	3	No
1969	*Teignmouth Electron*	Deserted	One-man crew, suicide	4	No
1969	derelict	Overturned	Found by *Maplebank* off northwest Africa	4	No
1969	yacht	(Looked abandoned)	Sighted by *Cotopaxi;* it was on automatic pilot; no ship that size was reported lost	4	No (?)

SHIPS (cont.)

Year	Name (Type)	Fate	Possible Explanation	Season[1]	In Triangle?
1969	derelict yacht	Over-turned	Unsolved. One report indicates it was encrusted with barnacles and may have been in the water for months	4	No (?)
1969	Brendan the Bold (sailboat)	Vanished	Never happened†	—	—
1970	Jillie Bean (cabin cruiser)	Vanished	Never happened†	—	—
1971	Elizabeth (LST)	Vanished	No data available*	—	—
1971	El Caribe (freighter)	Vanished	Possibly unseaworthy	2	Yes
1972	V. A. Fogg (tanker)	Sank	Explosion, near Texas	1	No
1973	Norse Variant & Anita (twin freighters)	Sank	Extremely high seas	3	No

[1]Year Quarter; 1=December, January, February; 2=September, October, November; 3=March, April, May; 4=June, July, August. The worst weather annually is in the first quarter above; the next worst is the second quarter, etc.

*No data can be found to prove even the existence of these ships.

†In both cases the boats were thought to be missing and newspapers reported their disappearance. The boats came into harbor a few hours or days later, but the sensation mongers overlooked news reports of their return.

PLANES

Name or type	Probable Explanation	Season	In Triangle?
1945 Avenger torpedo bombers	So-called "Lost Patrol," consisted of student pilots commanded by a man unfamiliar with area	1	Yes
Martin Mariner	Sent in search of the downed Avengers, it exploded	1	Yes
1947 Superfortress	Damaged by a severe up or downdraft in a cumulonimbus cloud. No independent data available	—	Yes

PLANES (cont.)

Name or type	Probable Explanation	Sea-son	In Tri-angle?
1948 Star Tiger	Unsolved	1	Yes
1948 DC-3	Basically unsolved, but radio was faulty and wind direction change could have taken plane off course	1	Yes
1949 Star Ariel (airliner)	Basically unsolved, but plane lost radio contact with ground during flight	1	Yes
1951 C-124 Globe Master	Exploded west of Ireland (usually dated 1950 by mistake)	3	No
1953 York Transport	Bad weather near Newfoundland	1	No
1954 Super Constel-lation	Unsolved	2	No (?)
1956 Martin Marlin	Exploded	2	Yes
1962 KB-50 aerial tanker	Unsolved	1	No (?)
Piper Apache	Never happened	—	—
1963 KC-135 aerial tankers (two)	Midair collision; reports of two widely separated areas of debris were in error	4	Yes
1965 C-119 Flying Boxcar	Unsolved	1	Yes
1967 YC-122 cargo plane	Unsolved	1	Yes
Beechcraft Bonanza	Engine trouble	1	Yes
Piper Apache	Unsolved	1	Yes
1970 Piper Comanche	Unsolved; pilot en route to Jamaica, did not have an instrument rating, yet half of flight was at night	2	Yes